Organizational Change for Corporate Sustainability

Since this classic book was first published in 2003, sustainability has increasingly become mainstream business for leading corporations, whilst the topic itself has also been a hotly debated political issue across the globe. The sustainability phase models originally discussed in the book have become more relevant with ever more examples of organizations at later stages in the development of corporate sustainability.

Bringing together global issues of ecological sustainability, strategic human resource management, organizational change, corporate social responsibility, leadership and community renewal, this new edition of the book further develops its unified approach to corporate sustainability and its plan of action to bring about corporate change. It integrates new research and brings illustrative case studies up to date to reflect how new approaches affect change and leadership. For the first time, a new positive model of a future sustainable world is included – strengthened by references to the global financial crisis, burgeoning world population numbers and the rise of China.

With new case studies including BP's Gulf oil spill and Tokyo Electric Company's nuclear reactor disaster, this new edition will again be core reading for students and researchers of sustainability and business, organizational change and corporate social responsibility.

Suzanne Benn is Professor of Sustainable Enterprise in the School of Management at the University of Technology, Sydney's Business School in Australia.

Dexter Dunphy is Emeritus Professor of Management at the University of Technology, Sydney, Australia.

Andrew Griffiths is Professor of Business Sustainability and Strategy and Dean of the Business School at The University of Queensland, Brisbane, Australia, where he is also Director of the Sustainable Business Unit.

Understanding Organizational Change

Series editor:
Dr Bernard Burnes

The management of change is now acknowledged as being one of the most important issues facing management today. By focusing on particular perspectives and approaches to change, particular change situations, and particular types of organization, this series provides a comprehensive overview and an in-depth understanding of the field of organizational change.

Titles in this series include:

Organizational Change for Corporate Sustainability

Third edition

Suzanne Benn, Dexter Dunphy
and Andrew Griffiths

Routledge
Taylor & Francis Group

LONDON AND NEW YORK

First edition published 2003
Second edition published 2007
Third edition published 2014
by Routledge
2 Park Square, Milton Park, Abingdon, Oxon OX14 4RN

and by Routledge
711 Third Avenue, New York, NY 10017

Routledge is an imprint of the Taylor & Francis Group, an informa business

© 2014 Suzanne Benn, Dexter Dunphy and Andrew Griffiths

The right of Suzanne Benn, Dexter Dunphy and Andrew Griffiths to be identified
as authors of this work has been asserted by them in accordance with sections 77
and 78 of the Copyright, Designs and Patents Act 1988.

British Library Cataloguing in Publication Data
A catalogue record for this book is available from the British Library

Library of Congress Cataloging-in-Publication Data
Dunphy, Dexter C. (Dexter Colboyd)
   Organizational change for corporate sustainability / Suzanne Benn, Dexter
   Dunphy, Andrew Griffiths. – Third edition.
      pages cm. – (Understanding organizational change)
   Includes bibliographical references and index.
   1. Organizational change. 2. Sustainable development. 3. Business planning.
   4. Social responsibility of business. I. Benn, Suzanne. II. Griffiths, Andrew,
   1969– III. Title.
   HD58.8.D862 2014
   658.4'06–dc23   2013041315

ISBN: 978-0-415-69548-0 (hbk)
ISBN: 978-0-415-69549-7 (pbk)
ISBN: 978-1-315-81918-1 (ebk)

Typeset in Times
by Keystroke, Station Road, Codsall, Wolverhampton

Printed and bound in the United States of America by Publishers Graphics,
LLC on sustainably sourced paper.

Contents

Figures

Tables

The authors

Suzanne Benn is Professor of Sustainable Enterprise in UTS Business School, University of Technology, Sydney, Australia. She researches and teaches in the area of change and leadership for sustainability and has consulted widely with government and business in these areas. Her work is published in three books and numerous journal articles and book chapters.

Dexter Dunphy is Emeritus Professor, UTS Business School, University of Technology, Sydney, Australia, and Senior Associate, UTS Centre for Corporate Governance. His main research and consulting interests are in corporate sustainability, the management of organizational change and human resource management. He has consulted to over 170 organizations and his research is published in more than 100 articles and 26 books.

Andrew Griffiths is Academic Dean and Head of the UQ Business School, Brisbane, Australia. He is a Professor in Sustainability and Strategy and the academic director of the Corporate Sustainability executive programme and the Sustainable Business Unit. Andrew is also Assistant Director at the Global Change Institute.

Series editor's preface to the Third Edition

I am extremely pleased to provide the preface for this third edition of *Organizational Change for Corporate Sustainability*. When Dunphy, Griffiths and Benn launched the first edition of this book in 2003, it was clear that environmental sustainability would be one of the major challenges of the twenty-first century. In the first edition, the authors argued that corporate 'greening' was central to achieving a sustainable world. The book also showed how corporations could begin to change themselves to achieve sustainability. The first edition was warmly welcomed and quickly became a leading text in the field. The second edition, published in 2007, consolidated its position as an indispensable text for anyone interested in the field of sustainability. Since the second edition was published, interest in the topic has grown considerably. Therefore, this new, updated and fully revised edition of the book is greatly to be welcomed for its timeliness, rigour and relevance. I am sure that, like the first two editions, it will be seen as the leading book on change and sustainability.

As well as making a considerable contribution to the sustainability debate, the new edition also makes significant contribution to the Routledge book series on *Understanding Organizational Change*. It is an accepted tenet of modern life that change is constant, of greater magnitude and far less predictable than ever before. For this reason, managing change is acknowledged as being one of the most important and difficult issues facing organizations today. This is why both practitioners and academics, in ever-growing numbers, are seeking to understand organizational change. This is why the range of competing theories and advice has never been greater, and never more puzzling.

Over the past 100 years, there have been many theories and prescriptions put forward for understanding and managing change. In the 1940s, Kurt Lewin created perhaps the most influential approach to managing change.

His Planned Approach, encapsulated in his three-step model, became the inspiration for a generation of researchers and practitioners, mainly – though not exclusively – in the USA. Throughout the 1950s, Lewin's work was expanded beyond his focus on small groups and conflict resolution to create the Organization Development (OD) movement. From the 1960s to the early 1980s, OD established itself as the dominant Western approach to organizational change.

However, by the early 1980s more and more Western organizations found themselves having to change rapidly and dramatically, and sometimes brutally, in the face of the might of corporate Japan. In such circumstances, many judged the consensus-based and incrementally focused OD approach as having little to offer. Instead a plethora of approaches began to emerge that, whilst not easy to classify, could best be described as anti OD. These newer approaches to change were less wary than OD in embracing issues of power and politics in organizations; they did not necessarily see organizational change as clean, linear and finite. Instead they saw change as messy, contentious, context dependent and open ended. In addition, unlike OD, which drew its inspiration and insights mainly from psychology, the newer approaches drew on an eclectic mix of sociology, anthropology, economics, psychotherapy and the natural sciences, not to mention the ubiquitous post-modernism. This has produced a range of approaches to change, with suffixes and appellations such as emergent, processual, political, institutional, cultural, contingency, complexity, chaos and many more.

It is impossible to conceive of an approach which is suitable for all types of change, all types of situations and all types of organizations. The aim of this series is to provide both a comprehensive overview of the main perspectives on organizational change, and an in-depth guide to key issues and controversies. The series will investigate the main approaches to change, and the various contexts in which change is applied. The underlying rationale for the series is that we cannot understand organizational change sufficiently, nor implement it effectively, unless we can map the range of approaches and evaluate what they seek to achieve, how and where they can be applied, and, crucially, the evidence which underpins them.

Bernard Burnes
Professor of Organisational Change
Stirling Management School
The University of Stirling

Acknowledgements

We would like to thank our families and colleagues for their ongoing support in our work. Our thanks are particularly due to Cristyn Meath from the University of Queensland Business School for her assistance in preparing this edition and to the Routledge team for their advice. Dexter would also like to express his gratitude for Suzanne Benn for the commitment, thought and hard work she devoted to revising the book for this edition.

Part I
Towards third wave corporations

1 Setting the agenda for corporate sustainability

Why corporate sustainability?

Since the previous editions of this book were published in 2003 and 2007, there has been a dramatic increase in interest in the fields of corporate sustainability and corporate social responsibility. Corporate managers, government agencies and regulators as well as academics and change practitioners are now engaged in the debate on the 'why' and 'how' of sustainability and social responsibility.[1] In 2014 we are still faced with an extraordinary situation. Never before in the history of the world has the viability of much of the life on this planet been under threat from humanity; never before have so many of the world's people experienced such material wealth and so many others lived in abject poverty; never before have so many had such interesting and fulfilling work and so many others such degrading work or no work at all. If we are to live healthy, fulfilling lives on this planet in the future, we must find new, life-affirming values and forge new patterns of living and working together. In the years since the first and second editions of this book, there have been some dramatic developments in our understanding of how business must change in order to achieve this aim. This new edition incorporates what we see as the most influential of these new understandings in terms of bringing about change. But we also explain why it is of increasing urgency to do so.

The critical situation in which we find ourselves has been brought about by multiple causes but one important contributing factor is the rise of the corporation. Corporations are the fundamental cells of modern economic life and their phenomenal success in transforming the earth's resources into wealth has shaped the physical and social world in which we live. The powerful dynamism of modern organizations has transformed nature and society. The central question to be answered is whether the current model of the corporation needs to be modified to contribute to the continuing health of the planet, the survival of humans and other species, the development of a just and humane society and the creation of work that brings dignity and self-fulfilment to those undertaking it. And if so, how?

In this book we build on arguments made in previous editions that some traditional organizational values and forms are not sustainable and, unless significantly reshaped, will continue to undermine the sustainability of society and the planet. Corporations have contributed to the problems outlined above and they must therefore be part of the answer. Fortunately their transformation is already underway, driven in part by the changing demands of modern society and also by the leadership of far-sighted and responsible people within and outside corporations who see the need for change. However, for the transformation to be successful, many more change agents are needed. Some of the most important changes in history have been created by people of vision and imagination who were not content simply to react to events about them but felt compelled to envisage the possibility of a different world and to initiate action to bring the new reality into being. They were often regarded as deluded or heretical at the time but later were celebrated for their foresight and courage.[2] Today senior executives from some of the world's largest and most profitable corporations – Toyota, Honda, GE, DuPont, PUMA, Swiss Re, Unilever – are actively seeking to transform their businesses to respond to sustainability issues. In their minds there is no doubt that we face serious issues such as climate change, resource scarcity, vulnerable ecosystems and poverty. This depletion of the services provided by nature to humankind requires a shift in how corporations think about and deal with sustainability. There is a compelling business case for sustainability as well as an ethical responsibility to find ways forward on these issues. Importantly, we also note in this new edition of the book that many smaller companies are now linking to the sustainability agenda. Some are responding to pressure from external stakeholders such as industry associations, government agencies or, increasingly, from larger companies along their supply chains. Others are assenting to demands from internal stakeholders concerned variously with ethical issues of production or supply, or the savings to be achieved from reducing waste and an efficiency approach to resource use.

This book is written to assist change agents to drive the necessary changes faster and farther while there is time. We discuss key issues in the debate around corporate sustainability. Our view is that the wider debate on sustainability and sustainable development will now be most fruitfully engaged through the process of reconstructing organizations so that they support a sustainable world. The current crisis is too urgent to wait for consensus; we need to start out on the path towards sustainability by generating new models of organizational action that support social relationships and the natural world. The time to debate abstract theories is past; what we need now is to embed our theories in action and to engage in dialogue around working models.

In our view, many corporations need to change significantly the way they do business. However, we are not arguing that corporations are the enemy. We are arguing that new circumstances require new responses. The crises faced by humanity can be resolved only by the use of concerted corporate action. Corporations are instruments of social purpose, formed within society to accomplish useful social objectives. If they do this, they have a right to a continued existence, a licence to use resources and a responsibility to produce socially beneficial products and services. However, if they debase human life, act with contempt for the community of which they are part, plunder and pollute the planet and produce 'bads' as well as 'goods', they forfeit their right to exist. They become unsustainable because they are unsustaining. The single-minded pursuit of short-term profitability for shareholders or owners does not justify a 'couldn't care less' approach to people and the planet. The prevailing economic value of unlimited and unending growth is the ideology of the cancer cell. Living within the natural limits of the earth's resources and exercising responsible resource stewardship is a universal requirement for all of us, individually and collectively.

This book continues the work of the two previous editions in examining the transition to the organization of the future that functions as an instrument both for the fulfilment of human needs and for the renewal of the biosphere. We define key steps along the way and indicate how to make an incremental transition from step to step or, in some cases, a transformative leap to the fully sustainable and sustaining corporation. This is therefore a guide book for corporate change agents – executives, managers and members of the workforce, external consultants, community activists – who are dissatisfied with the status quo in organizational life and who dream of a new organizational world where individuals are cherished, the community is supported and the natural environment is nourished as a matter of course as the organization goes about its core business. Nothing less than this is worthy of our humanity, our intelligence and our ingenuity.

The distinctive contribution of this book is that it concentrates on how to implement the changes that make organizations more sustainable themselves and also more sustaining of the environment and society. In this third edition, we again draw on leading-edge change theory from management and the social sciences which has evolved in the years since the previous edition, to deal more specifically with the challenges of implementing sustainability in the contemporary business context. So this book is a practical and informed tool for creating sustainable corporations that are part of the solution to keeping a world fit to live in. It is an invitation to you to be part of the future solution – a responsible agent of creative change.

For those who are prepared to act with purpose and direction in reshaping the organizational world, this is perhaps the most exciting period in human history. Each generation faces its challenges. But this and the next two or three generations will be decisive in determining whether more humans than have ever lived on this planet can create the collaborative institutional forms needed for our survival and the survival of those other precious life forms who share this planet with us. And beyond survival, to create innovative institutional forms to provide us all, and those who come after us, with a quality of economic, social and cultural life that nurtures and develops our human capabilities.

That is the challenge we deal with in this book. In meeting this challenge, we must redesign many of our organizations. So we begin here with a short discussion of the evolution of the institution which is the focus of our book: the corporation. Because corporations share so many common features and are so pervasive, we can easily assume that the corporation is an immutable social form. But it is not – it has already undergone substantial redefinitions over time. The question we address here is how can we redesign the corporation for human and ecological sustainability?

Redesigning the corporation

Over the years, corporate scandals such as James Hardie, Enron and Anvil Mining have been compounded by the recognized complicity of corporations in major environmental disasters, such as BP with the

Deepwater Horizon oil rig spill in 2010 where workers lost their lives and billions of dollars in damages awarded against BP reflected the huge impact on human welfare as well as on the natural environment. The tragic effect of the earthquake and subsequent tsunami on the Fukushima nuclear plant in Japan in 2011 had been heralded by numerous reports identifying poor safety records at the plant and came less than four years after a magnitude 6.8 quake shut the world's biggest atomic plant, also run by Tokyo Electric Power Co. Stanford researchers have calculated that the latter incident may eventually cause anywhere from 15 to 1,300 deaths and from 24 to 2,500 cases of cancer, mostly in Japan.[3] Such incidents highlighted the extent to which powerful corporate entities can write their own rules for action, regardless of the consequences for others. As a result there is increased public pressure for corporations to be made more accountable. The difficulties associated with holding organizations accountable for compliance with legal requirements and legitimate community expectations will be discussed in Chapter 4.

The rise of the multinational corporation and the internationalization of financial markets has taken the power of the modern corporation to the point where it can represent a formidable challenge to the authority of the nation-state, let alone small groups of citizens. Global corporations operate across political boundaries and so escape overall surveillance by particular nation-states. The wealth of the largest global companies exceeds that of most nations and this has given them unprecedented power. The existence of large-scale power discrepancies does not in itself guarantee that the power will be used irresponsibly but it does create the potential for the misuse of power. Throughout corporate history many corporate chieftains have used their power rapaciously and irresponsibly. For example, a coalition of oil companies and large construction firms in the USA planned and efficiently brought about the demise of the US railroad system to favour the construction of a vast network of interstate highways. More recently a small number of respected financial institutions were responsible for the irresponsible lending practices that caused the near meltdown of the world's financial system in 2008.

But of course, there are also plenty of instances of corporate leaders exercising social and environmental responsibility. In fact, there is a growing divide between those corporate leaders who have embraced the responsibilities and opportunities of corporate citizenship and those who, through ignorance or design, continue to exploit natural and human resources. The tide is turning in favour of the former group – for instance, a recent KPMG survey shows that from 2008 to 2011 the proportion of companies pursuing a sustainability strategy has risen from approximately 50 per cent to 62 per cent. This data comes from a survey on the significance of sustainability to their company of a sample of 378 companies in Europe, the USA, Canada and the Asia-Pacific region.[4] A previous KPMG survey on corporate responsibility reporting showed that 95 per cent of the 250 largest companies in the world (G250 companies) now report on their corporate responsibility (CR) activities.[5] Tellingly, two-thirds of non-reporters are based in the US.

Are corporations evil?

It is a naive and simplistic view that portrays corporations as evil by their very nature. Almost everything we depend on in our modern world is the product of corporations – from the food we eat, the clothes we wear to the phones and computers we use to communicate with each other. We cannot do without corporations. What is important, however, is that we exercise sufficient collective control over the way in which they operate to ensure that they support rather than destroy the ecological and social fabric we depend on.

Throughout the history of corporations, there has been a continuing debate over how the corporation should be defined, including its legal constitution, its social responsibilities, its role in environmental protection and the constituency to which it is accountable. The core of this debate can be summarized as the argument about whether the role of the corporation is simply to create financial wealth for its owners or to contribute to the well-being of a wider range of stakeholders, including the community, the environment and future generations.

This debate has gone on for as long as 'modern' corporations have existed and its history is too long and complex to trace here. The debate has included, for example, fierce critiques of the legitimacy of the slave trade; sabotage of the 'dark satanic mills' that blighted the lives of workers and devastated England's 'green and pleasant land'; large-scale demonstrations against nuclear power plants; experiments in 'industrial democracy'; the rise of 'green' political parties; organizational innovations such as 'the triple bottom line'; demonstrations against globalization. Since corporations came into being, each generation has engaged with and continued this debate which has shaped corporations as we know them today.

Most recently a critical issue in the debate has been the relative virtues of the prevailing neoliberal economics ('economic rationalism') versus 'stakeholder capitalism'. Neoliberal economics, led by the economist Milton Friedman, argues that the role of the corporation is simply to maximize short-term returns to shareholders. The widespread acceptance of this point of view, especially by economic advisers to governments, has been influential in shifting considerable power from the public to the private sector, the ongoing privatization of government services, the deregulation of major industries and markets and the creation of international competitive 'free trade' markets. Critics of this viewpoint argue that these changes have had destructive consequences for other important stakeholders – employees, customers, suppliers, governments, local communities, future generations, other species of planetary life and the environment. The drive for short-term profitability is underpinned by widespread acceptance hitherto of the logic of linear economic growth. However, increasingly powerful forces in government and business are recognizing the dangers of imposing linear economic growth logic on resources and ecological systems that do not grow in a linear fashion. The collapse of the 500-year-old cod-fishing industry off the coast of Newfoundland as a result of over-fishing, for example, is regarded as the archetypal example of how a subsistence relationship with nature can be destroyed by the onslaught of technological development at the cost, in this instance, of an estimated 30,000 jobs.

The nature of the modern corporation, and the philosophy of economic neoliberalism that supports it, has been strongly influenced by the success of the US economy and the history of leading US corporations. The culture of modern capitalism has evolved from the experiences of a multitude of corporations developing on a continent with enormous unexploited and virtually free natural resources. For example, at the time of European settlement, the number of bison on the North American continent was estimated at between 30 and 60 million. They were the most economically valuable wild animals that ever inhabited the American continent. When a halt was called to their slaughter in the late 1800s, only 600 survived. The passenger pigeon, once the most numerous bird in North America and on the planet, did not survive the onslaught of the hunters' guns – they were completely exterminated.[6] Despite depredations of this magnitude, the size of the continent ensured that, for the formative two centuries of US capitalism, the torrent of ecological destruction and the increasing waste and pollution emitted in converting resources into wealth could be absorbed by nature. The wealth that was generated enabled the USA to become the most powerful nation on earth, with a business culture dominating the late twentieth and early twenty-first centuries.

As a result, most corporations today operate under accounting rules and cultural assumptions that reward them for disregarding many of the social and environmental consequences of their activities. They 'externalize' many costs of ongoing operations to the community, the environment and future generations. Neoclassical economics, based on the experience of environmental plenty, still assumes that many inputs from the natural and social environments, like air and parenting, are free goods because there are no financial charges made for them. In addition, the goods and services produced by the firm are given value but the 'bads' and 'disservices' created at the same time are often neither identified nor costed and charged back to the corporation. The discourse of business and economics largely defines our ecological and community issues. Hence, in the most significant business decisions these issues are ignored because they are invisible – the decision makers have no cultural categories for them – or, if perceived, the issues are regarded as irrelevant or of marginal importance. In fact, they are of increasing importance for the survival of life on this planet and for social justice and they must become central to strategic decision making. We need a new economics that redefines economic capital to include nature and people.[7]

So we face a situation where corporate decision makers, many of whom are well intentioned, community-minded citizens, make decisions which cumulatively are having a catastrophic impact on the planet and on the global community. And they are supported in this pattern of decision making by consumers (us) who reward them by purchasing the goods and services that they produce. We are all captives of a culture of capitalism that, over 200 years, produced enormous wealth and an increased standard of living for large numbers of people. But the costs of continuing on this path, using the same methods, are now threatening to destroy our ability to use the wealth in the creation of healthy, satisfying lives and also threatening the viability of such a life for future generations. We have become, in the words of Tim Flannery, 'future eaters'.[8] Most of us have a stake in our current culture and are threatened by any substantial critique of it. We sense that we must, at least for the sake of our children and future generations, start to do some things differently. But the size and the complexity of the issues are daunting and we are caught in a spider's web of cultural categories that constrain our effective action. Change must begin with us – but where can we begin?

> Like it or not the responsibility for ensuring a sustainable world falls largely on the shoulders of the world's enterprises, the economic engines of the future.
>
> (Stuart Hart, Kenan Flagler Business School)[9]

Making a start

Wherever we are in society and the world of work, we can engage in the debate about the social role of the corporation. All of us can contribute to a redefinition of corporations to ensure they become major contributors to sustainability rather than social and environmental predators undermining a world fit to live in. There is a huge opportunity here to ensure that all corporations are instruments of a broader social purpose than the generation of short-term wealth for shareholders. Of course shareholders deserve a return on their investment. As we shall show, in most cases this return is enhanced rather than reduced by sustainable practices. We think it is vital that corporations make profits – but not at the cost of destroying the future viability of society and the planet. At this time, we have collectively overspent our credit card and are in danger of leaving our children with the debt.

Many well-informed scientists and social philosophers are warning that humanity is facing a potential environmental catastrophe of its own making and that we cannot continue to use up the earth's resources at an ever-increasing rate. Three examples:

> because we are advancing along this non sustainable course, the world's environmental problems *will* get resolved, in one way or another within the lifetimes of the children and young adults today. The only question is whether they will become resolved in pleasant ways of our own choice, or in the unpleasant ways not of our choice, such as warfare, genocide, starvation, disease epidemics, and the collapse of societies.[10]

> The life of nature demands a revolution in the way we live. And we have no time to lose.[11]

> Now is our last chance to get the future right.[12]

There is an urgent need to act intelligently now to protect ourselves and the unique ecology of this planet that supports us. Fortunately, as we wake up to the situation in which we find ourselves, we are searching for and finding new, sustainable ways of relating to the planet.

The sustainability debate is currently being engaged in three ways: first, at the intellectual level as the immensity of current unsustainable practices is documented and we all become aware of the considerable challenges of changing these practices; second, at the level of corporate action, as hundreds of thousands of members of boards of management, executives, managers, supervisors, members of the workforce, external consultants, non-government organizations and community groups take a multitude of actions on a daily basis that impact on issues of social and environmental sustainability; third, at the level of consumption, as we collectively create the powerful patterns of financial rewards that shape the economy. If we continue to purchase products that strew our world with waste and poison our environment, we cannot blame the captains of industry for the resulting destruction. If we are to make corporations instruments of renewal, the debate must be engaged at these three levels: through forging a powerful new ideology that creates a compelling vision of a future world fit to live in, and implementing the practical actions in the workplace and in our consumption patterns that will bring the vision into being.

A new approach to economics has developed in recent years to deal with the fact that traditional economics has largely taken the ecological and social environment for granted. This approach recognizes that economics must take 'natural capital' (ecosystems) and 'social capital' (relationships between people) into account. Neoclassical economics treats the economy as a closed system, with negative results, such as pollution, treated as 'externalities' which can be ignored in economic terms. Similarly some of the world's most critical resources are treated as 'free' inputs and accorded no value unless they acquire economic worth in the process of production. Ecological economics, by contrast, makes such externalities an integral part of the economic system. Ecological economics is a new field of study which integrates principles from ecology and economics. As a result of the increasing importance of these new approaches, economists are recognizing the implications of ecological functioning and resilience for human welfare. For instance, biological resources such as trees and fish and ecological services such as erosion control and climate stabilization depend on maintaining certain levels of ecosystem functioning.[13]

The depletion of natural and social resources and the accumulation of toxic wastes or rising crime rates can be consequences of economic decisions that seem 'rational' in traditional economic terms. But in the new economic models their social and ecological effects are included rather than excluded. It is fair to say that in these new models some 'rational' decisions begin to look insane. For instance, the decision to build bigger, more technologically efficient fishing fleets to maximize harvests of fish from the world's oceans looks rational – but only on the assumption that the supply of fish is inexhaustible.

This book makes a contribution at all three levels: to the intellectual agenda for change; to the strategies for corporate action; and to changing consumption patterns. We outline the need for sustainability, identifying the gap between where we are now and where we need to be, and then we provide a detailed discussion of the kinds of strategic actions that are needed to carry us forward.

In accomplishing this, we outline developmental phases that lead to the fully sustainable organization, that is, an organization that is itself sustainable because its stakeholders, including its employees, will continue to support it. But it is also a sustaining organization because it is sustaining the wider society and the ecological environment. Since 1992, when the leaders of the world's governments gathered in Rio to endorse the principles of sustainable development, they have struggled with the challenge of integrating the social, environmental and economic principles that sustainability requires. Since Rio +20 in 2012, it has become clear that key indicators such as levels of greenhouse gas emissions are not improving and that reductions in emissions from some developed countries are being cancelled out by the imports of goods from developing countries which do not have binding emissions targets.[14] Corporations which develop according to our integrated model will make a major contribution to ensuring that the world progresses along this path.

Phase models of sustainability

Various authors have described the historical processes by which corporations have moved towards supporting ecological sustainability.[15] Studies of historical stages underlying moves towards corporate social responsibility (or, as we refer to it here, human sustainability) are more rare. An exception is a model proposed by Austin. Austin proposed that corporations should develop relationships with other non-profit organizations according to a 'collaboration continuum'. In this continuum, the relationship can develop from the philanthropic phase through a transactional relationship, such as sponsorship, to an integrated phase. In this stage profit and non-profit share a common aim.[16] Our interest in phase theories such as this is not primarily to develop historical understanding, although that is useful, but more importantly to understand the paths corporations must travel to reach a full commitment to a comprehensive model of sustainability that covers both human and ecological issues. If we are to move corporations towards full sustainability, we must be able to identify the stage where they are now so that we can determine how to move forward.

Much can be learned by examining the history of moves towards sustainability in particular industries. For example, Hoffman has made a detailed analysis of the movement towards ecological sustainability in the chemical industry in the USA.[17] He distinguishes four stages, from 1962, when environmental issues were rarely discussed, to 1993, when the chemical industry and its key stakeholders increasingly adopted a proactive stance, viewing the environment as offering a set of strategic opportunities. In between, the chemical corporations reacted defensively and were met by tough governmental regulations; the initiative then moved from government to environmental activists. Finally, the leading US chemical companies absorbed what they had seen as 'heretical' ideas, acted more responsibly and found that the result was actually beneficial in business terms.

There is a great deal of overlap in models such as this, despite differences in the names given to the various phases and different numbers of phases. Clearly any generalized phase model is a high-level abstraction from the bewildering diversity of corporate life. Nevertheless, ideal-type models of this kind have a long history in the sciences – without such a model it is difficult to compare and contrast individuals, organizations, communities.[18]

In writing this book, we reviewed current models in the ecological and management literature and also drew on our own organizational experience and research. We also reviewed the parallel but unrelated literature on the developmental phases of the movement towards human sustainability in corporations.[19] The result is a comprehensive model of the developmental phases through which corporations progress towards both human and ecological sustainability. This model is central to the approach to change outlined in this book; we summarize it here and explain it in more detail in subsequent chapters.

The sustainability phase model

The phase model is designed as a tool for making meaningful comparisons between organizations to assess their current commitment to and practice of behaviours relevant to two kinds of sustainability: human and ecological. The phases outline a set of distinct steps organizations take in progressing to sustainability. There is a progression from active antagonism,[20] through indifference, to a strong commitment to actively furthering sustainability values, not only within the organization but within industry and society as a whole.

We can use the phases to characterize an organization's characteristic way of treating the human and natural resources it employs. We can also use them to trace the historical trajectory that the organization has taken in getting to where it is and to chart possible paths forward.

The six phases we distinguish are:

1 Rejection
2 Non-responsiveness
3 Compliance
4 Efficiency
5 Strategic proactivity
6 The sustaining corporation.

We do not assume that a firm necessarily progresses through the phases step by step on an 'improving' trajectory. To the contrary, an organization may leapfrog phases, or regress by abandoning previously established sustainability practices. Significant shifts are often triggered by changes such as the appointment of a new CEO, stakeholder pressure, new legislation, economic fluctuations or the loss of committed enthusiasts.

What are the distinguishing characteristics of each of these phases?

1 *Rejection* involves an attitude on the part of the corporation's dominant elite that all resources – employees, community infrastructure and the ecological environment – are there to be exploited by the firm for immediate economic gain. On the ecological side, managers disregard destructive environmental impacts of the organization's activities and expect the community to pay the costs of any remediation. On the human side, employees are regarded simply as industrial 'cannon fodder': there is no commitment to developing them, and health and safety measures are ignored or paid 'lip-service'. There is a strong belief that the firm simply exists to maximize profit and any other

claims by the community are dismissed as illegitimate. The firm disregards the destructive environmental impacts of its activities and actively opposes any attempts by governments, social advocates and 'green' activists to place constraints on its activities. We refer to these organizations as '*stealthy saboteurs and freeloaders*' because their opposition either actively sabotages movement toward a more sustainable world or leaves any costs of initiation of innovative sustainability practices to other organizations or the community.[21]

The prevailing theme for Phase 1 Rejection is: *exploit resources for maintaining short-term financial gain.*

2 *Non-responsiveness* usually results from lack of awareness or ignorance rather than from active opposition to a corporate ethic broader than financial gain. Many of the corporations in this category embody the culture of the past century, concentrating on 'business as usual', operating in conventional ways that do not incorporate sustainability issues into corporate decision making. The firm's human resource strategies, if they exist, are focused mainly on creating and maintaining a compliant workforce. Community issues are ignored where possible and the environmental consequences of the firm's activities are taken for granted and, if negative, disregarded.

We refer to these organizations as the '*bunker wombats*', as, like wombats, they prefer to avoid the light of day and hunker down in their dark bunkers away from where the action is taking place. The prevailing theme of Phase 2 Non-responsiveness is: *business as usual.*

3 *Compliance* focuses on reducing the risk of sanctions for failing to meet minimum standards as an employer or producer. In organizations at this stage, the dominant elite emphasizes being a 'decent employer and corporate citizen' by ensuring a safe, healthy workplace and avoiding environmental abuses that could lead to litigation or strong community action directed towards the firm. However, there is usually little integration between human resource and environmental functions. The organization may see itself as a responsible corporate citizen because it supports charitable community ventures which are usually irrelevant to its core business activities. But they are primarily reactive to growing legal requirements and community expectations for more sustainable practices. A recent shift has seen the development of co-regulatory practices. Instead of the traditional 'command and control' approach of governmental regulation, industry, NGOs and governments are collaborating to develop new systems of voluntary

compliance. This shift represents a transition from compliance towards later phases.

We refer to these organizations as '*reactive minimalists*', as they accept the demands of the environment to move toward more sustainable practices but limit their responses to what is required. Compliance is primarily a risk-minimization strategy designed to help the organization avoid fines for non-compliance with governmental legislation and regulation, reputational damage caused by community activism directed at exposing non-compliance to community expectations and the associated costs of time, energy and money in coping with antagonistic regulators and community groups. Compliance adds value by providing easier access to finance, improved relationships with regulators and the basis for a positive reputation as a good corporate citizen.

The central theme of Phase 3 Compliance is: *avoid risk*.

4 *Efficiency* reflects a growing awareness on the part of the dominant elite in the corporation that there are real advantages to be gained by proactively instituting sustainable practices. In particular, human resource and environmental policies and practices are used to reduce costs and increase efficiency. There is, for example, a growing awareness in many firms that what is defined as 'waste' derived from the production process may be a valuable resource to another firm. (For example, the spent hops from a brewery may be valuable as cattle feed and therefore sold rather than dumped.) Similarly, investment in training may involve expense but results in compensating added value, through increased quality of products and services. While moves towards sustainability may involve additional expense, they can also have significant payoffs in terms of generating income directly or indirectly. This is the beginning of the process of incorporating sustainability as an integral part of the business.

Value is added through: significant cost reductions, particularly through the elimination or reuse of what was formerly viewed as waste, increased employee productivity, involvement and engagement, better teamwork and lateral communication. There are not only cost savings from elimination of waste of physical resources, such as water, energy, heat and materials but also through formerly wasted human potential stemming from un-utilized people, turnover of important skills, absenteeism, lack of motivation, engagement and commitment, internal conflict and political processes and obsolescent and unintegrated work systems.

We refer to these organizations as '*industrious stewards*' because of the fundamental shift of attitude to support continuous improvement in eliminating waste and making maximum use of scarce and costly resources.

The central theme of Phase 4 Efficiency is: *do more with less.*

5 *Strategic proactivity* moves the firm further along the sustainability path by making sustainability an important part of the firm's business strategy. The focus is on innovation. The firm's strategic elite view sustainability as providing a potential competitive advantage. Consequently, they try to position the organization as a leader in sustainable business practices: with advanced human resource strategies that help make the organization an 'employer of choice', with 'corporate citizenship' initiatives that build stakeholder support and with innovative, quality products that are environmentally safe and healthy. The commitment to sustainability, however, is strongly embedded in the quest for maximizing longer-term corporate profitability, that is, it is motivated by intelligent corporate self-interest.

The commitment to eliminating waste that is the focus in the Efficiency stage is continued but the concept of waste is significantly enlarged and redefined. What is now recognized more clearly is the waste that occurs from unrealized or missed strategic opportunities. In particular, lost revenue and market share through lack of innovation, neglect of the advantages of up-skilling the workforce, failure to enter emerging markets and to develop more high value-added products which gain and secure market leadership, and too slow divestment of obsolescent operations.

We refer to these organizations as '*proactive strategists*' because they see sustainability as integral to business strategy and actively pursue its business advantages. Climate change and the transition to a carbon-neutral economy are seen not as threats to be resisted but as a source of business opportunity.

The central theme of Phase 5 Strategic proactivity is: *lead in value-adding and innovation.*

6 *The sustaining corporation.* In this final phase, senior executives and the majority of the members of the organization have strongly internalized the ideology of working for a sustainable world. With each advance toward this objective, the business environment supports the developing strategy of the organization, and the organization itself is actively redefining its environment.

If it is a 'for profit' company, the organization still pursues the traditional business objective of providing an excellent return to investors, but voluntarily goes beyond this by actively promoting ecological sustainability values and practices in the industry and society generally. Its fundamental commitment is to facilitate the emergence of a society that supports the ecological viability of the planet and its species, and contributes to just, equitable social practices and human fulfilment.

To achieve this, the organization actively participates in working with governments and communities to change 'the rules of the game', that is, public policy formulation that contributes to creating a more sustainable world. It cooperates with other organizations in its supply chain to ensure that the whole production process is fully sustainable. It builds human and relational capital within its own organization but also actively seeks to transfer best practice to other related organizations. It supports the dematerialization of production wherever possible, remanufacturing and recycling of resources and the growth of the knowledge-based economy. It models ecological and social sustainability best practice and supports and publicizes best practice elsewhere. It actively works to influence capital markets to support long-term value adding.

It participates in international agreements and seeks external independent auditing of progress towards its sustainability goals.

These organizations have developed the capability to create a business model that provides ongoing and continuing financial viability. Such organizations are either niche specialists in growing markets or have diversified to an extent that ensures continuity of performance for the whole organization. There is ongoing and integrated knowledge capture, storage and dissemination of the ways the organization ensures growth and viability. Continuity of performance is achieved by means of reliable and diverse sources of finance and human capital. Stakeholder involvement is ongoing and engagement is a strong and accepted aspect of the culture. There is an integrated approach to coordinating strategies in the three main streams of sustainability: economic, social and ecological. All key members of the supply chain are involved in well-coordinated sustainability practices, including a focused effort to improve the sustainable behaviour of customers and consumers. To achieve continuity in sustainable performance, effective change management becomes an ongoing and effective 'built-in' capability.

As a result of this approach, the organization is seen as exercising leadership for the global sustainability movement; its reputation is enhanced and it continues to build reputation and stakeholder support and involvement. Consequently its 'licence to operate' is continually endorsed. If it is a for-profit organization, its share value increases and it increasingly attracts and retains the most talented and highly motivated employees available. Sustainability is an integral element of the cultural DNA.

Again, waste is reinterpreted at this phase. Any operations that divert the organization from the sustainability goal for the organization and society are now considered wasteful. This includes products, services and processes that do not support or that actually undermine the organization's achievements and reputation as a sustainability leader. Additionally, failure to align corporate talent with the goal of sustainability or loss of talent needed to pursue that goal is regarded as waste. The overarching aim is to build a constructive culture that encourages openness, debate innovation and the participation of organizational members and key stakeholder groups.

We refer to these organizations as '*transforming futurists*' because they are not only concerned with the ongoing transformation of their own organizations to align with the requirements of a more sustainable world, but they are also actively involved in transforming the larger economy and society in the same direction.

The central theme of The sustaining corporation phase is: *transform ourselves: lead in creating a sustainable world.*

These are only broad summaries of these categories. For the sake of simplicity of presentation our summaries assume consistency in an organization's sustainability stance across the human and ecological areas. This is an oversimplification. In reality an organization can have quite different philosophies in each area. The organization as a whole, for instance, may have relatively enlightened human resource and social responsibility strategies that place it in Phase 5 for human sustainability (HS5), yet be simultaneously pursuing an unsustainable ecological strategy and so be in Phase 2 in ecological sustainability (ES2). For example, a mining company may invest strongly in the training and development of its employees and subcontractors and also in local community development (HS5), but it may operate environmentally polluting mining operations (ES2).

A fuller version of the model, which allows for differences of this kind, is given in the Appendix at the end of this chapter. We suggest that, on finishing this chapter, you skim-read this and identify where the organization you are involved in would be appropriately placed on these two important dimensions. As we mentioned above, we shall be dealing with each of these phases in much more detail later in the book and you can check out the specific implications of our argument for your particular organizational situation.

We have categorized the phases of sustainability according to three waves. These waves are set out in relation to the six phases of our phase model in Figure 1.1.[22]

Figure 1.1, modified from Kemp, Stark and Tantrum's diagrammatic version of our original phase model, shows an 'ideal type' model of the phases through which an organization that begins by exploiting the ecological and social environment might progress to eventually become a sustaining organization. The phases of our model are shown in the top line of arrows. The diagram shows (above the arrows) how the various phases fit into each of the 'waves' of corporate change. (The first wave, for example, is made up of organizations still in the phases of rejection and non-responsiveness). The second line provides a single word which characterizes the predominant attitudinal focus of senior executives at each phase. So, for example, in the rejection phase senior executives are focused on rejection of the relevance of sustainability attitudes to their business, while, by contrast, at the strategic proactivity phase their predominant focus is on achieving strategic advantage. The bullet points summarize some key characteristics of organizations at each phase – more detail is given in the relevant chapters in this book. Finally, the arrows at the foot of the diagram show how each phase affects the value of the organization. Rejection of sustainability, for example, actually destroys the value of the firm, as it increases risk; non-responsiveness limits value; compliance conserves value by reducing risk, and efficiency and strategic proactivity create value; finally, the sustaining corporation represents a transformation of the corporation into a truly sustainable business that is adding value for the business itself and also adding value for society as a whole and for the environment.

First wave		Second wave			Third wave
Opposition	**Ignorance**	**Risk**	**Cost**	**Competitive advantage**	**Transformation**
Rejection	Non-responsiveness	Compliance	Efficiency	Strategic proactivity	The sustaining corporation
• Highly instrumental perspective on employees and the natural environment • Culture of exploitation • Opposition to government and green activists • Community claims seen as illegitimate	• Financial and technological factors have primacy • More ignorant than oppositional • Seeks business as usual, compliant workforce • Environmental resources seen as a free good	• Focuses on reducing risk of sanctions for failing to meet minimum legal and community standards • Little integration between HR and environmental functions • Follows route of compliance plus proactive measures to maintain good citizen image	• HR systems seen as means to higher productivity and efficiency • Environmental management seen as a source of avoidable cost for the organization	• Focus on innovation • Seeks stakeholder engagement to innovate safe, environmentally friendly products and processes • Advocates good citizenship to maximize profits and increase employee attraction and retention	• Reinterprets the nature of the corporation to an integral self-renewing element of the whole society in its ecological context
Value destroyers	Value limiters	Value conservers	Value creators		Sustainable business

Figure 1.1 Waves of sustainability

Source: Modified from V. Kemp, A. Stark and J. Tantrum, *To Whose Profit: Evolution*, London: WWF-UK, 2004, see note 19.

Change agent roles and the phase model

The phase model represents the path forward to corporate sustainability. Progress on that path can take place only through the action of various change agents. In Chapter 9 we review the kinds of change agents who can impel the corporation forward on this trajectory and briefly outline their particular roles in the process. In that final chapter, we discuss these roles in more detail. Different change-agent roles are critical in different phases. Nevertheless, at this point you may wish to identify which kind of change agent you are, so that, as you read on, you can take particular note of how you can contribute to the progressive redefinition of those organizations you can influence. This will help to clarify how you can contribute to creating a more sustainable world.

The range of potential change agents includes those who work in corporations and those outside who wish to influence them. Internal change agents are board members, CEOs, executives, managers, supervisors, professionals in staff roles and other members of the workforce. External change agents include politicians and bureaucrats, investors, consultants, suppliers and subcontractors, financial analysts, social and ecological activists and other key stakeholders such as community groups, regulators and consumers. Throughout this book we shall argue that all have legitimate roles to play and that concerted action among different kinds of change agents will be needed to create the significant changes we are advocating.

The way these change agents exert influence varies – we shall take these up in more detail in Chapter 9, but some examples are useful here. Executives may exert influence through the exercise of authority: for example, through interpersonal influence in informal networks or through ensuring that their organization markets only sustainable products. Consumers may help to dramatize a key environmental issue or organize a boycott of company goods if they do not meet acceptable environmental standards. Concerted action between internal and external change agents can be particularly powerful in bringing about significant change and we shall be illustrating how this can be orchestrated. Leadership in corporate change is not only exercised by senior executives; in our final chapter we show how the most powerful force for shaping the sustainable corporation of the future will be the collaborative initiatives of a variety of change agents. We emphasize the importance of employees as change agents for sustainability and the importance of leadership which encourages diversity as a way not only to develop human sustainability but to increase the innovative capacity of the organization to progress towards ecological sustainability.

We hope that you now have an understanding of the exciting task we have set ourselves in this book and have begun to see where you can contribute to the significant social shift on which our collective future depends. The rest of the book will help you to deepen your understanding of your potential role and maximize your influence in this change process. To guide your path through the book, we give below a brief overview of the contents of each chapter. You may wish to read the chapters in a linear fashion or identify where you think your organization lies on the path to sustainability and leap ahead to read that first. This chapter outline will help assist you to decide which way to go.

However, we do suggest that you start by reading Chapter 2, 'The drivers of change'. Chapter 2 develops a broad overview of the political, economic and social environment in which we as change agents will be operating. We all need a realistic description and assessment of the forces that will restrain our attempts to influence corporate strategic action as well as those drivers of change that we can draw on to support what we are doing.

The story is told of a young emperor in ancient China who was exploring the labyrinthine interior of his palace. In his wanderings he came upon a room in which the palace butcher was carving carcasses. He watched the butcher at work for some time and was surprised to find that he didn't stop to sharpen his carving knife. The emperor inquired: 'My good man, I am surprised to see that you do not sharpen your knife. Surely with such work it must frequently become blunt?' The butcher replied: 'Your Highness is correct in perceiving that for this work the sharpest of knives is necessary. However, I seldom need to resharpen my knife as I cut where there is least resistance.' As change agents, we too need to learn how to work with the grain rather than against it, to act with skill and sure timing to ensure that our limited energy has maximum impact in bringing about movement towards the fully sustainable corporation.

Chapter 2 is designed to provide a basis for understanding the context of political and social forces in which our action is a small but potentially powerful part. If we understand the major forces that are transforming the world, we can align our energy with those forces already moving society in the direction we support. In this way even small actions may be amplified to create transformational change, rather than being neutralized and dissipated by countervailing forces. Chapter 2 presents the context for change while later chapters describe the goals for change and the means for achieving these goals. In Chapter 2 we highlight some of the major shifts that have occurred in the appreciation of the importance of sustainability and intangible value by individual organizations and across industry sectors since our first edition.

The remaining chapters then discuss the major steps organizations typically take as they move beyond the phases of rejection and non-responsiveness. Organizations in the first two phases are what we refer to as 'first wave corporations', in contrast to what we have termed the more progressive and forward-thinking 'second' and 'third wave' organizations. Their attitudes of antagonism or indifference to the compelling need to create a more sustainable world reflect the lingering persistence of a collapsing corporate model. In this 'first wave' model, the corporation simply exists to exploit human and natural resources for profit, regardless of the impact of this on the current world or the world of the future.

Chapter 3 deals with Phase 3 of our sustainability development model – compliance. In this phase, organizations seek to minimize the risk of ignoring the increasing demand, from governments, communities and activist organizations, for environmental protection and social justice. The chapter outlines the issues to be addressed at this stage in complying with relevant environmental and social legislation and in meeting the demands of key stakeholders. It places particular emphasis on the values, culture and learning characteristics that can enable organizations to move towards and beyond compliance. The chapter also points to the benefits for the corporation in going to 'compliance plus', that is, voluntarily exceeding legislative requirements and stakeholder expectations by playing a more proactive role in launching further sustainability initiatives.

This sets the scene for Chapter 4, 'Achieving sustainable operational efficiencies', which deals with Phase 4 of our model, efficiency. In this stage, organizations start to reap the positive rewards of concerted action on environmental and social issues. Chapter 4 discusses the nature of efficiency, enlarging the concept well beyond cost-cutting exercises. In particular it shows how the sustainability perspective creates a new mind-set that can reveal three successive and cumulative cycles of efficiency-orientated measures. Each of these cycles brings important business benefits as well as contributing to the well-being of the community and the natural environment. At this point organizations often discover how wasteful many of the traditional production or service processes are that they have used. Redesign of products, production flows and service systems generates significant returns. For example, recycling carpets (Interface) or remanufacturing office-machine components (Xerox; Fuji-Xerox) can save millions of dollars as well as benefiting the community and environment by eliminating toxic waste from landfill.

Chapter 5, 'Sustainability: the strategic advantage', moves on to Phase 5: strategic proactivity. At this phase, sustainability becomes important in the organization's strategic repositioning. New competitive advantages can be gained, for example, by moving into rapidly expanding markets for alternative energy (or becoming involved in projects designed to help regenerate communities). Strategic proactivity is an exercise in enlightened self-interest on the part of the corporation. However, Phase 6, the sustaining corporation, represents a move beyond enlightened self-interest to a reinterpretation of the nature of the corporation itself – its redefinition as an integral, self-renewing element of the whole society in its ecological context, which also actively seeks to sustain and renew the context in which it operates.

Chapters 3, 4 and 5 deal with what we regard as 'second wave corporations'. Second wave corporations represent the dominant business ideology in today's world, particularly the world of large corporations. Second wave corporations at least accept the rhetoric of adopting a view of enlightened self-interest, that is, promising policies that bring wider benefits than short-term financial returns to shareholders. Second wave corporations often fall short of these ideals for various reasons which we shall discuss later. What we are seeking in this book is to assist the transition of first wave corporations into second wave corporations; to find ways to turn the rhetoric of second wave corporations into the reality of realistic action and, where possible, to support the move of more second wave organizations into third wave organizations that are truly sustainable and sustaining.

The characteristics of our ideal organization of the future – The sustaining corporation – are discussed in Chapter 6. The sustaining corporation goes beyond self-interest to work actively for a fully sustainable world. If we are to lead change, we must have a view of what the ideal organization will be like. Sustaining corporations represent the third wave – the organizations of the future that act as constituent cells in a fully self-renewing world.

The final part of the book takes up the issue of the implementation of change. Corporate change is a theme that permeates the entire book, but in Part IV we concentrate on defining pathways towards sustainability, that is, on making corporate change that moves organizations towards sustainability.

Many organizations will prefer to make changes slowly, systematically building on the achievements of one phase as they move into the next. So in Chapter 7 we discuss how to progress incremental change.

Other organizations will want to make widespread, rapid and quite radical alterations to the business they are in, the way they do business, their structure, their corporate culture (or all of these). The choice of a transformative path is often driven by a desire to seize new strategic opportunities, or it may come from the organization facing a major threat to its viability. Chapter 8 includes an outline of how this transformational change can be done and provides examples such as DuPont, which has had several periods of transformative change, its most recent being in search of sustainability practices. It includes new material on systemic change and emergent change that is highly relevant to change for sustainability.

Finally, Chapter 9 takes up the issue of how corporate change can be led. We relate specific approaches to leadership to different phases of the phase model and discuss how a variety of change agents, occupying different kinds of roles and acting individually or collectively, can create the momentum needed to create more sustainable organizations. All of us can exercise leadership where we are. If you already are or wish to be a leader in creating this new social reality, the sustainable and sustaining organization, we dedicate this book to you. You will find it useful in the challenging task that lies ahead.

Appendix 1.1: phases in the development of corporate sustainability

 Phase 1: rejection

Human sustainability (HS1)

Employees and subcontractors are regarded as a resource to be exploited. Health and safety features are ignored or paid 'lip service'. Disadvantages stemming from ethnicity, gender, social class, intellectual ability and language proficiency are systematically exploited to advantage the organization and further disadvantage employees and sub-contractors. Force, threats of force and abuse are used to maintain compliance and workforce subjection. Training costs are kept to a minimum necessary to operate the business; expenditure on personal and professional development is avoided. The organization does not take responsibility for the health, welfare and future career prospects of its employees nor for the community of which it is a part. Community concerns are rejected outright.

Ecological sustainability (ES1)

The environment is regarded as a 'free good' to be exploited. Owners/managers are hostile to environmental activists and to pressures from government, other corporations, or community groups aimed at achieving ecological sustainability. Pro-environmental action is seen as a threat to the organization. Physical resource extraction and production processes are used which directly destroy future productive capacity and/or damage the ecosystem. Polluting by-products are discharged into the biosphere, causing damage and threatening living processes. The organization does not take responsibility for the environmental impact of its ongoing operations nor does it modify its operations to lessen future ecological degradation.

 Phase 2: non-responsiveness

Human sustainability (HS2)

Financial and technological factors dominate business strategies to the exclusion of most aspects of human resource management. 'Industrial relations' (IR) or 'employee relations'

Ecological sustainability (ES2)

The ecological environment is not considered to be a relevant factor in strategic or operational decisions. Financial and technological factors dominate business strategies to the

(ER) strategies dominate the human agenda, with 'labour' viewed as a cost to be minimized. Apart from cost minimization, IR/ER strategies are directed at developing a compliant workforce responsive to managerial control. The training agenda, if there is one, centres on technical and supervisory training. Broader human resource strategies and policies are ignored, as are issues of wider social responsibility and community concern.

exclusion of environmental concerns. Traditional approaches to efficiency dominate the production process and the environment is taken for granted. Environmental resources which are free or subsidized (air, water and so on) are wasted and little regard is given to environmental degradation resulting from the organization's activities. Environmental risks, costs, opportunities and imperatives are seen as irrelevant or are not perceived at all.

 ## Phase 3: compliance

Human sustainability (HS3)

Financial and technological factors still dominate business strategies but senior management views the firm as a 'decent employer'. The emphasis is on compliance with legal requirements in industrial relations, safety, workplace standards and so on. Human resource functions such as training, IR, organization development, total quality management (TQM) are instituted but there is little integration between them. Basically the organization pursues a policy of benevolent paternalism with the expectation of employee loyalty in response. Community concerns are addressed only when the company faces the risk of prosecution or where negative publicity may have a damaging impact on the company's financial bottom line. Compliance is undertaken mainly as a risk-reduction exercise.

Ecological sustainability (ES3)

Financial and technological factors still dominate business strategies but senior management seeks to comply with environmental laws and to minimize the firm's potential liabilities from actions that might have an adverse impact on the environment. The most obvious environmental abuses are eliminated, particularly those which could lead to litigation or strong community action directed against the firm. Other environmental issues, which are unlikely to attract litigation or strong community action, are ignored.

Phase 4: efficiency

Human sustainability (HS4)

There is a systematic attempt to integrate human resource functions into a coherent HR system to reduce costs and increase efficiency. People are viewed as a significant source of expenditure to be used as productively as possible. Technical and supervisory training is augmented with human relations (interpersonal skills) training. The organization may institute programmes of teamwork around significant business functions and generally pursues a value-adding rather than an exclusively cost reduction strategy. There is careful calculation of cost–benefit ratios for human resource expenditure to ensure that efficiencies are achieved. Community projects are undertaken where funds are available and where a cost benefit to the company can be demonstrated.

Ecological sustainability (ES4)

Poor environmental practice is seen as an important source of avoidable cost. Ecological issues that generate costs are systematically reviewed in an attempt to reduce costs and increase efficiencies by eliminating waste and by reviewing the procurement, production and distribution process. There may be active involvement in some systematic approach such as Total Quality Environmental Management (ISO 14001). Environmental issues are only addessed if they are seen as generating avoidable costs or increasing efficiencies.

 ## Phase 5: strategic proactivity

Human sustainability (HS5)

The workforce skills mix and diversity are seen as integral and vitally important aspects of corporate and business strategies. Intellectual and social capital are used to develop strategic advantage through innovation in products/services. Programmes are instituted to recruit the best talent to the organization and to develop high levels of competence in individuals and groups. In addition,

Ecological sustainability (ES5)

Proactive environmental strategies supporting ecological sustainability are seen as a source of strategic business opportunities to provide competitive advantage. Product redesign is used to reduce material throughput and to use materials that can be recycled. New products and processes are developed that substitute for or displace existing environmentally damaging products and skills are systematized to form the basis of corporate competences so that the organization is less vulnerable to the loss of key individuals. Emphasis is placed on product and service innovation and speed of response to emerging market demands. Flexible workplace practices are strong features of workplace culture and contribute to the workforce leading more balanced lives. Communities affected by the organization's operations are taken into account and initiatives to address adverse impacts on communities are integrated into corporate strategy. Furthermore, the corporation views itself as a member of the community and as a result contributes to community betterment by offering sponsorship or employee time to participate in projects aimed at promoting community cohesion and well-being.

processes or satisfy emerging community needs around sustainable issues (reforestation; treatment of toxic waste). The organization seeks competitive leadership through spearheading environmentally friendly products and processes.

 ## Phase 6: the sustaining corporation

Human sustainability (HS6)

The organization accepts responsibility for contributing to the process of renewing and upgrading human knowledge and skill formation in the community and society generally, and is a strong promoter of equal opportunity, workplace diversity and work–life balance as workplace principles. It adopts a strong and clearly defined corporate ethical position based on multiple stakeholder perspectives and seeks to exert influence on the key participants in the industry and in

Ecological sustainability (ES6)

The organization becomes an active promoter of ecological sustainability values and seeks to influence key participants in the industry and society in general. Environmental best practice is espoused and enacted because it is the responsible thing to do. The organization tries to assist society to be ecologically sustainable and uses its entire range of products and services to this end. The organization is prepared to use its influence to promote positive sustainability policies on the part society in general to pursue human welfare, equitable and just social practices and the fulfilment of human potential of all. People are seen as valuable in their own right.

of governments, the restructuring of markets and the development of community values to facilitate the emergence of a sustainable society. Nature is valued for its own sake.

Notes

1 We note for instance that the number of abstracts for refereed journal articles that refer to corporate social responsibility has increased by 280 per cent since 2002, while the total number of refereed articles has increased by 120 per cent.

2 D. Dunphy and A. Griffiths, *The Sustainable Corporation: Organizational Renewal in Australia*, Sydney: Allen and Unwin, 1998.

3 Stanford University, 'Global Health Impacts of the Fukushima Nuclear Disaster', *Science Daily*, at http://www.sciencedaily.com/releases/2012/07/120717084900.htm (accessed 5 April 2013).

4 KPMG, 'Corporate Sustainability a Progress Report', KPMG International, 2011.

5 KPMG, 'International Survey of Corporate Responsibility Reporting 2011', KPMG International, at http://www.kpmg.com/Global/en/IssuesAndInsights/ArticlesPublications/corporate-responsibility/Documents/2011-survey.pdf (accessed 4 April 2013).

6 T. Flannery, 'The lonesome prairie', *Good Weekend, Saturday Herald*, Sydney, 3 March 2001, 35–41; T. Flannery, *The Eternal Frontier: An Ecological History of North America and its Peoples*, Melbourne: Text Publishing Company, 2001.

7 P. Hawken, A. Lovins and H. Lovins, *Natural Capitalism: Creating the Next Industrial Revolution*, London: Earthscan, 1999.

8 T. F. Flannery, *The Future Eaters: An Ecological History of the Australasian Lands and People*, Port Melbourne: Reed Books, 1994.

9 S. Hart, 'Beyond greening: strategies for a sustainable world', *Harvard Business Review*, January–February, 1997, 67–76. This quote p. 76.

10 J. Diamond, *Collapse: How Societies Choose to Fail or Survive*, New York: Allen Lane, Penguin, 2005, p. 499.

11 R. Sheldrake, *The Rebirth of Nature*, London: Random Century Group, 1990, p. xv.

12 R. Wright, *A Short History of Progress*, Melbourne: Text Publishing, 2004, p. 132.

13 R. Costanza, R. d'Arge, R. De Groot, S. Farber, M. Grasso, B. Hannon, K. Limburg and M. Van den Belt, 'The value of the world's ecosystem services and natural capital', *Nature*, 1997, 387 (6630), 253–60.

14 C. Duncan, 'Has the Kyoto Protocol made any difference to carbon emissions?', at http://www.guardian.co.uk/environment/blog/2012/nov/26/kyoto-protocol-carbon-emissions (accessed 5 April 2013).

15 C. B. Hunt and E. R. Auster, 'Proactive environmental management: avoiding the toxic trap', *Sloan Management Review*, 1990, 31 (2), 7–18.

16 J. Austin, 'Strategic Collaboration between Non-profits and Businesses', Working Paper, Harvard University, 1999.

17 A. J. Hoffman, 'Institutional evolution and change: environmentalism and the US chemical industry', *Academy of Management Journal*, 1999, 42 (4), 351–7.

18 For a discussion and analysis of the stage model approach, see A. Kolk and A. Mauser, 'The evolution of environmental management: from stage models to performance evaluation', *Business, Strategy and the Environment*, 2002, 11, 14–31.

19 Dunphy and Griffiths, *The Sustainable Corporation*.

20 We do not imply here, of course, that all organizations start the journey from a position of active antagonism to sustainability. Some organizations are actually founded on strong ethical commitments (Phase 6) – they are, however, the exception, rather than the rule.

21 See S. Benn, D. Dunphy and B. Perrott, *Cases in Corporate Sustainability and Change: A Multidisciplinary Approach*, Prahan, Australia: Tilde University Press, 2011.

22 Our original phase model has been represented diagrammatically in V. Kemp, A. Stark and J. Tantrum, *To Whose Profit: Evolution*, London: WWF-UK, 2004. We have modified this diagram.

2   The drivers of change

- Dynamic natural environment
- Globalization
- Evolving forms of regulation
- New technologies and business models
- Conclusion

Dynamic natural environment

In this chapter we examine the key issues that are driving organizational change for sustainability. It is only in recent decades that we have become aware of the extent to which the dynamics of natural systems make them vulnerable to human intervention. But in that relatively short period in the history of industrialization, it has become increasingly evident that the damage wrought to the planet is such that without dramatic change in the behaviour of business organizations and our individual behaviour as consumers, life on the Earth as we know it is unsustainable. For the sake of the ecosystem upon which we all depend for the ultimate source of much of our aesthetic understanding of what is beauty and for what is left of the remaining great wilderness areas of the planet[1], we must question what we mean by business development. We can but stop to reflect on what will be left for the next generation of nature in all its wonder. It is the corporation that we must rely on for change, not just through the greening of a single organization but through the role it can play in interaction with other stakeholders.[2] To us, the reasons why business and its networks need to come on board are clear.

Climate change/global heating

In 2008, UN Secretary-General Ban Ki-moon warned that climate change is the 'defining challenge of the era'.[3] Four years later, the OECD Environmental Outlook to 2050[4] provided more evidence of the urgency with which action is needed on behalf of global ecological limits. It emphasizes that without more ambitious policies than those in force today, greenhouse gas emissions will increase by another 50 per cent by 2050 – primarily due to a projected 80 per cent increase in global energy demand and economic growth in key emerging economies. Global average temperature increase is projected to be 3°C to 6°C higher by the end of the century, exceeding the internationally agreed goal of limiting it to 2°C above pre-industrial levels. Temperature changes will be likely to be unevenly distributed but increases will be sufficient to alter precipitation patterns, melt glaciers, cause sea-level rise and intensify extreme weather events to unprecedented levels. They might also exceed some critical 'tipping-points', causing dramatic natural changes that could have catastrophic or irreversible outcomes for natural systems and society.

Regional attempts to improve energy intensity that are evident in emerging economies such as Brazil and Russia are not likely to address the increasing energy demand worldwide. So, while greenhouse gas emissions from land use and forestry are expected to decrease, that will not be enough to counterbalance the expected increases overall.

The implications of climate change are evident in economic scenarios that indicate that companies reliant on fossil fuel face major issues of long-term risk management. For instance, recent studies have shown that the benefits of a radical rethinking of our energy sources far outweigh the economic cost.[5] New research from Carbon Tracker and the Grantham Research Institute on Climate Change and the Environment at the London School of Economics published in the report 'Unburnable Carbon 2013: Wasted Capital and Stranded Assets' has revealed that fossil fuel reserves already far exceed the carbon budget to avoid global warming of 2°C. Yet '$674 billion was spent last year to find and develop new potentially stranded assets'. The research report 'calls for regulators, governments and investors to re-evaluate energy business models against carbon budgets, to prevent a $6 trillion carbon bubble in the next decade'.[6]

Other environmental impacts

The recent report *Natural Capital at Risk – The Top 100 Externalities of Business*, from the TEEB Coalition,[7] produced valuations of direct environmental impacts (that is, those produced by a company's own operations per sector and region). Examples of this work are at Table 2.1. The report notes that indirect impacts (from sources upstream in supply chains or downstream from product use or disposal or investments) are also crucial to understand. Even in the one industry sector there are differences across regions. Indirect impacts can be very high in some sectors such as the consumer goods sector, where impacts may be hidden upstream in the supply chain.

The findings of the most recent World Wide Fund for Nature (WWF) *Living Planet Report* (2012)[8] demonstrate the extent to which existing policies have failed to deal with the other planetary impacts of industrialization and globalization. The Living Planet Index measures the ecological health of the planet. While the Index for high-income countries shows an increase of 7 per cent between 1970 and 2008, that for low-income countries has declined by 60 per cent, a finding likely to be due to the differing capacities of high- and low-income nations to purchase and import resources. These figures indicate a potential catastrophe for biodiversity, for people living in certain regions of the world and for the planet as a whole. The box below shows the five greatest pressures on the planet according to this report.

Table 2.1 *Total direct environmental damage as a percentage of revenue for an illustrative selection of primary, manufacturing and tertiary sectors, using global averages*

Sector	Total direct impact ratio (natural capital cost as % of revenue)
Cattle ranching and farming	710
Wheat farming	400
Cement manufacturing	120
Coal power generation	110
Iron and steel mills	60
Iron ore mining	14
Plastics material and resin manufacturing	5
Snack food manufacturing	2
Apparel knitting mills	1

Source: Modified from TEEB, *Natural Capital at Risk – The Top 100 Externalities of Business*, TEEB, 2013.

The five greatest direct pressures on the planet

- *The loss, alteration and fragmentation of habitats* – mainly through conversion of natural land for agricultural, aquacultural, industrial or urban use; damming and other changes to river systems for irrigation or flow regulation.
- *Overexploitation of wild species' populations* – harvesting of animals and plants for food, materials or medicine at a rate higher than they can reproduce.
- *Pollution* – mainly from excessive pesticide use in agriculture and aquaculture, urban and industrial effluents, mining waste and excessive fertilizer use.
- *Climate change* – due to rising levels of greenhouse gases in the atmosphere, caused mainly by the burning of fossil fuels, forest clearing and industrial processes.
- *Invasive species* – introduced deliberately or inadvertently to one part of the world from another, they then become competitors, predators or parasites of native species.

(Source: Living Planet Report 2012, online. Available HTTP: <http://awassets.panda.org/downloads/lpr_2012_summary_booklet_final.pdf>, page 12 (accessed 4 March 2014)

For example, recent figures indicate:

- Nearly a quarter of all mammals and a third of all amphibians are threatened with extinction.
- Coral reefs are worth $172 billion a year to the human economy, but they are on the verge of extinction.
- Deforestation contributes to between 15 and 20 per cent of the world's carbon dioxide emissions.[9]
- Recent estimates from The Economics of Ecosystems and Biodiversity in Business and Enterprise (TEEB) Coalition are that the global top 100 environmental externalities are costing the economy worldwide around $4.7 trillion a year in terms of the economic costs of greenhouse gas emissions, loss of natural resources, loss of nature-based services such as carbon storage by forests, climate change and air pollution-related health costs.[10]

This book argues that business can and should be playing a leadership role in redressing these impacts on the natural world. Business can design more efficient production systems and more sustainable products. It can educate consumers to be more ecologically conscious and discriminating in their purchasing. It can work with governments and other stakeholders to develop viable and sustainable ways of delivering human and ecological sustainability so that landmark achievements associated with human development are not at the expense of our precious ecosystems.

For example, while the average life span in China has risen from 35 to 74.9 years in just over five decades, rising 3.43 years between 2000 and 2010,[11] China's leadership now publicly recognizes that environmental impacts will impede the continuing economic development of that country. A recent joint research report by a team from the World Bank and the Development Research Center of China's State Council argues that the current model of growth will not continue and that future growth and employment will rely upon China promoting innovation and green growth along with expanding health and education services. The compelling argument is that green growth can be stimulated in China through better design and enforcement of regulations to complement market incentives, such as taxes, fees, tradable permits and quotas, and eco-labelling.[12]

The destructive environmental and social side-effects of the combination of population growth and increased consumption have contributed to these challenges of global survival. The 2012 OECD report states the situation bluntly:

> Humanity has witnessed unprecedented growth and prosperity in the past decades, with the size of the world economy more than tripling and population increasing by over 3 billion people since 1970. This growth, however, has been accompanied by environmental pollution and natural resource depletion. The current growth model and the mismanagement of natural assets could ultimately undermine human development.[13]

How do we address these issues? What role should corporations, governments and individuals play in creating a more desirable future? Central to the resolution of these issues is the need for all sectors of society to cooperate in changes designed to promote human and ecological sustainability.

Globalization

Globalization has opened markets, dispersed capital and grown investments and has been endorsed by most leaders of developing and developed countries. Recent figures show that the value of world merchandise exports increased by 20 per cent in 2011 while exports of commercial services grew by 11 per cent.[14] The impact on human development is remarkable; the 2013 Human Development Report (HD Report) shows increasing convergence between nations, so that no nation had a lower Human Development Index (HDI) value in 2012 than in

2000. Yet the report also highlights the still uneven progress within and between nations. Globalization, while lifting many from poverty, is simultaneously contributing to the reinforcing and extending of inequities in human living standards as well as exacerbating climate change and other negative impacts listed above. As noted in previous HD Reports, the lower HDI nations will be most impacted by negative effects of climate change and in some areas of the world such effects are already manifest in drought, water shortages, floods and diminishing food security.

Pointing to shifting power differentials and sustainability risks and opportunities, key areas of development are in the South – Brazil, China and India, development that is being driven by technological advances and new business relationships between nations of the South. It seems that the future impact of globalization depends on how technology is utilized for human and ecological sustainability. Of equal importance is how relationships between business, civil society and government are harnessed for sustainable outcomes, countering risks from terrorism, nuclear warfare and social, environmental and financial instability.[15] As Ulrich Beck puts it – we are embedded in the conditions of 'the world risk society' where we are becoming increasingly concerned with the impacts of the modernization we have ourselves driven.[16]

'Globalization from above'

Two sets of actors have emerged on the global stage in reaction to these adverse social and environmental effects of globalization and industrialization. At one level, there is 'globalization from above', which represents groupings at the level of nation-states and international organizations. 'Globalization from below', on the other hand, represents groupings for local action that include citizens and not-for-profits.[17] So, from above, government representatives are negotiating international agreements, alongside with business, such as the response to diminishing world oil reserves, the nuclear non-proliferation treaties, General Agreement on Tariffs and Trade (GATT), the World Economic Forum, the World Trade Organization and intergovernmental agreements on the environment. The ineptness of national governments in dealing with climate change demonstrates the extent to which they experience difficulties in cooperating in the implementation of intergovernmental agreements concerning sustainability for various reasons, including unemployment, economic conditions and the activities of various interest groups. This puts the onus on multinational corporations to take more responsibility for their actions, confronting the hitherto dominant understanding of what should be regarded as business priority. Does the business world defend and take part in this system that contributes to social and environmental problems or does it shift mind-set and activities to become part of the solution?

To understand the countervailing pressures associated with 'globalization from above' we need to look at how sustainability has been interpreted in its global context. Sustainability can be defined as that *state* that results from the *process* of sustainable development[18] – or development which 'meets the needs of the present without compromising the ability of the future generations to meet their own needs'.[19] The term was thus defined by the World Commission on Environment and Development (WCED), established by the United Nations in 1983 and chaired by Gro Harlem Brundtland. The WCED report, *Our Common Future*, was the first attempt by an intergovernmental body to promote global dialogue on sustainability and sustainable development. This view of appropriate and sustainable development was promoted at the Second United Nations Conference on the Environment and Development (UNCED), held in 1992 in Rio de Janeiro. At the time, it was the largest-ever Heads of Government meeting, with more than 170 countries represented. The Conference endorsed the major action plan, Agenda 21, since widely taken as a blueprint for the implementation of sustainable development and the integration of economic growth with environmental responsibility. Along the way since 1992, the international community has developed a range of treaties and agreements which are designed to monitor 'progress' largely according to this definition. A number of global treaties and hundreds of regional and bilateral agreements have since been negotiated.

In the decades since Rio, the discourse of sustainable development has also been embedded within many governmental and intergovernmental documents and agreements. For example, the key concepts of sustainable development, interpreted as Education for Sustainability principles, are now espoused by many higher education institutions and enshrined in the UN Decade for Education for Sustainable Development. Also manifesting in the corporate sector, the World Business Council for Sustainable Development emerged post Rio as a CEO-led alliance of some of the world's biggest and most influential companies across sector and region claiming to pursue sustainable development and has since been involved in numerous multi-stakeholder arrangements that purport to address sustainability.

Effectiveness of 'globalization from above'

Given the extent to which business is clearly not internalizing environmental costs, one has to question the effectiveness of the top-down global-level approach in terms of what is lacking and what are possible improvements. Arguably, recent meetings conducted under the umbrella of the United Nations Framework Convention on Climate Change (UNFCCC) have exposed the limitations of existing global institutional arrangements for managing environmental impacts such as climate change.[20] Agreements or conventions that are largely constitutional, as with UNFCCC, face the problem that they are not designed to address compliance matters, and function largely as governance models. The Kyoto Protocol, on the other hand, from the outset included mandatory requirements concerning greenhouse gas emissions. According to Bodansky and O'Connor, stringency, participation and compliance are the factors necessary for intergovernmental arrangements to be effective, and neither UNFCCC or the Kyoto Protocol meet all three.[21] The problem is how to balance these characteristics so that the international standards and agreements are participatory, yet offer some commitment to setting standards of achievement.

The other question of note that is still unresolved in terms of environmental agreements in particular is the tension between national legislation and international agreements, exacerbated by the fact that environmental issues are inherently transboundary. Birds, fish and plants do not recognize those boundary lines we humans draw across the globe. World Heritage areas such as the Great Barrier Reef, for example, may be internationally protected, but threatened by local development which is quite lawful according to Australian legislation. Swedish Lapland, the last great European wilderness, could be similarly threatened by the Swedish extractive industry in neighbouring areas.

In fact many treaties and other cross-national arrangements do not result in effective action and often preserve existing inequities that favour the interests of the already privileged nations. Corporate and government irresponsibility and equity issues in the development of treaties and agreements are putting business under pressure to implement voluntary sustainability measures to supplement the international agreements.

In later chapters we discuss some of the voluntary codes, principles and agreements that industry organizations, multi-stakeholder arrangements and individual organizations have developed to restore their credibility.

At the World Economic Forum in Davos in 1999, UN Secretary-General Kofi Annan challenged business to support a Global Compact which he called 'Globalization with a Human Face'. The compact is intended to promote human rights, just labour standards and good environmental practices and marks an attempt by the UN to lead both the private and public spheres in the direction of a more equitable and ecologically sustainable model of development. As of 2012, figures for the number of participants show that the initiative has grown to more than 10,000 participants, including over 7,000 businesses in 145 countries around the world.[22] Linked in through UN action is the Global Reporting Initiative (GRI), a highly structured set of performance indicators to assist companies to report on sustainability performance.

Others include the Valdez Principles, the US Business Principles for Human Rights of Workers in China and the Business Charter for Sustainable Development. The Principles of Responsible Investment and The Economics of Ecosystems and Biodiversity for Business Coalition (TEEB) have both emerged through the agency of the UN Environment Program, with the latter a multi-stakeholder entity also supported by G8. TEEB activities focus on raising awareness of the business case for natural-capital accounting, research and supporting the development of harmonized methods for measuring, managing and reporting environmental externalities in business.

Twenty years on from Rio, the Rio +20 Conference, a three-day summit attended by 189 states and held in Brazil, produced the document titled 'The Future We Want'. Criticized for not going far enough in terms of gaining agreement around key measures such as phasing out subsidies for fossil fuels, the conference also provided some gains with particular implications for business sustainability. For example, the concepts of 'green economy' and 'integrated reporting' were endorsed and support groups were developed around these concepts.[23]

Overall, despite some advances, it seems that the ongoing inability of such global structures to deal effectively with what are blatant sustainability problems reflects an apparent impasse around the participatory and holistic principles upon which sustainability rests (Rio Declaration,1992: Principles 3, 4 and 10). They are well meaning, but are they so ambiguous, slippery, contested and readily politicized as to be inoperable?[24] The discourse has been criticized, on the one hand, as being inherently weak, in fact legitimating development by the wealthier countries of the North,[25] and questioned, on the other hand, in terms of the costs of attempting to balance environmental, social and economic development.[26] On a more positive note, we suggest that it is the very openness and breadth of the concept of sustainability and its associate, sustainable development, that allow other stakeholders to the table. This is evident in a parallel trend that has been labelled 'globalization from below'.[27]

'Globalization from below'

A powerful force is also swelling up from below to pressure corporate change. Organized by transnational NGOs and spread largely on the internet, 'globalization from below' is an initiative directed against the perceived self-seeking manipulations of elite nation-states and transnationals driving 'globalization from above'.[28] Work done by Inglehart and Welzel (2010) indicates a shift in industrialized countries towards what they term a self-expression society, concerned with environmental issues, freedom for self-expression and a high value placed on creativity,[29] argued as the key qualities needed for democracy to be effective. The most overt demonstration of this polarization between survival and self-expression is the Occupy Movement. This leaderless, global and still emergent phenomenon is represented in its website refrain:

> We are the 99 percent. We are getting kicked out of our homes. We are forced to choose between groceries and rent. We are denied quality medical care. We are suffering from environmental pollution. We are working long hours for little pay and no rights, if we're working at all. We are getting nothing while the other 1 percent is getting everything. We are the 99 percent.[30]

The aims of 'globalization from below' are diffuse and the vision for the future is not clearly specified. But the message is clear. The 'globalization from below' movement has spread from a criticism of Western 'imperialism' in the form of developmentalism, to a wider dissatisfaction with how global capitalism and lax national standards are contributing to destructive environmental and social conditions at the local level. It is not just a protest in Wall Street. In China, for example, pollution has replaced land disputes as the main cause of social unrest. China now sees 30,000 to 50,000 so-called mass incidents every year. Chen Jiping, a former leading member of the Chinese Communist Party's Committee of Political and Legislative Affairs, has claimed that increased use of mobile phones and the internet has allowed protesters to show their anger more effectively.[31]

Networks and alliances for sustainability

'Globalization from below' highlights two important points for corporations. First, globalization and the information revolution have also given the general public the means for self-critique and self-transformation. As awareness of the limitations of our traditional institutions spreads, we have continued to move towards what Hazel Henderson termed more than a decade ago 'the networked society'. Henderson noted then the emergence of a political trend in the form of citizen organizations and movements. They are now a distinct third sector in the world, holding the private and public sectors more accountable. More access to information has helped to empower citizens, consumer choice, employees and socially responsible investors. 'The information society has created new winners', as Henderson once said[32] – but what is now clear is that it has also created new losers . Examples abound of the power of viral networks in attacking corporate brands. In 2010 Greenpeace targeted Nestlé's famous KitKat product over concerns about the use of palm oil and the resulting impact on the habitats of orang-utans. A viral advertising campaign led Nestlé to announce that it would stop using ingredients that may be sourced as a result of rainforest destruction.[33] The Occupy Movement has utilized its crowd-sourcing mobilizing techniques to target major corporates such as the Bank of America. In Australia, NGOs such as Animals Australia and Voiceless have organized campaigns some of which have gone viral (such as those alleging cruelty against butchering methods of Australian cattle used in some Indonesian abattoirs). The impact of these campaigns can be enormous – for instance, causing the Australian government to temporarily call a halt to all live cattle exports until conditions were reviewed.

The second factor provoking business response is that manifest increased public awareness of sustainability issues and diminishing public trust in both corporations and governments are creating market expectations for more responsible corporate behaviour and sustainable products and services. In the wake of Rio +20 and widespread pessimism that governments will act to address issues such as climate change, the findings of a recent GlobeScan survey of 791 sustainability professionals from 74 countries are instructive (see Figure 2.1).

Alliances and networks forming around single issues such as climate change are now including social and natural scientists, business, local government, community and other social actors whose allegiances cross

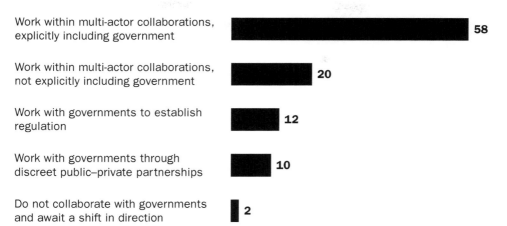

Figure 2.1 *Findings of GlobeScan and SustainAbility survey, 'What is the most effective approach companies can take?'*
Source: Modified from GlobeScan and SustainAbility, *Collaborating for a Sustainable Future. A GlobeScan/SustainAbility Survey*, 2012, p.6. http://www.sustainability.com/library/collaborating-for-a-sustainable-future#.UYULTpFaef8 (accessed 25 April 2013).

established disciplinary and role boundaries. Communities of practice are increasingly common and are forged by concepts or discourses acting as boundary objects across the different knowledge worlds of the participants.[34] The media, information systems and ad hoc coalitions of opposites, such as those between NGOs and business organizations discussed below, are increasingly influential in all aspects of society. The GRI, for instance, gathers input from environmental, human rights and industry association NGOs.

Consumer action and mass boycotts and protests, such as those targeted at Nike, Apple, IKEA and BP over the years are forcing corporations to defend their actions. The Australian company heavily involved in the woodchipping industry in some of the old growth forests in Tasmania, for example, has now gone out of business, unable to finance its operations after massive public campaigns led by a range of NGOs. The open-ended nature of the sustainability ethic gives it the power to bring together, at least at the discussion table, people and groups with very different political and ideological perspectives. Some supporters advocate greening of business models which work within the current model of capitalism and democracy and support continuing technological innovation and economic growth.[35] Others argue that this approach merely encourages the continuing exploitation of ecological resources, rather than guiding us

Company/NGO collaborations

Company and NGO partnerships are seen as the most traditional form of collaboration, with notable examples including Coca Cola and WWF, and Starbucks and Conservation International.

Company/Company collaborations

It is a fairly recent phenomenon that companies are working together in areas where they are directly competing. Ford and Toyota's collaboration on the development of an advanced new hybrid system for light trucks and SUVs being a notable case study.

Single-industry collaborations

Single-industry collaborations are where public, private and NGO actors from a single industry partner to achieve greater impact across a wider range of issues. A notable example of such a collaboration is the Sustainable Apparel Coalition, which has seen many of the top names in apparel and footwear partnering to reduce the environmental and social impacts of their industry.

Multi-industry collaborations

Single-issue collaborations see multi-actor partnerships formed across the boundaries of industry to tackle a single (often common) issue. High-profile examples include The Plant PET Technology Collaborative.

Figure 2.2 *Examples of collaboration*
Source: Modified from GlobeScan and SustainAbility, *Collaborating for a Sustainable Future. A GlobeScan/SustAinability Survey*, 2012, p. 4.

towards a more harmonious relationship with nature.[36] Other critics have argued in the past that a reliance on technical solutions for sustainable development and their diffusion to the countries of the South represents just another exploitative, special-interest-based relationship between North and South, although this situation is now changing with the huge upsurge in growth of South–South relationships.[37]

Alliances or collaborations around sustainability can be grouped according to their participants (see Figure 2.2):

- Company–company collaborations such as between Toyota and Ford around new hybrid technology for light trucks and SUVs.
- Multi-industry collaborations formed around a single issue such as the Plant PET Collaboration Initiative.

- Company–NGO collaborations such as Coca Cola and WWF, and Starbucks and Conservation International.
- Single-industry collaborations such as the Sustainable Apparel Coalition and the Sustainable Steel Certification Scheme in Australia.

Dynamic partnerships between these stakeholders can provide learning opportunities that have the potential to change corporate attitudes and practices. The GRI is a key example. Although costs may preclude smaller companies taking it up, there appear to be advantages in taking up opportunities and overall risk management. With 11,000 companies signed up, the GRI has clearly had an impact, although concerns are now being raised at the level of prescriptive standards.[38] In another instance, the NGO Global Forest Watch provides maps indicating the whereabouts of old-growth forests and other data for the IKEA corporation to enable purchasing of forest products according to sustainable criteria. Another example is the partnership formed between the WWF and Unilever, at the time the world's largest supplier of frozen fish, with the aim of developing incentives to support sustainable fishing. The Marine Stewardship Council was developed as a result of this alliance.[39] WWF has also partnered with Coca Cola to reduce water consumption.[40]

The Play Fair Alliance

Play Fair is a global campaign coordinated by international trade union federations and NGOs, namely, the International Trades Union Federation (ITUC), the International Textile, Garment and Leather Workers' Federation (ITGLWF), the Building and Wood Workers' International (BWI) and the Clean Clothes Campaign (CCC). The campaign calls on those who organize and profit from sports events to take specific steps to ensure that workers making sporting goods and building venues are not exploited, and that international labour standards are respected in the workplace as well as in the stadium. Campaigns began with the 2004 Athens Olympics and have continued across the 2008 Beijing Olympics, the 2010 Vancouver Winter Games and the 2010 South Africa World Cup. Campaigns aimed at event organizers, construction companies and sport-goods brands include the Ukraine and Poland European Championship, the London 2012 Olympics and the Sochi 2014 Winter Games. In an example of the activities of such alliances, research conducted in association with the Playfair London 2012 campaign found breaches of every one of the nine standards of the ethical code embraced by London Organising Committee of the Olympic Games and Paralympic Games (LOCOG) in factories in China producing official merchandise bearing the London 2012 Olympic Games logo.[41]

In a number of countries, networks and alliances that include corporations, state and local governments are addressing the lack of action by national governments on climate change. In Canada, the Network for Business Sustainability is part funded by the Canadian government and claims to move beyond disciplinary and organizational silos so that different aspects of society can work together. Influential reports and networking events emanating from such centres in many countries are pushing against corporate resistance.[42]

Supply chains as networks

While sustainability has been largely the domain of big business, small to medium-size enterprises (SMEs) are now taking some action because of pressures and requirements along supply chain networks. As mentioned above, major indirect sustainability impacts exist in some sectors and numerous sustainability advocacy bodies, consultancies and not-for-profits are working with companies to improve sustainability performance along their supply chains. For instance, the long-established advocacy organization CERES, with wide experience in working towards sustainable business, estimates that up to 60 per cent of a manufacturing company's carbon footprint is in its supply chain, and for retailers it is perhaps as much as 80 per cent – with an equally high supply-chain exposure to human rights and social issues.[43] Examples of companies that are implementing sustainable supply chain measures by working with CERES are PepsiCo (establishing a policy on the human right to water); the footwear and apparel industry's 'Eco-Index', a shared platform for companies to evaluate the environmental impacts of the design and manufacturing of their products; and the Electric Utility Sustainable Supply Chain Alliance, including the organization of a process to obtain multi-stakeholder input into the group's scope, criteria and disclosure mechanisms. Procter and Gamble has a sustainability scorecard against which it assesses its suppliers in terms of environmental factors such as waste management.[44]

While the rhetoric is strong that sustainable supply-chain management can deliver business gains in the form of reputational risk management, productivity and efficiency gains, clearly some organizations in certain industry sectors have major problems in managing their global supply chain according to these standards. As we write this chapter, for example, we read of another disaster in a Bangladeshi garment factory, a sadly repetitive story: a death toll of more than 200 workers, due to building collapse in a factory making clothes for foreign companies, claimed by activists to include Walmart, C&A, Benetton and Mango.[45]

Evolving forms of regulation

User pays

The 'user pays' principle is a regulatory approach easily applied through legislation that is driving corporate change, ensuring that those who create the risks pay for them. Taxes such as consumer fees for the disposal of appliances (applied in Japan), legislation for producer responsibility (in Sweden and the Netherlands) and pollution taxes in many countries are examples.[46] Incentives-based and polluter-pays strategies include load-based licensing and tradable permits to encourage reduction of pollution. In load-based licensing, companies are charged licence fees which vary according to the amount of pollution they discharge. Other economic policy tools include tradable rights to natural resources to encourage efficient resource management, innovative design and cleaner production. Examples of such incentives include vehicle emission quotas, landfill taxes and 'green taxes', such as carbon taxes (as in Denmark), congestion taxes (as in Singapore) and vehicle-return bonuses.

Co-regulation

Co-regulation means that government entrusts the attainment of various legislative objectives to 'parties which are recognized in the field (such as economic operators, the social partners, non-governmental organizations, or associations)'.[47] Since the Brundtland Report and the 1992 Rio Conference, business has been increasingly drawn into a system of co-regulation, where government, business and community are all expected to play a part in sustainable development. It is widely recognized that command-and-control forms of governance lack effectiveness in terms of changing behaviour and that, going beyond the setting of minimal standards, regulation needs to be a more participatory and reflexive process. Co-regulatory forms that have the potential to deliver on these requirements include legislation that incorporates a role for community consultative committees, frequently used to enable community response in legislation pertaining to mining operations, for example.

Porter and van der Linde's argument that regulation can force or 'enlighten' corporations to employ the environment as a 'competitive opportunity' has been taken up by some governments in Northern Europe and Japan.[48] These governments have initiated policies geared to encourage the emergence of a specific sector which focuses on the development of green technology, or environmental services. This powerful approach, termed 'ecological modernization', sees scientific and technological advances as an answer to the dilemma of how to provide for continued economic growth without negative impact on the environment. The basic argument is that we do not have to create a new political economy so as to achieve sustainability. It is enough to ensure that innovative environmental goods and services become a source of profit.[49] This approach is also co-regulatory, its proponents arguing that market, government and NGOs all have a role to play in industrial transformation incorporating more ecologically friendly principles.[50] Indeed, many of the governments, such as Japan, Sweden, Norway and Germany, which have been most successful in shifting the economy away from a dependency on unsustainable production technology and towards green production technology have a tradition of close associative relations between industry, business and government.[51]

Codes of conduct

The emergence of multiple forms of corporate codes is a relatively recent 'regulatory' phenomenon, where industry associations, individual firms or certain supply chains develop documents that set out specific standards of behaviour. Codes of conduct usually focus on ethical or socially responsible issues and are an example of the self-regulation of industry.[52] While voluntary, such codes are increasingly acting as de facto regulation, with some also having reporting requirements. In later chapters, we explore a range of codes of conduct and how they are becoming an instrumental form of regulation requiring compliance according to these standards. Although codes of ethics have a long history in business,[53] it is only relatively recently that corporate sustainability and corporate social responsibility (CSR) have been addressed comprehensively. Examples include the Nike Code of Conduct and voluntary sector-specific agreements such as the Responsible Care programme of the chemicals sector.[54]

New reporting requirements and concepts

Accompanying the push for greater regulation in one form or another is increased pressure on corporations to employ better assessment and measurement techniques in activities relevant to sustainability.[55] Companies are increasingly expected to report against non-financial as well as financial criteria. Pressure is coming from not-for-profit organizations such as the Carbon Disclosure Project, which leverages market forces including shareholders, customers and governments to motivate companies to reveal their carbon impacts. One third of the world's invested capital now calls for environmental data through this project.[56] Further evidence of the growing importance of reporting is that at Rio +20 a group of countries (Brazil, Denmark, France and South Africa) joined with GRI and UNEP to champion integrated reporting which combines financial data with information on organizations' performance on environmental, social and governance issues.

Recent research indicates that sustainability reporting not only increases transparency but can also change corporate behaviour. In a study where researchers applied an econometric model to data from 58 countries regarding laws and regulations that mandate a minimum level of disclosure on environmental, social and governance matters it was found that

> mandatory disclosure of sustainability information leads to a) an increase in the social responsibility of business leaders, b) a prioritization of sustainable development, c) a prioritization of employee training, d) more efficient supervision of managers by boards of directors, e) an increase in the implementation of ethical practices by firms, f) a decrease in bribery and corruption, and g) an improvement of managerial credibility within society.[57]

The paper notes a widespread increase in reporting of non-financial information, mostly on a voluntary basis, over the preceding decade. According to the GRI, only 44 firms followed GRI guidelines to report sustainability information in 2000. By 2010, the number of organizations releasing sustainability reports had grown to 1,973.

New technologies and business models

Innovation and technology

Aside from policy-focused recommendations, such as setting economy-wide greenhouse gas (GHG) mitigation targets to guide policy and investment decisions and setting a price on carbon, the recent OECD report[58] relies upon innovation as the way to avoid irreparable damage – presenting a clear role and opportunity for business. But it is an approach to business in collaboration with government and the not-for-profit sector that is needed to take up these opportunities.

For example, the leading environmental organization WWF has identified six key solutions to the challenge of meeting global energy demand without damaging the global climate:

1 improving energy efficiency
2 stopping forest loss
3 accelerating the development of low-emissions technologies
4 developing flexible fuels
5 replacing high-carbon coal with low-carbon gas
6 equipping fossil fuel plants with carbon capture and storage technology.[59]

According to the leading NGO Worldwatch Institute, new technologies embedded in advanced automotive, electronics and buildings systems will allow a substantial reduction in carbon dioxide (CO_2) emissions, at negative cost once the saving in energy bills is taken into account. The savings from these measures can effectively pay for a significant portion of the additional cost of advanced renewable energy technologies to replace fossil fuels, including wind, solar, geothermal and bioenergy.

New business models

A range of new business models are emerging in response to the evident negative social and environmental impacts of global capitalism. Shared value, Business at Base of the Pyramid, Fair Trade, natural capitalism, industrial ecology, biomimicry, collaborative consumption – these are just some of the new ways of doing business that we will explore in later chapters. Each can be linked to the phase model – some are more incremental and efficiency related, while others are more transformative and reflect a company really working to ensure long-term value for society and the environment as well as for its shareholders.

On a positive note, some world and corporate leaders are showing that they are willing to push for development which is more cautious, self-reflective and supportive of sustainable business as a means to foster learning and capacity building in local communities. For example, the major cleaning products company SC Johnson is integrating local farmers into its supply chain according to the Business at the Base of the Pyramid model.[60] Leading business academics, also, are proclaiming the need for business to shed an outdated understanding of value and to build shared value with society so that, by rethinking products and markets and building relationships along its supply chains and at and around its locations a company can not only reduce its externalities but build value for wider society.[61]

While there have been academic attempts to explode the 'myth of the ethical consumer',[62] new models of consumerism are offering more sophisticated approaches to purchasing that have less-negative social and environmental impact in the long term. According to the exponents of what is now a social movement, collaborative consumption through renting and sharing resources, or using services such as eBay, reflects a new trend in business, one based on communication where the use-value of objects or services is shared and where trust is an important aspect of the business equation.[63] In this model individuals act as brokers for goods and services that consumers would normally purchase from retailers – examples include the peer-to-peer rental services of various types, such as cars, landspace, rental rooms and tools. Benefits for the future are seen as breaking the consumer mind-set and reducing the environmental impact of our production systems.

Natural capitalism: the business advantage

Natural capitalism as a business model is based on the principle of increasing the productivity of natural resources. If firms persist with the win–win business logic of 'natural capitalism', profiting from increasing the productivity of natural resources, closing materials loops and eliminating waste, shifting to biologically inspired production models, providing their customers with efficient solutions and reinvesting in natural capital, they can gain a commanding competitive advantage.[64] Business advantage is also offered through the organizational restructuring required by following the principles of industrial ecology. Tracking material and energy flows over the whole producer–consumer cycle reduces the likelihood of suboptimal solutions and unintended consequences.[65]

At Hewlett-Packard (HP), for example, its Environmental Strategies and Solutions programme confirmed that sustainability does offer companies a strategic competitive advantage.[66] This conclusion was based on the premise that the planet is a closed system which will eventually face limits. In these circumstances, the firm would be in a new social and economic situation, and would have to deal with the challenges of a new business environment. According to Gabi Zedlmayer, Vice President, Sustainability and Social Innovation:

> HP's commitment to environmental sustainability helps guide the direction of our company, positions us as a leader in our industry, and drives the innovation of new products and solutions that make a positive impact in the world.[67]

Associated achievements at HP noted on the current website include a 20 per cent reduction in 2011 GHG emissions for HP operations, as compared with 2005.[68]

Cost avoidance and risk management

The most obvious internal pressures on managers are cost avoidance and risk management which drive corporate change for sustainability. But the firm now needs to consider potential costs to its reputation in the eyes of its employees as well as of external stakeholders such as shareholders, suppliers and consumers. The costs of non-compliance can be devastating for corporations, a point emphasized by the costs of oil spills to companies such as BP.[69]

Being competitive means reducing costs. As we have indicated, governments are still experimenting with measures to ensure increased sustainability. As we have shown above, most governments impose penalty measures for non-compliance. Corporations which do not address social and environmental requirements face fines, workers' compensation cases, criminal convictions and payment of clean-up costs. The potential for damage liability can make non-compliance a significant business risk.

Some examples:

- In the USA, the total corporate liability costs for asbestos-related diseases have been estimated at US$30 billion, far more than the product ever earned its manufacturers. In the UK the estimated future cost to the UK insurance industry of asbestos-related claims is £4–£10 billion.[70]

- The Deepwater Horizon oil spill in the Gulf of Mexico in 2010, when 11 men died, huge losses and damage to wildlife occurred and many fishermen went out of business, is expected to cost BP US$42 billion.[71]
- Costs to Tokyo Electric Power Co. of the Fukushima nuclear disaster in Japan in 2011 are estimated to be at least 11 trillion yen ($137 billion) and may be as high as three times that. Environmental and human costs are huge, with more than 150,000 people evicted from their homes and more nuclear material being discharged into the ocean than ever in history.[72]

Management of intangibles and associated performance measurement is emerging as a key driver of organizational sustainability. The Sustainability Balanced Scorecard, for instance, is an instrument that builds on the well-established Balanced Scorecard, adding social and environmental perspectives to the existing financial, customer, business process and learning and development perspectives and linking the perspectives with cause-and-effect chains.[73]

Key trends in risk management now include:

- the need for public trust
- the need for a partnership approach
- the role of personal leadership and workforce involvement
- the use of the law as a lever for safety management
- the public demand for a risk-free world.[74]

Business models that incorporate such risk management, and other approaches such as the natural capitalism and eco-efficiency models, are targeted at change according to the Efficiency stage of the sustainability phase model, developed in later chapters of this book. Other more transformative approaches look to a radical reconfiguration of what we value in business, with much more emphasis on recognition of the costs of natural capital and business performance, as well as on the value of community and employee relations to the long-term success of the company.

The costly effects of climate change are increasingly being recognized as an aspect of company value. However, the potential risks and opportunities associated with environmental impacts are not straightforward and differ markedly from sector to sector. Again referring to the recent 'Unburnable Carbon 2013: Wasted Capital and Stranded Assets' report, Professor Lord Stern comments:

Smart investors can see that investing in companies that rely solely or heavily on constantly replenishing reserves of fossil fuels is becoming a very risky decision. The report raises serious questions as to the ability of the financial system to act on industry-wide long term risk, since currently the only measure of risk is performance against industry benchmarks.[75]

Pressure from investors

Accordingly, risk management for large investors of necessity now includes sustainability assessment. In April 2006 United Nations Secretary-General Kofi Annan was joined by the heads of leading institutional investors managing combined assets worth more than $2 trillion to launch Principles of Responsible Investment. More informed shareholders are demanding a role in corporate decision making. Not only can shareholder activism be extremely damaging to the reputation of the corporation, but shareholders are now using sustainability as a measure of financial success. In January 2013, the Global Sustainable Investment Alliance (GSIA) released a report on the size and trends within the sustainable investment industry which finds that globally at least US$13.6 trillion-worth of professionally managed assets incorporate environmental, social and governance (ESG) concerns into their investment selection and management. Financial markets are generally requiring more information on standards of accountability and the financial services industry is now under considerable pressure to provide for ethical investment.[76]

The knowledge-based organization

In the information-based economy, corporations are looking to long-term survival through the development of knowledge systems, stores of social capital and a culture of innovation. These aspects of human sustainability in turn enable the firm to take a position of more environmental responsibility. A position of corporate sustainability requires a firm both to be responsible to employees and to look to its own needs for long-term survival. The bringing together of the corporate virtues of innovation and sustainability is the positive angle of change for sustainability – displayed already in the actions of leading organizations such as GE, Novo Nordisk,

Natura and Unilever, but now being taken up by smaller players – and implemented along their supply chains.

Knowledge management is also drawing attention to the value of an organization's human resources.[77] Motivation, qualifications and commitment, when combined with a significant store of 'corporate memory', are a major asset to the corporation. Companies are increasingly dependent on employees who can work cooperatively and contribute to the social capital of the organization.[78] Social capital is fundamental to the successful working of the new organizational forms such as the network organization and communities of practice.

As prized employees hunt for the firm with a strong sense of values, there are real rewards in becoming an employer of choice. Firms need employees who can give high levels of customer service and 'who are sufficiently motivated by the company's mission and prospects to stay and aspire to higher levels of productivity. The importance of teamwork, loyalty and skills is becoming doctrine in almost every industry.'[79]

Recent work also indicates a relationship between human resource policies, the successful implementation of the Environmental Management System (EMS) and its maintenance as a strategic business- and risk-management tool. Our own research shows a causal link between participation in EMS and employee commitment, connected with perception of good environmental performance by the organization.[80]

A culture of innovation

Managers are also recognizing the links between an organizational culture of innovation and one designed to deliver sustainability. Practices designed to enhance human sustainability and social capital within the organization (such as empowerment, teamwork and continuous learning) are linked to the capacity to innovate and escape from rigid models of operation and production. Arguably, implementing more sustainable practices creates an organizational culture that facilitates both resource productivity and product differentiation.[81]

A number of companies have been successful in employing a strategy of environmental product differentiation. Reinhardt points out that such a strategy will be successful if consumers are prepared to pay more, if the benefits can be communicated readily and if the innovation is unique long enough for a profit to be made.[82] Corporations face an accelerating rate of change and an increasingly complex society. For these business conditions, innovation depends on cultural and structural characteristics of the organization. Both sets of characteristics are linked to the organization's capacity to engage with sustainability. Cultural factors such as those associated with the learning organization also underpin a culture of precaution. Structural factors such as an internal network culture, employee participation and the capability to develop community partnerships also support human sustainability. In other words, innovation, business concept redesign and sustainability can be readily linked in a dynamic relationship aimed at delivering long-term business advantage.

Importantly, such qualities enable the corporation to be more responsive to the external drivers of change. An organization geared to innovation is ready to take up government incentives for ecological modernization; that is, it can readily translate social and moral issues into market issues and can exploit the potentially huge market that ecological sustainability, in particular, represents. But more than that, such an organization can more critically reflect on the possibilities of new relationships between nature, society and technology that will mark a new, more sustainable age.[83]

Conclusion

This chapter began by asking why organizations are moving to address the challenges of human and ecological sustainability. In large part, the answer is that the new reality for managers is that business success and sustainability are inextricably linked. Social and environmental health are essential aspects of corporate survival. Some managers are reacting primarily to the reputational and litigious risks associated with the increasingly global reach of corporations, to the actions of internationally mobilized human rights and environmental activists and to international and national agreements and regulations concerning environmental protection and social and environmental justice. International and national governments are experimenting with a variety of policy incentives and models of governance to ensure corporate accountability.

But many other managers are also taking proactive measures in the struggle to conserve resources, minimize waste and contribute to social and ecological renewal. More companies are moving beyond compliance with government regulations to accreditation under voluntary schemes such as ISO 14001. This delivers benefits from recognition by the community, customers and other stakeholders. Importantly, corporations are increasingly influenced by new alliances being formed across the range of corporate stakeholders. Community representatives and NGOs are working with firms to develop the knowledge and social capital required for the shift to sustainable products and processes.

Shareholders and investors are also looking to more than financial success in the assessment of performance. Their selection of investments increasingly takes into account reputation and performance on the longer-term factors of social and ecological sustainability. Investors are also placing more value on the human capabilities and commitment that the organization has built. In the new economy the building of knowledge systems, social capital and other strategies designed to increase and sustain human capability is vital to corporate performance.

More and more employees have strong expectations of workplace safety and heightened environmental awareness; they are searching for more meaningful work, particularly for work that makes a social and ecological contribution as well as providing an income.

In this context, the principles of community, interconnectedness and cooperation can be seen as a model for the way forward for corporations wishing to move towards sustainability. They provide a framework for new levels of resource productivity and generate new strategic directions. More importantly, they serve as a way of understanding the corporation as a moral entity.[84]

But we also need to recognize that there are countervailing forces tending to maintain the status quo, i.e. business as usual:

1 public lack of awareness of environmental (ecological and social) crises
2 difficulty of tracking and measuring sustainability improvements and difficulty in evaluating risks of inattention to sustainability
3 public cynicism about the ability of individuals to influence the course of events; moral disengagement, particularly in sections of the corporate world[85]
4 corporate disinformation campaigns (lies) around environmental issues led by those corporations with a strong stake in the status quo, particularly oil and mining companies; direct and indirect lobbying of governments at all levels

5 political coalitions around the politically conservative, particularly the fundamentalist religious right antagonistic to scientific knowledge on climate change

6 adherence to a capitalistic core belief that 'economic growth' (meaning increasing material consumption) is good

7 government distortion of resource markets, particularly energy, by subsidies, e.g. for carbon-based energy production, coal export etc. For example, in Australia fossil fuel subsidies in 2011 were A$12.2 billion vs. A$1.1 million spent on programmes to cut emissions and boost clean energy research. Yet these issues were little mentioned in the huge political debate in Australia around implementation of a carbon trading scheme or a carbon tax.

While there are increasing pressures to move toward a more sustainable world, we must never underestimate the power of the forces with an interest in the status quo. As the crisis increases, we can expect an increasing political reorientation and intensification of conflict; the old political division between capital and labour is already shifting to a division between those for maintaining 'business as usual' based on the old wasteful economic growth paradigm and those who stand for a sustainable economy based on alternative energy and remanufacturing and recycling.

Finally, we again make the point that energy is society's critical master resource.[86] We need it for everything we do. Therefore it is vital that we move rapidly to a carbon-neutral economy.

We also must recognize that increasing connectivity in global society leads to multiplier effects and the possibility of synchronous failure as problems occurring across interrelated systems coalesce, as, for example, with the Global Financial Crisis (GFC). Therefore we need to build resilience at all levels (e.g. nations and organizations) through buffering and redundancy. Combined energy, climate and pollution shocks challenge traditional capitalistic assumptions. Systems adaptation may still be possible, but it is a race against time. We need economic redirection as well as economic recovery.

The sustainability of cities will be an increasing issue. As seas rise, some cities and coastal communities will have to be relocated in whole or part; country communities built on flood plains will also need relocation as extreme weather conditions increase in frequency and scope (as is already happening in some regions across the world). Feeding city populations will also be an increasing problem as the costs of transportation rise with rising oil costs.

Our wealth has been funded on the exploitation of non-renewable resources and too-rapid use of potentially renewable resources. Many of the crises we have discussed are signals (Wrong Way: Go Back). We must green our economy, and in this, corporations, as powerhouses of economic change, must play a vital role. Fortunately, when we shift paradigms to think in terms of a sustainable future, we can plan corporate transformation that eliminates waste and increases productivity as well as preserving a world fit for human habitation for future generations. We need a working model for a truly sustainable global society and knowledge of how to create the transformative processes that will bring this about. This book concentrates on the role of corporations in this transformative process.

The following chapters take us along the spectrum of corporate sustainability stances. In the next chapter, we explain the changing picture of what compliance might mean for the contemporary organization and give examples of some of the ways the organization of today is moving to achieve these goals.

Notes

1 R. Mittermeier, C. Mittermeier, G. Pilgrim, J. Fonseca, G. Konstant and T. Brooks, *Wilderness: Earth's Last Wild Places*, Chicago: University of Chicago Press, 2002.
2 A. Jamison, *The Making of Green Knowledge*, Cambridge: Cambridge University Press, 2000.
3 UN News Centre, 'Climate Change Poses "Defining Challenge" of Our Time, Ban Says', 2008. Online. Available HTTP: <http://www.un.org/apps/news/story.asp?NewsID=28458#.UX-kwJFaef8> (accessed 1 May 2013).
4 OECD, *The OECD Environmental Outlook to 2050* (2012), OECD Publishing, p. 8. Online. Available HTTP: <http://www.oecd.org/environment/oecdenvironmentaloutlookto2050theconsequencesofinaction.htm> (accessed 1 May 2013).
5 N. Stern, *The Stern Review: Economics of Climate Change*, 2010. Online. Available HTTP: <http://webarchive.nationalarchives.gov.uk/+/http://www.hm-treasury.gov.uk/stern_review_report.htmreport> (accessed 20 April 2013).
6 Quoted from Carbon Tracker and the Grantham Research Institute, 'Unburnable Carbon 2013: Wasted Capital and Stranded Assets', London: LSE. Online. Available HTTP: <http://www.carbontracker.org/wastedcapital> (accessed 3 May 2013).

7 TEEB, *Natural Capital at Risk – The Top 100 Externalities of Business*, TEEB, 2013.

8 Living Planet Report 2012, Online. Available HTTP: <http://awassets.panda. org/downloads/lpr_2012_summary_booklet_final.pdf>, page 12 (accessed 4 March 2014).

9 New Economics Foundation, 'Natural Economies', 2103. Online. Available HTTP: <http://www.neweconomics.org/programmes/natural-economies> (accessed 21 April 2013).

10 TEEB, *Natural Capital at Risk.*

11 English.news.cn, *Life Expectancy Rises in China*, China: Xinhua, english.news.cn, 2012. Online. Available HTTP: http://news.xinhuanet.com/ english/china/2012-08/09/c_131773481.htm (accessed 20 April 2013).

12 World Bank, *China 2030: Building a Modern, Harmonious, and Creative High-Income Society*, Washington, DC: The World Bank, 2013.

13 OECD, *The OECD Environmental Outlook to 2050: The Consequences of Inaction*. Online. Available HTTP: <http://www.oecd.org/env/indicators-modelling-outlooks/oecdenvironmentaloutlookto2050theconsequencesof inaction.htm> (accessed 4 March 2014).

14 World Trade Organization, *World Trade Statistics*, WTO, 2012. Online. Available HTTP: <http://www.wto.org/english/res_e/statis_e/its2012_e/ its12_highlights1_e.pdf> (accessed 21 April 2013).

15 UNDP, *Human Development Report 2013*, UNDP, 2013. Online. Available HTTP: http://hdr.undp.org/en/media/HDR2013_EN_Summary.pdf> (accessed 25 April 2013).

16 U. Beck, *World Risk Society*, Cambridge: Polity Press, 1999.

17 Quoting Falk in U. Beck, *Risk Society: Towards a New Modernity*, London: Sage Publications, 1992.

18 S. Benn, and K. Kearins, 'Sustainability and organizational change', in D. Boje, B. Burnes and J. Hassard (eds) *Handbook of Organizational Change*, London: Sage Publications, 2012, pp. 535–51.

19 The World Commission of Environment and Development, *Report of the World Commission on Environment and Development: Our Common Future*, United Nations, 1987, p. 43. Online. Available HTTP: <http://www. un-documents.net/our-common-future.pdf> (accessed 4 May 2013).

20 I. Bluhdorn, 'The Sustainability of Democracy', 2011. Online. Available HTTP: <http://www.thenewsignificance.com/2011/07/12/ingolfur-bluhdorn-the-sustainability-of-democracy/> (accessed 26 April 2013); Doha Climate Change Conference, 2012. Online. Available HTTP: <http://unfccc.int/ meetings/doha_nov_2012/meeting/6815.php> (accessed 8 October 2013).

21 D. Bodansky and S. O'Connor, 'The Durban Platform: Issues and Options for a 2015 Agreement', 2012. Online. Available HTTP: <http://www.c2es.org/doc Uploads/durban-platform-issues-and-options.pdf> (accessed 25 April 2013).

22 United Nations, 'UN Global Compact, Participants and Stakeholders', 2012. Online. Available HTTP: <http://www.unglobalcompact.org/ParticipantsAnd Stakeholders/index.html> (accessed 26 April 2013).

23 WBCSD, 'Analyses of the Rio+20 Outcome document "The Future We Want"', 2012. Online. Available HTTP: <http://www.wbcsd.org/rio-20/rio20.aspx> (accessed 23 November 2013).

24 H. Tregidga, K. Kearins and M. Milne, 'The politics of knowing "organizational sustainable development"', *Organization & Environment*, 2013, 26 (102), 102–29 (originally published online, 20 January 2013).

25 S. Banerjee, 'Who sustains whose development? Sustainable development and the reinvention of nature', *Organization Studies*, 2003, 24 (1), 143–80.

26 B. Lomborg, *The Skeptical Environmentalist*, Cambridge: Cambridge University Press, 2001.

27 U. Beck, *Risk Society: Towards a New Modernity*, London: Sage Publications, 1992.

28 U. Beck, *World Risk Society*, Cambridge: Polity Press, 1999, p. 37; R. Falk, 'The making of global citizenship', in B. van Steenbergen (ed.) *The Conditions of Citizenship*, London: Sage Publications, London, 1994.

29 R. Inglehart, and C. Welzel, *Modernization, Cultural Change and Democracy*, New York: Cambridge University Press, 2010, p. 63.

30 Occupy Wall Street, 2013. Online. Available HTTP: <http://occupy wallst.org/> (accessed 2 May 2013).

31 Bloomberg News, 'Chinese Anger over Pollution Becomes Main Cause of Social Unrest', Beijing: Bloomberg News, 2013. Online. Available HTTP: <http://www.bloomberg.com/news/2013-03-06/pollution-passes-land-grievances-as-main-spark-of-china-protests.html> (accessed 22 April 2013).

32 H. Henderson, *Beyond Globalization: Shaping a Sustainable Global Economy*, West Hartford, CT: Kumarian Press, 1999.

33 KPMG and ICAA, *20 Issues on Building a Sustainable Business*, Business Briefing Series, Sydney: The Institute of Chartered Accountants in Australia and KPMG, 2011.

34 S. Benn, and A. Martin, 'Learning and change for sustainability reconsidered: a role for boundary objects', *Academy of Management Learning and Education*, 2010, 9 (3), 397–412.

35 E. von Weizsacker, A. Lovins and L. Lovins, *Factor 4: Doubling Wealth – Halving Resource Use*, London: Earthscan Publications, 1997.

36 J. Ehrenfield, 'Industrial ecology: paradigm shift or normal science', *American Behavioural Scientist*, 2000, 44 (2), 229–41; B. Szerszynski, S. Lash and B. Wynne, 'Introduction', in S. Lash, B. Szerszynski and B. Wynne (eds), *Risk, Environment and Modernity*, London: Sage Publications, 1996, pp. 1–26.

37 W. Sachs, 'Global ecology and the shadow of development', in W. Sachs (ed.) *Global Ecology*, London: Zed Books, pp. 3–21; Shiva, 'Greening of the global reach', W. Sachs (ed.) *Global Ecology*, London: Zed Books, 1993, pp. 149–56.

38 B. Tuxworth, 'GRI: a new framework?', *Global Sustainable Business Blog*, 2013. Online. Available HTTP: <http://www.guardian.co.uk/sustainable-business/global-reporting-initiative-updates> (accessed 22 April 2013).

39 WWF, 'History'. Online. Available HTTP: http://worldwildlife.org/about/
    history (accessed 8 September, 2013).
40 A. Giddens, *The Politics of Climate Change*, Cambridge: Polity Press, 2011.
41 Play Fair, 'Toying with People's Rights, A Report on Producing Merchandise
    for the 2012 London Olympic Games', 2012. Online. Available HTTP:
    <http://www.ituc-csi.org/IMG/pdf/play_fair_en_final.pdf> (accessed
    26 April 2013).
42 Network for Business Sustainability, 'News and Events', 2013. Online.
    Available HTTP: <http://nbs.net/category/news-events/> (accessed
    26 April 2013).
43 CERES, *Sustainable Supply Chains*, 2013. Online. Available HTTP:
    <http://www.ceres.org/issues/supply-chain> (accessed 28 April 2013).
44 Worldwatch Institute, *State of the World 2012: Moving towards Sustainable
    Prosperity*, Worldwatch Institute Report, 2013.
45 J. Manik and J. Yardley, 'Death toll rising in Bangladesh collapse',
    International Herald Tribune, 26 April 2013, p. 6.
46 T. O'Riordan and H. Voisey, *Transition to Sustainability*, London:
    Earthscan, 1998.
47 European Economic and Social Committee, 'Key Definitions'. Online.
    Available HTTP: <http://www.eesc.europa.eu/?i=portal.en.self-and-co-
    regulation-definitions-concepts-examples> (accessed 28 April 2013).
48 M. Porter and C. van der Linde, 'Towards a new conception of the
    environment–competitiveness relationship', *Journal of Economic
    Perspectives*, 1995, 9 (4), 97–118, p. 114.
49 J. Dryzek, *The Politics of the Earth*, Oxford: Oxford University Press, 1997.
50 A. Mol, 'Ecological modernization: industrial transformations and
    environmental reform', in M. Redclift and G. Woodgate (eds) *The
    International Handbook of Environmental Sociology*, Cheltenham:
    Edward Elgar, 1997, pp. 138–49.
51 M. Mason, *Environmental Democracy*, London: Earthscan Publications,
    1999.
52 S. Benn, and D. Bolton, *Key Concepts of Corporate Social Responsibility*,
    London: Sage Publications, 2011.
53 T. Jensen, J. Sandstrom and S. Helin, 'Corporate codes of ethics and the
    bending of moral space', *Organization*, 2009, 16 (4), 529–45.
54 Institute for Environmental Management (WIMM), *KPMG International
    Survey of Environmental Reporting 1999*, Amsterdam: KPMG, The
    Netherlands, 1999.
55 Ibid.
56 Carbon Disclosure Project, 2013. Online. Available HTTP: <https://www.cd
    project.net/en-US/Pages/HomePage.aspx> (accessed 28 April 2013).
57 I. Ioannou and G. Serafeim, *The Consequences of Mandatory Corporate
    Sustainability Reporting*, Harvard Business School Working Paper 11-100,
    Harvard Business School, 2012. Online. Available HTTP: <http://www.

hbs.edu/faculty/Publication%20Files/11-100_35684ae7-fcdc-4aae-9626-
de4b2acb1748.pdf> (accessed 20 April 2013).

58 OECD, *The OECD Environmental Outlook to 2050*, Paris: OECD, 2012, p. 8.

59 WWF, 'Climate Solutions, WWF's Vision for 2050', 2007. Online. Available
HTTP: <http://wwf.panda.org/about_our_earth/top_5_environmental_
questions/what_is_climate_change/> (accessed 19 April 2013).

60 R. Tieman, 'Sustainable business', *Financial Times*, 24 April 2012, p. 2.

61 M. Porter and M. Kramer, 'Creating shared value', *Harvard Business Review*,
January 2011. Online. Available HTTP: <http://hbr.org/2011/01/the-big-idea-
creating-shared-value> (accessed 3 May 2013).

62 M. Carrigan and A. Attalla, 'The myth of the ethical consumer – do ethics
matter in purchase behaviour?', *Journal of Consumer Marketing*, 2001, 18
(7), 560.

63 R. Botsman and R. Rogers, *Whats Mine Is Yours: The Rise of Collaborative
Consumption*, HarperCollins, 2010. Online. Available HTTP: <http://www.
wired.co.uk/news/archive/2011-10/13/rachel-botsman-wired-11> and
<http://www.sustainablebrands.com/news_and_views/behavior_change/
what-are-most-effective-ways-drive-changes-consumer-behavior> (accessed
20 April 2013).

64 A. Lovins, L. Lovins and P. Hawken, *Road Map for Natural Capitalism*,
New York: Back Bay Books, 2008.

65 J. Ehrenfeld, 'Industrial ecology: paradigm shift or normal science',
American Behavioural Scientist, 2000, 44 (2), 229–44, p. 226.

66 L. Preston, 'Sustainability at Hewlett-Packard', *Financial Times*, 2 June
2000.

67 Hewlett-Packard, 'About Environmental Sustainability', Online. Available
HTTP: <http://www8.hp.com/us/en/hp-information/environment/
sustainability.html#.UYS3OpFaef8> (accessed 4 May 2013).

68 HP Policy Position, Online. Available HTTP: <http://www.hp.com/hpinfo/
abouthp/government/ww/pdf/SER_Climate_Change.pdf> (accessed 5 March
2014).

69 International Business Times, 'BP Gulf of Mexico Oil Spill: Counting the
costs', 2013. Online. Available HTTP: <http://www.ibtimes.co.uk/articles/
462933/20130430/bp-deepwater-horizon-oil-spill-cost.htm> (accessed
3 May 2013).

70 GIR Seminar, 'UK Asbestos – The Definitive Guide', 2010. Online.
Available HTTP: <www.actuaries.org.uk/system/files/documents/pdf/
Lowe_0.pdf> (accessed 3 May 2013).

71 International Business Times, 'BP Gulf of Mexico Oil Spill'.

72 Environmental Health Policy Institute, 'Costs and Consequences of the
Fukushima Daiishi Nuclear Disaster'. Online. Available HTTP:
<http://www.psr.org/environment-and-health/environmental-health-policy-
institute/responses/costs-and-consequences-of-fukushima.html> (accessed
3 May 2013).

73 M. Wagner, and S. Schaltegger, 'Mapping the links of corporate sustainability', in *Managing the Business Case for Sustainability*, Sheffield: Greenleaf Publishing, pp. 108–27.

74 M. Brinded, 'Perception Versus Analysis: How to Handle Risk', speech to the Royal Academy of Engineering, London, 31 May 2000.

75 Carbon Tracker and the Grantham Research Institute, 'Unburnable Carbon 2013: Wasted Capital and Stranded Assets', Foreword by Lord Stern, p. 7.

76 T. Clarke, 'Balancing the triple bottom line', *Journal of General Management*, 2001, 26 (4), 16–27.

77 A. Wilkinson, M. Hill and P. Gollan, 'The sustainability debate', *International Journal of Operations and Production Management*, 2001, 21 (12), 1492–502.

78 S. Sagawa and E. Segal, 'Common interest, common good: creating value through business and social sector relationships', *California Management Review*, 2000, 42 (2), 105–23.

79 Ibid., p. 106.

80 S. Benn, S. Teo, and A. Martin, 'Working for the Environment and Intention to Stay, the Informal Economy', Academy of Management Conference, Boston, 2011.

81 R. Orssatto, 'The Ecological Competence of Organizations: Competing for Sustainability', paper presented to the 16th EGOS Colloquium, Helsinki, Finland, 1–4 July 2000.

82 F. Reinhardt, 'Bringing the environment down to earth', in R. Starkey and R. Welford (eds) *Business and Sustainable Development*, London: Earthscan Publications, 2000, pp. 53–64.

83 M. Hajer, 'Ecological modernization in cultural politics', in S. Lash, B. Szerszynski and B. Wynne (eds), *Risk, Environment and Modernity*, London: Sage Publications, 1996, pp. 246–68.

84 Ehrenfield, 'Industrial ecology: paradigm shift or normal science'.

85 J. White, 'Moral accountability in the corporate world', *Accountability in Research*, 2009, 16 (1), pp. 41–74.

86 T. H. Dixon, *The Upside of Down*, Melbourne: Text Publishing, 2006.

**Part II
Managing the persistent
past: dealing with first
wave corporations**

3 Compliance and beyond . . . management tools and approaches

Changing understanding of compliance

What is compliance?

Recurring reports of workplace incidents involving factory fires and building collapses, some with major losses of life, evidence of blatant tax avoidance by many of our leading multinationals and various food contamination scares point to persistent negligence on the part of business and political leaders. In China, for example, up to 150,000 protests are now recorded each year, reacting to news such as that of rat meat being sold as lamb and of milk and fish being treated with harmful chemicals.[1] In this chapter, we explore what these incidents reflect in terms of our current systems of compliance and what advances have been made to ensure business addresses the likelihood of negative social and environmental impacts. The definition of compliance is doing what you are required or expected to do.

One problem with our compliance definition is that it skips over the question of which stakeholder is the more legitimate in terms of setting such requirements. Unclear lines of responsibility and a lack of effective monitoring systems, particularly in international supply chains, can underpin major transgressions by industry in terms of human rights. They include the 2013 building collapse of the Rana Plaza garment factory in Savar, Bangladesh. The Bangladesh death toll of over 1,000 makes it the worst disaster in the garment industry and puts it near the level of the notorious chemical spill at Bhopal.[2] The factory was making clothes for leading European brands, now in risk-management mode as a result, with Disney, for instance, reported as considering taking its business out of Bangladesh. Underpinning the Rana Plaza disaster is the overlapping and complex human rights and environmental legislation in Bangladesh. Add in relentless consumerism in the developed world and, in the developing world, aspiring middle classes, all chasing for cheaper and cheaper goods, and corruption and exploitation are the result. Muhammad Yunus, the Nobel Prize winner and original developer of microfinance, argues that the only way out is for foreign buyers to set a minimum wage for the garment industry.[3] According to Yunus:

> We have to make international companies understand that while the workers are physically in Bangladesh, they are contributing their labour to the businesses: they are stakeholders. Physical separation should not be grounds to ignore the wellbeing of this labour.[4]

Foxconn, a Chinese-based supplier to Apple, Dell and numerous other multinationals in the consumer electronics market, provides us with another example of the complexity of a compliance issue involving multiple stakeholders across different national regimes, tiers of suppliers and raised consumer demand. Under the spotlight as a result of worker suicides, in 2012 Foxconn was investigated by the Fair Labor Association (FLA), resulting in a finding of serious and pressing noncompliances with Foxconn's Workplace Code of Conduct and Chinese labour law. Excessively long working hours were a prominent concern, although Foxconn justified its policies with claims of queues of would-be workers.[5] On the other hand, Apple was accused of earning massive profits from products such as iPhones, with little left over to be shared along the value chain, let alone to the worker. Apple was further accused of channelling profits into off-shore companies to avoid payment of domestic taxes. Also in 2012, the NGO China Labour Watch produced the report 'Beyond Foxconn: Deplorable Working Conditions Characterize Apple's Entire Supply Chain', based on interviews of 620 workers in ten diverse factories making Apple products in China. The report delivered findings including that human rights transgressions occurred throughout Apple's supply chain and that working conditions in some suppliers were even worse than at Foxconn. Extraordinarily long working days and dangerous working conditions were reported.[6]

The second problem with our definition of compliance is that it ignores the difference between the spirit and the letter of the law. The ongoing debate around the meaning of compliance as it applies to corporate sustainability and responsibility hinges on this difference. Contrary to the more traditional view that the corporation can legally address a wider social or environmental agenda only if it is of direct financial benefit to the shareholders,[7] the compliance approach to corporate sustainability or corporate social responsibility (CSR) is that even if shareholder gain or corporate profit is reduced, companies should abide by the letter of the law. According to the American Law Institute, in that way a corporation is no different to a 'natural person'.[8] According to some critics, however, the constraints of the market economy impose serious limits on corporate virtue.[9] In other words, compliance with the spirit of the law is a vexed question and raises issues of governance.

New forms of governance

The 2011 EU communication *A Renewed EU Strategy 2011–2014 for Corporate Social Responsibility* states that CSR is the responsibility of every company – an example of the spirit of the law. In the US, a number of legislatures have implemented corporate constituency statutes which can incorporate CSR and sustainability into the letter of the law. While a number of these statutes are specifically designed to deal with hostile takeovers, others permit directors to consider the effect that their decision making may have on employees, suppliers and local communities. What is in the 'best interests' of the corporation may now take other factors than those of shareholders' financial interests into account.

These decisions reflect the emergence of new forms of governance. As Clarke and Branson argue,

> the industrial world is confronting two inescapable tasks: the first is the necessity to rejuvenate mature industries and to create new, innovative industries. The second and much greater challenge, is to achieve social and environmental sustainability in all economic activity. It is difficult to see how the 'market mechanisms and shareholder value of the Anglo-American corporate governance model could possibly contribute to either of these challenges. New modes of governance will be required to achieve balance and sustainability.[10]

In the aftermath of the GFC, new forms of governance that could more effectively ensure corporate responsibility are under consideration. These include regulatory structures that bring together public and private entities and that focus on information giving and sharing as 'compliance' tools. They are reflexive, designed to bring about learning by doing rather than through command-and-control measures. They include monitoring arrangements that have been imposed on well-known firms such as America Online, KPMG, Boeing, Monsanto and AIG.[11]

Network-based governance, for instance, where relationships between firms and other organizations such as government bodies and NGOs representing a wide range of interests are coordinated according to a range of social contracts, is an evident trend with implications for sustainability compliance. Where the pace of regulatory change is particularly slow, as occurs with toxic chemicals because of the intensive testing required before chemicals can be banned and taken off the market, government agencies are now seeking partnerships and voluntary agreements with chemicals companies in order to reduce more rapidly the use of chemicals with suspected toxic effects. For example, recently the US Environmental Protection Agency (EPA) called together a group of chemical companies and environmentalists to discuss how to control perfluorooctanoic acid (usually called PFOA), a chemical in waterproof clothing and nonstick cookware. As a result, each company voluntarily agreed to curtail its use of the substance. Companies and environmentalists, while frequently operating from opposite sides of the fence, are in agreement that issues like greenhouse gases, endangered forests and genetically modified crops will inevitably impact on their operations, and they want to participate in setting them. DuPont, for instance, includes environmentalists on its internal biotechnology advisory panel. 'Our ability to get product to market is moving faster than the EPA's ability to get rules out, and we want to agree in advance on what the rules of the road should be,' said Linda J. Fisher, DuPont's chief sustainability officer.[12]

Governments have a choice as to whether to force consumers into restricted access to unsustainable products, such as through legislation preventing the sale of non-energy-efficient light globes, or to educate consumers through more comprehensive product labelling or information programmes.[13] So for example, using the latter approach, provision of information via Restricted Substances Lists is a key government-led strategy to make products safer by means of a checklist of flagged chemical ingredients. The lack of consumer response to such programmes is causing governments to rely more on incentive programmes, on partnership arrangements with corporates or on supporting various forms of sustainable supply-chain management to encourage industry to develop more sustainable products. For example, the chemical company BASF maintains a database called SELECT (Sustainability, Eco-Labeling and Environmental Certification Tracking), which is tracking 270 programmes, a number that has tripled over the last few years.[14]

In effect, the revolving door between business and government means that the managers of many companies actively contribute to government rule making. So-called partnerships between government and business appear to generate some shared learning around sustainability,[15] to pre-empt policy changes and to adopt precautionary measures before being required to do so. They can progress human and ecological sustainability measures, enhance participants' reputations and allow them to take leadership in order to increase competitiveness.

Because network and other collaborative approaches to governance tend to focus on information sharing and transparency they can be utilized to break the nexus between consumerism and 'unsustainability'. Various certification systems, often monitored by NGOs, have arisen to qualify products according to a range of voluntary standards and there does seem to be some evidence that these systems can result in financial benefits associated with addressing reputational risk and the delivery of supply-chain efficiencies and chain-of-custody management.

Global principles for action

One major impact of the GFC is that reputation, communications, disclosure, transparency and trust are now interconnected issues for organizations. If any one of these factors fails, all others are affected and the path back to rebuilding them is a long one. Nike's experience also shows this: after a series of reputational problems, Nike has endorsed the Environmental Code of Conduct of the Coalition for Environmentally Responsible Economics (CERES). While this does not mean that CERES endorses Nike's practices, it does mean that Nike will communicate with CERES members. The code requires companies to adopt environmentally friendly policies and perform annual self-audits. Sets of principles and codes such as CERES which provide a formal statement of business practices and values have proliferated since the late 1990s. They differ in author organization and in code content. All are directed at improvement in social and environmental company behaviour according to principles of self-regulation.[16]

Company codes can play a major role in facilitating the organizational learning required for the transition to compliance and beyond (see Table 3.1). Despite this potential, there are obvious drawbacks. The overwhelming majority of codes have no implementation methods. In particular, there are five major drawbacks of company codes – they can be:

Table 3.1 *Classification of codes of conduct*

Company trade association	Responsible Care (chemical industry)
Company	Examples: Nike code of conduct, Levi Strauss code of conduct
Intergovernmental	OECD guidelines for multinational enterprises
Multi-stakeholder	CERES principles, Global Compact, Global Reporting Initiative, ILO
NGO	ISO, AccountAbility, Transparency International

Source: Modified from K. Bondy, D. Matten and J. Moon, 'Codes of conduct as a tool for sustainable governance in MNCs', in S. Benn and D. Dunphy (eds), *Corporate Governance and Sustainability*, London: Routledge, 2009.

- vaguely defined – corporate codes often do not specify precisely the limits of their responsibility
- incomplete – many company codes exclude the right to organize, refer only to a specific issue such as child labour or are incomplete in other ways
- not implemented – an important flaw in company codes of conduct is the lack of information on whether or how these codes are being implemented or monitored
- not independently monitored – internal monitoring assumes a public willingness to take the company at its own word but the public is often distrustful
- subject to personal bias of senior managers.[17]

Role of reporting and management tools

Certification and self-reporting

An alternative to the adoption of self-generated codes is for a company to seek independent certification of the company's products or processes or to adopt systematic processes of disclosure. Sustainability audits include various instruments: ISO 26000; AccountAbility; Global Compact; Global Reporting Initiative (GRI); Transparency International.

In general these instruments provide principles and guidelines for voluntary adoption and implementation. All assume that sustainability/CSR actions will utilize existing organizational change and reporting tools. The Global Compact has principles and assumes implementation through GRI or something similar. Table 3.2 sets out the ten social dimension principles of the Global Compact. Examples of other operating functions of these systems are that GRI mandates reporting

Table 3.2 *Social dimension principles of the Global Compact*

Human rights	Principle 1: Businesses should support and respect the protection of internationally proclaimed human rights. Principle 2: Business should make sure that they are not complicit in human rights abuses.
Labour standards	Principle 3: Businesses should uphold the freedom of association and the effective recognition of the right to collective bargaining. Principle 4: The elimination of all forms of forced and compulsory labour. Principle 5: The effective abolition of child labour. Principle 6: The elimination of discrimination in respect of employment and occupation.
Environment	Principle 7: Businesses should support a precautionary approach to environmental challenges. Principle 8: Businesses should undertake initiatives to promote greater environmental responsibility. Principle 9: Businesses should encourage the development and diffusion of environmentally friendly technologies.
Anti-corruption	Principle 10: Businesses should work against all forms of corruption, including extortion and bribery.

Source: Modified from UN Global Compact, 'The Ten Principles', http://www.unglobalcompact.org/AboutTheGC/TheTenPrinciples/index.html (accessed 21 April 2013).

categories but selection is 'voluntary', and Transparency International promotes 'whistleblowing' and undertakes selective interviews/surveys.

The Global Compact provides a blueprint (Figure 3.1) of how these ten principles can be incorporated into sustainability leadership.

In one example of a leading company which has deployed certification systems to apparent advantage, Sappi, one of the largest paper manufacturers in the world, has long used a data collection system to keep track of its production systems and to collect data for annual reports and sustainability reports. The company used that data to reduce costs and inefficiencies. Sappi claims its European operations were the first in the European pulp and paper industry to achieve joint ISO 9001, ISO 14001 and Eco-Management and Audit Scheme (EMAS) certification, and to be the first paper company to achieve multi-site, cross-border Group chain-of-custody certification for its entire European operations under both the Forest Stewardship Council (FSC™) and the Programme for the Endorsement of Forest Certification (PEFC) schemes. Its management systems are certified under the international health and safety, environmental and quality standards OHSAS 18001, ISO 14001, EMAS and ISO 9001.[18]

Implementing the ten principles into strategies and operations

1. Full coverage and integration across principles
2. Robust management policies and procedures
3. Mainstreaming into corporate functions and business units
4. Value chain implementation

1. CEO commitment and leadership
2. Board adoption and oversight
3. Stakeholder engagement
4. Transparency and disclosure

Taking action in support of broader UN goals and issues

1. Core business contributions to UN goals and issues
2. Strategic social investments and philanthropy
3. Advocacy and public policy engagement
4. Partnerships and collective action

Engaging with the UN Global Compact

1. Local networks and subsidiary engagement
2. Global and local working groups
3. Issue-based and sector initiatives
4. Promotion and support of the UN Global Compact

Figure 3.1 *Implementing the ten Global Compact social dimension principles*
Source: Modified from UN Global Compact, 2012, <http://www.unglobalcompact.org/HowTo Participate/Business_Participation/blueprint_for_corporate_sustainability_leadership.html> (accessed 21 April 2013).

The latest count by EcoLabel Index puts the number of programmes that qualify products according to various environmental or sustainable resource credentials at 433 across 246 countries. Figure 3.2 demonstrates the extent of this trend to certification, while Figure 3.3 provides the specific example of marine certification systems.

Benefits of compliance and self-reporting

It has long been claimed that strengthening regulation around environmental impacts will encourage business innovation.[19] Another argument is that corporates also benefit from newer, more collaborative forms of governance through setting new pathways for competitive advantage. Examples frequently given are Nike's campaign to regulate its supply chain to ensure that suppliers do not breach human rights conventions and Novo Nordisk's award-winning approach to 'dilemma reporting' on access to drugs in the biotechnology industry.[20]

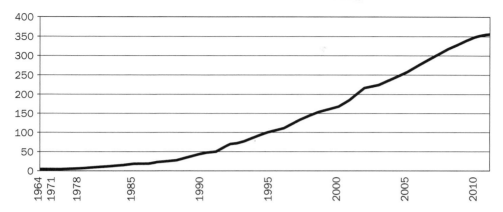

Figure 3.2 *Number of ecolabels registered per year*
Source: Modified from Steering Committee of the State-of-Knowledge Assessment of Standards and Certification, *Toward Sustainability: The Roles and Limitations of Certification* (Executive summary), Washington, DC: RESOLVE, Inc., 2012, p. ES 4.

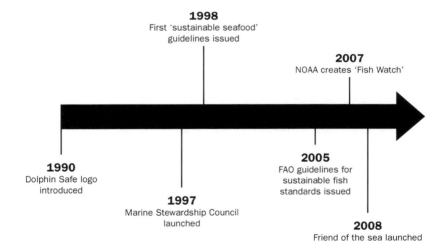

Timeline of the emergence of marine certification programmes

Figure 3.3 *The case of marine certification*
Source: Modified from Steering Committee of the State-of-Knowledge Assessment of Standards and Certification, *Toward Sustainability: The Roles and Limitations of Certification* (Executive Summary), Washington, DC: RESOLVE, Inc., 2012, p. ES 10.

Using examples of how compliance can shift a company to a more innovative approach, Westervelt claims a relationship between compliance, profit and innovation. Each of these examples, set out in the box below, also shows how compliance requirements can force companies to generate more data about their production and supply systems, leading eventually to wider business benefits.[21]

Case examples: positive outcomes of compliance

Varian Medical Systems used software to help it collect and analyse all the necessary data to meet the European Union's Registration, Evaluation, Authorization and Restriction of Chemicals (REACH) and Restriction of Hazardous Substances Directive (RoHS), with which it will have to comply in the coming few years. Easy access to data about its products has enabled Varian to re-engineer products in five days, as opposed to the 18 days such work once required.

Seagate, the hard-drive manufacturer, has similarly established itself as a sustainability leader by moving far beyond compliance in every regulatory framework and using data to continuously improve its product. It's a move that has often given the company a competitive advantage. In 2009, for example, when its competitors' hard drives were failing, due to bromine contamination, Seagate took the opportunity to tell the world about its bromine-free drives. By opting for eco-friendly design, the company had also designed a disk drive that was more resilient and robust.

Source: see note 21.

The success of such initiatives is dependent upon the development and implementation of new management tools: systems, processes and programmes that often involve collaboration between business organizations, government and NGOs.

Associated with the rapidly multiplying voluntary standards and certification systems and a new emphasis on transparency issues, is the need for new reporting and management tools. The extent to which the corporation can or should be required by legislation to reveal information about practices such as those that relate to CSR or sustainability is variable across national regimes. As we mentioned in Chapter 2, Ioannis Ioannou and George Serafeim's important study explored the value of forcing corporations to report on non-financial matters, showing that benefits for the business and for society as a whole included a broader managerial understanding on the part of board members and better treatment of employees. National regimes with stricter reporting requirements on non-financials were more likely to have more responsible business leaders as well as more substantial investments in employee training. Third parties were found to play an important role in the auditing or verifying of the reporting.[22]

Global watchdogs for sustainability

The massive expansion of information technology has led to a growing awareness of the risks and impacts of corporate irresponsibility. More-informed consumers and investors have pushed corporations into a new arena of competing for reputation and for access to the benefits of relationship building with other corporations, suppliers, clients and NGOs. NGOs such as Amnesty International, Greenpeace, WWF and Human Rights Watch act as monitors of environmental and social standards across the world and have had a major impact on how corporations perceive compliance. Corporations failing to comply with standards set by these alert watchdogs can be targeted and their transgressions given huge publicity.

Sustainability reporting tools

In previous editions we have noted the burgeoning interest in sustainability and CSR reporting, prompted by a perceived need to shore up reputation and manage risk. Associated with this trend is an increasing role being played by the accountancy profession. A spate of reports by the large accountancy firms and the professional associations testify to raised professional standards around sustainability and to the perception of potentially increased demand for accounting services in this area.[23] A key driver for improved sustainability reporting remains the Global Reporting Initiative (GRI). As noted above, GRI is increasingly accepted as a reporting tool, particularly in larger organizations. The GRI Reporting Framework aims to provide a means for all organizations to measure and report sustainability performance. Examples drawn from the social dimensions of the GRI are reproduced in Table 3.3.

A wide range of standards are now used to assist in sustainability reporting. For example, ISO, the International Organization for Standardization, has launched an International Standard providing

Table 3.3 *Social dimensions of the Global Reporting Initiative*[24]

Human rights examples [HR 1–11]	Aspects: investment and procurement practices; non-discrimination; freedom of association and collective bargaining; child labour; forced and compulsory labour; security practices; indigenous rights; assessment; remediation HR1 – Percentage and total number of significant investment agreements and contracts that include clauses incorporating human rights concerns, or that have undergone human rights screening. HR7 – Operations and significant suppliers identified as having significant risk for incidents of compulsory labour, and measures to contribute to the elimination of all forms of forced or compulsory labour.
Labour practices and decent work examples [LA 1–15]	Aspects: employment; labour/management relations; occupational health and safety; training and education; diversity and equal opportunity; equal remuneration for women and men LA1 – Total workforce by employment type, employment contract and region, broken down by gender. LA7 – Rates of injury, occupational diseases, lost days and absenteeism, and total number of work-related fatalities, by region and by gender. LA10 – Average hours of training per year per employee by gender, and by employee category.
Society examples [SO 1–10]	Aspects: local communities; corruption; public policy; anti-competitive behaviour; compliance SO1 – Percentage of operations with implemented local community engagement, impact assessments and development programmes. SO2 – Percentage and total number of business units analysed for risks related to corruption.
Product responsibility examples [PR 1–9]	Aspects: customer health and safety; product and service labelling; marketing communications; customer privacy; compliance PR1 – Life-cycle stages in which health and safety impacts of products and services are assessed for improvement, and percentage of significant products and services categories subject to such procedures. PR6 – Programmes for adherence to laws, standards and voluntary codes related to marketing communications, including advertising, promotion, and sponsorship.

Source: Global Reporting Initiative (GRI), https://www.globalreporting.org/ (accessed 11 September 2013).

guidelines for social responsibility (SR), named ISO 26000. The standard for environmental management, ISO 14000, is long established and widely used. SA8000 is another specific framework established for social accountability. Supporting frameworks for GRI and SA8000 include the AA1000 principles (see http://www.accountability.org/), which aim to 'Set the Standard for Corporate Responsibility and Sustainable Development'.

AA1000 Principles

Inclusivity – For an organization that accepts its accountability to those on whom it has an impact and who have an impact on it, inclusivity is the participation of stakeholders in developing and achieving an accountable and strategic response to sustainability.

Materiality – Materiality is determining the relevance and significance of an issue to an organization and its stakeholders. A material issue is an issue that will influence the decisions, actions and performance of an organization or its stakeholders.

Responsiveness – Responsiveness is an organization's response to stakeholder issues that affect its sustainability performance and is realized through decisions, actions and performance, as well as communication with stakeholders.[25]

Another supporting management tool enabling better reporting is provided by Transparency International (see http://www.transparency.org/). The focus here is on elimination of corruption in societies.

Sustainability reporting is grounded in the people, planet, profit principles of the Triple Bottom Line (TBL), developed as a reporting concept by John Elkington.[26] Although it is now widely accepted in corporate rhetoric, TBL is frequently criticized for being overly reductionist and not allowing for the holistic principles of sustainability to be assessed. Recently, attempts have been made to promote a more integrated approach enabling a more overall view of corporate performance.

Integrated reporting

Integrated reporting is now emerging as a replacement to separate sustainability reporting. It refers to the intent to have environmental and social impact reporting included with financial reports, with the aim of presenting a concise picture of the overall performance of the organization. Proponents of integrated reporting argue that it links strategic management and practice, planning, governance and performance in a way that highlights the critical interdependencies of an organization's economic, social and environmental concerns. The International Integrated Reporting Committee (IIRC) represents leaders from the corporate, investment, accounting, securities, regulatory, academic, civil society and standard-setting sectors. The aim is to develop an agreed internationally convergent set of principles for integrated reporting that reflects organizational impact on the stores of different kinds of capital: financial, manufactured, natural, social, intellectual and human.

According to the IIRC, the key principles of integrated reporting include:

- strategic focus
- connectivity of information
- future orientation
- responsiveness and stakeholder inclusiveness
- conciseness, reliability and materiality.

These principles should be applied in determining the content of an Integrated Report, based on the key content elements summarized below:

- organizational overview and business model
- operating context, including risks and opportunities
- strategic objectives and strategies to achieve those objectives
- governance and remuneration
- performance
- future outlook.[27]

The reporting emphasis is on materiality – that is, the factors that create and increase business value over time. Table 3.4 summarises the differences between integrated reporting and traditional reporting.

Table 3.4 *How is integrated reporting different?*

Thinking	→	Isolated	→	Integrated

Because traditional reporting occurs in silos, it encourages thinking in silos. Integrated reporting, on the other hand, reflects, and supports, integrated thinking – monitoring, managing and communicating the full complexity of the value-creation process and how this contributes to success over time. Integrated reporting demonstrates the extent to which integrated thinking is occurring within the organization.

Stewardship	→	Financial capital	→	All forms of capital

An integrated report displays an organization's stewardship not only of financial capital, but also of the other 'capitals' (manufactured, human, intellectual, natural and social), their interdependence and how they contribute to success. This broader perspective requires consideration of resource usage and risks and opportunities along the organization's full value chain.

Table 3.4 *Continued*

Focus	→	*Past, financial* →	*Past and future, connected, strategic*

Annual reporting at present is largely focused on past financial performance and financial risks. Other reports and communications may cover other resources and relationships, but they are seldom presented in a connected way or linked to the organization's strategic objectives and its ability to create and sustain value in the future.

Time-frame	→	*Short term* →	*Short, medium and long term*

Much of the media and regulatory attention in response to the global financial crisis has focused on 'short-termism' as one contributory factor. Although short-term considerations are important in many ways, placing them in context is also essential. Integrated reporting specifically factors in short-, medium- and long-term considerations.

Trust	→	*Narrow disclosures* →	*Greater transparency*

Financial reporting focuses primarily on a narrow series of mandated disclosures. Although an increasing number of organizations are improving their transparency, for example, through voluntary sustainability reporting, in absolute terms that number is still low. By emphasizing transparency, for example, covering a broader range of issues and disclosing the positive with the negative, integrated reporting helps to build trust.

Adaptive	→	*Rule bound* →	*Responsive to individual circumstances*

Today's reporting is often said to be too compliance orientated, reducing the scope for organizations to exercise an appropriate amount of judgement. While a certain level of compliance orientation is necessary to ensure consistency and enable comparison, integrated reporting offers a principles-based approach that drives greater focus on factors that are material to particular sectors and organizations. It permits an organization to disclose its unique situation in clear and understandable language.

Concise	→	*Long and complex* →	*Concise and material*

Long and complex reports are often impenetrable for many readers. A key objective for integrated reporting is to de-clutter the primary report so that it covers, concisely, only the most-material information.

Technology enabled	→	*Paper based* →	*Technology enabled*

Source: Modified from *Towards Integrated Reporting*, 2010, p. 9. Available HTTP: http://theiirc.org/wp-content/uploads/2011/09/IR-Discussion-Paper-2011_spreads.pdf, p. 9 (accessed 22 November 2013).

Sustainable supply-chain management

Given that procurement can take up a high percentage of corporate budgets, purchasing can obviously play a leading role in sustainable management. Supply-chain choices can be a major way companies can reduce their indirect emissions and environmental impacts, as well as limit reputational risks associated with human rights issues along the supply chain. Seuring and Muller define sustainable supply-chain management (SSCM) practices as:

> the management of material, information and capital flows as well as cooperation among companies along the supply chain while taking goals from all three dimensions of sustainable development, i.e., economic, environmental and social, into account which are derived from customer and stakeholder requirements.[28]

The environmental and human rights credentials of suppliers are now influencing supplier selection, as rating systems are being utilized to accredit and thus compare supplier performance according to the demands of individual sectors.[29] As part of the supplier assessment process, organizations typically require suppliers to attain third-party certificated accreditation to various codes and standards, including the ISO 9001 series for quality management, ISO 14000 and EMAS. Codes for ethical sourcing include the Base Code of the Ethical Trading Initiative (ETI), International Labour Organization (ILO) conventions and SA 8000.[30] Sustainable supplier programmes also impose sustainability along the supply chain through coercive forces. An example of this is the Walmart's Supplier Sustainability Index.[31] Industry associations also play a role. The box below provides an example of collaborative action along a specific supply chain that has potential to impact on the entire system of steel production in Australia.

Steel Stewardship Forum[32]

In 2008, the Steel Stewardship Forum (SSF) was formed in Australia with representatives from industry, government and NGOs in response to the Asia-Pacific Economic Cooperation Ministers Responsible for Mining discussion in February 2007 that steel stewardship would make a positive contribution. The formation of the SSF body was underpinned by its drive to maximize the value of steel to society whilst minimizing the negative commercial, social and environmental impact across the life-cycle. The SSF

continued

body aims to develop steel stewardship across the entire steel supply chain within the Australian market and to act as a template or 'best practice' model for the region.

The SSF concept brings together representatives from all major sectors of the Australian steel product life-cycle from mining through steel manufacturing, processing, product fabrication, use and reuse and recycling. Industry associations are also members. The focus is the shared responsibility of working together to optimize the steel product life-cycle. The process will use sustainability principles which include minimizing the impact of steel on the environment and maximizing its social and economic benefits.

Optimizing the steel product life-cycle using sustainability principles is important, as steel is necessary for the functioning of the global economy, and there is a significant environmental impact arising from its production process. Ensuring a more sustainable product is seen as key to Australia's medium- to long-term competitiveness in this industry for which Australia is a major source of raw materials.

Source: see note 32.

Specific change management approaches

Specific change management approaches geared to sustainability are required to address the changes needed to move an organization from rejection or non-responsive phases to compliance. Sustainability principles need to be integrated into the change process and set as a specific target to be achieved. For example, The Home Depot, one of the largest home improvement retailers in the world, moved towards sustainability by implementing the Natural Step Principles into its business model. The Natural Step Principles are:

- Substances from the earth's crust cannot systematically increase in the biosphere.
- Substances produced by society cannot systematically increase in the biosphere.
- The physical basis for the productivity and diversity of nature must not be systematically deteriorated.
- There must be fair and efficient use of resources to meet human needs.[33]

At The Home Depot the change programme for sustainability began in 1998, when these principles were integrated into an intensive training programme for senior management which included systems mapping of the organization so that managers could develop an awareness of the sustainability impacts of its operations and its 40,000 products. Top-to-bottom commitment to sustainability is the target – to be achieved by ongoing education and awareness programmes at all levels of the organization. The firm has now progressed to developing a sustainable procurement policy, selecting vendors who themselves have sustainability policies in place.[34] Similarly, McDonalds Sweden has achieved major sustainability outcomes by engaging top leadership support for Natural Step Principles, conducting a comprehensive sustainability analysis and educating suppliers into the Principles. Achievements include cutting waste by 85 per cent and major reduction in heavy metals used in toys and construction.[35]

Another example from the fast food industry in Sweden is Max's Hamburgers, a McDonalds competitor. Max's Hamburgers is a family-owned chain with 75 restaurants and 3,000 employees. It is a major sustainability award winner and has quintupled its profits since 2003.[36] Table 3.5 shows how Max's Hamburgers has applied the Natural Step Principles.

Table 3.5 *The Natural Step Principles at Max's Hamburgers*

Sustainability principles 1-4 *In a sustainable society, nature is not subject to systematically increasing:*	*How Max is changing its business to meet this principle:*
1 concentrations of substances extracted from the earth's crust	• All restaurants are powered by 100% wind energy. • Toys requiring batteries have been removed from kids' meals. • All company vehicles are low carbon.
2 concentrations of substances produced by society	• No GMOs are used in Max products. • All used fry oil is converted into biodiesel. • High recycling rates (e.g. cardboard, food wastes, metal, electronic equipment, etc.)
3 degradation by physical means	• All fish procured from well-managed ecosystems (MSC-certified). • Most paper products are FSC-certified. • Reforestation through Plan Vivo-certified projects in Africa.
4 and, in that society, people are not subject to conditions that systematically undermine their capacity to meet their needs	• No use of transfats. • Product lines have been remade into the healthiest of the industry (by 2005). • More than half of the restaurants have at least one staff member with a mental disability. • Max leadership programme includes sections on sustainable leadership that are based on the FIRO (Fundamental Interpersonal Relations Orientation) theory.* • Max has partnered with TNS's Real Change program to research social sustainability.

* W. Schutz, *FIRO: A Three Dimensional Theory of Interpersonal Behaviour*, New York: Holt, Rinehart, & Winston 1958.

Source: Modified from The Natural Step, *A Natural Step Case Study, Max Hamburger and the Natural Step*, 2010, p. 2.

Individual industry characteristics need to be considered so as to generate these specific approaches to sustainability. For example, Marcuson *et al.*[37] highlight the challenges that mining poses for sustainability:

- Metal and mineral resources are non-renewable.
- Economic mineralization often occurs in remote areas that are rich in biodiversity, with many sites of cultural importance to indigenous inhabitants. The mining company develops essential infrastructure. Its activities irreversibly alter both the natural and social environments.
- The mining sector is diverse in size, scope and responsibility. It comprises government and private organizations, major corporations and junior miners and exploration companies.
- The mining industry has a poor legacy.
- The risks and hazards in production, use and disposal are not well understood by the public and are often poorly communicated.
- In contrast to manufacturing, which involves primarily physical change, the processing of metals involves chemical change, which inherently is more polluting.

These writers argue that the major sustainability challenges relate to the fact that many of the negative impacts are at the very local level, while the benefits may accrue globally. It follows that key principles that the sustainability programme must follow include:

- Diversity – modern mining is not labour intensive; only a small proportion of the local population will be employed in the operation. Additionally, many people may choose a lifestyle that does not fit the manufacturing mode. They have to feel welcome in the community. The sustainability programme has to take this into account, for example, support for pastoral communities.
- Equity – the community provides equitable, but not equal, opportunities and outcomes for all of its members, particularly the poorest and most vulnerable.
- Interconnectedness – local groups have to be connected both internally and externally.
- Quality of life – commitments to improve the quality of life must include; (a) employment and training, (b) small-business development, (c) individual capacity development and (d) support for diversity in lifestyles and aspirations.

- Democracy and governance – the quality of self-governance directly affects the outcome of the process. Agreements must be aimed at achieving a high quality of self-governance and independence from the state.

Summary: the case for moving to compliance

The previous sections outlined a broad case for corporations to adopt a proactive approach to compliance. In summary, the reasons are:

- the emergence of more widespread and increasingly sophisticated forms of government regulation
- increasing scrutiny by NGOs
- public access to information technology and the risks to corporate reputation of public perception of poor corporate citizenship
- the opportunities which compliance can provide to improve the firm's competitive situation
- the benefits of building cooperative relationships with regulators
- the risks associated with delays in achieving compliance. While rejection or non-responsiveness to regulation may delay costs and assessments, these approaches can result in much higher costs being paid for non-compliance and in more negative assessments by regulators and the public.

As we noted in Chapter 2, the relationship between risk management and climate change is sensitizing a range of industry sectors to sustainability. Moving to compliance is largely a matter of incremental change. In Chapter 7 we take up again issues relating to the move to compliance. In that chapter we concentrate on substantive issues in the move, that is, what to do.

Appendix 3.1: phases 1–3 in the development of compliance

 ## Phase 1: rejection

Human sustainability (HS1)

Employees and subcontractors are regarded as a resource to be exploited. Health and safety features are ignored or given 'lip-service'. Disadvantages stemming from ethnicity, gender, social class, intellectual ability and language proficiency are systematically exploited to advantage the organization and further disadvantage employees and subcontractors. Force, threats of force and abuse are used to maintain compliance and workforce subjection. Training costs are kept to a minimum necessary to operate the business; expenditure on personal and professional development is avoided. The organization does not take responsibility for the health, welfare and future career prospects of its employees nor for the community in which is a part. Community concerns are rejected outright.

Ecological sustainability (ES1)

The environment is regarded as a 'free good' to be exploited. Owners/managers are hostile to environmental activists and to pressures from government, other corporations or community groups aimed at achieving ecological sustainability. Pro-environmental action is seen as a threat to the organization. Physical resource extraction and production processes are used which directly destroy future productive capacity and/or damage the ecosystem. Polluting by-products are discharged into the biosphere, causing damage and threatening living processes. The organization does not take responsibility for the environmental impact of its ongoing operations nor does it modify its operations to lessen future ecological degradation.

 ## Phase 2: non-responsiveness

Human sustainability (HS2)

Financial and technological factors dominate business strategies to the exclusion of most aspects of human resource management. 'Industrial relations' (IR) or 'Employee relations' (ER) strategies dominate the human

Ecological sustainability (ES2)

The ecological environment is not considered to be a relevant factor in strategic or operational decisions. Financial and technological factors dominate business strategies to the exclusion of environmental concerns.

agenda with 'labour' viewed as a cost to be minimized. Apart from cost minimization, IR/ER strategies are directed at developing a compliant workforce responsive to managerial control. The training agenda, if there is one, centres on technical and supervisory training. Broader human resource strategies and policies are ignored, as are issues of wider social responsibility and community concern.

Traditional approaches to efficiency dominate the production process and the environment is taken for granted. Environmental resources which are free or subsidized (air, water and so on) are wasted and little regard is given to environmental degradation resulting from the organization's activities. Environmental risks, costs, opportunities and imperatives are seen as irrelevant or not perceived at all.

 ## Phase 3: compliance

Human sustainability (HS3)

Financial and technological factors still dominate business strategies but senior management views the firm as a 'decent employer'. The emphasis is on compliance with legal requirements in industrial relations, safety, workplace standards and so on. Human resource functions such as training, IR, organization development, total quality management are instituted but there is little integration between them.

Ecological sustainability (ES3)

Financial and technological factors still dominate business strategies but senior management seeks to comply with environmental laws and to minimize the firm's potential liabilities from actions that might have an adverse impact on the environment. The most obvious environmental abuses are eliminated, particularly those that could lead to litigation or strong community action directed against the firm.

Notes

1 J. Fenby, 'Scandals undermine China's regime', *Guardian Weekly*, 20 May 2013, p. 20.
2 J. Manik, and J. Yardley, '17 days after collapse, cries of save me!' *International Herald Tribune*, 11–12 May 2013, pp. 2–4.
3 M. Yunus, 'A way to start the healing at Savar', *Guardian Weekly*, 17 May 2013, p. 18.
4 Ibid.
5 J. Stern, 'Apple Foxconn Investigation: Serious Worker Rights Issues Reported: Major Changes for Chinese Workers Promised', ABC News, 2012. Online. Available HTTP: <http://abcnews.go.com/Technology/apple-

foxconn-production-lines-china-fair-labor-association/story?id=16006516>
(accessed 20 April 2013).

6 China Labor Watch, 'Beyond Foxconn: Deplorable Working Conditions
   Characterize Apple's Entire Supply Chain', Online. Available HTTP:
   <http://www.chinalaborwatch.org/news/new-415.html> (accessed 21 May
   2013).

7 J. Bakan, *The Corporation*, New York: Free Press, 2004.

8 Australian Government Corporations and Markets Advisory Committee,
   Corporate Social Responsibility Discussion Paper, Canberra:
   Commonwealth of Australia, 2005, p. 13.

9 D. Vogel, *The Market for Virtue*, Washington, DC: Brookings Institution
   Press, 2005.

10 T. Clarke and D. Branson, 'Introduction', in T. Clarke and D. Branson (eds)
   The Sage Handbook of Corporate Governance, 2012, London: Sage, p. 31.

11 C. Ford, 'Lessons from financial regulation', *Wisconsin Law Review*, 2010, 2,
   pp. 441–87.

12 C. Deutsch 'Companies and critics try collaboration', *New York Times*,
   17 May 2006. Online. Available HTTP: <http://www.nytimes.com/2006/
   05/17/business/businessspecial2/17partner.html?_r=1&fta=y&oref=slogin>
   (accessed 21 May 2006).

13 P. Monaghan, 'Consumer Product Red List', 2012. Online. Available HTTP:
   <www.infrangilis> (accessed 2 February 2013).

14 BASF (2012) 'BASF SELECT™ Eco-Label Manager nearly Triples in Size',
   2012. Online. Available HTTP: <http://www.basf.com/group/corporate/
   us/en_GB/news-and-media-relations/news-releases/news-releases-usa/
   P-12-131> (accessed 20 April 2013).

15 N. J. Roome and F. H. Wijen, 'Stakeholder power and organizational learning
   in corporate environmental managment,' *Organization Studies*, 2006, 27 (2),
   235–63.

16 K. Bondy, D. Matten and J. Moon, 'Codes of conduct as a tool for sustainable
   governance in MNCs', in S. Benn and D. Dunphy (eds), *Corporate
   Governance and Sustainability*, London: Routledge, 2009, pp. 165–86.

17 Ibid., p. 170.

18 A. Westervelt, 'Turning Compliance into Innovation and Profit', 2012.
   Online. Available HTTP: <http://www.greenbiz.com/blog/2012/04/02/
   turning-compliance-innovation-and-profit> (accessed 21 April 2013).

19 M. E. Porter and C. van der Linde, 'Toward a new conception of the
   environment-competitiveness relationship', *Journal of Economic
   Perspectives*, 1995, 9 (4), 97–118.

20 Novo Nordisk. Available at http://www.novonordisk.com/sustainability/
   sustainability-approach/awards-and-recognition.asp (accessed 22 April 2013).

21 A. Westervelt, 'Turning Compliance into innovation and Profit',
   Greenbiz.com, 2012. Online. Available HTTP: <http://www.greenbiz.
   com/blog/2012/04/02/turning-compliance-innovation-and-profit> (accessed
   21 April 2013).

22 Global Leadership Summit, *The Growing Power of Non-financial Reports*,
    London: London Business School, 2013. Online. Available HTTP:
    http://gls.london.edu/news-and-articles/40/95/The-growing-power-of-non-
    financial-reports.html (accessed 22 April 2013).
23 KPMG and ICAA, *Governance Risk and Compliance*, Sydney: ICAA and
    KPMG, 2012.
24 Global Reporting Initiative (GRI). Online. Available HTTP: https://www.
    globalreporting.org/ (accessed 11 September 2013).
25 AccountAbility (2012) 'Standards'. Online. Available HTTP: <http://www.
    accountability.org/standards/aa1000aps.html> (accessed 24 April 2013).
26 J. Elkington, *Cannibals with Forks: Triple Bottom Line of 21st Century
    Business*, Oxford: Capstone Publishing Ltd, 1999.
27 Towards Integrated Reporting (2010). Online. Available HTTP: <http://the
    iirc.org/wp-content/uploads/2011/09/IR-Discussion-Paper-2011_spreads.pdf>,
    p. 3 (accessed 22 November 2013).
28 S. Seuring and M. Muller, 'From a literature review to a conceptual
    framework for sustainable supply chain management', *Journal of Cleaner
    Production*, 2008, 16 (15), 1699–710, p. 1700.
29 S. New, K. Green and B. Morton, 'An analysis of private versus public sector
    responses to the environmental challenges of the supply chain', *Journal of
    Public Procurement*, 2002, 2 (1), 93–105.
30 M. Blowfield, 'Ethical supply chains in the cocoa, coffee and tea industries',
    Greener Management International, 2003, Autumn (43), pp. 15–24.
31 Walmart Sustainability Index. Available HTTP: <http://corporate.walmart.
    com/global-responsibility/environment-sustainability/sustainability-index>
    (accessed 25 November 2013).
32 Steel Stewardship Forum. Online. Available HTTP: http://steelstewardship.
    com/ (accessed 11 September, 2013).
33 The Natural Step, 2006. Online. Available HTTP: <http://www.naturalstep.
    org> (accessed 28 May 2006).
34 Home Depot, Wood Purchasing Policy. Online. Available HTTP:
    http://corporate.homedepot.com/CorporateResponsibility/Environment/
    WoodPurchasing/pages/default.aspx (accessed 5 match 2014).
35 McDonalds Sweden– A Case Study. Online. Available HTTP: http://www.
    designinnovation.ie/downloads/mcdonalds_sweden.pdf (accessed 5 Macrh
    2014).
36 The Natural Step, *A Natural Step Case Study, Max Hamburger and the
    Natural Step*, The Natural Step, 2010. Available HTTP: <http://www.natural
    step.org/sites/all/files/Max-TNS-CaseStudy-FINAL.pdf> accessed
    24 November 2013).
37 S. Marcuson, J. Hooper, R. Osborne, K. Chow and J. Burchell, 'Sustainability
    in nickel projects: 50 years of experience at Vale Inco', *Engineering and
    Mining Journal*, 2009. Online. Available HTTP: <http://www.e-mj.com/
    index.php/features/117-sustainability-in-nickel-projects-50-years-of-
    experience-at-vale-inco> (accessed 22 April 2013).

Part III
The dominant current reality: understanding and reconstructing second wave corporations

4   Achieving sustainable operational efficiencies

Beyond low-hanging fruit

'Picking the low-hanging fruit' is an expression that managers use to describe the easily achieved efficiency gains made within their corporations. However, once all the low-hanging fruit is picked, where are new efficiency gains to be achieved? This chapter takes the search for efficiency beyond the obvious cost-reduction exercise. We identify three paths to efficiency:

- efficiencies via cost reduction
- efficiencies through value adding
- efficiencies through innovation and flexibility.

These are not mutually exclusive paths to efficiency. Together, they represent a radical shift in the way that corporations approach efficiency – both human and ecological. They form the basis of a strong and compelling business case for managers to engage in sustainability activities.

The Scandic hotel chain provides insights into how organizations can capitalize on these three paths to efficiency. Today, Scandic is the dominant operator of full-service 3–4 star hotels in Scandinavia and one of the major hotel chains in Europe. However, this was not the case in

1992, when the chain was in crisis. The newly appointed CEO, Roland Nilsson, instigated a major turnaround project that lasted two years. The successes achieved in the turnaround enabled the corporation to shift its focus from crisis management to future strategy. Central to this achievement was a change in values and philosophy. The company adopted 'profound caring' as its value statement. This reflected a commitment to care for all major stakeholders: customers, employees, shareholders, communities and the environment.

Environmental and social responsibility became a central focus of the organization. A corporate-wide programme, The Natural Step, was instigated to instil the new values approach throughout the corporation. Nilsson, the CEO, viewed The Natural Step as a powerful tool for communicating the importance of achieving sustainable outcomes. All managers and employees were exposed to the ideas of The Natural Step through workshops. Scandic managers and employees then sought to translate the principles of The Natural Step into concrete actions that would reduce the 'ecological footprint' of the corporation and simultaneously harness efficiencies to deliver in a practical way on the commitment to 'profound caring'.[1]

The first efficiency impacts at Scandic were felt almost immediately. Employees identified many 'low-hanging fruit', ripe for picking. For instance, the overall amount of soap and shampoo used was reduced by 25 tons annually, and refuse by 8.5 tons. This was achieved by the introduction of recyclable soap and shampoo and the elimination of waste by the use of refillable containers. The implementation of ideas such as these continues to generate cost efficiencies for Scandic. As a consequence of these initiatives, Scandic is now developing a hair- and skincare range for 2013 in partnership with FACE Stockholm. To be introduced in all hotels, the scheme will allow Scandic to cut plastic consumption by 21 tonnes per year.[2]

Second, Scandic moved towards efficiency gains through the adoption of value-adding activities. In order to generate value-adding outputs, the company had first to build the capability of its employees. Anticipated efficiency gains were shared with employees by investing in their skills. Emphasis was placed on developing and training employees (enhancing human capital) to identify value-adding opportunities. Employees developed and used a range of metrics such as environmental barometers (quarterly benchmarking reports) and an environmental index. In addition, a resource hunt was initiated to gain resource efficiencies in energy, water, waste and dematerialization. In its first year, average energy consumption in Scandic's Nordic hotels was reduced by 7 per cent, water consumption by 4 per cent and unsorted waste by 15 per cent. This resulted in estimated financial benefits of US$800,000. Scandic has continued to build on these developments by reducing water consumption by 13 per cent and energy consumption by 24 per cent.[3] Through investment in such value-adding activities, Scandic built on its initial cost-cutting approach to deliver more fundamental efficiency improvements in resource utilization. This strategy is now being applied to Scandic's supply chain and procurement practices.

Finally, at Scandic innovation has become another means of gaining further sustainable efficiencies. Renewing and refurnishing are major investment activities in hotels. One major innovation which Scandic has developed is the 97 per cent recyclable 'eco-room'. Rooms are designed and built for disassembly and all components that cannot be reused or recycled are sold. Currently, the Scandic chain has created over 10,000 environmental rooms and is tracking daily use of energy, unsorted waste, water and fossil carbon dioxide in its live Sustainability Report. The chain is committed to eliminating all fossil fuels emissions by 2025.[4] Innovation – a change in mind-set – has led to huge cost savings, has reduced ecological impacts and has enhanced the reputation of the corporation with its customers. Scandic has also sought to add value in other areas of its operations. For instance, the hotel demands that its suppliers share Scandic's corporate values and are responsible to both the environment and society. In order to demonstrate transparency, Scandic has made its terms for suppliers' agreement available on its website.

The Scandic case reinforces two important messages contained in this chapter. First, the move to efficiency often starts with an emphasis on using cost measures to capture short-term efficiencies. However, to achieve sustainable longer-term gains, the appropriate human systems and cultural values must be built to support value adding and innovation. For instance, staff training is a key aspect of the sustainability programme implemented at Scandic by The Natural Step. All employees are provided with environmental guidelines, are involved in special environmental meetings and participate in the drawing up of action plans.[5] Second, in a world where population is still increasing, the stewardship of natural and social resources is critical. An economy made up of efficient organizations may simply devastate the natural and social world more efficiently by, for example, using up natural resources at a greater rate or generating a larger pool of unemployed. Efficiency is a contestable term that can be defined only by reference to values. At Scandic Corporation, efficiency gains are shared with employees and a broader set of stakeholders, as well as being used to build internal competencies and the reputational capital of the firm. These strategies create a virtuous circle of steadily increasing efficiencies. The three-pronged approach to sustainability that is exemplified by Scandic provides a compelling business case for sustainability.

In this chapter, we detail these three approaches to efficiency: cost reduction, value adding and innovation. While we discuss all three, we emphasize the importance of the latter two in creating positive benefits for the natural and social world. We refer to these as the high road to sustainability. Cost reduction alone is not necessarily a positive achievement for the organization, society or the environment. However, it can become a significant first step on the journey towards achieving sustainable competitive advantages and benefiting society and the environment. Some commentators, such as Renato Orsato, have provided a compelling case for understanding under what conditions and strategies corporations should engage with sustainability practices (cost or differentiation) in order that they may be able to generate long-term value and potential competitive advantages.[6] His work further reinforces the business case for sustainability.

What is efficiency?

Efficiency is a concept that means different things to different people. So what is efficiency? How can efficiency contribute to creating a more sustainable world? Who owns the increased efficiency? And how is the payoff shared?

The search for corporate efficiencies has a long history that provides a useful framework for understanding current approaches. As organizations became larger and more complex in the late nineteenth century, a movement emerged which focused on controlling the complexities that had arisen in these new factories. Frederick Taylor, the father of scientific management, was one leader who responded to this challenge. He involved himself in studying the new factories and trying to improve their productive efficiency. Taylor aimed to tame organizational complexity through the systematization of work and to increase organizational profitability through incremental improvements to the efficiency with which work was performed. Taylor's scientific management was only one historical source of traditional bureaucratic attempts to improve the efficiency of organizations. A comparable European source was the work of Henri Fayol. Both Taylor and Fayol had visions of more-productive organizations which they and their followers were able to implement in the real world.[7] Their ideas on what constitutes efficiency were, however, limited in scope and unrelated to issues of sustainability.

The principles generated by these approaches were simply an extension of Newtonian science. Success in scientific endeavour had been achieved by breaking the whole into duplicate parts with highly specialized functions and making these parts interchangeable. Scientific management extended these principles to the creation of a logical, linear workflow, the selection of applicants best suited to the job, training workers in the skills needed, measuring output and motivating workers by suitable rewards for performance. One result was the assembly line, which dominated manufacturing through most of the last century.

The systematizing of work that Taylor captured in his *Principles of Scientific Management* still remains an influential concept in much work redesign. Many of the principles embodied in Taylor's work were later taken up by industrial engineers and incorporated in operations management, the application of mathematical and technical solutions to solving managerial problems.

More recently, business process re-engineering (BPR) has built on these earlier incremental approaches to creating corporate efficiencies. It has attempted to do this by designing organizational transformations which 'bust silos', that is, break down the boundaries between functional management areas such as marketing, manufacturing and sales. The aim is to reorganize corporations into discrete lateral process and/or product flows.[8] Re-engineering can result in positive benefits such as a reduction in the number of levels in the organizational hierarchies, a refocusing of activities and resources on the core business, elimination of non-value-added activities, the outsourcing of non-core businesses and simplification of workflows that cross traditional functional boundaries. This in turn requires the devolution of authority and in some cases the introduction of team-based work.[9] With BPR, efficiency moved from being treated as simply an operational issue to being a corporate-wide performance improvement strategy. However, issues of social responsibility, the systematic building of human capability in the workforce and environmental regeneration were largely ignored by BPR specialists.

So how do we understand corporate performance? Hilmer identified three factors affecting organizational performance: cost, value and flexibility.[10]

We shall deal with each of these potential components of performance in turn.

If they are working within a conventional business perspective, corporations seeking efficiency are primarily concerned with the first factor – cost. If a firm is to compete against other firms producing similar products or services on price alone, then cost becomes the vital factor in success, and the search for ongoing cost reductions is the way to sustain success. This may include reducing the costs of inputs; redesigning work, product and process flows to generate internal efficiencies; reducing labour inputs and creating better utilization of company resources (see Figure 4.1). Most firms compete on cost to some extent, but cost is less likely to be the most important factor in success where the firm has developed a unique product, service or production process. In other words, many cost advantages are short lived. Take for example a beverage company that introduces new water-saving technologies as part of an eco-efficiency initiative and in the process doubles its water efficiency in five years. For instance, the Carlton United Brewery at Yatala in Queensland previously used six litres of water per litre of beer brewed; it has now reduced this to two litres. However, as one manager put it: 'We need to keep extending our efficiencies and looking for new breakthroughs. It won't be long before our competitors follow.'

A second approach to performance improvement comes from improving the quality of the product or service through adding value of some kind. Innovation around adding value is a potential source of performance improvement. Being an innovator is a strategic choice, with very different implications from competing primarily on cost, because adding value

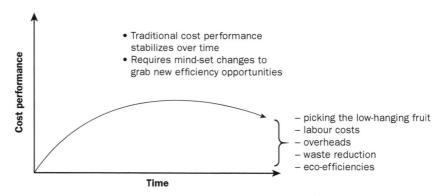

Figure 4.1 *Traditional cost efficiencies*

usually incurs extra costs, such as those associated with research and development and new product design. In the words of Orsato, 'being green costs more, a differentiation strategy is the only way out for the company to pay off ecological investments'.[11]

Environmental performance at SC Johnson

The case of SC Johnson demonstrates how a company can build innovation in sustainability by valuing people, place and environment. SC Johnson is a leading manufacturer of household products for floor, furniture, air care and insect control, a family-owned company established in 1886. Its headquarters are located in the United States but the company operates in over 60 countries. The firm currently does US$9 billion in sales annually, employs nearly 13,000 people globally and sells products in virtually every country around the world. The firm has a long history of philanthropy and corporate social responsibility. When faced with increasing consumer awareness and a resulting pressure for regulatory compliance, the management of the company initiated an eco-efficiency approach to improve the environmental performance of its manufacturing operations. Rowledge *et al*. point out that, initially, 'it was not a particularly explicit or integrated strategy designed to carefully position itself in customer minds . . . it was clear that there were business benefits to be won from reducing waste, improving efficiency and minimising liabilities'.[12]

SC Johnson's strategy at first focused on improving operational efficiencies by finding engineering and technical solutions in the areas of waste management, filtering, recycling and in some cases the use of gas from landfill to produce steam power. However, as the programme of change continued, its success became more reliant on company-wide educational programmes, eco-efficiency workshops, communication strategies and developing the capabilities of its people. The experiences of this company highlight a central theme of this book: that it is important to make a start somewhere, where at least small wins may be readily made. But where a company ends up may be very different from what management envisaged in the beginning. SC Johnson's initial endeavours were devoted solely to the capturing of eco-efficiencies and reducing risk by removing noxious chemicals. But now the emphasis has changed and the company is asking: 'How can we create products without any chemicals at all?'

Eco-efficiency often starts with the idea of improving the environmental performance of existing operations. However, its inherent logic carries those involved into a more substantial change process. SC Johnson has continued to add value to these initial improvements via its Greenlist programme. The Greenlist programme forces the company to invest in research and development in order to look for replacement natural resources that are environmentally best or better than existing products. For example, each potential ingredient in an SC Johnson product is rated as 'Best', 'Better',

continued

'Acceptable', or '0-rated' for materials that can be used only in special circumstances. Since 2001, the firm has increased the percentage of 'Better' or 'Best' ingredients from 18 per cent to 50 per cent. Furthermore, the company has sought energy, waste and greenhouse gas improvements as part of its overall innovation drive. SC Johnson completed its 2006–2010 corporate energy and emissions goals, including sourcing 40 per cent of total electricity usage worldwide from renewable sources and cutting greenhouse gas emissions from global factories by 26 per cent since 2000. The Waxdale operation, its largest global manufacturing site, has installed two massive wind turbines which are predicted to enable 100 per cent electricity generation on site.[13] Finally, in 2012, the firm was awarded the SmartWay(r) Excellence Award from the United States Environmental Protection Agency (EPA) as a leader in freight supply-chain environmental performance and energy efficiency. This award is the EPA's highest recognition for demonstrated leadership in supply-chain goods movement.

A third approach to performance improvement comes from increasing flexibility through innovation; that is, maintaining the ability to monitor, respond to or even anticipate changing market demands. The key to success here is to move in speedily with appropriate products or services to meet emerging demands. Innovation, speed to market and organizational flexibility become key components of success in this approach to creating a high-performance organization. The emphasis is placed on competing by developing unique bundles of competencies and organizational capabilities, particularly those involved with reshaping the organization.

The efficiency approach to sustainability is therefore not only a way of reducing costs to ensure competitive advantage but also an approach that can involve investments in value-adding and innovation-based activities which lead on to strategic sustainability initiatives. When managers apply efficiency approaches to ecological issues, for example, they initially recognize that poor environmental practice may result in fines, boycotts or expensive clean-up operations. Product or service redesign may eliminate these risks, which are avoidable costs. On the human sustainability side, efficiency-driven organizations regard employees as a necessary resource required to make returns to the corporation, but a significant source of expenditure. Reducing employee numbers by process redesign can minimize these costs. But this denominator-driven approach is only one way to achieve this end. Another way to increase profitability is to make better use of the workforce to increase the numerator. Adding value through more effective use of employees is another approach to efficiency.

This is clearly the path that has been pursued by organizations such as Scandic and SC Johnson.

Efficiency approaches to sustainability are recognition of the scarcity of organizational resources and are about finding efficiency improvements through changing the resource mix or through better utilization of resources. We argue that these latter two approaches to efficiency require significant mind-set changes within organizations.

How can the search for efficiency contribute to sustainability?

Efficiency rests on value judgements – particularly about whose interests will be served by the changes. For instance, there is 'efficiency for the firm on the cheap'. It is relatively easy to increase the efficiency of any subunit of an organization or of society by externalizing costs to others. A simple example from managing a household economy is to throw the garbage over the neighbour's fence or onto the common. All this does is transfer the costs to someone else. While efficient in the short term, we do not see it as leading to sustainability. Similarly, we may reduce household costs in the short term by chopping up the floorboards for heating and selling off basic facilities like the refrigerator and stove. In this case, we have externalized costs to the future. So when we are evaluating efficiencies, we cannot evaluate them solely on whether they benefit the organization: we also have to look at their impact on the environment and society.

In many cases, the efficiency approach to sustainability is a natural extension of an organization's engagement in compliance activities. Compliance involves reviewing and monitoring organizational performance in order to identify inefficiencies. Efficiency approaches to sustainability have been particularly popular with organizations engaged in activities that significantly impact on the environment, such as those operating in the resource-extraction industries, in manufacturing and in petrochemicals.[14] Companies in these industries have typically moved over time beyond compliance activities and towards the adoption of efficiency approaches to sustainability.

In other words, the new lens of sustainability helps management and others to see current organizational activities in a fresh light so that new opportunities to make efficiency improvements become apparent. This is crucial for organizational change for sustainability, as senior management commitment to significantly moderate influences such as from government, public concern and perceptions of competitive advantage has been found.[15] As we have previously pointed out, this new lens of sustainability also highlights the importance of generating efficiencies along the supply chain. A Trucost study for the United Nations Principles for Responsible Investment (UN PRI) found that of the $2.15 trillion of environmental damage caused by the world's largest 3,000 companies annually, 49 per cent comes from impacts hidden within supply chains. As pointed out in a recent article on *Newsweek*'s Green Rankings: 'Integrating this information into the management of business can help companies mitigate risk, reduce costs, and reduce their impact.'[16]

The UK food retailer Sainsbury's is an example of a firm that has focused on efficiency measures that have had a major impact in terms of reducing waste to landfill. At the same time, it has addressed a number of human sustainability targets by meeting some community needs. According to Justin King, Sainsbury's Chief Executive:

> We're very proud of hitting our target for zero waste to landfill which we set three years ago. We know times are tough for many customers but they still rightly expect Sainsbury's to lead the way on the things that will always matter to all of us including caring for our environment.[17]

Efficiency measures at Sainsbury's

Sainsbury's has reached its target of zero waste to landfill seven years ahead of schedule by means of working up and down its supply chain.

- Any surplus food that Sainsbury's cannot donate to its food-charity partners is sent to processors to be turned into animal feed.
- All general waste from stores is either recycled or turned into fuel.
- The waste and recycling firm Biffa collects and treats organic and dry waste on behalf of the chain. Waste is backhauled from larger stores, while Biffa collects material directly from convenience stores in towns and cities.
- Techniques such as anaerobic digestion are used to reduce waste and any dry waste that cannot be recycled is disposed of via energy from waste.
- Vegetables and fruit that are slightly damaged, previously sent to waste, are now sold, as an aspect of a consumer awareness-raising campaign.[18]

The message is simple: the efficiency approach represents a natural move towards sustainability because it builds on existing operational and technical capabilities and is a natural extension of installing compliance systems and the application of quality management principles. However, efficiency defined solely as cost reduction and the simplification of product, process and service flows is insufficient to achieve fully sustainable communities and a sustainable world. Some commentators argue that the 'greening of industry' associated with these initiatives is not sufficient to deal with the significant environmental and social shocks that organizations may face under conditions of discontinuous change.[19] In addition, such efficiencies will provide only limited competitive advantages for the organization, as efficiencies of these kinds are readily copied by competitors. Nevertheless, the cost-efficiency paradigm can help organizations to lay the foundation for a more comprehensive approach to becoming a strategically sustainable organization.

We argue that a radical rethink of efficiency is required. The Scandic case highlights this in practical terms. The Scandic change programme started with a cost-cutting focus but went on to initiate value-adding and innovation approaches. There are many detailed examples of efficiency and resource gains to be made in organizations and societies as they engage seriously with protecting the natural environment.[20] The examples given in this literature demonstrate the need for a mind shift in how managers look at and value natural resources. For example, Hardin Tibbs argues that a paradigm shift in thinking on resource usage is required:

> At the moment, the industrial system is less a system than a collection of linear flows. Industry draws materials from the earth's crust and the biosphere, processes them with fossil energy to derive transient economic value and dumps the residue back into nature. For every 1 kilogram of finished goods we buy, about 20 kilograms of waste have been created during production, and within six months 0.5 kilograms of our average purchase is already waste.[21]

In other words, if close to 95 per cent of the material used in the production process doesn't make it into the final product, then there must be dramatic opportunities for more efficient use of the waste and for major productivity increases. There is a need to replace the current 'extract and dump' mind-set with one that seeks to create virtuous cycles of resource usage and utilization.[22] For instance, this can be achieved through developing an industrial ecology where we begin with the principle of maximizing overall benefit to the total system. Efficiency based on value adding places the full cost of disposing of anything

106 • The dominant current reality

dangerous or not used (waste) on the producer. This leads the producer to initiate a search for 'beginning of pipe' design solutions to eliminate pollution and waste, to maximize use of all resources and to recycle material output. This in turn can lead to the creation of new industries which use waste as valuable inputs to further production. Such industries represent new strategic opportunities.

While technologies are important in generating new efficiencies, as in the case of Carlton United Breweries, fundamental shifts in mind-sets are also required to maximize the value of new technologies so that they contribute towards value-adding and innovation-based approaches to efficiency. As the Scandic case highlights, human capabilities are crucial in creating and capitalizing on these higher-level efficiencies. In a rapidly changing world, marked by unforeseen discontinuities, such dynamic capabilities that allow for flexible response and the ability to change and to reshape the organization to meet new challenges are vital for competitiveness.[23] Therefore, it is false to imagine that anything which reduces this capacity to create higher-level efficiencies is itself an efficiency. It is easy to cut costs in the short term by putting off skilled and experienced staff and cutting back on investing in capabilities and competencies. But these human capacities are crucial to generating long-term competitiveness. Roland Nilsson, the former CEO of Scandic, has the last word here when discussing Scandic's decision to invest in people and the environment:

> So we can accept a higher investment today, because it will lower the cost in the future. It hasn't cost us anything. No one can claim that this has cost us more money.[24]

Potential benefits of efficiency

There are potential benefits to the organization, society and the ecosystem from adoption of efficiency initiatives that build on compliance activities. First, efficiency approaches to ecological sustainability are the front line of action on sustainability for the majority of organizations today. Efficiency initiatives of this kind usually take place within the functional 'silos' of these organizations. These ecological initiatives can be relatively isolated and limited interventions such as the implementation of 'end of pipe' filtering systems and the use of programmes such as total quality environmental management or design for the environment. Alternatively, they can be much more comprehensive interventions such as the development of fully integrated industrial ecosystems or the launch of corporate-wide programmes such as The Natural Step. Central to the successful adoption and utilization of such programmes is the development of a high degree of engineering, operational and technical competence and the use of compliance-based monitoring systems to drive ongoing business performance. The benefits for the organization of the development of such programmes are:

- the building of technical capabilities
- the development of integrated human-resource management systems
- cost savings through waste reduction
- the development of corporate specific knowledge on product design, process and service layouts that can result in future competitive advantages.

There can also be societal benefits from the application of efficiency approaches to sustainability. These include the more efficient use of scarce natural resources and the development of industrial ecosystems that protect and promote healthy communities by recycling and reusing industrial waste. Similarly, there may be some forms of community involvement – such as the funding of public programmes or the establishment of community consultative committees.

Finally, efficiency approaches can have positive benefits for the natural environment. For example, according to a recent World Bank document, environmental degradation and depletion costs in China are currently estimated at 10 per cent GDP overall and four of China's cities are listed in the top ten cities in the world that are most vulnerable to rising sea levels. The World Bank argues that these costs can be alleviated if China implements a range of policies to drive resources efficiency. These include the 12th Five Year Plan commitment to implementing a carbon capping and trading scheme or other policy initiatives such as the pricing of environmental resources such as oil, gas, water, so as to reflect environmental costs as well as scarcity value.

> As a result of these policies, returns to investments in green products and services will increase, and 'brown' industries will be discouraged. More important, the expansion of green industries will contribute to economies of scale in production and to R&D. Competitiveness honed in the domestic market could accelerate the competitiveness of Chinese green firms in a rapidly growing international market. Net job creation is likely to be positive. In the long run, green development will derive from new product and process opportunities afforded by innovation aimed at addressing environmental concerns, more efficient

use of resources through the removal of price distortions that lead to environmentally harmful practices, more rigorous appraisal of the costs and benefits of alternative government policies and public investments, and lower economic costs associated with growing green now rather than growing now and greening later.[25]

China also provides us with an example of an industry sector where economic and environmental efficiencies work together. Its solar photovoltaic industry is the lowest-cost producer of solar panels in the world, thanks in no small part to the country's large domestic market. The industry's annual production value now exceeds $45 billion, imports and exports have topped $22 billion, and the industry employs around 300,000 people.[26]

It is important to consider the argument of Lovins *et al*.: 'It turns out that changing industrial processes so that they actually replenish and magnify the stock of natural capital can prove especially profitable because nature does the production; people just need step back and let life flourish.'[27] The full range of potential benefits of efficiency can be realized only when efficiency is maximized simultaneously for the organization, society and the environment. As we indicated earlier in this chapter, however, it is important to remember the extent to which sustainability priorities and benefits can vary by sector. As shown in Table 4.1, a recent McKinsey global survey of more than 3,000 respondents highlighted significant sectoral differences in perceptions of sustainability value creators.[28]

Efficiency choices: high or low paths to competitive advantage?

Efficiency is the dominant concern of many organizations today; so the key issues here are understanding what efficiency is and making it happen. Some of our own research on Australian organizations has indicated that the business case for energy efficiency, for instance, is poorly understood by accountants and business managers and largely remains dealt with within narrow technical silos.[29] This relates to a failure to understand that the drive towards enhanced corporate performance through efficiency gains diverges in two directions: the first path is based primarily on the search for internal efficiencies and cost reductions and is related to competition on cost alone. The second path leads to the development of specific capabilities and strategies that can add value – a major feature of high-performance organizations. Organizations can often choose the direction they take. If they follow the first path, they run the

Table 4.1 *Value creation and industries – value varies by industry*

Value-creation levers		% of respondents (N=3,203)	Industry, top three most-cited activities[a] with potential to create significant value over the next 5 years
Growth	Committing R&D resources to sustainable products	17	Energy (2), high tech/telecom (3), manufacturing (1)
	Leveraging sustainability of existing products to reach new customers or markets	15	Health care/pharma (3)
	Managing portfolio to capture trends in sustainability	20	Energy (1), extractive services[b] (3), finance (2), high tech/telecom (1), manufacturing (2), retail (3), transportation (2)
Return on capital	Achieving higher prices or market share because of sustainable products	13	
	Improving employee retention and/or motivation related to sustainability activities	11	Finance (3), retail (3), transportation (1)
	Managing impact of products throughout the value chain	13	Retail (2), transportation (3)
	Reducing emissions from operations	10	
	Reducing energy use in operations	15	Extractive services (3), retail (3), transportation (1)
	Reducing waste from operations	13	Retail (2), transportation (3)
	Reducing water use in operations	9	
Risk management	Managing corporate reputation for sustainability	20	Energy (3), extractive services (1), finance (1), health care/pharma (1), high tech/telecom (1), manufacturing (2), retail (3), transportation(2)
	Mitigating operational risk related to climate change	8	
	Responding to regulatory constraints or opportunities	13	Energy (3), extractive services (2), health care/pharma (3)

Notes: [a] Numbers (1), (2) and (3) indicate the first, second and third most frequently chosen activities within each industry.
[b] This group includes respondents from the coal, metal, oil and gas extraction, petroleum and natural gas distribution, petroleum refining and other mining sub-industries.

Source: Modified from Bonini and Görner, 'The Business of Sustainability, McKinsey Global Survey Results', 2011, http://www.mckinsey.com/insights/energy_resources_materials/the_business_of_sustainability_mckinsey_global_survey_results (accessed 19 June 2013).

risk of creating only temporary competitive advantages that are ultimately easy to imitate so that the immediate advantage can be leap-frogged by more strategically focused organizations. If they follow the innovation and flexibility path, new opportunities for business growth and sustainability emerge.

In support of our argument, Bos-Brouwers presents the results of a study on sustainable innovation activities in the rubber and plastics industry.[30] This work shows that many incremental sustainable innovations are directed at the improvement of technological processes (eco-efficiency) and to lowering costs of production, but that companies with sustainability integrated into their orientation and innovation processes show value creation associated with the development of products new to the market and new forms of cooperation with stakeholders. The findings of this study are particularly relevant to SMEs in their struggle to build value through innovation.[31]

As Jenkinson and Putt del Pino have argued, investing in innovative and more resource-efficient products can pay off for first movers.[32] Along with GE, Kimberly Clark, Marks & Spencer, Nike and IKEA, these writers give the following examples of companies who are benefitting from such investments:

- Procter & Gamble, the consumer goods giant, which generated $40 billion from sales of a slew of self-defined 'sustainable innovation products', such as cold-water laundry detergents, between July 2007 and June 2011.
- Philips, the Dutch healthcare, lifestyle and lighting company, which already generates 30 per cent of total revenues from green products, and is doubling R&D investment in such product innovation to €2 billion by 2015.
- Kingfisher, the European home-improvement group, whose revenue from independently verified eco-products reached £1.1 billion in 2010–11, representing 10.5 per cent of its total retail sales.[33]

That executives are increasingly recognizing these possibilities is reflected in the McKinsey Global survey, which found that 'seventy-six per cent of executives say engaging in sustainability contributes positively to shareholder value in the long term while only 50 per cent saw value creation as being short-term'.[34] Such findings reflect the fact that the high road to efficiency can provide both organizations and societies with greater choices and significant added value.[35]

Sony and the high road to ecological efficiency

Sony provides us with an example of an organization that is attempting to pursue the high road to ecological sustainability. Sony is a leading Japanese multinational company involved in the development, design and provision of consumer and industrial electronic equipment and devices.[36] Sony's first attempts at ecological efficiency in the 1970s focused on the reduction of hazardous waste in the production process and the introduction of health and safety initiatives for its workforce. These initial efficiency approaches were 'production' orientated and focused on process improvements – much in the same vein as quality management. However, these production-orientated approaches became the springboard from which the company launched and extended its efficiency approaches to ecological sustainability. For instance, the company has gone about implementing environmental management systems, furthering its work on process efficiencies, product redesign for the environment and product recycling.[37]

Sony's benchmarking strategies such as its product-assessment check-sheet have been noted as a simple yet effective tool allowing for environmental performance measurement and long-term planning.[38] Sony Corporation is now moving beyond the production and cost-efficiency basis of earlier initiatives to integrate environmental issues into its corporate strategy, involving its employees in Eco Challenge initiatives and energy-awareness programmes for its leaders.[39]

Creating eco-efficiencies

In the previous chapter, the case for compliance was examined. Compliance-based companies focus primarily on the implementation of monitoring and performance-based systems and the early experimentation with programmes that bring the organization into alignment with external stakeholder demands. The major aim is to reduce the organization's exposure to liability and the risk of penalty, fines and loss of reputation. As we pointed out, the failure to do so by many organizations can be costly in terms of the loss of reputational and social capital and the organization's overall ability to develop internal competencies. However, we now discuss positive examples of organizations creating eco-efficiencies. We build on the distinction made earlier between low and high approaches to efficiency, concentrating on examples of corporations following the high road.

What is eco-efficiency? The World Business Council for Sustainable Development and the United Nations Environment Program (UNEP) define eco-efficiency in this way:

> Eco-efficiency is reached by the delivery of competitively priced
> goods and services that satisfy human needs and bring quality of life
> while progressively reducing ecological impacts and resource
> intensity, through the life-cycle, to a level at least equal with the
> Earth's estimated carrying capacity.[40]

The World Business Council for Sustainable Development and the United
Nations Environment Program have also outlined what they regard as the
major principles of eco-efficiency. These include:

- reducing material intensity of goods and services
- reducing energy intensity of goods and services
- reducing toxic dispersion
- enhancing material recyclability
- maximizing sustainable use of renewable resources
- extending product durability
- increasing the service intensity of goods and services.[41]

Pursuing these changes amounts to the more efficient use of
environmental resources. The efficiencies, however, provide benefits both
to the firm and to the environment. Lovins *et al.* refer to this as Natural
Capitalism. In attempting to implement these changes, they recommend
that managers seek to address four key areas:

1 Increase the productivity of natural resources through changes to the
  production design, layout and technologies of operations.
2 Use biologically inspired production models, that is, closed-loop
  production systems.
3 Develop new business models based on value and service.
4 Reinvest in natural capital.[42]

Organizations, particularly those based in the manufacturing sector, are
increasingly using these principles to design their eco-efficiency
programmes. This efficiency approach to ecological sustainability is
driven primarily by technocultures associated with engineers and
scientists. Eco-efficiency builds incrementally on the compliance
approaches and revolves around the establishment of and commitment to
environmental programmes and the introduction of technologies to
capture these benefits or the design of better facilities.

One effect of changing forms of governance and new perspectives on
compliance has been that multinationals such as GE and Nike, once
vilified by environmental and anti-globalization activists for their lack of
responsibility to the environment, employees and other stakeholders, are
leading the way in improving their capability to innovate in relation to

sustainability efficiencies that lead to wider benefits to society and the environment. In the past, for example, GE has been in trouble with regulators over the dumping of chemicals in the Hudson River in New York State. GE, at that time either in the non-responsive or rejection phases, is now committing to an 'eco-imagination plan'. Under the plan, launched in 2005, GE committed to doubling its research and development into clean technology for its customers, doubling its sales of new technologies and products that conserve water and reducing its own greenhouse gas emissions by 1 per cent over the next seven years. In 2012, the initiative, operating as both an internal corporate sustainability drive and a development programme for products and services that can be used by GE's supply chain and other third parties, was marked as reaching more than $105 billion in sales and services since its launch.[43]

Likewise, Nike's 2005 report published a complete list identifying all its suppliers, reversing its previous position of rejection concerning public disclosure of its supply chain. Since then, Nike has publicly acknowledged that its massive returns (it grossed more than $20.9 billion in 2011–12) will be threatened by rising energy costs, increasingly scarce natural resources and human rights demands, unless it makes all its operations more transparent. In 2011 Nike announced it would eliminate all releases of hazardous chemicals across its global supply chain by 2020. This is a major challenge for a firm with an estimated supply chain comprising 900 contract factories, employing over one million workers, who make more than 500,000 different products. Recent announcements are that Nike is providing its suppliers with online tools to help it reach these targets.[44]

Rockcote is another example of this.

Rockcote Sustainable Design Centre[45]

Eco-efficiency highlights:

- The creation of a sustainable design centre – that generates its own energy needs, recycles and has closed its water loop.
- Waste-free factory and the formation of partnerships with other eco-friendly organizations that exist in the same geographic area.
- Valuing employee input and ownership of the programme to generate home-grown sustainability and eco-efficiency initiatives.
- The creation of a new range of eco-paints and a focus by the research and development section on eco-products.

Eco-efficiency is characterized by a variety of programmes such as: total quality environmental management; industrial ecology; end-of-pipe solutions; design versus labelling; and environmental management systems. While these systems are primarily technological, they also involve developing the human capabilities that enable the effective use of these systems. These capabilities include identifying, collecting and understanding information, and taking action to implement these programmes.

Furthermore, it appears that several key issues drive corporations towards the pursuit of eco-efficiency. These include the degree of alignment between market opportunities and eco-efficiencies, the internal structure and culture of the company and pressure from external stakeholders demanding action. We have discussed the full range of these pressures for change in Chapter 2.

We also look to the example of the Canon Group. Facing increasing regulation over the use of toxins in its manufacturing operations and increasing consumer awareness, Canon instigated technical and cultural changes designed to deliver eco-efficiencies. Emura states that Canon's corporate philosophy is 'Kyoseri' – harmonious co-existence.[46] This has been interpreted as co-existence both within human communities and with the natural environment. As Emura points out:

> the pursuit of Q (quality), C (cost) and D (delivery) are allowable only under conditions that fulfil environmental protection and . . . businesses that cannot protect the environment have no right to manufacture products. Under the EQCD policy, the E (environment) must be given higher priority than management efficiency.[47]

What are the strategies that Canon has employed to create a high-value road to eco-efficiency? The first initiative was to improve resource productivity, through efforts to reduce energy consumption, reduce waste and thereby save on resources and the removal of hazardous substances from production. In the second initiative, the environmental focus shifted from these product and process improvements to the issue of eco-design. Eco-design has involved the examination of the environmental impact of Canon's products and the introduction of environmental considerations in the initial stages of the product-design process (see Table 4.2).

The third initiative in the Canon approach to eco-efficiency has been to reorganize the supply chain through the use of 'green' procurement policies and accreditation systems. Emura states: 'Canon requested 1200 suppliers in Japan . . . 200 suppliers in South East Asia and China and

Table 4.2 *Characteristics of product eco-efficiency at Canon*[48]

Resource conservation	Ease of recycling	Ease of disposal
Energy consumption	Energy conservation	Environmental preservation
Resources	Ease of assembly	Ease of disposal
Layout	Ease of sorting	
	Ease of reusing	

100 suppliers in North America to supply environment-conscious products.'[49] In the 1960s and 1970s Japanese automotive producers introduced quality improvement and just-in-time programmes to create lean production systems. Similarly today, Canon is using its influence over the supply chain to set standards for 'green' products and provide suppliers with the capabilities to develop 'green' components.

The final initiative in the eco-efficiency strategy at Canon is inverse manufacturing – or product recycling (remanufacturing). Along with other companies such as Volvo and Fuji-Xerox, Canon realizes that eco-efficiency is a transition phase to strategic sustainability. The pursuit of eco-efficiency enables the firm to develop and build broad environmental management capabilities signified by environmental management system (EMS) accreditation and environmental management information systems and environmental accounting systems that leverage this transition.[50] Canon sees that its environmental mission is to move the focus from internal company changes to broader societal changes requiring community cooperation, particularly through 'green' procurement, product recycling and environmental disclosure. Reflecting this broader understanding of sustainability, in 2003 the company shifted its ten-year-long policy of producing global environmental reports and began to integrate economic and social disclosures into a global sustainability report.[51]

While much of the efficiency drive in corporates to date has been focused on energy, water is also a key resource of increasing concern to companies. At Ford, for example, a Global Water Management Initiative began in 2000, setting an initial target of 3 per cent year-over-year reductions. Between 2000 and 2012, Ford reduced its total global water use by 62 per cent, or 10.6 billion gallons (see Figure 4.2), by cutting water use across manufacturing operations. Ford claims that this reduction is equivalent to the water used annually by nearly 99,000 US residences.[52]

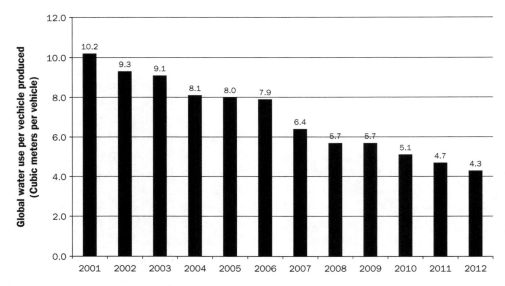

Figure 4.2 *Global water use per vehicle at Ford*
Source: Ford, 'Ford Progress in Reducing Water Use', 2013, <http://corporate.ford.com/microsites/sustainability-report-2012-13/water-reducing> (accessed 20 June 2013).

Key issues in creating eco-efficiency

What lessons can we draw from these examples of collective organizational attempts to become eco-efficient? The characteristics of a winning formula for the creation of eco-efficient organizations are:

- establishment of measurement systems to monitor performance in key areas of energy, waste and quality, for example, systems such as Life Cycle Assessment, Eco Productivity Index, or Design for Environment;
- development of environmental programmes, similar to the quality management initiatives of the 1980s, that provide guidelines, tools and basic knowledge which can be diffused to line managers and employees alike or, alternatively, rather than using such tools, development of an internally generated approach closely tailored to the needs of the particular organization;
- building strong support of these initiatives by middle management (if the initiatives are isolated to functional or business units) and by senior management (if these programmes are corporate-wide). For instance, Interface's mission is to become the first company to be fully sustainable – with zero negative impact. This is its Mission Zero which it aims to achieve by 2020. Interface has set stretch targets and goals to

reduce greenhouse gases and become footprint neutral. Specifically, it has established a range of eco and social metrics. Figure 4.3 shows a leading example of the firm's ability to monitor and progress against set targets in the areas of Footprint Reduction, Product Innovation and Culture Change.[53] Interface's extraordinary sustainability programme will be discussed further in Chapter 6;[54]

- systematically identifying significant inefficiencies, unnecessary steps in the production or service process, poor layout, physical waste, old technologies and wasteful procedures. For example, buildings are now being redesigned using various types of smart or dynamic glass that come with a coating that can be tinted electronically according to lighting levels, controlling solar glare and heat gain, in turn cutting energy costs;[55]
- accessing the tools available to address these issues: total quality environmental management (TQEM); environmental management systems; new technologies; industrial ecology opportunities and eco-design. Off-the-shelf solutions are generally less useful than combinations of these approaches;
- using the tools identified above to introduce extensive value-adding activities such as eco-design, recycling of products and conversion of products into services;

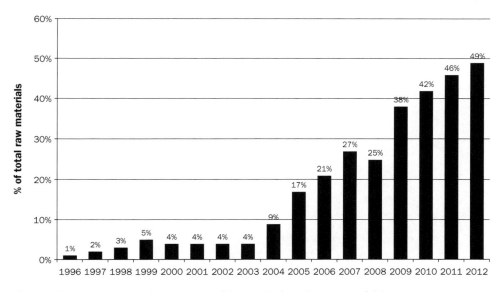

Figure 4.3 *Recycled and biobased material use (% of total raw materials)*
Source: Interface, 'Interface Our Progress', 2013, <http://www.interfaceglobal.com/Sustainability/Our-Progress.aspx> (accessed 20 June 2013).

- piloting initiatives in a variety of business units and then progressively integrating them across the organization;
- measuring and monitoring the costs of the improved systems using both 'hard' measures (financial improvements, waste reduction, production quality) and 'soft' measures (capability development, knowledge transfer, change-agent development, consumer awareness and value changes in employees). For example, Ford is the first automotive company to have joined the Carbon Disclosure Project Water Disclosure and has now begun to track process water discharge at its manufacturing plants globally;[56]
- including external stakeholders in the sustainability/eco-efficiency process through adopting, for example, procurement and supply-chain management practices that involve suppliers also adopting eco-efficiency approaches. For example, BHP Billiton's 2013 Business in the Community award-winning programme has invested $50 million in transforming opportunities for suppliers in Chile which has achieved $121 million cost savings, while supporting projects that reduce environmental impact;[57]
- linking human capabilities and knowledge to generate new value-adding and innovation opportunities. For instance, Electrolux, Clorox and Procter & Gamble have all continued to invest in environmental product lines, despite the GFC. As Nidumolu, Prahalad and Rangaswami point out, they are looking beyond 'the public-relations benefits to hone competencies that will enable them to dominate markets tomorrow'.[58]

We have emphasized here both the technical elements of generating a winning formula for eco-efficiencies and the vital links that must be made to human sustainability to maximize gains for both the organization and society. As Tibbs states:

> Change in either values or in technology alone is not enough: the two must happen in conjunction. One of the reasons for this is that technology – and new technology in particular because it is more powerful – can either help provide solutions or make the situation worse. What makes the crucial difference is human intention.[59]

A recent IBM report identified that energy efficiency and waste reduction are seen by organizations as providing best return on investment. Technology is clearly important to implementing such initiatives but it needs to be complemented with the capability building in project management and project evaluation that underpin and support key tactics for reducing energy use and improving environmental performance such as the introduction of operational improvements, investment in building retrofit projects and implementation of space-management programmes.[60]

Creating human efficiencies

We have all heard the mantra: 'People are an organization's most valued asset.' In many cases they are only its most valued asset until the organization experiences a crisis, and then they are seen as disposable.

Even when the organization does not downsize, the stated value placed on people is often demonstrated by low pay and failure to invest in employee-competency development or to use fully employees' knowledge and skills. Many corporations have been trading on rhetoric for decades and in the process they have been losing their intellectual capital and consequently the basis for competition in the knowledge economy:

> If employers do not bridge the current gap between their rhetoric and workplace reality, then the likely outcome will be an exodus of bright and enthusiastic people to organizations that do. For true corporate sustainability, an organization must recognize value and promote the capability of its people. For human resource sustainability to be achieved, therefore, the HR policies and practices need to be integrated for sustained business performance and positive employee outcomes of equity, development and well being.[61]

Placer Dome and Scandic Hotels

The case of Placer Dome, a gold mining company, highlights the potential conflict between narrow and broader views of human sustainability. In the 1990s Placer Dome's human resource policies and strategies had a strong focus on employee development, training and safety, and on valuing employee contributions to the company's sustainability efforts. A range of human sustainability initiatives were aimed at developing the capabilities of both employees and local communities affected by mining operations. However, a dramatic decline in the gold price caused a setback in the pursuit of sustainability. Its decision to downsize led to a substantial reduction in one area of its core capabilities: for instance, at the Marcopper mine site a retrenched employee was rehired to undertake negotiations with key stakeholders when executives realized that he was the only one in the company who had developed a strong and trusting relationship with the community stakeholders. This example is an instance of a managerial decision,

---

continued

made in the name of efficiency, which can threaten the corporate capabilities required for future competitive advantages.

The Placer Dome approach is similar to the approach initially adopted by Scandic Hotels during its period of crisis. However, after the implementation of turnaround management strategies which lasted two years, Scandic's CEO realized that the best way to deal with future problems was to develop the human capital and competencies of its people that would enable the corporation to adapt. Therefore investments were made in training people to deliver on the hotel chain's stated value of 'profound caring'. In the process, Scandic rebuilt its reputational capital and shared the efficiency gains with a range of stakeholders.[62]

Corporations can achieve human efficiency by downsizing and retrenchments. While these policies provide short-term financial benefits and efficiency gains for companies, they provide few, if any, efficiency benefits for the societies in which they operate. Efficiency approaches dominated by such practices as cost cutting through downsizing and poor work environments, such as exist in many call centres, may create short-term efficiencies for corporations. However, they may also create long-term inefficiencies for the company and significant inefficiencies for society as a whole.

For instance, in the USA, Marriott Hotels was finding it difficult to attract new recruits and to retain good managers. The company had a strong culture of 'face time', that is, managers stayed at their hotel and pretended to work even if they had completed their work! In the Marriott culture, having managers put in long hours at the hotel was regarded as a benefit for the corporation. But there were heavy hidden costs in increased turnover and difficulty in recruiting new managers. When these costs were identified, the senior executive team instigated a programme of 'flexible work' which encouraged managers to adopt a different approach. If they had a busy week and put in more hours at work, they were encouraged to work fewer hours in down times. The pilot programme proved successful and Marriott reaped the rewards of these new efficiencies, reflected in a reduction of management turnover.[63]

What, then, is human efficiency? The high road to human efficiency involves organizations making maximum use of their human capabilities; that is, efficiency for the organization is primarily about ensuring that the organization has the requisite number of people, the mix of skills to perform its goals effectively and a strong base for future development. In the drive towards efficiency through added value, the human resource function increasingly develops an integrated approach to the management of a corporation's human capital. This is evidenced through:

- the development of human resource information systems
- the identification of core competencies
- focused training and organization development initiatives to enhance managerial and supervisory skills or to create core competencies
- introduction of displacement technologies
- outsourcing of those areas identified as not cost efficient.

The development of well-organized corporate human resource capabilities makes a significant contribution to human efficiency. Furthermore, current research has identified a strong link between a company's investment in its workforce and outcomes such as productivity.[64] These are characteristics of the value-adding and innovation approaches to efficiency.

Human sustainability can also be thought of as allowing employees to thrive. Thriving at work is defined in the literature as the joint experience of learning and vitality, in that 'thriving individuals are growing, developing, and energized rather than stagnating or feeling depleted'.[65] The interesting work of Spreitzer *et al.* on six case organizations shows that:

> organizations can increase the potential for employees to thrive when they: (1) enable decision-making discretion, (2) provide information about the organization and its strategy, (3) minimize incivility, (4) provide performance feedback, and (5) create a climate that promotes diversity. In one study, by focusing on just four of these factors, thriving across the six organizations increased 42 per cent.[66]

Cisco, Microsoft and Southwest Airlines are all quoted as organizations that have encouraged thriving in their employees through using one or another of these tactics. These authors also point out that learning and vitality can also be increased by engaging employees in activities outside work, such as by joining a community organization board.

We also note that our framework allows interesting dilemmas to be highlighted in the creation of sustainable corporations. Gaming organizations, for example, may be pursuing an efficiency approach to sustainability. However, many would argue that their products (gaming equipment) can damage the social fabric of communities and most ethical investment groups avoid investment in gaming activities. Gaming corporations respond that they have initiated programmes on responsible gambling and have created community benefit funds. This debate illustrates the usefulness of our framework, which can point to the real contribution of a firm like a gaming organization in one area of human sustainability (employee and community relations) and raise issues about its impact in another – social responsibility. We do point out, however, that research shows that participation in perceived 'sin' industries such as tobacco and nuclear power increases firms' cost of equity, indicating the link between social responsibility and economic sustainability.[67]

The external stakeholder relations of the organization can also contribute significantly to efficiency because they are often strongly affected by the reputation of a company. There is an increasing realization of the value of reputational capital. Reputational capital takes years to build, cannot be bought but can be quickly and easily damaged. As Petrick *et al.* note, organizations that systematically build this aspect of intangible assets do so by demonstrating: trustworthiness to employees; credibility with investors (through profitability); reliability to customers and suppliers; and responsibility with communities for stewardship of community and natural resources.[68] The paybacks can be significant, with companies such as Microsoft having generated massive amounts of reputational capital. In other words these corporations have added value via their enhanced reputations and public profiles.

So how does reputational capital contribute to efficiency? As organizations gain cost efficiencies by picking the low-hanging fruit, that is, by using their resources more effectively, increased emphasis is placed on leveraging those fewer resources that the organization has so as to increase value. As McIntosh *et al.* state: 'As businesses have become leaner, tighter organizations with fewer staff, key relationships and brand image are the company's greatest assets and their management becomes more important.'[69] That is, organizations need to leverage the resources that they have, such as reputation, more effectively to gain further value-added outcomes.

Steps to the creation of reputational capital

Petrick *et al*. suggest four practical steps that managers can take to build reputational capital in the area of sustainability:

1 Provide leadership education to managers and all levels of the organization in the areas of stewardship, behavioral skills so that sustainability competencies become commonplace.
2 Create senior executive roles for co-ordination of stakeholder relations that impact on reputational capital.
3 Conduct an annual audit of global reputation.
4 Use competitions for various product, organizational, social and leadership rewards to develop and maintain reputational capital.[70]

For organizations that seek to compete on efficiency there is a clear choice. The challenge is to look beyond a simple-minded cost-cutting approach – the low-cost path. The value-adding route to efficiency offers greater returns to the organization, the society and the natural world. In this approach, the organization continues to reinvest in technologies, in research and development and in developing knowledge-based competition. This in turn involves a shift away from an unskilled or semi-skilled workforce to a workforce with high skill levels and an extensive knowledge base. Organizations taking the added-value path have an efficiency focus in the present, but it is tempered by a future vision of adding value and innovating.

Ray Anderson, founder and chairman of Interface Inc., took an approach to eco-efficiency and industrial ecology that was based on employee involvement and engagement. As Borial states, 'the participative program 'QUEST' (Quality Utilising Employee Suggestions and Teamwork) . . . [was] designed to foster involvement in and environmental awareness covering all the company's activities'.[71]

As a result, companies that have a future vision of value adding do not cut costs in a way that would jeopardize the progressive development of a highly skilled, well-paid workforce and the customizing of products and services. This choice involves a fundamentally different way of leading and managing organizations: it demands new structural forms and flexible work systems for the organization, a transformed approach to work design and new cultural values that reflect the shift to a knowledge-based economy. Managers who locate their organizations within the paradigm of value-adding/innovation efficiency are in a prime position to move to the next phase of developing a strategic approach to sustainability. Take the case example of BHP Billiton's supply-chain development programme in Chile.

BHP transforming opportunities for suppliers in Chile[72]

Business benefits:

- The programme delivered $121 million of direct savings in the cost of inputs, goods and services up to December 2012.
- The company has enhanced supplier relations from service provision to collaboration.
- BHP has improved its reputation through improved public perception and government relations.

Supplier and societal benefits:

- Forty-three innovation projects have been developed with 36 suppliers, focusing on water, energy, health, safety, environment and community (HSEC), human capital and operational efficiency.
- One third of the projects are creating environmental benefits, including energy generation from waste.
- Suppliers benefit from increased efficiency, access to finance and new revenue-generation opportunities.

Potential pitfalls in pursuing human efficiencies

Several key issues for organizations emerge in the pursuit of human efficiencies. First, HR managers often find it difficult to convince senior management and line managers that their efficiency programmes work, because of the intangible nature of the benefits of many HR programmes and also because of the longer time-frame involved before the efficiency gains become apparent. The contrast is between short-term cost efficiencies but medium- to long-term negative impacts (as in the case of downsizing or re-engineering) versus short-term increased costs (such as in training and development) and medium- to long-term benefits. However, as shown in Table 4.3, evidence has been accumulating over the last 30 years showing that advanced human resource policies, procedures and practices do contribute to the performance and financial competitiveness of organizations. More recently, these case-based examples of advanced human resource performance are supported by surveys of large numbers of organizations.[73]

Second, efficiency alone will not deliver sufficient long-term competitive advantage in turbulent and competitive markets. Skinner has referred to 'the productivity paradox'. He found that organizations that were obsessed with increasing the productivity of labour capital and

Table 4.3 *Human sustainability orientation*

Compliance	Cost efficiency	Value added/ innovation efficiency
Characteristics:	*Characteristics:*	*Characteristics:*
• Industrial relations emphasis on awards, legal agreements, formal negotiations	• Early capability development often subjected to cost cutting in times of crisis • Downsizing for realignment • Core values focus on short- to-medium-term profitability and returns on investment	• Capability enhancement • Integration of sustainability programmes at all levels of the organization • Value added and flexibility enhancement are linked to long-term financial goals
Aims:	*Aims:*	*Aims:*
• Survival, 'licence to operate'	• Utilize resources to maximize financial returns from resources	• Increasing emphasis on employee rewards • Capability building • Adding value, cost minimization (without damaging capabilities and flexibility)

technology became locked in a vicious cycle of their own making and that this inhibited their ability to develop new ways of competing and enhancing their performance.[74] The relentless search for short-term productivity gains or efficiencies resulted in long-term decline. One danger of adopting a single-minded cost-efficiency focus is that, in tough times, it can lead managers to cut programmes designed to up-skill the workforce and create positive corporate cultures, thereby reducing the organization's ability to pursue a value-adding path.

Hamel and Prahalad make a similar point in their discussion of the way management fervently embraced re-engineering. They argue that re-engineering focuses too much attention on immediate efficiencies and neglects the vision for future innovative strategies; so there are real limits to an organization's ability to develop a fully sustainable human and ecological approach based on cost-efficiency alone. In an extension to these ideas, some commentators argue that the pursuit of efficient and lean organizational designs increases the potential vulnerability of organizations to disruptive change events by reducing slack resources and hence the ability of the organization to adapt to changes in its external environment.[75] Managers need to ensure that cost cutting today lays the

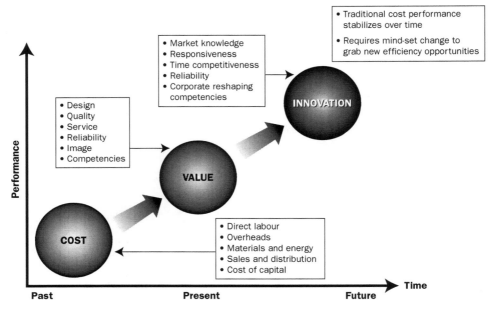

Figure 4.4 *The changing nature of performance*

organizational basis for moving towards the next phase of sustainability, the adoption of the strategic paradigm, rather than undermining it.[76]

How to add value through efficiency

So how can an organization pursue efficiency goals in a way that lays the basis for adding value? Figure 4.4 identifies sources of such value. Here are some guidelines:

- Where possible, managers need to establish the costs of compliance and present an emerging business case to the organization's senior managers based on piloting efficiency measures, which are then used to offset the costs of compliance-based activities.
- Shift the efficiency orientation of the organization away from cost and towards value and innovation. This can be achieved by demonstrating the value of building human capital and by changing management reward systems to ensure that they do not encourage short-term cost-cutting measures that destroy human capabilities for enhanced performance in the medium and long term (see Figure 4.1 on building cost-reducing, value-adding and innovation cultures).

- Develop and implement systems which reflect increases in human capital, reputational capital and intangible assets at the corporate level. At the operational level, demonstrate the value-added contribution of HR programmes to operations.
- At the corporate level, develop integrated human resource information systems (HRIS) that enable the HR professional to identify the organization's existing core competencies so that they can provide informed advice to senior managers about human-capital competency areas of the organization.
- Initiate and implement trials of high-performance work environments and practices such as multi-skilled teams, value-adding programmes, culture-change programmes.
- Protect innovative units of the organization from cost-cutting initiatives until they have had a reasonable time to demonstrate the value of their innovations to the corporation.
- Diffuse demonstrably successful high-performance practices and experiment with new organizational structures such as virtual teams, networks and communities of practice.
- Give line managers responsibility for the human sustainability agenda, establish support networks which include line and staff innovators and use corporate HR as a centralized resource facility to encourage and inform value-adding initiatives.
- Integrate and or establish links between corporate human resources and sustainability departments to generate complementary programmes – i.e. linking HR reward systems and training with sustainability initiatives.
- Recognize that not all areas of the organization will be value adding and develop appropriate policies to maintain cost efficiencies in these areas.
- Seek opportunities to build reputational capital and develop monitoring systems that measure the movement away from physical and financial assets to intangible assets.
- Ensure that the head of the HR function is included in senior management and board decisions regarding corporate strategy.
- Challenge the organization to calculate the costs of eco-services (land, energy, water) to generate broader awareness of emerging business opportunities by valuing innovation.

The challenge: integrating human and ecological efficiency

Integrating the human and ecological approaches to efficiency is a key challenge at this stage of the journey to sustainability. Initially energies are often directed to one approach or the other, or initiatives are undertaken independently. It is only as these initiatives have been implemented that opportunities emerge to develop an integrated approach to efficiency. However, as organizations move further down the efficiency path, particularly in the development of eco-efficiencies, human capabilities become more important to the success of these programmes.[77]

Daily and Huang found that human sustainability factors, such as senior management support, environmental training, empowerment, teamwork and reward systems, were key elements in the implementation of environmental management systems.[78] This evidence has more recently been backed up by research that has found that operational-level employees in the Canadian chemical industry contributed significantly in reducing pollution and in undertaking environmental initiatives.[79] The evidence suggests that the pursuit of value-orientated eco-efficiencies is reliant upon the parallel development of human capabilities. However, the development of human capabilities is not reliant upon eco-efficiencies.

Who leads in the pursuit of eco and human efficiencies? The cases presented in this chapter show that senior managers play an important role in championing efficiency programmes. The case evidence also suggests that responsibility for making efficiency measures work belongs with line managers. They must take on the major responsibility for building future capabilities and for identifying future value-added opportunities. Efficiency approaches, by their very nature, are operational in focus and content. Efficiency programmes, whether human or eco-based, focus on such measures as the application of new technologies, the development of integrated and systematic information systems, cost and waste reduction and the effective utilization of a company's human, physical and resource assets. Line managers play an important stewardship function in addressing these issues: they must make the overall approach work.

Moving beyond efficiency approaches

In this chapter we have outlined a case for a radical rethinking of efficiency approaches to sustainability. We have argued that cost-reduction approaches are only one path which corporations can use to achieve efficiency gains. For corporations to develop long-term competitive advantages and position themselves to make the leap to strategic sustainability there is a need to invest in capabilities and competencies that capitalize on value-adding and innovation paths to efficiency.

The cases we have used demonstrate that once people become committed to developing human and ecological sustainability, the momentum builds. In the cases presented here, all organizations started with simple cost-reduction measures but went on to adopt a value-added/innovation approach to efficiency performance. In the process they found that this value-added approach unleashed a momentum of its own that led to the development of distinctive competencies. These competencies can be turned into competitive advantages. Technology initiatives are easily imitated; however, configurations of organizational capabilities – such as those found at Scandic or Canon – are harder to emulate. This is particularly so when these investments lead to and enhance the firm's reputational capital. Efficiency approaches based on adding value and innovation provide organizations with a strong impetus for moving into the next phase of achieving strategic sustainability. This is the subject of the next chapter.

 Appendix 4.1: phase 4: efficiency

Human sustainability (HS4)

There is a systematic attempt to integrate human resource functions into a coherent HR system to reduce costs and increase efficiency. People are viewed as a significant source of expenditure to be used as productively as possible. Technical and supervisory training is augmented with human relations (interpersonal skills) training. The organization may institute programmes of teamwork around significant business functions and generally pursues a value-adding rather than an exclusively cost-reducing strategy. There is careful calculation of cost-benefit ratios for human resource expenditure to ensure that efficiencies are achieved. Community projects are undertaken where funds are available and where a cost-benefit to the company can be demonstrated.

Ecological sustainability (ES4)

Poor environmental practice is seen as an important source of avoidable cost. Ecological issues that generate costs are systematically reviewed in an attempt to reduce costs and increase efficiencies by eliminating waste and by reviewing the procurement, production and distribution processes. There may be active involvement in some systematic approach such as Total Quality Environmental Management (ISO 14001). Environmental issues are ignored unless they are seen as generating avoidable costs or increasing efficiencies.

Notes

1   The sustainability strategy pursued by Nilsson was significantly embedded into the culture and values of Scandic. In 2001 the Hilton Group acquired Scandic and has continued to expand its sustainability initiatives.

2   'Scandic Joins Forces with FACE Stockholm – Cutting Plastic Consumption by 21 tonnes in the Process'. Available HTTP: http://news.cision.com/scandic/r/scandic-joins-forces-with-face-stockholm—cutting-plastic-consumption-by-21-tonnes-in-the-process,c9387467 (accessed 25 November 2013).

3   Scandic, *Environmental Common Sense*, 2003, p. 5.

4   *The Independent*, 'The rise of the urban eco-hotel', *The Independent*, 2008. Online. Available HTTP: <http://www.independent.co.uk/travel/news-and-advice/the-rise-of-the-urban-ecohotel-921460.html> (accessed 17 June 2013); Scandic, 'Scandic Live Sustainability Report', 2013. Online. Available HTTP: <http://www.scandic-campaign.com/livereport/default.asp?lang=en> (accessed 17 June 2013).

5   N. Pegram, 'A Natural Step Case Study: Scandic Hotels', 2008. Online. Available HTTP: <http://www.thenaturalstep.org/en/system/files/Scandic+Hotels+Case+Study_Dec+2008.pdf> (accessed 17 June 2013).

6   R. Orsato, 'Competitive environmental strategies: when does it pay to be green?', *California Management Review*, 2006, 48 (2), 127–43.

7   D. Dunphy and A. Griffiths, *The Sustainable Corporation*, Sydney: Allen and Unwin, 1998.

8   M. Hammer and J. Champy, *Reengineering the Corporation*, London: Nicholas Brealey, 1990.

9   Ibid.

10 F. Hilmer, *Coming to Grips with Competitiveness and Productivity*, Canberra: Economic Planning Advisory Council Paper 91/01, 1991; D. Stace and D. Dunphy, *Beyond the Boundaries: Leading and Re-Creating the Successful Enterprise*, Sydney, Australia: McGraw-Hill, 2nd edn, 2001, p. 143.

11 Orsato, 'Competitive environmental strategies', p. 135.

12 L. Rowledge, R. Barton and K. Brady, *Mapping the Journey: Case Studies in Strategy and Action toward Sustainable Development*, Sheffield: Greenleaf Publishing Company, 2000, p. 131.

13 SC Johnson, 'SC Johnson Sustainability Report', 2012. Online. Available HTTP: <http://www.scjohnson.com/en/commitment/report.aspx> (accessed 17 June 2013).

14 J. Keegan, 'Corporate Environmentalism and Market Performance: An Analysis of US Corporate Annual Reports 1988–1999', Honours dissertation, Brisbane: School of Management, Queensland University of Technology, 2002.

15 S. Banerjee, E. Iyer and R. Kashyap, 'Corporate environmentalism: antecedents and influence of industry type', *Journal of Marketing*, 2003, 67 (2), 106–22.

16 J. Salo, 'Beyond the Brand: Leaders in Supply Chain Environmental Sustainability', 2012. Online. Available HTTP: <http://www.thedailybeast.

com/newsweek/2012/10/22/beyond-the-brand-leaders-in-supply-chain-environmental-sustainability.html> (accessed 17 June 2013).

17 JC Sainsbury, 'Sainsbury's Puts All Store Waste to Positive Use', 2013. Online. Available HTTP: <http://www.j-sainsbury.co.uk/media/latest-stories/2013/20130613-sainsburys-puts-all-store-waste-to-positive-use/> (accessed 20 June 2013).

18 V. Delgado, 'Sainsburys Achieves Zero Waste to Landfill Seven Years Early', 2degrees network, 2013. Online. Available HTTP: <https://www.2degreesnetwork.com/groups/water-risk-strategy/resources/sainsburys-achieves-zero-waste-landfill-seven-years-early_2/> (accessed 25 November 2013).

19 M. Winn and M. Kirchgeorg, 'The siesta is over: a rude awakening from sustainability myopia', in S. Sharma and M. Starik (eds) *Research in Corporate Sustainability*, Cheltenham, UK; North Hampton, MA: Edward Elgar, 2006.

20 E. von Weizsacker, A. Lovins and L. Lovins, *Factor Four: Doubling Wealth – Halving Resource Use*, London: Earthscan Publications, 1997; P. Hawken, A. Lovins and L. Lovins, *Natural Capitalism: Creating the Next Industrial Revolution*, Boston, MA: Little Brown, 1999; H. Tibbs, 'The technology strategy of the sustainable corporation', in D. Dunphy, J. Beneviste, A. Griffiths and P. Sutton (eds) *Sustainability: The Corporate Challenge of the 21st Century*, Sydney: Allen and Unwin, 2000, pp. 191–216.

21 Tibbs, 'The technology strategy of the sustainable corporation', p. 203.

22 Ibid., p. 210.

23 V. Ambrosini and C. Bowman, 'What are dynamic capabilities and are they a useful construct in strategic management?' *International Journal of Management Reviews*, 2009, 11 (1), 29–49.

24 B. Nattrass and M. Altomare, *The Natural Step for Business: Wealth, Ecology and the Evolutionary Corporation*, Gabriola Island, BC: New Society Publishers, 1999, p. 80.

25 World Bank 2013 *China 2030, Building a Modern, Creative and Harmonious Society*. Washington, DC: World Bank. Online. Available HTTP: <http://documents.worldbank.org/curated/en/2013/03/17494829/china-2030-building-modern-harmonioius-creative-society>, at page 45 (accessed 5 March 2014

26 Ibid., p. 241.

27 P. Hawken, A. Lovins and H. Lovins, *Natural Capitalism: Creating the Next Industrial Revolution*, London: Earthscan, 1999, p. 155.

28 S. Bonini and S. Görner, 'The Business of Sustainability, McKinsey Global Survey Results', 2011. Online. Available HTTP: <http://www.mckinsey.com/insights/energy_resources_materials/the_business_of_sustainability_mckinsey_global_survey_results> (accessed 19 June 2013).

29 S. Benn, P. Crittenden, P. Brown and D. Brown, 'Leadership and Change for Energy Efficiency for Accountants and Business Managers, Training Needs Analysis', 2013. Online. Available HTTP: <http://www.business.uts.edu.au/energyefficiency> (accessed 21 June 2013).

30 H. Bos-Brouwers, 'Corporate sustainability and innovation in SMEs: evidence of themes and activities in practice', *Business Strategy and the Environment*, 2009, 19 (7), 417–35.
31 Ibid.
32 K. Jenkinson and S. Putt del Pino, 'Big Business on the Sustainability Offensive', 2012. Online. Available HTTP: <http://insights.wri.org/news/2012/03/big-business-sustainability-offensive> (accessed 21 June 2013).
33 Ibid.
34 McKinsey, 'How Companies Manage Sustainability: McKinsey Global Survey Results', 2011. Online. Available HTTP: <http://www.mckinsey.com/insights/sustainability/how_companies_manage_sustainability_mckinsey_global_survey_results> (accessed 19 June 2013).
35 A. Griffiths and R. Zammuto, 'Institutional governance systems and variations in national competitive advantage: an integrative framework', *Academy of Management Review*, 2005, 30 (4), 823–42.
36 Rowledge, Barton and Brady, *Mapping the Journey*, pp. 129–50.
37 Sony has also instigated new approaches to the collection, use and recycling of electrical goods. It has taken part in a pilot programme in Minnesota. See: 'US begins to wrestle more earnestly with electronic waste', *CutterEdge Environment*, environment@cutter.com.
38 S. Schvaneveldt, 'Environmental performance of products: benchmarks and tools for measuring improvement', *Benchmarking: An International Journal*, 2003, 10 (2), 137–52.
39 Sony, 'Promoting Efficiency Energy Use', 2013. Online. Available HTTP: <http://www.sony.net/SonyInfo/csr_report/environment/climate/ghg/site/index3.html#block3> (accessed 21 June 2013).
40 World Business Council for Sustainable Development and the United Nations Environment Program (UNEP), *Cleaner Production and Ecoefficiency: Complementary Approaches to Sustainable Development*, Geneva: WBCSD and UNEP, 1992, p. 3.
41 THE *UN GLOBAL COMPACT*. MODULE 4 from *Principle to Practice*, Online. Available HTTP: <www.unep.fr/shared/publications/other/.../Module4%20-%20Session1.ppt> at slide 25.
42 A. Lovins, H. Lovins and P. Hawken, 'Road map for natural capitalism', *Harvard Business Review*, May–June 1999, 145–58.
43 See GE, 'GE EcoImagination Report'. Online. Available HTTP: <http://files.gecompany.com/ecomagination/progress/GE_ecomagination_2011Annual Report.pdf> (accessed 17 June 2013).
44 O. Balch, (2013) 'Nike Reveals a New, Innovative Game Plan for Sustainability', 13 May 2013, *Guardian Professional Network*. Online. Available HTTP: http://www.guardian.co.uk/sustainable-business/nike-sustainability-report-social-environmental-impact> (accessed 17 June 2013); see also Nike, 'Nike Reporting and Governance', 2013. Online. Available HTTP: <http://nikeinc.com/pages/reporting-governance> (accessed 17 June 2013).

45 A. Griffiths, *Rockcote: A Case in Sustainable Entrepreneurship, Case Study*, Brisbane: University of Queensland Business School, 2006.

46 Cited in Y. Emura, 'Environmental management of Canon group', in P. Allen (ed.) *Metaphors for Change*, Sheffield: Greenleaf Publishing, 2001, p. 57.

47 Ibid., p. 58.

48 Ibid.

49 Ibid., p. 60.

50 Ibid., p. 59.

51 Canon, 'Sustainability Management', 2013. Online. Available HTTP: <http://www.canon.com.au/About-Canon/Sustainability-Environment/Sustainability-Management> (accessed 21 June 2013).

52 Ford, 'Ford Progress in Reducing Water Use', 2013. Online. Available HTTP: <http://corporate.ford.com/microsites/sustainability-report-2012-13/water-reducing> (accessed 20 June 2013).

53 Interface, 'Interface Our Progress', 2013. Online. Available HTTP: <http://www.interfaceglobal.com/Sustainability/Our-Progress.aspx> (accessed 20 June 2013).

54 Interface, 'Interface Gobeyond', 2013. Online. Available HTTP: <http://www.interfacegobeyond.com.au/> (accessed 20 June 2013).

55 H. Clancy, 'Sage Builds a Bright Outlook for Smart Glass', 2013. Greenbiz.com. Online. Available HTTP: <http://www.greenbiz.com/blog/2013/06/17/sage-builds-brighter-future-smart-glass> (accessed 17 June2013); Sage, 'Sage Glass', 2013. Online. Available HTTP: <http://sageglass.com/sage glass/> (accessed 20 June 2013).

56 Ford, 'Ford Progress in Reducing Water Use'; for sustainability indicators at the firm level, see D. Tyteca, 'Sustainability indicators at the firm level', *Journal of Industrial Ecology*, 1999, 2 (4), 61–77.

57 Business in the Community, 'BHP Billiton – World Class Supplier Programme in Chile', 2013. Online. Available HTTP: <http://www.bitc.org.uk/our-resources/case-studies/bhp-billiton-world-class-supplier-programme-chile> (accessed 20 June 2013); Business in the Community, 'Sustainable Supply Chain Award, Big Tick, 2013'. Online. Available HTTP: <http://www.bitc.org.uk/services/awards-recognition/responsible-business-awards/categories/sustainable-supply-chain-award> (accessed 20 June 2013).

58 R. Nidumolu, C. K. Prahalad and M. R. Rangaswami, 'Why sustainability is now the key driver of innovation', *Harvard Business Review*, September 2009, 1–10.

59 Tibbs, 'Technology strategy of the sustainable corporation', p. 201.

60 IBM Software, 'Crossing the Sustainability Chasm: Strategies and Tactics to Achieve Sustainability Goals', 2012. Online. Available HTTP: <http://www.ibm.com/smarterplanet/global/files/se__sv_se__none__sustainability-chasm.pdf> (accessed 15 July 2013).

61 A. Wilkinson, M. Hill and P. Gollan, 'The sustainability debate', *International Journal of Operations and Production Management,* 2001, 21 (12), 1492.

62 J. Benveniste and D. Dunphy, *The Path Towards Sustainability: A Case Study of Placer Dome Asia Pacific*, New South Wales: Centre for Corporate Change, Australian Graduate School of Management, University of New South Wales, 1999.

63 B. Munck, 'Changing a culture of face time', *Harvard Business Review*, November 2001, 64 (4), 125–54.

64 M. A. Delmas and S. Pekovic, 'Environmental standards and labor productivity: Understanding the mechanisms that sustain sustainability', *Journal of Organizational Behavior*, 2013, 34, 230–52.

65 G. Spreitzer, C. L. Porath and C. B. Gibson, 'Toward human sustainability: how to enable more thriving at work', *Organizational Dynamics*, 2012, 41(2), 155.

66 Ibid., p. 158.

67 S. El Ghoul, O. Guedhami, C. C. Y. Kwok and D. R. Mishra, 'Does corporate social responsibility affect the cost of capital?' *Journal of Banking & Finance*, 2011, 35 (9), 2388–406.

68 J. Petrick, R. Scherer, J. Brodzinski, J. Quinn and M. Fall Ainina, 'Global leadership skills and reputational capital: intangible resources for sustainable competitive advantage', *Academy of Management Executive*, 1999, 13 (1), 58–69, p. 60.

69 M. McIntosh, D. Leipziger, K. Jones and G. Coleman, Corporate Citizenship, London: Financial Times Management, 1998, p. 62.

70 Petrick *et al.*, 'Global leadership skills', p. 60.

71 O. Borial, 'The impact of operator involvement in pollution reduction: case studies in Canadian chemical companies', *Business Strategy and Environment*, 2005, 14(6), 339–60.

72 BHP Billiton, 'BHP Billiton – World-Class Supplier Programme in Chile', 2013. Online. Available HTTP: <http://www.bitc.org.uk/our-resources/case-studies/bhp-billiton-world-class-supplier-programme-chile#> (accessed 1 July, 2013).

73 J. Pfeffer, *Competitive Advantage through People*, Boston, MA: Harvard Business School Press, 1994.

74 W. Skinner, 'The productivity paradox', *Harvard Business Review*, 1986, July–August, 64 (4) 55–9.

75 A. Griffiths and M. Winn, 'Slack and Sustainability', Academy of Management Conference Paper, Hawaii, August 2005.

76 G. Hamel and C. K. Prahalad, *Competing for the Future*, Boston, MA: Harvard Business School Press, 1992.

77 A. Griffiths, J. Petrick and V. Fung, 'Proactive Environmental Management of Ecological Information', Brisbane: Technology and Innovation Management Centre, University of Queensland, unpublished manuscript, 2002.

78 B. Daily and S. Huang, 'Achieving sustainability through attention to human resource factors in environmental management', *International Journal of Operations and Production Management*, 2001, 21 (12), 1539–52.

79 Borial, 'The impact of operator involvement in pollution reduction'.

5 Sustainability: the strategic advantage

- Turning sustainability to advantage
- The importance of strategy
- What is strategic sustainability?
- How strategic sustainability contributes to competitive advantage
- Risks of the strategic approach
- Beyond rhetoric and greenwash
- The winning formula
- Moving beyond strategic sustainability
- Appendix 5.1: phase 5: strategic proactivity

Turning sustainability to advantage

> To avoid making the same mistakes, managers must recognize environmental improvement as an economic and competitive opportunity, not as an annoying cost or an inevitable threat. Instead of clinging to a perspective focused on regulatory compliance, companies need to ask questions such as: what are we wasting? And how could we enhance customer value? The early movers – the companies that can see the opportunity in sustainability first and embrace innovation-based solutions – will reap major competitive benefits.[1]

The above quotation from the early work of Porter and van der Linde, two of the world's leading strategy theorists and free market proponents, was a manifesto to managers and corporations alike: It is now time to link the firm's competitive advantage to environmental issues. Many firms have already responded to this emerging challenge and are developing corporate strategies that make sustainability a critical component of competitive success. Leading CEOs are now outlining the challenges of sustainability – not only in terms of their own businesses but also in terms of its potential impact on society at large. Their calls to action do not amount to 'greenwash' but rather are a rallying point for further corporate action and strategic change on sustainability and challenges of climate change (see box 'What CEOs are saying'). This shift is a significant one, but those organizations that succeed in making the new integration will be the strategic leaders in the new economy.

What CEOs are saying

We see climate change as a business issue . . . and we're accelerating our efforts to find solutions.

(Bill Ford, CEO Ford Motor Co)[2]

We believe climate change is one of the most significant environmental challenges of the twenty-first century and voluntary action alone cannot solve the climate change problem.

(Henry Paulson, Chairman Goldman Sachs)[3]

The vision is not just to change our company and eliminate our environmental footprint, but through the power of our influence on others become restorative.

(Ray Anderson, previous Chairman, Interface)[4]

The Unilever Sustainable Living Plan (USLP) inspires us to grow in line with our new purpose to make sustainable living commonplace. The lens of sustainable living is helping us to drive brands that have a strong purpose in people's lives, to reduce costs and take waste out of the system and to drive innovation that will make a positive difference to the environmental and social challenges facing us all. The Plan pushes us to think ahead, reducing risk and making the business more resilient for the long term.

(Paul Polman, CEO Unilever)[5]

I believe that only a sustainable company, with sustainable growth, is able to deliver sustainable solutions. To demonstrate the seriousness of our vision, the Volvo Group has revised our CSR and sustainability strategy and is incorporating it into our daily work. I feel that we have a method that is clearly connected to our business model and our strategies. The model handles risks, supports our business and contributes to sustainable development.

(Olof Persson, President and CEO, Volvo)[6]

Previous chapters have demonstrated that managers increasingly face consumer boycotts, public scrutiny, internet blog sites and activism, regulatory monitoring and fines over any failure to meet expectations around sustainability issues. The wish to avoid liability and reduce risk is a major driver for companies to review their strategies to include sustainability objectives. But sustainability can also be seen as presenting opportunities rather than potential problems. There is a better way of doing business that enables corporations to progress beyond pursuing efficiency measures to improve financial outcomes. The key to achieving this is to link corporate strategy to innovation around sustainability and to progressively build relevant capabilities to support that strategy. In the UK, for example, recent research shows 'that UK businesses have the opportunity to unlock around £100 billion a year in value from new innovation opportunities that address social and environmental challenges'.[7] Siemens is a leading firm which has applied this logic.

Sustainability at Siemens

Siemens is an example of a company which has taken innovation for sustainability as a guiding principle of its corporate strategy. Its key focus on innovation-driven growth markets is enabled by its expansion of its Environmental Portfolio. The following outcomes support its claim that its environmental portfolio is a significant growth driver.

In 2011–12 the company generated €33.2 billion in revenues from products and services within its Environmental Portfolio, representing 42 per cent of Group revenue and enabling customers to cut CO_2 emissions by 332 million tonnes.

The company spends more than €1billion per year on environmental R&D and holds about 14,000 patents for climate protection and environmental technologies.

Siemens argues that its technologies assist its clients to make massive reductions in their environmental footprint. So, for example, Siemens energy specialists assisted the City of Houston to convert its traffic lights to LED technology, replacing 40,000 incandescent lights bulbs and saving the city nearly 9.8 million kilowatt hours of electricity consumption per year, as well as replacement costs of the old globes.

As part of that project, Siemens also set up a traffic light database to lower operating costs even further. In another example, its use of ultra-supercritical technology at the Waigaoqiao III plant in Shanghai enables the plant to operate at an exceptionally high efficiency of 46 per cent, making it the world's most efficient coal-fired power plant. The plant uses approximately half the amount of hard coal as the standard plant.

While its connections with a fossil fuel-dependent industry mean we cannot categorize Siemens in our ideal phase of sustainability, it is the integration of environmental technologies into its core business as well as the major achievements made in its own operations and its strong focus on corporate governance and anti-corruption that place it in the strategic phase. Recognizing these achievements, the company has been a leader in the Diversified Industrials section of the Dow Jones Sustainability Index and featured a number of times in the Carbon Disclosure Project's (CDP) Global 500 Carbon Disclosure Leadership Index (CDLI). As well as a top position in the major sustainability rankings it has won Germany's Most Sustainable Strategies (Corporation) award. In Chapter 9 we discuss some of the leadership strategies that Siemens has utilized to further its sustainability agenda.

(Source: www.siemens.com; Marks & Spencer & Accenture, 2013)[8]

Corporations willing to adopt a strategic approach to sustainability can generate important ecological and community benefits that can also have other positive outcomes for the organization.[9] These may include:

- the generation of brand and reputational capital; for example, Nokia, HP, Honda, Unilever, Anheuser-Busch InBev, Swiss Re, Toyota and Westpac are consistently singled out as leading corporations in strategically managing social and environmental resources;
- the development of innovative products and services for emerging markets;
- local community support for the organization's activities;
- difficult-to-imitate human and knowledge capabilities that are the basis for future competitive advantage; for example, Nucor Steel in the United States and Hewlett-Packard and Unilever worldwide;
- industry leadership and, in some cases, the creation of a new industry. For instance, the development and release of the hybrid Toyota Prius created new product and industry divides. Consequently, Toyota and Honda put other automotive manufacturers on notice. Some of their competitors have found themselves lacking in terms of their research and development capabilities. History is now repeating itself with the recent success of Tesla, the start-up electric car company. With highly positive reviews and consumer response, on 9 May 2013 Tesla posted its first profit, recording $11.2 million in first-quarter net income. With its corresponding rise in share price resulting in market capitalization reaching $8 billion, Telsa is now more valuable than the 113-year-old Italian car company Fiat. Even Ford Motor executive chairman Bill Ford is recorded as saying 'My hat's off to them'.[10]

The example of the electric car highlights a point to be made throughout this chapter, namely, that to establish long-term success around emerging environmentally sound technologies and markets, companies need not only visionary leadership but, less obviously, also the ability to collaborate with would-be competitors to turn the market around. So, for example, Tesla is apparently collaborating with other car manufacturers to share charging stations, a strategy that could help to expand the market so that batteries would become cheaper.

Amory Lovins, Research Director of the Rocky Mountain Institute, argues that our current corporate strategies, structures, cultures and norms prevent us from seeing solutions that can be both environmentally and economically beneficial. Similarly, Stead and Stead argue that 'achieving sustainability is not just about changing how humans do things; it's about changing how humans view things'.[11] Taken together, the collective view emerging from sustainability academics, practitioners, investment funds and managers is that the relationship between corporations and their environment is too complex to represent as either win–win or win–lose.[12] There are costs in incorporating sustainability objectives into corporate strategy but there are also very significant potential gains. This chapter builds the case for corporations to adopt a strategic approach to sustainability.

The importance of strategy

The last two decades have been a critical time for traditional organizations. In the preceding period of economic growth and relative stability, strategy was seen as developing and implementing top-down corporate plans and annual monitoring to see whether plan outcomes and objectives had been achieved. Like the five-year plans of the command economies of the former Soviet Union, corporate planning sometimes did not reflect the realities of corporate activity but nevertheless remained an important corporate ritual. Corporate strategic planning and its implementation is a very different process today and, to see why, we shall briefly review how the field developed.

The field of corporate strategy emerged in the 1960s from the work of several managerial thinkers, particularly Philip Selznick, Kenneth Andrews, Alfred Chandler and H. Igor Ansoff. They were actively involved as consultants to some of the leading US companies, including multinationals. These companies were confronting a series of problems emerging out of the growing pace of environmental change and the increasing size and complexity of their organizations. The executives were seeking more effective ways to control the activities of these growing organizations and to develop strategies to seize industry leadership and ensure the success of their international operations.[13]

Strategic management was subsequently popularized and developed further by the leading consulting companies, particularly the Boston Consulting Group and McKinsey's in the 1960s and 1970s. By the early 1970s, most large corporations were attempting to develop or had developed a corporate strategic approach with long-range plans to deal with environmental threats and opportunities. However, they were using what Lynda Gratton refers to as the top-down model of strategy.[14] The top-down model is characterized by senior management formulating strategy and then pushing it down through the organization.

This approach to strategy suffered from several major limitations. First, it assumed that managers were rational decision makers who could make accurate forecasts and that organizations were passive tools to be directed to produce the desired outcomes. In fact, accurate forecasting is increasingly difficult in a turbulent world and organizations are often more political, chaotic and disorganized than a rational decision-making model implies. In addition, the environment was generally taken to mean only the competitive market environment. Other major political and social factors (including the ecological environment) were generally left out of the analysis. Finally, strategic planning often focused on the content of strategy and neglected the process of achieving it.[15] The assumption was that, if the strategy was formulated by the senior executive team, it would be automatically implemented throughout the organization.

The overly rational assumptions of the early strategic planners were widely questioned and led to a major debate in the field about the value of deliberate and emergent strategies.[16] As a result of this debate, researchers are now paying much more attention to three key issues that were formerly ignored:

1 the open-ended nature of strategy
2 the impact of political groups in shaping the strategy process
3 the importance of an organization's resources and dynamic capabilities in shaping its ability to respond rapidly to turbulent and competitive environments.[17]

In particular, the debate on strategy has shifted beyond the traditional external elements of strategy such as industry structure, positioning and resources.[18] Current debates now emphasize that sustainable competitive advantages can be achieved by implementing value-adding strategies and by developing organizational innovation and agility. These strategies require the development of particular bundles and sets of capabilities that are not easily imitated and that can be used to transform and adapt the organization to changes over time.

Tactics underpinned by capabilities, such as design thinking based in cross-disciplinary and cross-functional collaboration and research, are being utilized to understand customer needs and forge innovative directions in companies such as Google and Amazon. According to a leading researcher in this area, Sam Bucolo, Professor of Design and Innovation, University of Technology, Sydney:

> The current processes of innovation just aren't leading to those 'Aha!' moments. So what we're trying to use design thinking for is a way of

actually better understanding needs in the market, opportunities and then responding to them at an organizational level.[19]

In other words, these capabilities are future orientated and dynamic.[20] This approach to strategy can be characterized as a learning process which brings people together in an active engagement to design the future of the company.[21] In this chapter, we outline how strategic thinking will develop further as business grapples with challenges such as global competition and the limiting of natural resources.

Hitt, Keats and DeMarie argue that the following capabilities and competencies play an integral role in achieving strategic outcomes. We have linked some sustainability issues to these concepts:[22]

- *Strategic flexibility.* The capability to adapt to fast-paced environmental change. The implication for sustainability is the ability to respond quickly to consumer and community demands and to create business opportunities.
- *Strategic leadership.* The ability to develop a vision and mission and help build the values of the company that will achieve the stated intent of the mission. The challenge here is to incorporate sustainability objectives into the mission which can be acted upon.
- *Dynamic core competencies.* The development and evolution of core skills and training and competency development. This requires investment in resources and people. Sustainability strategies require the development of core competencies to create value-adding opportunities.
- *Developing human capital.* Focus on the development of organization learning, capturing and developing employee knowledge, and identifying when to develop or rely on contingent workers. This amounts to a capability of higher-order learning – found in organizations such as Hewlett-Packard.[23] The focus is on long-term competency development.
- *Effective use of new technology.* Extension of information systems into systems of procurement and supply management for value adding; design of environmentally responsive technologies and products/services. For instance, Interface has pursued a strategy based on the pursuit of long-life leasing deals for its products.
- *Engaging in valuable strategies.* Taking advantage of global opportunities and developing strategic alliances and cooperative strategies. An extension of this to the ecological approach focuses on the development of partnerships with key stakeholders and local communities to review and monitor performance, to redesign products

or services or to build local community capacity. Unilever is an organization known for this approach as it works with new business models such as Business at the Base of the Pyramid that we will discuss in the next chapter.

- *Developing new organizational structures and cultures.* Valuing human capital and contributing to the sustainability outcomes and strategic goals of the organization. Such structures are designed to enhance and reward continuous innovation – this may be product or process orientated. The implication for sustainability is that the development of human and ecological competencies is reliant upon changes in structure and culture, creating the conditions whereby these competencies become the basis upon which future competitive advantages are generated.

We think that Hitt *et al.*'s points are perceptive but we would add one further key characteristic of successful strategy: strategy is more than a set of business goals, financial objectives and means for pursuing competitive advantage in the marketplace.[24] This is the traditional province of business strategy but it means nothing if the strategy is not known to all the members of the organization, strongly committed to by them and actionable in their terms. To be effective, strategy must be clearly articulated and embodied in specific action plans for every unit and individual in the organization.

We have explained how the current view of strategy differs from the traditional strategy model. But the current model of business strategy is only now beginning to take into account the importance of the ecological environment and human factors in achieving success. This is the issue we take up now. How can the strategy field incorporate the new demands of sustainability?

What is strategic sustainability?

What is meant by the term 'strategic sustainability'? There is no clear-cut definition and several parallel interpretations exist. The first interpretation is the use of the word sustainability to mean corporate longevity and survival. If we were interested in how to achieve this kind of strategic sustainability, then we would examine characteristics of those corporations that are long lived and strong performers.[25] For instance, the seminal work of de Geus has identified four characteristics of long-living companies. They show fiscal responsibility – these companies are not high-risk takers in the financial arena. They are aware of and in tune with their environment; they scan it constantly and respond quickly to emerging consumer demands. They have developed ways to experiment and to examine peripheral ideas and turn these into core activities or important side businesses. Finally, these companies have a sense of identity and community, and they work at maintaining good communal relationships.[26]

Long-living companies value innovative capacities in their staff so that they can reinvent themselves. For example, Nokia was once a pulp manufacturer before it moved to electricity and then to mobile phones. The world's oldest limited liability company, Stora Enso, began as a copper miner and is now a leading paper and pulp company. Such long-living companies appear to value human capital and seek to integrate the development of human capabilities into their long-term strategic approach.[27]

Take DuPont's approach to innovation. While this firm expresses pride in its 37,000 patents and its early history as a gunpowder manufacturer and claims it as proof of its commitment to innovation, at the same time it acknowledges that inventions are not enough to keep the company operating from day to day. Careful strategic planning and application of its human capital are also necessary. So, for example, DuPont implemented a new rule in 2010 that mandated that 30 per cent of revenue must come from innovations the company has created in the last four years – a move that could help to reassure investors who might complain at the company's $2 billion research and development budget.[28]

There are limitations to adopting longevity as the measure of sustainability. Longevity is a poor indicator of whether an organization is pursuing goals that sustain the natural environment or society. However, the characteristics of long-living organizations do provide insights into how organizations adapt to changing environments. They are therefore useful in creating sustainable organizations.

The second use of the term sustainability focuses on an organization's engagement with its ecological environment.[29] According to this approach, organizations which are seeking to realize strategic opportunities from the natural environment will develop a range of capabilities for understanding, processing and acting on ecological threats and opportunities. This includes the generation of green products and services, refinement of supply-chain procurement practices and the implementation of environmental management programmes, practices and techniques. Hoffman uses Volvo as an example of a company that was able to shift from environmental management to environmental strategy because it was able to adopt environmental values rapidly. In Volvo's case, the new environmental values were congruent with its existing values of safety and corporate responsibility. This enabled it to enlarge its existing values base to take in these other aspects of sustainability. Nevertheless, Hoffman claims that the adoption of a strategic sustainability perspective requires a cultural and behavioural shift within firms.[30] Such shifts do not occur easily or overnight but the resulting capabilities are hard to imitate and are a key source of competitive advantage.[31] Interface provides us with the paradigmatic example of an organization that has been successful in such an engagement with the environment.

Interface

In 1994 Ray Anderson, Interface CEO and founder, instigated QUEST: a corporate programme designed to address the environmental consequences of manufacturing commercial carpets made primarily from petrochemicals. Anderson confronted the issue of huge quantities of Interface's carpets ending up in landfill around the world.[32]

QUEST was aimed at waste minimization through a variety of processes, including the recycling of carpet. However, for QUEST to succeed as a programme, the organizational members needed to be strongly motivated to address the negative environmental impacts of key elements of the Interface 'value-adding' chain. This required a dramatic shift in the mind-sets and motivation of everyone in the organization, from Ray Anderson to shopfloor workers.

While QUEST was a company-wide programme, decisions on how it was to be undertaken were delegated to each of the individual production facilities. Plants in individual countries were given the autonomy to pursue the QUEST programme according to local needs.[33] In facilities across the world, small teams were established to address internal issues, such as waste reduction and minimization, and external issues, such as customer and supplier requirements. Company processes were then altered so that they aligned with the new focus on quality, waste reduction and recycling. For example, individuals and groups of employees were rewarded for attaining these goals. At Interface, the distinction between human and ecological issues has been increasingly integrated; new structures and processes have been established that reward progress in both areas and encourage the pursuit of excellence in each. Some of the impressive achievements are due to sustainability being embedded in the firm through managers spreading employees' personal energy-saving suggestions and communicating five-year goals. Recent outcomes of its sustainability programme have been:

continued

- The carbon footprint of the average Interface product is down 19 per cent since 2008. This reduction was achieved primarily by increasing the use of recycled raw materials in products and by improving process efficiency to cut required raw materials and waste. About 70 per cent of the carbon footprint of carpet tile is in the raw materials and manufacturing stage. The remaining 30 per cent is associated with the carpet tile's delivery and installation, maintenance and end of life.
- 49 per cent of the total raw materials used by the company in 2012 were recycled or bio-based, including 36 per cent of yarn and 51 per cent of carpet backing.
- In 2012, Interface's ReEntry® 2.0 recycling programme diverted 15 million pounds of carpet and carpet scraps from landfill, bringing the 18-year total for ReEntry 2.0 to £268 million diverted.
- Energy use per unit of production is down 39 per cent since 1996. Renewable sources provide 36 per cent of the energy Interface uses.
- Greenhouse gas emissions per unit of production from manufacturing facilities are down 41 per cent since 1996. Direct use of green electricity in Europe, improved efficiency and process changes have contributed to this reduction.
- Water intake per unit of production is down 81 per cent since 1996.

(Source: Interface, 'Interface Our Progress', 2013. Online. Available HTTP: <http://www.interfaceglobal.com/Sustainability/Our-Progress.aspx> (accessed 20 June 2013); D. Dunphy, J. Beneviste, A. Griffiths and P. Sutton (eds) *Sustainability: The Corporate Challenge of the 21st Century*, Sydney: Allen and Unwin, 2000)

The third use of sustainability focuses on strategic sustainability as a suite of human resource practices and clusters of human capabilities that lead to high performance and enduring competitive advantages. Such HR practices include the redesign of jobs to develop autonomy in decision making, the use of skills training to increase the organization's flexibility and the adoption of team-based organizational architectures to enhance work and increase innovation.[34] High-performance workplaces require organizational systems which integrate HR practices such as particular approaches to recruitment and selection, the distribution of resources to value-adding activities, and knowledge management systems. Consequently, within this tradition, the focus of strategic development has been on creating value-based corporate cultures made up of committed individuals and supportive organizational systems.

Hewlett-Packard, for example, has built its strategic sustainability success on the commitment, pride and trust of its employees – its competitive advantage has been based on the development and utilization of its human capital to design new products, processes, services and community engagement, that in turn can lead to success in implementing environmental or social initiatives which may otherwise not be included in strategy setting, as well as positive economic outcomes.[35] According to Gratton, the development of human capital is a complex task that requires years of management commitment, action and skill. But the result is sustainable high performance.[36]

A key factor in Hewlett-Packard's success has been the effective development of a workplace culture which attracts and retains skilled people committed to working in an entrepreneurial team-based environment that supports innovation. Hewlett-Packard has achieved a global reputation for building and utilizing human capital in the creation of new, innovative products and processes. One aspect of the firm's competitive advantage is its sustainable design programme, which focuses on reducing materials used in the making, packaging and delivery of products. By minimizing the amount of packaging, costs of transport are reduced. Product designers are trained in the company's 'Design for Environment Principles' as well as in regulations around the world which need to be addressed at the design stage.[37]

Research has demonstrated the interconnection between investment in human capital and sustainability and environmental investments. For example, adoption of environmental standards has been shown to be associated with increased employee training and interpersonal contacts, which contribute to improved labour productivity, increased communication among workers with diverse capabilities and, ultimately, knowledge transfer and innovation.[38] For the purposes of this book, we identify strategic sustainability as being an organizational commitment to achieving competitive advantage through the strategic adoption and development of ecologically and socially supportive production processes, products and services and innovative human and knowledge resource management practices. What distinguishes our approach from the earlier strategic approaches that we identified is the integration of the human and ecological sustainability traditions as a means of generating long-term competitive advantages. We have combined elements from all three traditions of strategic sustainability to define strategies to sustain the organization, society and the environment.

How strategic sustainability contributes to competitive advantage

What is the evidence that the strategic approach to sustainability can provide corporations with a basis for enduring competitive advantages? Research shows a positive relationship between a firm's performance on environmental indicators and its economic growth. When it comes to developing capabilities around sustainability, it pays to be green.[39] But the model of strategy we are advocating here goes beyond environmentalism: throughout this book, we have viewed sustainability as including both human and ecological factors. Effective strategy in the future will draw competitive advantage from both areas. In this section we outline how this can be achieved and provide examples.

There is, however, an important point to make before we do this. Strategic sustainability represents more than the rhetorical commitment to human and ecological sustainability principles found in the glossy reports published by some corporations. These reports can be public relations exercises designed to conceal the corporation's lack of care for the community and the environment rather than an exercise in transparency. Strategic sustainability, by contrast, is a demonstrated commitment by the executive team and the board actively to pursue and develop corporate capabilities, products and processes that align sustainability initiatives with the corporation's overall strategic orientation.

Strategic sustainability is also about the development and utilization of corporate competencies in both the human and the ecological areas. The two are loosely linked because developing ecological competencies within the organization necessarily relies on the development of proactive advanced-level human capabilities. Take the example of the Xerox Corporation, where proactive designers and managers working in teams generated new products that were recyclable and reusable. This approach adopted by Xerox defied current trends that built in product redundancy and therefore waste. The team's zero-waste vision resulted in the establishment of a manufacturing plant that created virtually no waste.[40] More recently, Xerox has been focused on integrating sustainability across the business, helping customers to reduce costs while reducing their environmental impact. According to Patricia Calkins, President of Environment, Health and Safety for Xerox Corporation, this exemplifies the principle of 'shared value', as espoused by Porter and Kramer in their recent *Harvard Business Review* article and which we discuss more fully in following chapters.[41] As Calkins says:

> For sustainability to be worthwhile, it must be integrated throughout your business operations. From inception to a product's end of life cycle, you should think about every component that makes up your products and its potential effect on the environment. Sustainability, separate and apart from your core business, means it's not part of your everyday thought process. While it is important to deliver shareholder value; there's a widely held misconception that green responsibility carries a high cost. That's simply not true. In reality, green innovation helps the bottom line by reducing cost, increasing revenue and enhancing brand value.[42]

This approach pursued by Xerox and other firms such as HP – focused on product stewardship – contrasts in almost every respect with the 'old strategy' of limited product lifetimes pursued by firms in the new consumable markets of plasma and LCD television technologies. Opportunities exist for companies to take strategic leadership in redefining these dated strategies. Similarly, there are advantages to be gained by extending these strategies to include reorganizing supply chains so that all stages of the chain contribute to the sustainability strategy.

Strategic sustainability involves the organization in developing processes that institutionalize and systematize these capabilities so that they no longer depend on key individuals but are embodied in systems that act as an organizational memory. Based on a statistical analysis of change in over one hundred organizations, Turner and Crawford argue that high-performing organizations require both operational and transformational capabilities.[43] Operational capabilities contribute to the efficiency and effectiveness of day-to-day activities while transformational capabilities support change and strategic repositioning. This also holds true for organizations pursuing strategic sustainability.

Gratton argues that human capital contributes to the competitive advantage of organizations in three ways: first, when it is rare, that is, something other competitors lack; second, when it is valuable, that is, it has an impact on bottom-line performance; finally, when it is difficult to imitate. Gratton goes on to argue that only human capacity can create these competitive advantages for corporations. She builds a strong case for managers to develop and integrate human capital into the core strategic directions of corporations in order to build long-term, sustainable competitive advantages.[44]

Talent management at Westfield

The case of the Westfield Group illustrates key steps that can be taken to implement strategic human sustainability. Over the last 50 years the Westfield Group has expanded from its Australian origins to now encompass 119 shopping centres in UK, USA and Australia. Its success in revamping its lacklustre Finance function in Australia into a high-performance unit was dependent upon creating a talent pool through key interventions such as increasing interdependency and collaboration across the organization, introducing a range of measures to attract and retain talent and focusing on eliminating wasted time and effort. Reward structures were instigated which included more open promotion schemes and a flexible approach to roles and career planning. Partnerships, both internal and external, were encouraged.

(Dunphy and Perrott, 2011)[45]

However, in analysing what strategic sustainability might mean for the individual organization, it is important to recognize the considerable differences between the way small to medium-sized privately held business enterprises and large, publicly listed companies view the link between strategic value and sustainable business practices.[46] Differences include:

- Large, listed companies are more concerned with equity, while small, privately held companies are more concerned with debt.
- Large, listed companies have significant reputation issues connected with their public profile – brand, media.
- Small companies may be required as suppliers, or followers, to imitate large-company approaches to sustainable development. However, small companies are more nimble and can find these requirements sometimes overly bureaucratic and counter-productive.
- Large companies need formal systematic approaches to achieve consistency across their operations, whereas small companies may not have sufficient resources or need for such approaches.
- Large companies tend to have a longer-term strategic planning time-frame than small companies.
- Large companies have greater market power than small companies.
- Large companies can act differently and retain their competitiveness more readily.

Other research indicates that the main reason fast-growing SMEs invest in environmental measures is to improve working conditions and hence employees' motivation and performance.[47] As an example of how SMEs approach strategic sustainability through enhancing human sustainability and focusing on their supply-chain relationships, we can look to the case of Blackmores.

Enhancing sustainability at Blackmores

Blackmores is a moderately sized organization, a leader in the Vitamin, Herbal and Mineral Supplement (VHMS) market in Australia which has won a number of sustainability-related awards. Some of its products are heavily monitored along the sustainability supply chain in terms of their natural product requirements. For example, it sells the only krill oil in Australia that is certified by the Marine Stewardship Council. Blackmores has a strong values-based culture, reflected in the way employees are recruited and treated in the workplace. Strategic sustainability objectives were built into executive annual plans (shared operational responsibility), linked to performance pay, so that the required actions are implemented and cascaded into managers' and staff plans. It is one of a number of Australian organizations whose investment into sustainable business practices in one way or another has been shown to deliver a much faster return on investment than initially predicted. For example, a move to centralize the firm into a new five-star building with trigen operations to provide energy, water treatment plant to provide 70 per cent of water needs and with wide amenity for employees, including a wellness centre, resulted in 26 per cent productivity gains within two years.[48]

(ICAA, 2011)

Clearly, whether for SMEs or for larger organizations, managing relationships along the supply chain is crucial to an organization achieving strategic sustainability. Figure 5.1 modifies our phase model to reflect what transition to strategic sustainability might mean for the overall supply chain. So, for example, taking a strategic approach to sustainable supply-chain management entails an emphasis on transparency, certification and integrating human and ecological sustainability.

Management

Illustrating the pressure that can be applied along supply chains by public concern, the food industry is currently under scrutiny in the wake of horsemeat scandals in Europe and generally wider interest on the part of

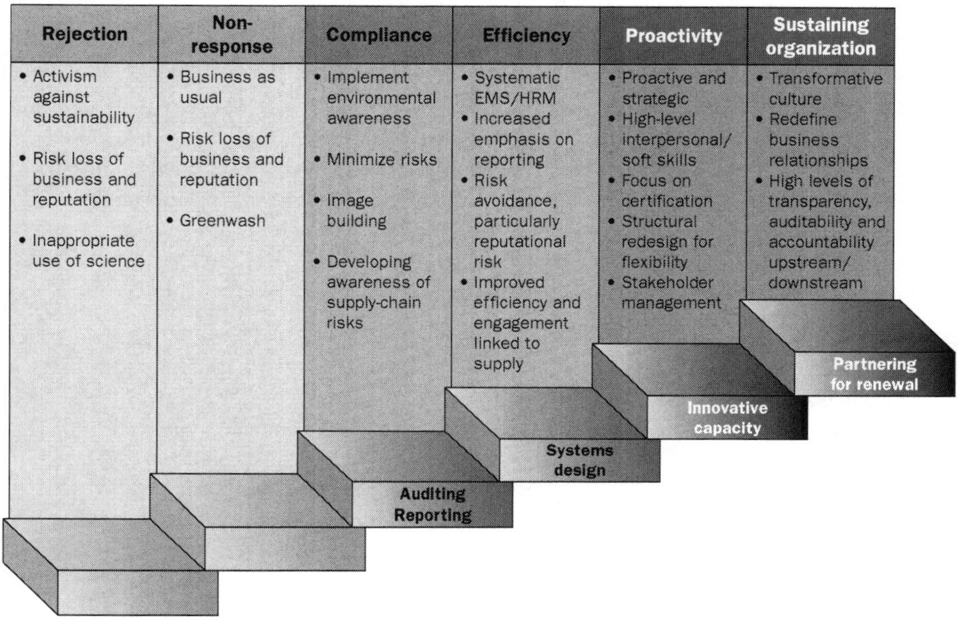

Rejection	Non-response	Compliance	Efficiency	Proactivity	Sustaining organization
• Activism against sustainability • Risk loss of business and reputation • Inappropriate use of science	• Business as usual • Risk loss of business and reputation • Greenwash	• Implement environmental awareness • Minimize risks • Image building • Developing awareness of supply-chain risks	• Systematic EMS/HRM • Increased emphasis on reporting • Risk avoidance, particularly reputational risk • Improved efficiency and engagement linked to supply	• Proactive and strategic • High-level interpersonal/ soft skills • Focus on certification • Structural redesign for flexibility • Stakeholder management	• Transformative culture • Redefine business relationships • High levels of transparency, auditability and accountability upstream/ downstream

Auditing Reporting

Systems design

Innovative capacity

Partnering for renewal

Figure 5.1 *Applying the sustainability phase model to the sustainable supply chain*

consumers in food safety. McDonald's reaction is to attempt to show a lead in more sustainable procurement. It has recently launched a Quality Scouts initiative where members of the public are invited to visit its supply chain and report back. In 2013, it has become the first UK restaurant to serve 100 per cent Freedom Food pork across its menu.[49] For us this example also serves to illustrate the complexity of classifying the sustainability activities of major companies. Do we applaud McDonalds for taking this lead in sustainable supply-chain management or do we argue, as Paul Hawken does, that sustainability at McDonalds is irrelevant given that '"Sustaining" McDonald's requires a simple unsustainable formula: cheap food plus cheap non-unionized labor plus deceptive advertising = high profits'.[50]

Adding to the complexity of the challenge, for many companies, taking a strategic approach to supply-chain management means considering what strategic sustainability might mean in large developing countries where many suppliers, including SMEs, may be sited. The case of what sustainable business might mean in China illustrates this point.

Challenges for strategic sustainability in China

Most research on corporate sustainability and corporate social responsibility has focused on Western companies. Despite the economic significance of China, for example, surprisingly fewer studies have been conducted on Chinese companies. What studies have been done show considerable differences in how Chinese and international companies enact sustainability. Kolk *et al.* (2010) show that Chinese retailers report more on economic dimensions, including philanthropy, and place relatively less emphasis on contentious labour issues and the environment, while international organizations focus more on product responsibility.[51]

Manufacturing enterprises in China have been singled out for their negative environmental impacts and excessive use of resources. Given the complexity of the task of implementing sustainable forms of manufacturing and the comparative lack of relevant experience, green manufacturing strategies in China require long-term continuous improvement based on the establishment of the greener management strategy; the setting of appropriate objectives; environmental auditing of the enterprise; selection of green technologies; risk assessment of the exercise; performance measurement and aligning of suitable human resources.[52]

The huge numbers of SMEs (estimated at more than 50 million) in China face particular difficulties such as the low levels of awareness of environmental concerns of many companies that are family owned, with little in the way of specialist technical expertise, lack of technological absorptive capacity, lack of financial resources and access to capital, and short-term economic perspective.[53] Since China appears to be facing an emergent green era, it is likely many SMEs will struggle to comply with rapidly changing government legislation in this area unless their capacity is raised through such measures as implementing environmentally sound technology.[54]

Up to this point, we have argued that strategic sustainability generates competitive advantages when ecological and human sustainability elements have been effectively integrated. Now we show that this integration can be achieved in different ways which result in significantly different sustainability strategies. Each of these strategies provides a different form of competitive advantage. To develop this approach, we combine two influential theoretical frameworks; the first, by Hart and Milstein,[55] outlines different strategies for the creation of sustainable shareholder value and applies these strategies to the sustainability imperative. The second framework, developed by Orsato, outlines a contingent set of circumstances for when it pays to be green.[56]

Hart and Milstein start from a simple assumption (see Figure 5.2) – that shareholder value is a multidimensional construct. On the vertical dimension (today versus tomorrow), managers can make decisions favouring short-term outcomes such as investing in pollution-saving technologies now, or they can make decisions for the longer-term future such as investing profits in new products and markets. On the horizontal dimension (internal versus external), managers can choose to build their current internal capabilities, by for example, purchasing new equipment, or they can choose to gather new information, ideas and innovations from external sources. The choices that managers make about these issues determine their dominant strategy and how the firm goes about creating value.

Hart and Milstein argue that this framework can be used to understand a firm's sustainability strategy. For instance, firms can choose between a pollution-prevention strategy – that is, a short-term, cost-reduction efficiency strategy (short-term, internal) – or shift their orientation to a future-oriented, clean-technology strategy (future, internal). Both strategies create shareholder value; however, they have different implications for capability development and represent different strategic orientations. Defining your firm's strategy in this way provides strategic

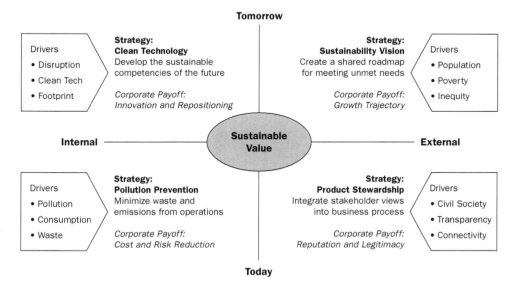

Figure 5.2 *Sustainable value framework*
Source: S. Hart and M. Milstein, 'Global sustainability and the creative destruction of industries', *Sloan Management Review*, 1999, 41 (1), 60.

focus and helps to clarify the kinds of sustainability strategies the firm needs to develop and implement.

The Hart and Milstein framework elaborates how companies can create sustainability value. Similarly, Orsato's work outlines a specific set of environmental strategies that firms can pursue in order to generate competitive value (see Figure 5.3). For instance, Orsato argues that firms can pursue either a differentiation or a low-cost strategy (competitive advantage) and then can decide whether they improve products/service or organizational processes (competitive focus). For instance, some firms can generate competitive advantages via the pursuit of eco-efficiency strategies – such as firms in the beverage industry that need to reduce water consumption. The world's biggest brewer, Anheuser-Busch InBev, for example, reported that in 2012 it had reached its three-year goal of using a leading-edge 3.5 hectolitres of water per hectolitre of production within a three-year period. This represents an 18.6 per cent reduction in water usage across its global operations against a 2009 baseline. This is equivalent to the amount of water needed to produce approximately 25 billion cans of AB InBev products, which is about 20 per cent of one year's production'[57] The Belgian brewer has also just announced an ambitious set of five-year environmental goals setting further targets for

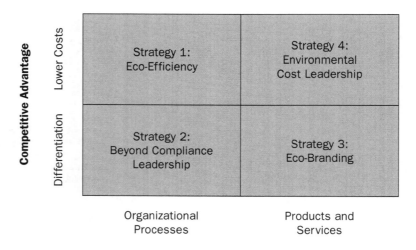

Competitive Focus

Figure 5.3 *Generic competitive environmental strategies*
Source: R. Orsato, 'Competitive environmental strategies: when does it pay to be green?', *California Management Review*, 2006, 48 (2), 131.

water and energy use, while setting also its first targets for packaging reductions and eco-friendly coolers.[58]

As we discussed in previous chapters, firms can also pursue ISO and other forms of certification as a means of branding and differentiating their product from that of their competitors.[59] This would fit within the clean-technology and processes quadrant of the Hart and Milstein model. A clear example of a long-term sustainability vision is the introduction by Toyota and Honda of hybrid cars – the Toyota Prius and the Honda Insight. Although other brands are now in the growing hybrid market, the Toyota and Honda models still lead the way. Taking this long-term strategy in the face of predictions of the growing cost of fossil-based fuels and regulatory imposts also means the both companies are equipped to enter the electric and hydrogen fuel market, when and if infrastructure needs are addressed to the extent that such vehicles can be competitive.

The two frameworks appear to be converging on a new approach to differentiating sustainability strategies (see Table 5.1).

We now outline some of the strategic human capabilities required for these four strategy types (our preferred term for each of these strategies is shown in italic print below):

1 Pollution prevention/*eco-efficiency*: The human capabilities that are required to further this strategy involve the development of engineering and technical understandings and skills for addressing environmental issues. These capabilities focus on reducing resources waste, particularly for water, energy and materials. Many of these types of technical capabilities can be located at the operator level but need to be fully integrated into an overall strategic plan.
2 Clean technology/*beyond compliance*: The human capabilities involved here focus on both the development of innovative R&D approaches and the ability to use metrics to further sustainability goals. For instance, to measure and then reduce greenhouse gas emissions demands either the development of new technologies or the application

Table 5.1 *Comparing competitive environmental strategies*

Hart and Milstein	Orsato
1 Pollution prevention	1 Eco-efficiency
2 Clean technology	2 Beyond compliance leadership
3 Product stewardship	3 Environmental cost leadership
4 Sustainability vision	4 Eco-branding

of new technologies to existing production and service systems. This requires high levels of innovation, increased investment in research and development and external environmental scanning for potential new solutions.

3   Product stewardship/*environmental cost leadership*: The focus of capabilities in this area will be around the creation of new ranges of low-cost products for emerging and existing markets or streamlining supply chains and current operations.

4   Sustainability vision/eco-branding: The focus of human capabilities in this area is on developing the relationship skills needed to integrate external stakeholders into the organization; to develop innovative future-oriented strategies and product offerings, and the leadership capabilities needed to influence others in the organization's supply chain to follow this visionary leadership.

Risks of the strategic approach

While the previous section outlined positive examples of corporations that were seeking to gain competitive advantages through the pursuit of strategic sustainability, this approach has some inherent risks. A focus on sustainability alone is clearly not enough to deliver competitive advantages. If the strategy is not viable in business terms, then a focus on sustainability will not save the organization.

Similarly, managers of organizations engaging in strategic sustainability need to understand that, as corporations, they must be profitable, add value and provide quality products and services. These are the conventional elements of any viable corporate strategy. For instance, The Body Shop was long held up as a successful example of a company pursuing strategic sustainability – starting with a tiny shop selling 30 products and expanding to 2,500 stores worldwide, while keeping to its core commitment of selling products composed of natural ingredients that were ethically sourced and cruelty free. However, it began to experience problems in maintaining the financial viability of the business, apparently losing ground to competitors because its product line was ageing and in need of revamping.[60] Elkington argues that this demonstrates the need for managers to maintain their focus on financial and strategic issues as well as social and ecological ones.[61]

An analogy can be made between current efforts to institutionalize green strategies and earlier corporate experiences with the implementation of flexible manufacturing systems. At the height of competition between US and Japanese manufacturing firms, Jaikumar showed that Japanese firms outperformed US firms using the same or similar technologies.[62] Why? It appears that US firms used traditional organizational structures, systems and processes and did not modify their strategy to take account of the flexibility benefits associated with the new technologies. The Japanese, on the other hand, not only introduced the new technology, but also changed their structures and strategies to maximize the competitive advantages associated with its introduction. The story serves as a powerful reminder of the importance of linking the pursuit of sustainability with organization systems and strategic outcomes. It should also act as a warning: in the haste to develop corporate sustainability strategies, we should not overlook the need to make these strategies deliver competitive advantages.

Another potential risk is that the organization outstrips the understanding of the key external stakeholders on whom the organization's future depends. This is particularly the case with shareholders and financial analysts, whose viewpoints on sustainability are often highly conservative. However, as discussed in Chapter 2, there is some evidence that the investor interface is changing, with investors starting to price in the costs and liabilities associated with social, ethical and environmental issues. Recent work by Barnett and Salomon found that firms with low corporate social performance (CSP) have higher corporate financial performance (CFP) than firms with moderate CSP, but firms with high CSP have the highest CFP. These writers claim that their work supports the theoretical argument that capacity for stakeholder influence underlies the ability to transform social responsibility into profit.[62] Consequently, the organization pursuing strategic sustainability initiatives needs to devote time and energy to keeping shareholders and other stakeholders informed of the value being added to their investment through these strategies.

Beyond rhetoric and greenwash

What can we learn from our discussion of the risks of the strategic approach and from the successes of corporations such as Interface, Hewlett-Packard and Toyota, which continually re-emerge as leaders in areas of strategic sustainability? One conclusion we could draw is that strategic sustainability can be fragile and difficult to maintain.

For instance, in the 1990s, Monsanto was hailed as a company that had achieved a remarkable turnaround. It adopted a strategy of moving from being a major polluter to pushing the boundaries of biotechnology and the new agriculturally based industries. In generating this transformation, the issues of strategic sustainability were key drivers. Monsanto's internal sustainability initiatives were promoted as being forerunners to creating the sustainable corporation.[64] They included the establishment of sustainability teams, a focus on waste and pollution reduction, and executive leaders who appeared to support key principles of strategic sustainability. Monsanto executives were keen to turn around the company's negative reputation concerning ecological and human resources. They set out to build a new image of an organization that valued community concerns, emphasized building human capabilities and was determined to move away from polluting industrial processes.[65] However, by the late 1990s and into 2000, Monsanto was once again attracting the ire of green and civil liberties groups and its commitment to sustainability was being questioned (see Figure 5.4). What had gone wrong?

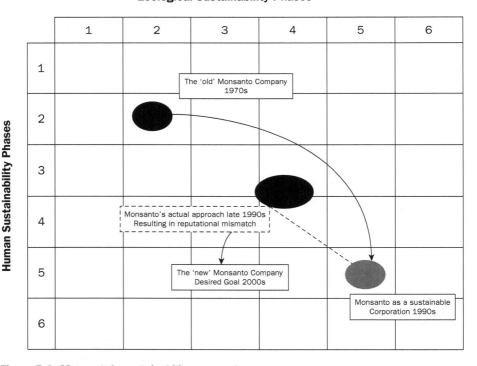

Ecological Sustainability Phases

Figure 5.4 *Monsanto's sustainability approach*

Monsanto had moved strategically to develop a range of genetically modified products. This was a product line which many outside Monsanto found ethically unacceptable. Environmentalists almost universally condemn Monsanto's ethics and its development and promotion of these products. In the case of Monsanto, first-mover advantages were quickly lost due to external stakeholder criticism, which was very public and evoked broad consumer cynicism. Strategic proactivity in the new areas of biotechnology and genetic engineering requires the application of the precautionary principle: that 'when an activity raises threats of harm to human health or the environment, precautionary measures should be taken even if some cause and effect relationships are not fully established scientifically'.[66] Monsanto provides an illustration of how easily a company can overlook this fundamental requirement of strategic sustainability. Had Monsanto maintained active and open links between strategic decision makers and third-party monitoring groups, it would have received an early warning that its developments in this area were unacceptable. These consumer concerns about genetic modification have now spread to food manufacturers, with many food manufacturers, particularly in the European Union, discarding genetically modified foods in order to avoid having to display GM food labels. As Robert Hadler, Corporate Affairs Director of Goodman Fielder, stated at the time: 'The customer is always right and the customer is concerned about the effects of GM ingredients. The major retailers don't want products with GM in them.'[67]

Despite the strong commitment of its CEO and the introduction of sustainability teams, Monsanto found that strategic sustainability can be fraught with potential problems and hazards. In a thought-provoking article, Stuart Hart and Sanjay Sharma argue that companies such as Shell, Nike and Monsanto had experienced legitimacy problems generated by remote but increasingly connected 'fringe stakeholders'. They ask, how is it that a company that had broken no laws in the pursuit of its strategy and engaged all key stakeholders managed to get it so wrong?[68] As Figure 5.4 illustrates, Monsanto started out as a low-margin polluting chemical company. From 1993 to 1998 it made around $8 billion in acquisitions as it implemented its strategy of being a life-sciences company – a significant commitment of which was to become a sustainable corporation. However, questions were increasingly asked over genetic modification of crops and food, and farmers from Canada to India were concerned about Monsanto protecting its patent ownership.[69] As fringe stakeholders found collective and connected voices, a mismatch appeared between Monsanto's stated goals and where the company was seen to be. By the year 2000 Monsanto's $8 billion vision of being a global life-science company had disappeared – the company was bought out by competitors.[70]

There are some lessons to be learned from the Monsanto case. To achieve sustainability, companies need to remain nimble and to continually reinvest in ecological and human sustainability capabilities. They need to maintain active and open links between strategic decision makers and third-party monitoring groups. In particular, strategic proactivity in the new areas of biotechnology and genetic engineering requires the application of the precautionary principle and transparency in operations.

The building of the human and ecological capabilities of an organization also contributes to its reputational capital. In their efforts to turn around poor or bad reputations, companies sometimes turn to 'spin doctors' and advertising, but this can expose the gap between what the organization says and what it does. Reputation must be realistic, monitored and constantly assessed, particularly in the global economy. We have mentioned already the reputational risks associated with the global supply chain. These were clearly demonstrated in the fall-out from the recent factory fires in Bangladesh for various international clothing companies whose brands are now associated with poor conditions of worker health and safety. In the aftermath, some companies have committed millions of dollars to upgrade worker conditions in their supplier factories.[71]

Table 5.2 outlines false postures that organizations sometimes adopt in dealing with sustainability issues. If your organization is adopting one of these postures, attempting to pass this off as strategic sustainability, then the deception will almost certainly be uncovered.

The winning formula

What is the winning formula to achieve strategic sustainability? What can we learn from our discussions of company cases and emerging research about how to integrate sustainability into strategy? First, corporations moving towards the attainment of strategic sustainability focus on building key capabilities for value adding and innovation. Second, they develop and utilize the corporate competencies needed to develop and enact these business strategies in the human and ecological spheres.[72] Third, the corporation develops processes that institutionalize and

Table 5.2 *Strategic sustainability: false postures*

What strategic sustainability is not	Risk to the organization
Greenwash The use of corporate reports and misinformation to promote the public image of being sustainable.	Damage to reputational capital as a cynical public votes with their dollars and shifts loyalties. For instance, Exxon lost US\$3 billion in shareholder value after the *Exxon Valdez* incident. Similarly, protests and consumer boycotts over its factories in developing countries hurt Nike's bottom line and pushed that organization into more responsible management of its supply chain.
Green marketing Green product labels and the use of animals such as dolphins to create the image of green branding while obscuring the actual environmental impact of a company's processes, products and services.	Consumer backlash against the organization and heightened cynicism about corporate and institutional pledges of self-regulation.
EMS/TQEM These tools are useful in addressing complex sustainability issues but will not in themselves deliver strategic sustainability.	A technological fixation: organizations can slip into the assumption that the implementation of such tools necessarily generates sustainability outcomes. A focus on tools alone can lead to missing strategic advantages, which are eventually developed by competitors.
Fad surfing in the area of human resources Rhetoric about teams, virtual organizations, empowerment, culture change. Most employees have heard it all before. If translated into strategically relevant actions these concepts may help build sustainable capabilities and employee capital; but if rhetoric only, they create cynicism and resistance.	Alienation/cynicism and the flight of human capital as employees leave to find better employment prospects and to pursue their own values in a more honest corporate environment.

systematize these capabilities so that the organization is no longer reliant upon key individuals for best-practice operations. The capabilities are embodied in the organization's systems and culture and are simply seen as 'the way we do business around here'. Finally, corporations must be embedded into local communities so that they are sensitive to community needs. Strategically sustainable organizations will therefore give priority to cutting-edge human resource practices and look towards the creation of values-based cultures for sustainable outcomes. They will aim to become high-performance organizations (see Figure 5.5).

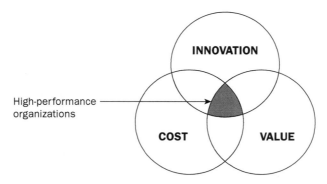

Figure 5.5 *The strategic target*

Achieving successful strategic sustainability also involves the following:

- *The move from efficiency to strategy.* Building capabilities around achieving strategic goals involves moving beyond the compliance and efficiency phases to a strategic approach to sustainability. Strategic proactivity is much more externally focused and involves calculated risk taking. This is a significant value shift because the compliance phase reinforces risk avoidance and the efficiency phase reinforces cost minimization. By contrast, the development of new strategic options demands thoughtful risk taking and investment in R&D. Consequently, many organizations have to run an 'analyser' strategy, that is, they pursue a low-cost, low-risk strategy in traditional operational areas while accepting higher costs and significantly greater risks in areas involving new strategic developments.[73] To be successful this requires a more flexible managerial approach. IKEA is an example of a company that has moved from the efficiency stage to the strategic phase. It initially engaged with sustainability because it was the 'right thing to do' and to reduce costs from waste. In more recent times, it is taking an approach whereby it pursues sustainability as integral to its business model. This includes engaging directly with communities to increase local community employment, developing e-learning programmes to engage a range of stakeholders with sustainable living concerns and advice, fostering innovative operational initiatives around logistics and goods transfer and developing various means to reduce emissions.[74]
- *Introducing new tools and techniques.* Various tools and techniques can be used to guide the development of strategic sustainability initiatives and in third-party monitoring and audits. One well-known example is the use of the triple bottom-line (TBL) and the deployment

of that approach into the Global Reporting Initiative, as discussed in previous chapters. John Elkington defines TBL as: 'sustainable development [that] involves the simultaneous pursuit of economic prosperity, environmental quality and social equity. Companies aiming for sustainability need to perform not against a single, financial bottom line but against the triple bottom line.'[75] A range of organizations including Hewlett-Packard, DuPont and numerous universities have experimented with the Balanced Environmental Scorecard, which links environmental performance to four key indicator areas: financial, customer, business processes and organizational learning.[76]

Figure 5.6 shows how sustainability can be integrated into the Balanced Scorecard.[77]

• *Linking operational processes to sustainable strategy.* This involves the systematic and rapid translation of successful experimental ventures into standard operating procedures company-wide. For instance, Texas

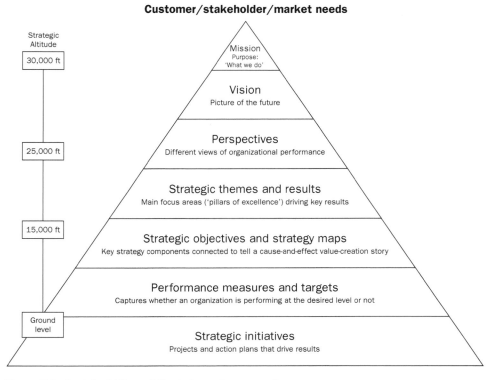

Figure 5.6 *Sustainability and the balanced scorecard*

Industries operates a steel mill reliant on recycled scrap. A separate division, in the same town, then turns the slag from the mill into the raw material for its cement works. This has created synergies in product, resource usage and a reduction in energy waste, while increasing profits.[78]

- *Creating new product and service process-improvement opportunities.* A strategic approach to sustainability enables an organization to look for new opportunities to create new markets, reinvent existing products or add value to services. The Toyota Prius illustrates how Toyota has made significant strategic research and development investments in hybrid technologies and then integrated those into Toyota's lean production systems to create new products and consumer demand.

- *Creating enabling structures and design.* The development of sustainable business models and new organizational architectures can enhance an organization's responsiveness to environmental and social issues. Many traditional organizations have structures and designs that actually impede the development of sustainable business models. Networks and alliances in particular are appropriate to supply-chain reorganization, recycling and stakeholder involvement. For example, Nike has recently joined with NASA, the US Agency for International Development and the US Department of State to convene 150 materials specialists, designers, academics, manufacturers, entrepreneurs and NGOs to catalyse action around the sustainability of materials.[79] Groups such as the Electronic Industry Citizenship Coalition, of which IBM and a number of other electronics providers are members, cooperate in areas such as up-skilling and capacity, minerals and working hours.[80]

- *Building employee knowledge and commitment.* Firms adopting innovative and value-adding approaches to sustainability have emphasized the development of employee capital and corresponding competencies and have acknowledged their importance for long-term competitive advantages. They have set about creating commitment rather than control-based cultures and structures.

- *Executive leadership and stewardship.* Innovative firms and corporations committed to the attainment of strategic sustainability have executive teams which support the development of sustainable products, services and processes for existing, emerging and future markets. Building an informed executive team takes time and may involve some change of membership.

- *Developing differentiated stakeholder strategies.* This involves designing and implementing various strategies that reflect the needs and interests of different stakeholders.[81] To achieve this, stakeholder representatives need to be actively involved. For example, Interface has given a commitment to have its 'green' products independently tested and verified by external parties.

We shall now expand on each of these points in the remainder of the chapter.

The move from efficiency to strategy

What does a review of the existing literature and case examples tell us about what the shift from the efficiency phase to the strategic phase involves? First, it is important to note that much of the literature in this area concentrates on environmental management rather than human sustainability. We shall deal with this literature first. Andrew Hoffman argues that the move from environmental management to environmental strategy requires organizations to shift their cultures, structures, reward systems and job responsibilities. In his view, the shift to strategic sustainability requires a radical overhaul of how corporations value their assets and how they define what is an asset.[82] The current strategic approaches are only starting to recognize the importance of culture and human capital in the attainment of strategic outcomes.

Furthermore, Hoffman argues that engagement with sustainability issues requires a holistic change. Piecemeal solutions such as retrofitting, fire fighting, end-of-pipe solutions and other technical programmes such as total quality environmental management (TQEM) and environmental management systems (EMS) are not enough. To be effective these programmes must be accompanied by a series of broader supporting organizational changes. Hoffman acknowledges that technical solutions can provide efficiency gains. However, he argues that they are easily imitated and will not provide long-term competitive advantages.[83] Increasingly, companies will also require that their suppliers adopt a strategic approach to sustainability. For instance, the movement from efficiency to strategy has implications for a range of small- and medium-sized companies. In their pursuit of new markets for green products and services, larger corporations will increasingly require their suppliers to obtain environmental accreditation and reach quality standards. The implication for those companies that supply the larger corporations is clear. They must act now to avoid the risk of having such systems imposed or, worse still, of losing market share to others who have already implemented such systems. This has happened in some cases. IKEA, for example, now requires its furniture manufacturers, subcontractors, transport and logistics companies to implement and adhere to IKEA's high environmental standards. Customers are demanding high environmental standards and IKEA insists that those who participate in its supply chain deliver on IKEA's commitments to meet them.[84]

Key steps to strategic sustainability

This section outlines the five key steps required to shift an organization from an efficiency focus to strategic sustainability.

Step 1: Top team elaboration of corporate goals relating to sustainability. For corporations to shift to strategic sustainability, corporate goals need to measure and be redefined to include sustainability. This involves a thorough assessment of the strategic advantages that sustainability can provide. The executive team then needs to work with line managers to turn the revised goals into actionable strategies for individual business units. This is an iterative process as each individual business unit searches for new business opportunities in line with the corporation's overall sustainability agenda. Individual managers can also build on initiatives already undertaken through TQEM/EMS programmes or on skills-development programmes, job redesign and pilot-teaming initiatives. In the process, widespread involvement of staff at all levels leads to upward feedback about the goals and strategies, which may result in some modification of them. It is important at this stage that the projects developed have clear strategic relevance and are not simply the ad hoc projects of individual enthusiasts.

Step 2: Development and systematic alignment of measurement systems with corporate goals. This step involves the design and use of measurement systems to monitor ecological and human performance. Such systems are aligned with corporate objectives and linked to broader performance systems such as the triple bottom line. The aim is to use the resulting information to further drive the development of capabilities in product and process design to increase sustainability.

Step 3: Diagnosis of opportunities. Opportunities for 'quick wins' are identified and resources channelled into those areas. In other areas of business activity, a constant scanning is taking place of internal opportunities to achieve strategic sustainability. Resources are shifted into research and development and future opportunity areas. Competitors and potential allies are identified. Resources are also shifted to the individual business-unit level to support new developments there. Culture-change programmes are designed, aimed at modifying corporate culture to support the drive to achieve sustainability goals.

Step 4: Implementation and diffusion of successful practices both internally and externally. Successful product and service practices, measurement systems and human resource approaches are then diffused internally. Slow-moving business units are linked to 'star' or good performers to improve the performance of these areas. At the senior management level, more time is devoted to engaging suppliers and other external parties to take part in the initiatives. At the grass-roots level, business-unit performance is supported by the provision of new resources, training and development initiatives and the development of key performance indicators (KPI) for all relevant staff.

Step 5: Review, monitoring and alignment. Results of initiatives on both the ecological and human-sustainability fronts are made available internally and externally. Third-party auditors are invited to review the strategic directions, challenge strongly held corporate assumptions and generate ideas for future opportunities for competitive advantage.

Employees and managers alike are rewarded for strong performance on triple-bottom-line measures. Feedback mechanisms are used to further develop and enhance human and ecological capabilities and develop the next range of sustainable products, processes and services.

Introducing new tools and techniques

The movement towards strategic sustainability has raised new issues over the tools, techniques and methods that corporations use to monitor their performance (for example, various reporting systems and certification schemes described in Chapter 3) and inspire corporate transformation (such as The Natural Step). Earlier chapters referred to programmes and systems such as TQEM and EMS. In this section, we outline the benefits of such programmes – particularly the measurement systems that enable organizations to collect information on their performance and that enable them to set targets and goals. This monitoring of human and ecological performance, established in the compliance phase, is an essential element in the attainment of strategic sustainability. We shall examine first the operational benefits of such systems, then move on to explore how they can be used to inform the strategic directions of corporations and, finally, outline some risks involved with the use of measurement systems.

As we saw in Chapters 3 and 4, moving through the compliance and efficiency phases requires that organizations develop systems for collecting and evaluating information on performance. Generally, in these early stages, monitoring and data-collection systems focus on operational activities. For example, environmental reporting systems may focus on monitoring pollution or waste levels, with the goal being to use TQEM programmes to move towards zero waste or zero emissions at particular business-unit locations. In pursuing human sustainability in the compliance and efficiency modes, organizations will often monitor their performance in terms of operational factors, such as health and safety incidents and absenteeism. Such monitoring systems allow individual managers and business units to comply with legislative requirements and track costs. These systems form the base from which broader strategic sustainability initiatives can be launched.

As corporations develop strategic sustainability initiatives, they systematize and expand such information systems. The Fuji Xerox Eco Manufacturing plant in Sydney, Australia, exemplifies this approach. When it began to retrieve components of its damaged office equipment, instead of allowing them to be thrown into landfill, it found that it could analyse where faults had occurred and why. This product information was then used to redesign components to extend their life. For instance, the redesign of a small roller spring, worth only 5 cents, saved millions of dollars by significantly extending the working life of each roller. Or in the case of its new team-based organization, teams become responsible for collecting information on their own performance in terms of product, processes and customers. They use this information to leverage further performance improvements, identify gaps in their skills and knowledge base and develop proactive programmes to address these limitations.

Corporations that have moved into the strategic phase increasingly align their internal tools and systems with other reporting initiatives of environmental and social performance. For instance, such ambitious initiatives are being undertaken by ABB, Daimler-Benz, BT and Toyota. In 2001 Clarke noted the following trends in the movement towards broader measurement systems:[85]

- an increased willingness to use such systems to engage with a broader range of stakeholders interested in different elements of the company performance;

- a shift towards complementing the measurement of tangibles with those of intangibles – that is, the social capital of the firm;
- the broadening of social and environmental reporting both within the organization and in public forums and the development of more systematic ways of reporting;
- the creation of a sense of legitimacy in the process by increasing involvement of external parties in the auditing and verification process.

We now see the shift to Integrated Reporting, where the sustainability report is brought together with the financial report and the focus is on value creation through bringing together strategy, risk, performance and sustainability.[86] Finally, however, as with any reporting system, there exist some inherent challenges such as bringing together the Global Reporting Initiative approach focused on materiality and Integrated Reporting focused on value creation.

Linking operational processes to sustainable strategy

We mentioned earlier in this chapter that, in the efficiency phase, the prime focus of sustainability initiatives was on creating effective operational systems. As the organization moves into the strategic phase, these systems have to be linked to the emerging sustainability strategies so that they can support them.

However, to be effective, the linking of operational systems to sustainability strategy requires a shift in values and culture. Hoffman has identified the need to change traditional values, the way managers typically view organizations and technical problems.[87] Value shifts by employees, engineers and other key stakeholders are important prerequisites in identifying innovative solutions to existing problems and potential new opportunities.

For instance, Hawkins, Lovins and Lovins provide examples of how strategic knowledge can be linked with operational processes and emphasizes the importance of changing values to identify such opportunities: realizing that changes in the size of pipes could modify the flow of processes in a plant and result in efficiencies for business units.[88] This case provides a clear example of the linking of operational knowledge, embedded in the minds of scientists, engineers and employees of the organization, with the strategic approach of gaining long-term sustainability outcomes, embedded in the minds of executives.

In other words, organizations need to create cultures which provide opportunities for employees to undertake 'out of the box' thinking and play 'maverick roles' in identifying strategic sustainability opportunities. The human sustainability tradition already has developed processes which can be utilized to solve problems – such as total quality management (TQM) practices. However, TQM systems are tightly controlled and managed problem-solving approaches and must be modified to provide for creative thinking if organizations are to integrate operational and strategic practices. Operational thinking cannot be allowed to dominate: managers also need creative thinking for strategic initiatives. Contradictions need to be managed so that the two mind-sets can co-exist.

At a more macro level, the new field of industrial ecology also provides insight into the benefits of linking operational and strategic processes. The operational processes revolve around finding synergies in the industrial eco-system in order to create closed-loop systems. This involves the creation and management of strategic alliances between different firms within the industrial eco-system. It requires the development of competencies in the management of strategic alliances, in the exploration of industrial interconnections and in the management of trust. Cohen-Rosenthal believes that central to the success of effective industrial ecology applications are skills in human decision making, imagination and learning.[89] He reports a comment made by Tachi Kiuchi, managing director of Mitsubishi Electric and chairman of the Future 500, a high-level group exploring industrial ecology:

> When I visited the rainforest, I realized that it was a model of a perfect learning organization. A place that excels by learning to adapt to what it doesn't have. A rainforest has almost no resources. The soil is thin. There are few nutrients. It consumes almost nothing. Wastes are food. Design is capital. Yet rainforests are incredibly productive. They are home to millions of types of plants and animal, more than two thirds of all biodiversity, so perfectly mixed that the system is more efficient, and more creative than any business in the world. Imagine how creative, how productive, how ecologically benign we could be if we could run our companies like rainforests.[90]

Creating enabling structures and designs

Organizations will fail to address ecological and social issues unless systems, designs and structures are changed to support sustainability initiatives. Organizations can impede the attainment of sustainability in three ways: first, rigid corporate structures can insulate organization systems and processes from a broad range of relevant information: systems that rely on inspired leaders rather than establishing structural or systemic solutions are particularly vulnerable; second, the established routines and systems of many corporations promote and protect the status quo: sustainability initiatives, particularly in the strategic sustainability phase, can be a threat to command-and-control-style management systems, managers who have risen to power in the command-and-control systems frequently resist the transition to alternative enabling organizational structures; finally, many current organization designs limit or deny access to a range of stakeholders whose participation is vital for the pursuit of sustainable initiatives. Traditional organizations tend to be focused on a limited set of stakeholders, in particular boards of directors and shareholders. Other stakeholders, such as unions, green groups and community groups, are often seen as hostile forces that may harm current organizational performance. Redefining these groups as resource and information opportunities rather than problems demands a significant shift of perspective.

However, organizational design can play an important contributing role in the development of human and ecological capabilities. Hierarchies are killers of creativity and initiative and impede the use of employee knowledge. Companies such as Xerox found that team-based structures are more conducive to the generation of employee knowledge and empower employees to use such knowledge. Team-based structures enable employees to have input, discretion over decision making and provision of information. Team-based organization architectures, which include project teams and virtual teams based on new information technologies, provide the basis for capturing and utilizing employee knowledge and competence in real-time situations.

Building employee knowledge and commitment

Strategic sustainability requires employee input and commitment. The successful implementation of various operational programmes such as TQEM is reliant on human capital and workforce skill. The experience of firms such as Interface demonstrates the need to develop and utilize employee capital and knowledge to achieve innovation, agility and high performance.

Organizations that have shifted to the strategic approach value human resource practices around new workplace cultures, enhanced adaptability, team-based work and project work and are keen to experiment with new ventures, such as virtual teams, that characterize 'silo busting' approaches to sustainability. The focus in these organizations is on developing and promoting talent, increasing autonomy and being responsive and flexible. Similarly, these firms typically create reward structures that allow managers to foster these conditions and that encourage employees to look beyond their organization by rewarding their efforts in community assistance and community building.

In a empirical study, it was found that within organizations there exist at least four distinct categories of understanding of corporate sustainability. These included: a corporation working towards sustainable long-term economic performance; a corporation working towards positive outcomes for the natural environment; a corporation that supports people and social outcomes; and a corporation with a holistic approach. One implication from this study is that the change agents guiding strategic-sustainability programmes can motivate people by designing change-management programmes to appeal to people holding these different views, to deliver sustainability products and services.[91] We would add a another implication – that it is important to define very carefully the outcomes to be achieved by any sustainability strategy, rather than to leave the strategy couched in ambiguous abstractions like 'sustainability' and 'corporate social responsibility'.

The innovative performance of Nucor Steel, a US-based firm, is reliant in part upon the development and utilization of its human capital. At the heart of this strategy lies a social ecology that enables Nucor to: create knowledge internally through the encouragement of experimentation; acquire external knowledge as a consequence of good reward structures and a reputation for being an 'ideal employer'; and, finally, retain and use the knowledge it has developed. By social ecology, we mean the culture, structure, information systems, processes, people and leadership that enable the company to pursue its knowledge-management approach. The concrete actions that Nucor has taken include: the use of group incentive schemes; the encouragement of experimentation and 'play'; risk taking; rewards for knowledge sharing; and transfers within the company to diffuse knowledge. These have helped to create Nucor's innovative approach to knowledge management and human-capital development.[92]

Building executive leadership and stewardship

Strategic proactivity is a demonstrated commitment by the senior executive team and the board to actively pursue and develop corporate capabilities, products, processes and designs that align sustainability with the corporation's overall strategic orientations. Strategic proactivity encourages the use of distributed leadership approaches – rewarding innovation and initiatives that drive the company further towards its sustainability goals. Strategic proactivity opens the corporation to third-party scrutiny, as a way of improving or embedding sustainability practices within the organization. In particular, one of the key drivers of sustainability performance for an organization is the commitment by the executives to the large-scale changes and reforms required for sustainability to take place. They outline and live a compelling vision for the organization.

While executive leadership is crucial for sustainability, such leadership needs to be reinforced by the corporate values, the funding of corporate change programmes and willingness to transform organizations towards these ends. CEOs of companies that have achieved outstanding sustainability outcomes, such as Westpac, Interface and Rockcote, highlight the importance of social strategies in building and developing the human capital of the organization. These executives believe that it is important for CEOs and other senior managers to address people's needs and expectations and to reward their efforts by taking time to communicate openly and honestly. They not only believe in these values but enact them in their day-to-day activities. Because they model these values with integrity, others follow their example and the values then become 'human capital assets' within the organization.

The success of senior managers in this area is also determined by the skill with which they draw together different sustainability initiatives within the overall strategy of the organization and its ongoing programmes and operations. The senior executive role is not only about formulating commitment but about integrating the transformation into the business strategies of the organization.[93] Reinhardt argues that 'Managers need to go beyond the question: "Does it pay to be green?" and ask instead: "Under what conditions do particular lines of environmental investment deliver benefits to shareholders?"'[94]

Developing differentiated stakeholder strategies

Business alone cannot achieve sustainability. To achieve sustainability, corporations also require inputs from both governments and communities. Some organizations have already built capabilities associated with forming internal communities of practice that are fluid structures formed around areas of interest and expertise in organizations. An example of a community of practice may be a community of professionals who gather and share information around particular technical problems or solutions. Such communities generate the diffusion and acceptance of tacit knowledge that can be transferred into innovative solutions and actions within organizations. Their contribution to the attainment of sustainability outcomes for organizations lies in their ability to collect, process and diffuse knowledge of a technical and specialized nature to find rapid and innovative solutions. This is a vital component of strategic success.

One method to use in developing a stakeholder strategy is values-based environmental management. It is an approach that aims to develop a strong relationship between corporate strategy and how stakeholders view the organization. The questions proposed by values-based environmental management include: Do stakeholders value your performance? Do products and services contribute to solving environmental issues? Does the stakeholder see you as a problem or part of the solution?[95]

Analysing stakeholders

It is vital to engage key stakeholders and to ensure that they understand and support the new strategic thrust of the organization.

Polonsky suggests a four-step process to analyse stakeholder approaches and identify strategic actions:

Step 1: Identify the stakeholders. That is, identify those who have a vested interest in the outcomes of environmentalism.

Step 2: Determine the stakes. What is each group's stake in the issue? Is it large or small? What specific issues do they revolve around?

Step 3: Determine how expectations are met. Use this to assess the gap between expectations and performance.

Step 4: Adjust the strategy. Strategy is adjusted to minimize/deal constructively with the stakeholder expectations and the gap in performance.[96]

Moving beyond strategic sustainability

Hart and Milstein state:

> To capture sustainable opportunities managers must fundamentally rethink their prevailing views about strategy, technology and markets. Managers who treat sustainable development as an opportunity will drive the creative destruction process and build the foundation to compete in the twenty-first century.[97]

We agree with Hart and Milstein. To attain strategic sustainability managers must develop ecological and human capabilities within the organization. These capabilities enable the organization not only to keep abreast of sustainability issues but to obtain sustainable competitive advantages.

This chapter has outlined some organizational pathways to strategic sustainability. The challenge now, for those who aspire to move beyond strategic sustainability, is to generate the new business models of corporations that move beyond the pursuit of competitive business advantage in order to contribute to a fully sustainable society. This emerging model of business we take up in the next chapter.

Appendix 5: phase 5: strategic proactivity

Human sustainability (HS5)

The workforce skills mix and diversity are seen as integral and vitally important aspects of corporate and business strategies. Intellectual and social capital are used to develop strategic advantage through innovation in products/services. Programmes are instituted to recruit the best talent to the organization and to develop high levels of competence in individuals and groups. In addition, skills are systematized to form the basis of corporate competencies so that the organization is less vulnerable to the loss of key individuals. Emphasis is

Ecological sustainability (ES5)

Proactive environmental strategies supporting ecological sustainability are seen as a source of strategic business opportunities to provide competitive advantage. Product redesign is used to reduce material throughput and to use materials that can be recycled. New products and processes are developed that substitute for or displace existing environmentally damaging products and processes or satisfy emerging community needs around sustainable issues (reforestation; treatment of toxic waste). The organization seeks placed on product and service innovation and speed of response to emerging market demands. Flexible workplace practices are strong features of workplace culture and contribute to the workforce leading more balanced lives. Communities affected by the organization's operations are taken into account and initiatives to address adverse impacts on communities are integrated into corporate strategy. Furthermore, the corporation views itself as a member of community and, as a result, contributes to community betterment by offering sponsorship or employee time to participate in projects aimed at promoting community cohesion and well-being.

competitive leadership through spearheading environmentally friendly products and processes.

Notes

1 M. Porter and C. van der Linde, 'Green and competitive: ending the stalemate', *Harvard Business Review*, 1995, September–October, pp. 121–34, at page 130.
2 D. Cogan, *Corporate Governance and Climate Change: Making the Connection, CERES*, Boston: Investor Responsibility Research Centre, 2006, p. 14.
3 Ibid.
4 R. Anderson, *Interface Celebrates Ten Years of Sustainability in Action.* Corporate Report, Interface, 2004.
5 Unilever, 'Unilever CEO Review 2012'. Online. Available HTTP: <http://www.unilever.com/sustainable-living/ourapproach/messageceo/> (accessed 12 July 2013).
6 Volvo, 'CEO Comment'. Online. Available HTTP: <http://www.volvo group.com/group/> (accessed 27 June 2013).
7 Marks & Spencer & Accenture, 'Fortune Favours the Brave', 2013. Online. Available HTTP: <http://www.accenture.com/SiteCollectionDocuments/PDF/accenture-fortune-favours-brave-full-report.pdf> (accessed 9 July 2013).
8 Ibid.
9 J. Bryson, and R. Lombardi, 'Balancing product and process sustainability against business profitability: sustainability as a competitive strategy in the property development process', *Business Strategy and the Environment*, 2009, 18 (2), 97–107; E. Fraj-Andrés, E. Martínez-Salinas *et al.*, 'Factors

affecting corporate environmental strategy in Spanish industrial firms', *Business Strategy and the Environment*, 2009, 18 (8), 500–14.

10 B. Walsh, 'Tesla beats the odds – and the haters – but now comes the hard part', *Time Business and Money*, 9 May 2013. Online. Available HTTP: <http://business.time.com/2013/05/10/tesla-beats-the-odds-and-the-haters-but-now-comes-the-hard-part/> (accessed 5 July 2013).

11 Amory Lovins, Research Director of the Rocky Mountains Institute, quoted in E. Stead and J. Stead, *Sustainable Strategic Management*, London: Sharpe, 2004, p. 28.

12 P. Hawken, A. Lovins and L. Lovins, *Natural Capitalism: Creating the Next Industrial Revolution*, London: Earthscan, 1999.

13 D. Dunphy and A. Griffiths, 'Corporate strategic change', in M. Warner (ed.) *International Encyclopaedia of Business and Management*, London: Thomson Learning, 2002.

14 L. Gratton, *Living Strategy: Putting People at the Heart of Corporate Purpose*, London: Financial Times/Prentice-Hall, 2000.

15 A. Pettigrew, *The Awakening Giant,* Oxford: Basil Blackwell, 1985.

16 H. Mintzberg and J. Waters, 'Of strategies deliberate and emergent', *Strategic Management Journal*, 1985, 6 (3), 257–72; H. Mintzberg, *The Rise and Fall of Strategic Planning*, New York: Free Press, 1995; Gratton, *Living Strategy*.

17 Dunphy and Griffiths, 'Corporate strategic change'.

18 M. Porter, *The Competitive Advantage of Nations*, New York: Free Press, 1990.

19 S. Bucolo, 'Design: the Latest Buzzword in the Financial Sector', ABC News, 2013. Online. Available HTTP: http://www.abc.net.au/news/2013-06-24/design-the-latest-buzz-word-in-the-financial-sector/4777254 (accessed 25 June 2013).

20 K. Eisenhardt and J. Martin, 'Dynamic capabilities: what are they?', *Strategic Management Journal,* 2000, 21 (10–11), 1105–21; C. Prahalad and G. Hamel, 'The core competence of the corporation', *Harvard Business Review*, May–June 1990; V. Ambrosini, and C. Bowman, 'What are dynamic capabilities and are they a useful construct in strategic management?', *International Journal Of Management Reviews*, 2009, 11 (1), 29–49.

21 Gratton, *Living Strategy*.

22 The basic competencies outlined are based on: M. Hitt, B. Keats and S. DeMarie, 'Navigating in the new competitive landscape: building strategic flexibility and competitive advantage in the 21st century', *Academy of Management Executive*, November 1998, 12 (4) 22–47; M. Hastings, 'Oil companies in sensitive environments', *Business Strategy and Environment*, 1999, 8, 267–80; S. Sharma and H. Vredenburg, 'Proactive environmental strategy and the development of competitively valuable organizational capabilities', *Strategic Management Journal*, 1998, 19 (5), 729–53.

23 Gratton, *Living Strategy*.

24 M. Hitt, B. Keats and S. DeMarie, 'Navigating in the new competitive landscape: building strategic flexibility and competitive advantage in the

21st century', *Academy of Management Executive*, November 1998, 12 (4) 22–47.

25 A. de Geus, *The Living Company*, Boston, MA: Harvard Business School Press, 1997; J. Collins and J. Porras, *Built to Last*, London: Century, 1994.

26 de Geus, *The Living Company*.

27 K. Kittleson, 'Can a Company Last forever?', 2012. Online. Available HTTP: <http://www.bbc.co.uk/news/business-16611040> (accessed 25 June 2013).

28 Ibid.

29 J. Aragon-Correa, 'Strategic proactivity and firm approach to the natural environment', *Academy of Management Journal*, 1998, 14 (5), 556–67; M. Starik, *Management and the Natural Environment*, Fort Worth, TX: Dryden Press, 1997.

30 A. Hoffman, *Competitive Environmental Strategy: A Guide to the Changing Business Landscape*, Washington, DC: Island Press, 2000.

31 S. Hart, 'A natural resource based view of the firm', *Academy of Management Review*, 1995, 20 (4), 986–1014.

32 Interface, 'Interface Celebrates 10 years of Sustainability in Action, Corporate Communication', Interface, 31 August 2004.

33 A. Griffiths, 'New organisational architectures: creating and retrofitting for sustainability', in D. Dunphy, J. Benveniste, A. Griffiths and P. Sutton (eds) *Sustainability: The Corporate Challenge of the 21st Century*, Sydney: Allen and Unwin, 2001, pp. 219–35; R. Orsato, 'Competitive environmental strategies: when does it pay to be green?', *California Management Review*, 2006, 48 (2), 127–43.

34 J. Pfeffer, 'Producing sustainable competitive advantage through the effective management of people', *Academy of Management Executive*, 2005, 19 (4), 95–106.

35 D. Raths, '100 Best Corporate Citizens', *Business Ethics Magazine*, 2006, 20 (1), pp. 1–9.

36 Gratton, *Living Strategy*.

37 J. Chelliah and S. Benn, 'Hewlett Packard's supply chain', in S. Benn, D. Dunphy and B. Perrott (eds), *Cases in Corporate Sustainability and Change*, Prahan, Australia: Tilde University Press, 2011.

38 M. Delmas, and S. Pekovic, 'Environmental standards and labor productivity: understanding the mechanisms that sustain sustainability', *Journal of Organizational Behavior*, 2013, 34 (2), 230–52.

39 M. Russo and P. Fouts, 'A resource based perspective on corporate environmental performance and profitability', *Academy of Management Journal*, 1997, 40 (3), 534–59; M. Orlitzky, F. Schmidt and S. Rynes, 'Corporate social and financial performance: a meta-analysis', *Organization Studies*, 2003, 24 (3), 403–41.

40 P. Senge and S. Carstedt, 'Innovating our way to the next industrial revolution', *MIT Sloan Management Review*, 2001, Winter, 42 (2) 24–38.

41 M. Porter and M. Kramer, 'Creating shared value', *Harvard Business Review*, 89 (1–2), January–February 2011, 62–77.

42 R. Kahani, 'Xerox Corporation: A Pioneer in Environmental Sustainability', 2012. Online. Available HTTP: <http://www.forbes.com/sites/rahimkanani/2012/03/27/xerox-corporation-a-pioneer-in-environmental-sustainability/> (accessed 27 June, 2013).

43 D. Turner and M. Crawford, *Change Power: Capabilities that Drive Corporate Renewal*, Sydney: Business and Professional Publishing, 1998.

44 Gratton, *Living Strategy*, p. 11.

45 D. Dunphy and B. Perrott, 'Westfield talent management: creating a high performance culture in Australian operations finance', in S. Benn, D. Dunphy and B. Perrott, *Cases in Corporate Sustainability and Change*, Prahan, Australia: Tilde University Press, 2011, pp. 121–37.

46 D. Goldsmith and D. Sansom, 'Sustainable Development and Business Success: Reaching beyond the Rhetoric to Superior Performance', *A report of the Australian Business Foundation and the Foundation for Sustainable Economic Development at the University of Melbourne*, 2005, pp. 2–68.

47 E. Masurel, 'Why SMEs invest in environmental measures: sustainability evidence from small and medium-sized printing firms', *Business Strategy and the Environment*, 2007 16 (3), 190–201.

48 Institute of Chartered Accountants in Australia, *Integrating Sustainability into business Practices: A Case Study Approach*, Blackmores, Sydney, Australia: Institute of Chartered Accountants in Australia, 2011.

49 See McDonalds, 'Want to Know More About Our Quality Scouts', 2013. Online. Available HTTP: <http://www.mcdonalds.co.uk/ukhome/whatmakes mcdonalds/articles/faqs-to-become-a-quality-scout.html> (accessed 6 July 2013).

50 P. Hawken, 'McDonalds and Corporate Social Responsibility?', 2002. Online. Available HTTP: <http://www.sustainablebusiness.com/index.cfm/go/news.feature/id/820 accessed 6 July 2013> (accessed 6 July 2013).

51 A. Kolk, P. Hong and W. van Dolen, 'Corporate social responsibility in China: an analysis of domestic and foreign retailers' sustainability dimensions', *Business Strategy and the Environment*, 2010, 19 (5), 289–303.

52 C. Li, F. Liu and Q. Wang, 'Planning and implementing the greener manufacturing strategy: evidences from western China', *Journal of Science and Technology in China*, 2010, 1 (2), 148–62.

53 R. J. L. Stevens and R. J. Stevenson, 'Harnessing Environmental Sound Technology for Chinese SMEs' Environmental Sustainable Development', *Proceedings of the 9th International Conference on Innovation and Management*, 14–16 November 2012, Eindhoven, The Netherlands, pp. 315–20.

54 R. J. L. Stevens, M. M. Moustapha, P. Evelyn, and R. Jean Stevenson, 'Analysis of the emerging China green era and its influence on small and medium-sized enterprises development: review and perspectives', *Journal of*

Sustainable Development, 2013, 6 (4), published online at http://ccsenet.org/journal/index.php/jsd/article/view/24795, pp. 86–105.

55 S. Hart and M. Milstein, 'Global sustainability and the creative destruction of industries', *Sloan Management Review*, 1999, 41 (1), 22–33.

56 S. Hart, 'Creating sustainable value', *Academy of Management Executive*, 2003, 17 (3), 56–67; Orsato, 'Competitive environmental strategies'.

57 Anheuser-Busch InBev, 'Social Responsibility Report', 2012. Online. Available HTTP: <http://www.abinbev.com/go/social_responsibility/environment/water_use.cfm#sthash.gKDpOLMF.dpuf> (accessed 30 June 2013).

58 M. Dorazio, 'Anheuser-Busch InBev: Less Water, More Beer', 2013. Online. Available HTTP: <http://greenplug.nu/anheuser-busch-inbev-less-water-more-beer/> (accessed 30 June 2013).

59 M. Reed and D. Chiang, 'Eco-advantage strategies and supply chain effects', *Journal of Supply Chain and Operations Management*, 2012, 10 (1), 212–25.

60 Finally, when The Body Shop was sold to the international giant L'Oreal, which does not have the same commitment against animal testing, its founder, Anita Roddick, argued that she would be able to influence policy from the inside. *Guardian*, 'A brief history of The Body Shop', 2011. Online. Available HTTP: <http://www.guardian.co.uk/fashion/fashion-blog/2011/nov/21/brief-history-of-body-shop> (accessed 15 November 2013).

61 J. Elkington, *Cannibals with Forks: Triple Bottom Line of 21st Century Business*, Oxford: Capstone Publishing, 1997, p. 333.

62 R. Jaikumar, 'Postindustrial manufacturing', *Harvard Business Review*, November–December 1986, 64 (6), 69–76.

63 M. L. Barnett, and R. M. Salomon, 'Does it pay to be really good? Addressing the shape of the relationship between social and financial performance', *Strategic Management Journal*, 2012, 33 (11), 1304–20.

64 S. Hart, 'Beyond greening', *Harvard Business Review*, 1997, January–February, 66–76; J. Magretta, 'Growth through global sustainability', *Harvard Business Review*, 1997, January–February, 75 (1), 79–88.

65 J. Elkington, *The Chrysalis Economy*, Oxford: Capstone, 2001.

66 Wingspread Statement 1998, Wingspread Conference on the Precautionary Principle. Online. Available HTTP: <http://www.sehn.org/wing.html> (accessed 15 September 2013).

67 M. Metherell, 'Gene labels scare off food makers', *Sydney Morning Herald*, 15 November 2001, 1.

68 S. Hart and S. Sharma, 'Engaging fringe stakeholders for competitive imagination', *Academy of Management Executive*, 2004, 18 (1), 7–18.

69 Ibid.

70 Ibid.

71 Ethical Corporation, 'Briefing Supply Chains; Patagonia Footprint', 2012. Online. Available HTTP: <http://www.patagonia.com/us/footprint/suppliers-map/> (accessed 12 July 2013).

72 R. Orsato, 'The ecological competence of the organization: competing for sustainability', paper presented to the *16th EGOS Colloquium, Helsinki, Finland*, July 2000.

73 R. Miles and C. Snow, *Fit, Failure and the Hall of Fame*, New York: Free Press, 1994.

74 B. Perrott and D. Dunphy, 'IKEA: a company's progression to a strategic approach', in S. Benn, D. Dunphy and B. Perrott, *Cases in Corporate Sustainability and Change: A Multidisciplinary Approach*, Prahan, Australia: Tilde University Press, 2011, pp. 48–63.

75 Elkington, *Cannibals with Forks*, p. 3.

76 Balanced Scorecard Institute, 'Balanced Scorecard Adopters', 2013. Online. Available HTTP: <http://balancedscorecard.org/BSCResources/Aboutthe BalancedScorecard/BalancedScorecardAdopters/tabid/136/Default.aspx> (accessed 3 July 2013).

77 Balanced Scorecard Institute, 'Linking Sustainability to Strategy using the Balanced Scorecard', 2013. Online. Available HTTP: <http://www.balanced scorecard.org/Portals/0/PDF/LinkingSustainabilitytoCorporateStrategy UsingtheBalancedScorecard.pdf> (accessed 3 July 2013).

78 Anon., 'Case studies: visionary leadership', *Business Week*, 3 May 1999.

79 Nike, 'Sustainability'. Online. Available HTTP: <http://nikeinc.com/ sustainability> (accessed 5 July 2013).

80 Ethical Corporation, 'Briefing Supply Chains'.

81 B. Hirsh and P. Sheldrake, *Inclusive Leadership*, Melbourne: Information Australia, 2000, p. 20.

82 Hoffman, *Competitive Environmental Strategy*; Stead and Stead, *Sustainable Strategic Management*.

83 Hoffman, *Competitive Environmental Strategy*.

84 B. Nattrass and M. Altomare, *The Natural Step for Business*, Gabriola Island: New Society Publishers, 1999, pp. 47–74.

85 T. Clarke, 'Balancing the triple bottom line: financial, social and environmental performance', *Journal of General Management*, 2001, 26 (4), 1–11.

86 See Integrated Reporting Discussion Paper at http://www.theiirc.org/ discussion-paper/ (accessed 5 July 2013).

87 Hoffman, *Competitive Environmental Strategy*.

88 Paul Hawken, Amory Lovins and Hunter Lovins (2010) *Natural Capitalism: The Next Industrial Revolution*, London: Earthscan.

89 E. Cohen-Rosenthal, 'A walk on the human side of industrial ecology', *American Behavioral Scientist*, 2000, 44 (2), 245–64; J. Benyus, *Biomimicry: Innovation Inspired by Nature*, New York: William Morrow Paperbacks, 1997.

90 Cohen-Rosenthal, 'A walk on the human side', p. 259.

91 S. Russell, N. Haigh and A. Griffiths, 'Understandings of Corporate Sustainability', *Academy of Management Conference*, Atlanta, 2006.

92 A. Gupta and V. Govindarajan, 'Knowledge management's social dimension: lessons from Nucor Steel', *Sloan Management Review*, 2000, 42 (1), 71–80.

93 S. Banerjee, 'Managerial perceptions of corporate environmentalism: interpretations from industry and strategic implications for organizations', *Journal of Management Studies*, 2001, 38 (4), 479–513.

94 F. Reinhardt, 'Bringing the environment down to earth', *Harvard Business Review*, 1999, July–August, 77 (4), 149–56, esp. p. 150.

95 J. Blumber, A. Korsuold and G. Blum, 'Value based environmental management and sustainability', in G. Wilson and D. Sasseville (eds) *Sustaining Environmental Management Success*, New York: John Wiley, 1999, p. 220.

96 M. Polonsky, 'Incorporating the natural environment in corporate strategy: a stakeholder approach', *Journal of Business Strategy*, 1995, 12 (2), 152–5.

97 Hart and Milstein, 'Global sustainability and the creative destruction of industries', p. 32.

6   The sustaining corporation

Generating a future reality

In this chapter we aim to present a vivid image of the 'sustaining corporation', that is, the corporation which fully incorporates the tenets of human and ecological sustainability into its own operations and which also works actively to support the application of sustainability principles throughout the rest of the society.

We freely admit that there are few if any organizations today that fully embody this socio- and eco-centric ideal. To date the ones most cited, such as Patagonia, have not been public companies but are relatively small and privately owned. Some of these innovative smaller companies have not always been able to maintain the advances they have made, particularly through the transitions of takeover or CEO succession. This indicates that a CEO's leadership plays a crucial role in shaping a company's corporate sustainability strategy. The challenge is to learn from these early adventures in sustainability and extend that learning to larger public corporations. There is, however, another source of learning. Many larger companies have experimented successfully with aspects of sustainability and we illustrate the ideal with case examples of what some of these organizations have achieved.

For instance, Green Mountain Coffee Roasters (GMCR), a publicly listed company since 1993, has developed an extensive form of community engagement and consultation in supporting both communities and the environment from locations where it sources coffee beans.[1] Reflecting this commitment, the company is already one of the largest purchasers in the world of Fair Trade Certified Coffee. Building on this history, the 2012 Sustainability Report notes three new areas of focus: Resilient Supply Chains, Sustainable Products and Thriving People and Communities. Reflecting the benefits of this integrated approach, GMCR delivered a 46 per cent increase in net sales in 2012 while also improving energy efficiency, recycling more waste and reducing the proportion of waste sent to the landfill. Highlights of the fiscal 2012 report include:

- GMCR more than tripled the amount of waste chaff, burlap, coffee, powder, and tea that it composted, and increased recycling of corrugated boxes, boxboard, paper and plastics by 50 per cent in its facilities, compared to the previous year.
- Over $10 million in grant money was allocated to supply-chain communities, including food-security projects for over 20,000 coffee-farming families around the world.
- The company maintained an employee retention rate of approximately 90 per cent.
- Sixty-five per cent of full-time employees volunteered through a company-sponsored programme called Café Time, which allows employees up to 52 paid hours per year to volunteer.[2]

GMCR's goals for fiscal 2013 include continuing financial support for projects addressing food security in coffee-growing communities, increasing the sourcing of sustainable coffees and further reducing the amount of waste sent to landfills.

According to GMCR President and CEO, Brian P. Kelley:

> There's significant value at the intersection of innovation, relationships, and sustainability. Producing this report benchmarks our achievements and provides important transparency into our challenges. We're creating a blueprint that integrates sustainability more deeply into our operations and across our value chain.

Others, such as SC Johnson, have moved into the development of environmentally safe products and the reduction of greenhouse gas emissions, while some state-owned enterprises, such as the Canadian electricity company BC Hydro, are striving to become 'footprint neutral'. BC Hydro is already one of the lowest greenhouse gas emitters in North America and has committed to initiatives to support clean energy, such as developing expertise around plug-in vehicles.

None of these organizations yet meets the ideal, but collectively they help us create an image of how a fully committed organization would operate.

The future is emerging around us, if we have eyes to see it, as innovative companies explore sustainability practices in a range of operations. The analogy is of constructing a jigsaw puzzle – we assemble one piece from one organization, another piece from another organization, until we have an overall image of the organization of the future which is modelling sustainability in its own operations and supporting the wider sustainability movement. The sustaining organization is not only sustainable itself but is also promoting and supporting the further development of sustainability principles throughout society and for future generations.

This image may seem a dream. It is. Managerial leadership is increasingly about having ambitious dreams and then ensuring that these dreams are realized. Ian Lowe writes: 'in fact, practically all desirable features of modern life were once utopian visions made real by visionaries who worked systematically to achieve their dreams of a better world'.[3] We have said in previous editions that such dreams are only reality waiting to happen. But now the new reality is upon us as smaller companies are being pushed by their supply chains to measure up to procurement requirements. For example, IBM is requiring its suppliers to deploy a corporate responsibility and environmental management system and to establish sustainability goals, measure their performance against them, as well as to publicly disclose their results.[4]

The internet was once a dream – until it was put in place and revolutionized the economy and society. Our argument here is that transformational social change is now happening at incredible speed and that the onset of the 'third wave' will make achieving corporate sustainability a political, economic and social priority. For instance, a KPMG survey in 2005 found for the Global 250 companies that Corporate Responsibility reporting had increased from 45 per cent in 2002 to 52 per cent in 2005 and, if integrated annual reports were included, the figure was 64 per cent.[5] The challenge is to turn dreams into corporate visions and visions into concrete, practical actions.

It is ridiculous that we allow businesses to continue to destroy our planet. The bottom line is now simple – people are dying because of environmental degradation, people are forced into working for subsistence wages because companies need to increase their profitability, those who resist the progress of capitalism are subjected to torture and even murdered by the state because they have campaigned for human rights. Yet business still operates in concert with the institutions and governments which cause such suffering and people still buy its products. Doing business in countries which abuse human rights and torture citizens means that you accept that practice. Not protesting when your opponents are hanged is tantamount to killing them yourself. To buy the products of such a company is to agree with its actions.[6]

These are strong statements, but we are moving to a society where more people will support these views and act on them. More ethical investment funds are being created around the world and the capital invested in these funds is growing every day. At first glance, it seems strange that radical green activists and conservative financial institutions are now working together to ensure that corporations act responsibly, but this is a regular occurrence now. We have examined the way that powerful drivers of change are converging to change the ground rules for corporate activity. The result is that old-style companies face increasing pressure from social and environmental activists and can no longer assume that they will be supported even by financial institutions. The future lies with those organizations that anticipate changes such as this and take the lead as the changes unfold.

The third wave

So we go on to outline the nature of the third wave. The third wave sees society moving into a new paradigm where complexity and interconnectedness are central, where transformational change is more widespread and occurs over shorter time periods, where direction and momentum are achieved through alliances, shared commitment to common goals, high levels of innovation and loose coupling. In this world, there will be an increase in the number of temporary organizations formed for specific purposes. Whether long-lasting or temporary, these organizations of the future will be strongly value driven. They will be responding to an emerging shift in global values that is already becoming evident in a number of ways:

- growing scientific consensus and concern about the looming environmental crisis;
- international co-operation between governments, corporations and environmental groups to protect the environment;
- increasing questioning of the value of the dominant neoliberal economic model, accompanied by the rise of ecological economics as an alternative;

- increasing use of the precautionary principle as a policy tool;
- development of international regulatory agreements to promote social justice and protect the environment;
- the rise of post-modern philosophy questioning the association between positivist science and materialistic views of progress, and rejecting social and environmental exploitation in favour of care for all humans, other species and the natural world.[7]

This last point represents a re-emphasis on spirituality and the emergence of a new way of conducting science so that it is embedded in values that affirm biodiversity and social justice. Happily, this is taking place as professional scientists set up ethics committees and sign public statements about critical issues of sustainability such as global warming.

The most successful of these sustaining organizations will act both locally and globally, will put a premium on speedily repositioning themselves strategically to take advantage of new market opportunities and will add value through providing new levels of customized service. In this regard, they are acting strategically. For these organizations, sustainability is central to their corporate strategies and a vital ingredient in how they assess their effectiveness. They see success as dependent on developing active stakeholder relationships with a variety of community groups – they build 'stakeholder capital'. They regard their success as dependent also on the 'intellectual and skill capital' of their workforce. Therefore, they systematically develop the skills of those in the core workforce and contribute to skill development in the workforces of suppliers and alliance partners. They are consciously committed to actions that increase the human capability base of society and that maintain and restore the biosphere. For those who contribute to the leadership of these organizations, the corporation is a vital link in the ecology itself and in the intergenerational continuity of society. They are 'sustaining organizations'.

We contrast this world with the world of the first wave, where organizations were discrete and enduring entities with clear boundaries, were primarily cost driven, emphasized hierarchy and control, and maintained traditional ways of doing things, resisting change unless the traditional ways were clearly failing. We also contrast the third-wave world with the second wave, where organizations sought to establish radically new levels of efficiency and to develop more forward-looking business strategies to ensure their futures.

First-wave organizations largely took the ecological and social environment for granted. At worst, some actively opposed (and still do) moves to protect the biosphere from destructive exploitation, or pressure for their active involvement in community development. Typically, they argued that business exists simply to make a profit. Or they ignored sustainability issues, concentrating on a narrowly defined business concept, and treating the natural and social environment as a 'free good' or a regrettable source of cost. At best, they emphasized compliance with legal restraints (health and safety regulations, waste treatment) and pursued positive sustainability policies only when these measures reduced costs or provided a clear competitive advantage. Both first-wave and early second-wave organizations tended to ignore the wider issues of ecological and social responsibility, generally failing to recognize and measure the negative impacts of their activities on communities and on the ecological carrying capacity of the environment (unless public reaction compelled them to do so). Issues of social and environmental responsibility were, at best, regarded as marginal to the core business of the company and to its business strategies. They emphasized the goods and services they provided and conveniently ignored the 'bads' and 'disservices' they contributed. This, however, undergoes a significant change as organizations move into Phase 5: strategic proactivity.

> The basic development patterns of the industrial era are not sustainable.
> (P. Senge, in *Sloan Management Review*[8])

If we are to turn around the serious social and environmental degradation we have created, there must be a radical departure from past practices. We argue for a reinterpretation of the role of the corporation in society and for a reintegration of the economy into ecology and the global community. Economics cannot be separate from issues of species survival, social justice and spirituality. Similarly, science and technology cannot operate without regard to the risks they create for survival, health and human happiness. And businesses cannot ignore the costs, to future generations, of operations that outrun the rate of resource replacement. Hoffman argues that more and more businesses are seeing opportunities and rapidly moving to make the most of them.[9] However, currently many other corporations use accounting practices that ignore the social and environmental costs of their business practices. We are all part of a living system that is dependent on a delicate balance of gases in the atmosphere and a thin residue of soil created over millennia. Our activities must preserve and enrich this precious life support system, not degrade it.

Similarly, we all come into this world as helpless infants and depend for our subsequent development as mature human beings on a society that provides caring relationships, socialization and education. Traditional economics tends to ignore these functions, for example, of parents caring for their children in the home. The proper function of the economy is to support a healthy biosphere and quality of social life for the earth's human population. Consequently, the sustaining organization will create a social and ethical balance sheet and be accountable for it. An important step in recognizing these accountabilities was the development of the United Nations Guiding Principles on Business and Human Rights, endorsed by the United Nations in 2011.[10] A number of companies are working with these Principles to address their specific human rights issues. For example, in partnership with BSR, Microsoft states that it has undertaken an approach based on four key elements:

1 An enquiry-based approach involving consulting with a wide cross-section of Microsoft employees which helped to define a human rights strategy tailored to Microsoft's specific products, technologies and business model.
2 A Global Human Rights Statement: Publishing this allowed Microsoft to set out its commitment to human rights, as well as key beliefs about how the company could most effectively respect human rights.
3 Human rights impact assessments: This allows Microsoft to look across all of its operations.
4 Ongoing work: Microsoft uses the findings from the assessments to inform its work going forward.[11]

Such initiatives reflect the shift in academic and practitioner interest towards collaborative relationships rather than the past obsession with competition, 'winners' and 'winning'. Underpinning this shift is the recognition by business that dealing with current global realities is reliant upon capabilities such as systems thinking. For example, many organizations that have moved to the strategic proactivity phase have incorporated industrial ecology principles that draw on life-cycle approaches to materials and energy flows. Although often highly technical, these approaches are also reliant for their success upon iterative cycles of human interaction and collaboration that lead to knowledge development.

The third wave departs from the other waves in that it is essentially regenerative, organizations deploying radical, emergent approaches to business such as Shared Value, Business at Bottom of the Pyramid (BoP), Biomimicry and Collaborative Consumption – all of which are crucially dependent on partnering and collaboration. Each of these models for how business might work in a new, more responsible and sustainable reality is grounded in cooperation and takes its key principles from social systems approaches.[12] A summary of these new business models in terms of their key principles and implementation examples is at Table 6.1.

Table 6.1 *Models for sustainable business*

Business principles	Core concepts	Example
Shared Value	Companies can create shared value opportunities: • by reconceiving products and markets • by redefining productivity in the value chain • by enabling local cluster development.[a]	Revolution Foods provides 60,000 fresh, healthful and nutritious meals to students daily at a higher gross margin than traditional competitors.[a]
BoP	Targeting BoP market can lead to innovation and more sustainable livelihood for the very poor. Business profits are associated with low margins but high unit sales.	Proliferation of micro-lending in the informal economy (e.g. Grameen Bank). Products such as affordable renewable energy devices targeted at rural poor.[b]
Biomimicry	Design innovations and ways of doing business based on principles utilized in nature such as piggy-backing on other efforts already in place.	Front end of Shinkansen Bullet train modelled on beak of kingfisher. Velcro and the self-cleaning Lotusan paint are both products inspired by living organisms.[c]
Collaborative Consumption	Traditional approaches to sharing, lending, swapping, etc. redefined through technology and peer communities.[d]	Business models include tiered subscription, initial membership plus usage. eBay and numerous firms sharing cars, accommodation, etc.

Notes: [a] M. E. Porter and M. R. Kramer. 'Creating shared value', *Harvard Business Review*, 89 (1–2), January–February 2011, 1–17.
[b] C. Prahalad and S. Hart, 'The fortune at the bottom of the pyramid', *Strategy +Business*, 26 (2), first quarter 2002, 54–67.
[c] See more business ideas inspired by nature at Biomimicy, Green Biz. 'Dandelions Leverage Free Energy', http://www.greenbiz.com/slideshow/2013/01/11/dandelions-leverage-free-energy (accessed 11 July 2013).
[d] R. Botsman, 'Purpose with Profits: Collaborative Consumption Business Models', 2011, www.nesta.org.uk/ (accessed 12 July 2013).

Putting the jigsaw together

What, then, are the characteristics of the sustaining corporation?

A new social contract

We begin with the corporation's connection with its key stakeholders and the notion of a social and ecological contract negotiated by management with these stakeholders or their representatives. This social contract provides the rationale for the corporation's continued existence, for it defines the mutually valuable exchanges that will sustain the firm's ongoing network of relationships. It also defines the organization's mission and legitimizes the organization's right to operate, to produce valued goods and services, and its responsibility not to produce 'bads' (pollution, waste and so on) and 'disservices' (socially or ecologically destructive processes). Concomitant with this is the development of a stakeholder accountability process that emphasizes transparency and openness in reporting on delivery to stakeholder expectations. For example, the 2011 KPMG Survey showed that 95 per cent of the 250 largest companies in the world (G250 companies) now report on their corporate responsibility (CR) activities, showing a dramatic increase from the 52 per cent we stated in a previous edition of this book as measured by the same researchers. Currently two-thirds of non-reporters are based in the USA. Revealing rapid gains in some developing countries, the survey showed, for example, that almost 60 per cent of China's largest companies already report on CR metrics.[13]

That new business models are now having an impact in terms of business and, crucially, investor decision making, is further demonstrated by the rapidly increasing number of responsible investment funds on the global market and the relatively high performance of these funds to date. For example, the 2011 Benchmark Report of the Responsible Investment Association Australasia showed that the average responsible investment fund delivered higher returns than the average mainstream fund in every one of the 12 categories covered in the report (across one, three, five and seven years, and for Australian, overseas and balanced funds).[14]

But all this begs the question: Who are the stakeholders? There is now a substantial body of work delineating stakeholder theory.[15] There are differences of opinion expressed in this literature about whether to confine the definition of stakeholder to those individuals and groups who are vital to the survival of the firm or to expand it to a wider set of groups whose interests are affected by the firm's actions. These views correspond to the two major uses of the word 'sustainability', which cause considerable confusion in the field: (a) the firm's ability to sustain itself, versus (b) its impact on the sustainability of its social and ecological environment.

Both definitions are useful and some writers suggest that we distinguish between 'primary' and 'secondary' stakeholders.[16] Primary stakeholders are those engaged in some transactions with the firm and without whom the firm would cease to exist. Secondary stakeholders are those who are not essential for the firm's survival but who can influence the firm or who are influenced by the firm (or both). The distinction makes it clear that, to pursue its own immediate self-interest, the firm must concern itself with the expectations of primary stakeholders; however, it also has ethical responsibilities to secondary stakeholders.[17] In a similar vein, Hart and Sharma differentiate between core stakeholders and peripheral stakeholders. Much of the strategy literature has been obsessed by the core stakeholders of an organization. This focus on a limited number of key stakeholders has had disastrous consequence for some organizations – such as Monsanto (covered in Chapter 5). For others, such as HP and Unilever, the recognition of the importance of peripheral stakeholders has created new product and business opportunities and the formation of new social contracts with communities.[18] Unilever, for example, has taken up the challenge of BoP in Africa, marketing products such as low-cost, climate-stable margarine that does not require refrigeration, using informal sellers – a strategy that, the company argues, itself enables social and economic well-being. A wide range of stakeholders are identified in its Sustainable Living Plan, which commits the company to address sustainability across its value chain, including consumers. Associated activities include setting greenhouse gas targets that have resulted in a 6 per cent decrease per consumer since 2010 (in 2012), but it commits to halving the water associated with the consumer use of its products by 2020.[19]

The potential list of stakeholders includes shareholders and owners, suppliers, customers, government, the community, future generations and the rest of nature: that is, all 20 million or so species on earth. Each organization must decide which are primary and which are secondary. Given the insights provided by Hart and Sharma, we argue for a broad definition of the potential range of stakeholders – one that includes future generations, the good of society as a whole and the natural world.

The social contract that emerges out of a company's interaction with its stakeholders has its visible form in clear, written policies and principles that relate to human resource development, community relations and the ecological environment. It is evident also in the firm's core business strategies and in the way they are interpreted in the process of day-to-day decision making. It is clear that the commitment to sustainability matters because it shows up in decisions about what the corporation both does and does not do. It does not exploit its workforce or pollute the planet with its products or emissions. It does work collaboratively with a variety of community bodies to solve social and environmental problems and to identify and take up opportunities that build community. It does actively help workforce members to develop their personal and professional capabilities; it works actively to foster a healthy biosphere. Smaller companies may find it difficult to generate the resources needed for technical sustainability improvements around sustainability reporting and assurance but, on the other hand, may be able to enact more freely the values of their owners. Take the example of a New Zealand organization which plays out the strong sustainability values of its owners, unhindered by the short-term decision making so prevalent in many of our large business organizations.

State of Grace

State of Grace is a small, family-directed New Zealand funeral business. Its founders were inspired by the vision of establishing their own business which would offer socially and environmentally responsible services to their clients. A key to their services is natural burial – not offering embalming, for instance, unless specifically required. Sustainable timber caskets and natural fibre linings and shallow graves to allow for composting remains are other features of their ecologically responsible services. The owners see their determination to encourage ownership of the burial procedures by the bereaved family as playing out the social responsibility of the business. Families are encouraged to participate in all aspects of the preparations for burial. In that sense, they therefore encourage community engagement and responsiveness. While competition is emerging in the form of mainstream funeral services adding on 'green' options, the owners of State of Grace apparently do not see that as a threat but as a lever for reducing the costs of some of their infrastructure expenses. Certainly, in this case integrating sustainability into the business model made economic sense as well. In 2010, when we accessed this case, it was reported that the most popular option selected by clients of State of Grace was a cardboard-lined wooden coffin – on burial the cardboard could be removed and the timber coffin reused, making it much cheaper, as well as environmentally responsible.[20]

We have noted that many companies worldwide have significantly modified their traditional approach of measuring the effectiveness of their operations through financial measures alone, adapting the Balanced Scorecard to the Environmental Scorecard, for example. Ensuring that performance measures include these concerns and engaging in dialogue around them keeps the firm in touch with the interests of those groups that can affect its future. It assists the firm to co-evolve with its life companions in the way that bumble-bees have co-evolved with flowers.

A focus on human sustainability

We move on now to the issue of how the corporation handles human sustainability. In this area, the organization accepts responsibility for the process of contributing to and upgrading human knowledge and skill formation within the organization itself. It acts this way because it makes good business sense to develop the intellectual and social capital of the workforce, particularly in areas relevant to the organization's mission.[21] This upgrading is also valuable for its own sake and reflects the organization's commitment to treating people as having value in their own right. It also contributes to a society where human capabilities are enhanced rather than degraded and this process of continuous up-skilling improves the quality of life in society as a whole.

Capability enhancement includes developing the organization's capacity for reshaping itself; that is, its ability to identify future strategic opportunities and to initiate action which effectively repositions particular products or services, repositions the organization as a whole to take advantage of changing markets, or proactively redefines the industry or a significant segment of it. There is an intimate connection between creating the capacity for organizational and for individual change. Flexible organizations need and develop proactive, flexible individuals who take responsibility for their own personal, professional and spiritual growth. In turn, they are able to raise the level of organizational innovation. Today we find more examples of organizations progressing human sustainability in 'hi-tech' companies in IT, software development, the arts and the service sector.

Consistent with this emphasis on innovation is strong support for a policy of workplace diversity, participation in decision making, gender equity and work–life balance. In addition, the organizational architecture reflects the emphasis on adaptability, flexibility, innovation and speed of response. It is a non-hierarchical, continuously evolving net of interrelated groups and individuals. For example, the Danish maker of hearing aids, Oticon, abandoned all formal structures, supervisory positions, job descriptions, budgets and policies in its head office, established a true paperless office, encouraged any and all of its head office employees, including its R&D staff, to form themselves on their own initiative into working groups around innovative projects and made all information on its IT system (except trade secrets) available to all employees. Its multi-story office building was reorganized to encourage people to communicate informally. After an initial period of disorientation, the result was a significant improvement in the company's market position. This resulted from doubling the rate at which new products were developed, halving new product lead time and growing sales at 20 per cent per annum when global markets were shrinking.[22] These results were achieved under the leadership of Lars Kolnid, CEO from 1988 to 1998. His successor, Niels Jacobson, received the prestigious Employee Empowerment Pioneer Award in New York in 1998 on behalf of Oticon, and stated:

> Our goal is to do business in a manner that positively contributes to society in every country where we do business. We support the principle that industry has a responsibility to society and that we have a collective responsibility to the environment.[23]

One critical challenge for the company of the future will be to attract and retain highly talented people, as either 'permanent employees' or contract workers. There are some managers who imagine that, because there is significant unemployment in most societies, building and retaining a skilled workforce is not problematical. But there is intense global and national competition for highly talented professionals and a firm's success is increasingly dependent on attracting, developing and retaining such people. Many executives are responding to this perceived need by trying to define their company as 'the employer of choice'. The fact is that talented professionals are highly mobile, in many cases define the world as their sphere of activity and take for granted that they will be well paid. The deciding factor in choosing an employer is the opportunity that an organization provides for meaningful work, autonomy and professional development. Consequently human resource management strategies become critical for building a high performance culture that provides challenge, work satisfaction and effective career development. The success of companies such as Hewlett-Packard and Ericsson comes in part from their development of comprehensive human resource policies that recognize this.

> I don't think just trying to maximize profits is a very good long-term strategy for a business. It doesn't inspire the people who work for you.
> (John Mackey, CEO Whole Foods Market[24])

Human sustainability also has an external as well as an internal focus. It involves adopting a strong and clearly defined corporate ethical position based on multiple stakeholder perspectives. It identifies key stakeholders with interests in human sustainability, builds positive relationships with them or their representatives, listens to their concerns, identifies their needs and communicates the organization's mission and strategies to them. This ethical commitment also makes good business sense in that it provides, for example, an up-to-date customer knowledge base which signals previously unidentified customer needs or emerging interests – these represent potential future business opportunities. It also builds customer loyalty. Customers and other key stakeholders ask: 'Why would we go elsewhere when our needs are being identified and met so effectively here?'

> Research drawing from the resource-based view argues that a capability of integrating knowledge from stakeholders such as suppliers and customers will help firms design products for the environment; empirically it has been shown that a stakeholder integration capability helps a firm generate knowledge from collaborative and adversarial stakeholders for continuous learning and innovation around sustainability and for generating competitive imagination and ensuring corporate survival.[25]

Cultural diversity

> We recognize and value our multi-cultural background as a company. We draw on the wealth of diversity as a unique strength to preserve, promote and protect the rich culture and character of countries, communities and local regions. We value the variety of our diversity content, which represents our heritage and the world's cultural diversity and we strive to deliver competitively superior services to our local markets.
> (Vivendi Universal website)[26]

The sustaining organization seeks to exert influence on stakeholders, other industry participants and society in general to pursue human welfare, equitable and just social practices, and to create the social circumstances that contribute to the fulfilment of human potential in all citizens. The concern here is global and multigenerational: 'citizens' includes citizens of other countries as well as our own and future generations. Sustaining organizations are aiming to use their influence to create a generative society. This is not considered an 'add on' to the organization's activities, as a charitable exercise, but as a demonstration of the organization's integrity as a responsible corporate citizen. We like the story of the organization that always keeps an empty chair at the table when the board meets to consider the organization's strategies. The chair represents unborn generations; it stands as a constant reminder to consider seriously the long-term impact of decisions on the future.

Patagonia is one company that has consistently acted on this principle. Patagonia manufactures sports clothing and gear and has built a strong reputation for quality and innovation. The company's environmental commitment is evidenced, for example, by its use of recycled materials and its decision to convert its entire sportswear line to 100 per cent organically grown cotton fibre even though this incurs higher costs. Patagonia has a reputation for very strong supply-chain sustainability across is global supply chain, enabled through high levels of transparency assurance. For example, its website offers Patagonia's Footprint Chronicles, which shows consumers a world-map view of its suppliers. A customer can see photos of each factory and details such as which Patagonia products are made there, factory demographics and more. The company claims that the website will eventually link back to Patagonia's e-commerce page to allow customers to make purchase decisions based on a product's environmental and social specifications.[27] The site also offers other reference materials enabling consumers to make responsible choices. While such tactics clearly benefit the firm's own business model its approach illustrates that of a regenerative company. Despite the sportswear being more expensive, sales have grown, showing that there is public support for environmentally responsible action of this kind.

Furthermore, Patagonia's partnership with eBay in the Common Threads Recycling Program is a radical approach to reducing consumption, with the company advertising on its website its own second-hand clothing as a further extension of its desire to create closed-loop systems.[28] In conjunction with research partners in Japan, Patagonia is now able to accept back polyester clothing for recycling into new products. Driving these innovations has been the founder's passion for ecological and social sustainability, and also the willingness to invest in technical and non-technical solutions to social and environmental challenges.[29] The acceptance of these principles has an observable impact on the way the corporation operates. It is strongly and proactively committed to traditional occupational health and safety measures, ensuring that the workplace is safe and healthy. It is also strongly committed to equal opportunity and proactive in recruiting from minority groups and ensuring career progression for women and minorities. It adopts family-friendly policies. But it goes beyond these concerns to place importance on the design of work for job satisfaction, personal and professional development, and on creating a learning environment. It also actively encourages all members of the organization to be involved in community activities in which they contribute in their own right and as members of the organization. In 2013 the founder and owner, Yvon Chouinard, announced a new venture: the launch of $20 Million & Change, an internal fund to help responsible start-up companies to bring about benefit to the environment.[30] After four decades of successful operation, this company is evidence that strongly held values need not impede sustainability in any sense of the word. The company has built a brand which, in a sense, self-promotes through its own group of evangelists – those who see the social and environmental values of the company as contributing to the evident quality of the products.

Purposive, value-based action

Sustaining corporations are value based and attract members who are strongly committed to the same values – people who want to make a difference. In such organizations people feel that their work is meaningful and the process of innovation and strategy implementation flows more readily because of the basic alignment between the values of the organization and the majority of those working there. They want to see innovations with positive environmental impact and they are keen to make the developing environmental strategy work.

The sustaining corporation has a codified set of company values – a corporate value statement or credo – that is used as a reference point in decision making at all levels of the organization. This is actively workshopped and discussed throughout the organization and, where appropriate, modified so that it attracts widespread commitment. The company specifies guidelines for how the company will treat its members, the community and the environment. An external body is chosen to collaborate in conducting an independent ethical audit of the company's internal and external relations and its report forms an integral part of the company's annual report published on the company website. All this demands much more disclosure, transparency and accountability than has been the practice in the traditional firm.

One firm that has based its existence on sustainability values is the US chain of quality food supermarkets, Whole Foods Market. This is a chain of food stores that actively markets delicious and nutritious foods that are mostly organic. Its core values are:

- selling the highest-quality natural and organic products available
- satisfying and delighting our customers
- team member happiness and excellence
- creating wealth through profits and growth
- caring about our communities and environment with our commitment to community giving of more than 5 per cent of net profits per year.[31]

In 2013 Whole Foods Market is described not only as posting impressive profits but as widening its market through growth, moving into new areas with new stores and all the time realizing economies of scale.[32]

The range of activities emphasized in sustaining organizations means that different capabilities and skills are developed within the organization – the organization generally needs a broader range of skills than a traditional organization and the emphasis is on process skills. In particular, members develop higher-order skills of personal resilience, self-confidence, adaptation and learning, empathy, communication and influence, coaching, negotiation and conflict resolution. Chapter 9 discusses how leadership becomes increasingly diffused throughout the organization and how leaders develop these qualities.

Some sustaining organizations are not-for-profit and we are confident that, as third-wave thinking spreads, we shall see more organizations of this kind emerging, committed to social ideals other than profitability.

As more third-wave organizations develop, they will begin to bring pressure to bear on politicians to support the development of third-wave economies, that is, economies which value people and use resources to develop their capabilities, invest in environmental renewal and redefine progress in ways that are more meaningful than GNP. They will lobby governments to withdraw subsidies from unsustainable industries, to invest in social capital, to encourage innovation and the innovative industries of the future. They will also form alliances with like-minded companies whose activities are complementary to their own. In some cases, the organizations in these alliances will co-locate their production facilities to form what are known as 'industrial clusters' or 'industrial ecosystems'. In these clusters, materials flow in closed loops. As Tibbs points out, this has the potential to create a massive increase in the efficiency of materials use because 'about 95 per cent of all the materials we use end up as waste before the finished product is even purchased'.[33] Imagine the productivity increase possible if this material were fully utilized and recycled! The evidence is that focused industrial clusters like this can be highly productive in business terms and support a healthy environment and society. This brings us to the issue of ecological sustainability.

Focus on ecological sustainability

In the area of ecological sustainability, the sustaining organization seeks to define itself as an integral part of the ecology: like an earthworm, it takes up resources from the environment, processes them and, in returning them to the earth, ensures its own growth and enriches the environment. The sustaining organization ensures that resources are economically recycled or returned to the environment in a form which is not destructive of environmental value or actually helps to restore and enrich the environment where it has been damaged. This is in contrast to most current industrial processes whose major output is waste, often poisonous waste. The British retailer Marks & Spencer has instigated a 'shwopping' initiative, encouraging customers to bring back their used clothing to any one of its 342 stores – in partnership with Oxfam. Since 2008, 10 million items have been donated, worth an estimated £8 million. While there is some criticism that such schemes can marginalize the smaller charities,[34] the overall contribution is to change the consumer mind-set, and the model of shwopping is emerging as one of the approaches to consumption now challenging traditional ways of doing business.

Marks & Spencer

Operates in over 50 territories worldwide and employs almost 82,000 people. Founding values of Quality, Value, Service, Innovation and Trust.

Plan A 2007: sustainable sourcing, 'shwopping', closed loop through partnership with the global poverty campaigner Oxfam.

2012 achievements:

- M&S-operated stores, offices, warehouses and delivery fleets in the UK and Republic of Ireland became carbon neutral, making it the first major retailer to achieve this;
- 28 per cent reduction in the volumes of waste and a 32 per cent reduction in food waste since 2008/09;
- health and well-being initiatives include calorie information on the menu boards in employee cafes.

(Marks & Spencer websites)[35, 36]

In the sustaining organization, environmental best practice is espoused and enacted because it is the responsible thing to do. The organization becomes an active promoter of ecological sustainability values and seeks to influence key participants in the industry and in society in general. It is prepared to use its influence to promote positive sustainability policies on the part of governments, the restructuring of markets and the development of community values to facilitate the emergence of a sustainable society. Green Mountain Coffee Roasters, Patagonia, Whole Foods Market and now the major retailer Marks & Spencer represent third-wave firms that have pioneered better relationships with the community and their customers while emphasizing environmental responsibility in their sourcing. In third-wave firms, the environment is treated as integral to a viable global economy that is sustainable into the future for the benefit of generations to come as well as those alive today.

This has some important consequences for how firms with a material production process can operate in the future. They will be far more concerned about the initial design of products than with their ultimate disposal. Much of the problem of pollution and waste can be eliminated at the design stage by the choice of environmentally friendly, non-polluting materials and designing out waste. In natural systems there is no waste and our material production processes can increasingly emulate natural processes.

In 1992, Hewlett-Packard initiated a product stewardship programme:

> Under this program, Hewlett-Packard strives to prevent or minimize
> any negative impacts to human health or safety, or to the ecosystem,
> that may occur at any point in the life of an HP product – from when it
> is designed until it is no longer used.[37]

The programme guidelines outline five key principles in the attempt to
design environmentally friendly products:

1 Minimize the energy consumption of our products, fewer raw
  materials, and increase our use of recyclable materials.
2 Reduce waste and emissions from our manufacturing processes.
3 Use less material overall and more recyclable material in our
  packaging.
4 Form local covenants for the collection, disposal and recycling of
  computer equipment – taking responsibility for products from cradle to
  grave.
5 Develop products that are easier to reuse or recycle.[38]

Hewlett-Packard regularly reports progress against these guidelines.

Sustaining organizations conduct a life-cycle assessment for all products.
They are concerned with the full production flow from extraction of raw
materials to their disposal, even where their own operation may control
only one link in the total chain. Where this is the case, they will actively
negotiate collaborative solutions to social and environmental problems
with other firms in the chain. In this way, they build voluntary
partnerships committed to working to raise their awareness of key
interdependencies and to eliminate the – often unintended – negative
impacts of the production process on the community or the ecology.
Collectively, they view themselves as stewards of the resources they use:
they either continue to recycle them or return them to the earth in a form
that feeds the earth.

The sustaining organization seeks partnerships with relevant 'green'
groups, actively supports their involvement in assessing the firm's
environmental performance and works collaboratively with them to
develop improved environmental practices. It goes beyond compliance to
develop and update a knowledge base relevant to its core production
processes (for example, a register of chemical pollutants), to build a
general awareness of environmental issues within its workforce and a
commitment to progressive elimination of pollutants, product redesign for
improved environmental impact and support for the 'dematerialization' of

physical processes. It collaborates with an external 'green' group to conduct an externally verified environmental audit of its operations and publishes this as an integral part of its annual report and on its website. This is an increasingly common practice in a number of the companies, as we have discussed in previous chapters.

Frankel argues that there are four principles which companies must adopt to make genuine progress towards ecological sustainability.[39] The first is '*towards zero waste*': rather than reducing waste, every company must eliminate it entirely. Examples of major corporations committed to achieving zero emissions are Ogihara and Chichibu Cement in Japan, and DuPont in the USA. An example of a company working towards zero waste is Walmart, the world's largest company, while Marks & Spencer achieved carbon neutrality by means of reducing energy consumption, changing to renewables and utilizing carbon offsets in 2012.

The second principle is '*whole system thinking*', which fosters the reinvention rather than redesign of industrial processes. The third principle is '*look outward*', which means that companies have to go beyond cleaning up their own operations by helping smaller companies with fewer resources to put their houses in order. It also means working in concert with other companies to create symbiotic cycles of industrial ecology, that is, capitalizing on the notion that one company's waste is another's resource. And in addition, it means creating alliances to capitalize on large-scale business opportunities in the greening process.

Principle four is '*remember sustainable development*'. Businesses need to think more broadly than the ecological environment. As we have pointed out above, sustainable development involves social issues as well as ecological ones. Because these issues are integral to the core strategies of the organization, they are not considered to be the sole responsibility of an environmental manager or a human resource manager. There may be an environmental manager and a human resource manager, but they are regarded as technical experts who are there to provide the specialized input which other senior executives need so as to implement sustainability strategies.

At any one time there will be a range of environmental initiatives being run on a project basis; all of these will also have human resource implications. As a consequence, lateral coordination is at least as important as vertical.

What are the advantages for the firm of pursuing ecologically sustaining policies with such ardent commitment? We argue that, as the ecological crisis deepens and the third wave moves the values of society towards this ideal, it will be the bold but foolish organization that persists in environmentally destructive practices. As recognition of resource limits and the negative environmental impacts from pollution intensifies, there will be increasing pressure on firms to be 'squeaky clean' environmentally if they are to continue to have a 'licence to operate'.[40] But proactive policies in particular can provide a comparative advantage in the marketplace as consumers, investors and governments increasingly discriminate in favour of firms that are ethical in their approach to their people, their community and the natural world. As we have noted, this is shown in the performance of the ethical investment fund industry. In the Australian share market, for example, ethical funds appear to have outperformed the mainstream by 8 per cent in 2012–13, a margin which has been maintained since 2002.[41] Again, however, such claims need to be taken in context and we accept that the meaning of 'ethical investment' is highly variable and ethical investment standards cannot be set universally.

As in the social arena, we are also witnessing a trend to the development of more not-for-profit organizations devoted to environmental protection and renewal. One well-known organization of this kind is Greenpeace, which operates globally and has had a powerful influence on international, national and enterprise-level environmental policies. Another that is having a significant impact on the corporate world and in raising community campaigns is WWF. But there is a plethora of such organizations and we are confident that we shall see many more. In addition, a range of new jobs, such as 'environmental manager', 'sustainability manager' and 'corporate sustainability manager' are being established in organizations.

The sustaining corporation is currently a visionary ideal – but it is one that we illustrate with partial case examples to show that there are firms moving towards the ideal. Its visionary nature raises the issue of how the transition can be managed for those corporations that wish to move in this direction. We refer the reader to Chapters 7 and 8, where we deal with the process of managing change, particularly to our discussion of the need for both incremental and transformative change processes and how the latter relates to specific approaches to leadership. The transition to the third wave represents a significant value shift. Therefore, the core of the transformative process that will bring about third-wave organizations has to be culture change. We deal here with some of the characteristics of culture change but refer the reader forward to Chapters 7 and 8, where culture change is dealt with in more detail.

Building strategy into the culture

Many standard texts on strategic management describe it as a process that is logical, rational and non-problematical. Empirical studies of strategic management show that in reality strategic management differs substantially from this model. Strategy is created in a political environment where stakeholders have differing and sometimes conflicting interests. Within the organization itself, executives are seldom in full agreement about an appropriate strategy and sometimes in active conflict. This is not surprising because they face differing environments (for example, customers versus suppliers) and have differing career interests. There is, in fact, no single shared environment for the firm: there is a multitude of environments changing at different rates; there are too many factors to consider and there are legitimate differences of opinion about which are important signals of future trends. When we expand this confusing reality to the organization as a whole, we can conceive of the organization as a constellation of groups all perceiving differing environments, having differing interests and having close relationships with some groups but seldom or never relating to others.

In addition, strategic planning is not only a rational process. Any attempt to define a future rouses strong emotions. People care about the future, as Mark Twain remarked, because it is where they will spend the rest of their lives. Strategic planning is an attempt to envision a desirable future and to take action to bring that future into being. Even where the senior executive team reaches consensus on a strategic plan, there is no assurance that the plan will be implemented as conceived. It relies for its implementation on the actions of other members of the organization, all of whom have interests at stake. Large-scale strategic shifts necessarily involve transforming the established culture (or cultures) of the organization and integrating strategic reorientation and sustainability into the corporate culture itself.

> A shift from environmental management to environmental strategy requires a concurrent and supporting shift in organizational culture, structure, reward systems, and job responsibilities.[42]

But what exactly is corporate culture and why is it so important?

Organizational culture is usually defined as 'the way we do business around here'. Organizational culture consists of the basic assumptions, values and norms, symbols, myths and 'wisdom' that define the collective approach to day-to-day decision making and action. Culture centres on the creation and continuity of meaning for organizational members. Much of it may be unreflective and unarticulated – it is the 'world taken for granted' – often more visible to visitors than to inmates. One of the most powerful ways to create organizational change is to confront, develop or remould the core cultural values of an organization so that people experience a profound change in their understanding and purpose and, as a result, act differently. Leaders play a major role in this because they can embody a new cultural profile in their speech and action, and become catalysts for cultural change.

In their book, *Blown to Bits*, Evans and Wurster discuss the forces that are massively reorganizing global and local markets and challenging our understanding of what corporations are and how they should do business.[43] They emphasize that the leader's first task is to create a culture and the second task is to develop a strategy. They then search for a way to define the core identity of the corporation of the future. They conclude:

> Theorists have variously seen the corporation as a set of physical assets, a set of property rights, or a body of core competencies. Those can all be deconstructed. What *resists* deconstruction is the idea of the corporation as defined by its culture and its strategy. The corporation as *purposeful community*. And if all else fades, perhaps purposeful community becomes the essence of identity, of management, of leadership. In a world of impersonal, technical change, that is a refreshingly human thought.[44]

To move to the sustaining organization involves members of the organization at all levels internalizing the values of sustainability so that these values become a core theme in their work as a purposeful community. This does not mean that there will necessarily be unanimity about the solutions to be sought to emergent sustainability issues. However, it does mean the development over time of a strong and pervasive shared ideology. The members of the organization derive meaning from their ability to create useful goods and/or services that contribute to the community's quality of life and sustain the natural environment. In reality, this is reflected in the fact that all members of the organization, as well as its subcontractors and suppliers, make day-to-day decisions on the basis of a deeply held, internalized commitment to sustainability values. This ideology does not negate the value of work in providing financially for the needs of the workforce or running a profitable enterprise. But it does define financial returns to organizational members and shareholders as the appropriate exchange for providing something of real value to society and the environment.

Culture is the glue which holds the pieces of the jigsaw puzzle firmly together so it cannot fall apart. A positive culture blends human and ecological sustainability seamlessly.

Proactive leadership

Critical to this culture-building process is proactive leadership consciously developed and practised at all levels of the organization. Ideally, this starts with a fully committed executive team which has reached agreement that sustainability is central to the firm's ongoing strategy or strategic reorientation. The executive team emphasizes creating a strong corporate identity around sustainability values and creates shared experiences and reward systems that reinforce the emerging values. Culture is not created by fiat; rather, it grows organically from the experience of working together successfully on meaningful tasks. Leaders are the shapers of the corporate culture and they must embody the core cultural values of sustainability in their actions.

Culture change involves creating an ongoing drama in which the members of the organization are both actors and audience. It is a drama in which heroes and heroic groups emerge who forge new meaning for themselves and others and whose success is embodied in powerful stories and myths. Leaders become attractors and role models, inspiring others to move in the same direction, so multiplying the momentum of change. This surge of human energy and meaning making is the matrix from which the new culture arises, is invigorated and becomes a powerful shaper of the work-related behaviour of all organizational members. The process of continuing cultural innovation is an organizational endeavour to support and renew, rather than exploit and degrade, the world, the community and the planet. It is a process which restores a fuller meaning to human work than the accumulation of capital and material goods.

I fully expect that we'll no longer be talking about economic, environmental and societal values as being distinctly different, but see them as integral and interlocking aspects of every business process and activity.

(Paul Tebo, Vice President for Safety,
Health and the Environment, E. I du Pont de Nemours)[45]

Conclusion

Corporations are the fundamental cells of the modern economy. If we are to transform our economy to make it sustainable and sustaining, then we must make significant changes to the way corporations operate. Corporations also control most of the resources of our global society; if we are to have effective leadership of the sustainability movement, then much of that leadership must come from the corporate sector. Building sustainable organizations requires a fundamental shift of mind-set from traditional mainstream business thought and practice. In the future, the corporation will remain profitable by becoming an active partner in the ongoing renewal of global society and of the earth's biosphere.

However, the path to creating the sustaining organization is not travelled quickly and easily. Having sketched the ultimate goal in this chapter, in the remaining three chapters, we outline the incremental (Chapter 7) and transformational change strategies (Chapter 8) required to create sustaining corporations. In Chapter 9 we also outline the change-agent roles and leadership actions required in creating fully sustainable organizations.

 ## Appendix 6.1: phase 6: the sustaining corporation

Human sustainability (HS6)

The organization accepts responsibility for contributing to the process of renewing and upgrading human knowledge and skills formation in the community and society generally, and is a strong promoter of equal opportunity, workplace diversity and work–life balance as workplace principles. It adopts a strong and clearly defined corporate ethical position based on multiple stakeholder perspectives and seeks to exert influence on the key participants in the industry and in society in general to pursue human welfare, equitable and just social

Ecological sustainability (ES6)

The organization becomes an active promoter of ecological sustainability values and seeks to influence key participants in the industry and in society in general. Environmental best practice is espoused and enacted because it is the responsible thing to do. The organization tries to assist society to be ecologically sustainable and uses its entire range of products and services to this end. The organization is prepared to use its influence to promote positive sustainability policies on the part of governments, the restructuring of markets and the development of practices and fulfilment of the human potential of all. People are seen as valuable in their own right.

community values to facilitate the emergence of a sustainable society. Nature is valued for its own sake.

Notes

1 D. Raths, '100 Best Corporate Citizens for 2006', *Business Ethic Magazine*, Spring 2006, 20 (1). Online. Available HTTP: http://www.business-ethics. com/ whatsnew/100best.html (accessed August 2006).

2 GMCR, 'Sustainability Report Fiscal 2012'. Online. Available HTTP: <http://www.gmcr.com/~/media/Sustainability/PDF/ReportsDisclosures/ Sustainability%20Report%20Summary%20Fiscal%202012.ashx> (accessed 7 July 2013); see GMCR-C, 'Green Mountain Coffee Roasters, Inc. Releases Fiscal 2012 Sustainability Report', Business Wire, 2013. Online. Available HTTP: <http://www.businesswire.com/news/home/20130318005293/en/ Green-Mountain-Coffee-Roasters-Releases-Fiscal-2012> (accessed 7 July 2013).

3 I. Lowe, *A Big Fix: Radical Solutions for Australia's Environmental Crisis*, Melbourne: Black Inc/Schwartz Publishing, 2005, p. 109.

4 K. Perkins, '5 Reasons Why Small Businesses Should Care About Sustainability', Greenbiz.com, 2010. Online. Available HTTP: <http://www. greenbiz.com/blog/2010/10/13/5-reasons-why-small-businesses-should-care-about-sustainability > (accessed 20 July 2013).

5 KPMG, *International Survey of Corporate Responsibility Reporting*, KPMG Global Sustainability Services and University of Amsterdam Graduate Business School (2005), Amsterdam.

6 R. Welford, *Hijacking Environmentalism: Corporate Responses to Sustainable Development*, London: Earthscan Publications, 1997.

7 W. Fox, cited in J. Dryzek, *The Politics of the Earth: Environmental Discourses*, Oxford: Oxford University Press, 1997, p. 156; M. Fox, *The Reinvention of Work: A New Vision of Livelihood for Our Time*, San Francisco: Harper, 1994.

8 P. Senge, 'Innovating our way to the next industrial revolution', *Sloan Management Review*, 2001, Winter, 43 (2), 1–15.

9 A. Hoffman, 'Climate change strategy: the business logic behind voluntary greenhouse gas reductions', *California Management Review*, 2005, 47 (3), 21–46.

10 See United Nations, *UN Principles*, Business and Human Rights Resource Centre, 2013. Online. Available HTTP: <http://www.business-humanrights.org/Links/Repository/1017820> (accessed 8 July 2013).

11 D. Bross, 'BSR Insight How Microsoft Did It: Implementing the Guiding Principles', Business and Human Rights, 2012. Online. Available HTTP: <http://www.bsr.org/en/our-insights/bsr-insight-article/

how-microsoft-did-it-implementing-the-guiding-principles-on-business-and-humanrights> (accessed 9 July 2013).

12 T. B. Porter, 'Managerial applications of corporate social responsibility and systems thinking for achieving sustainability outcomes', *Systems Research and Behavioral Science*, 25 (3), 397–411.

13 KPMG, 'International Survey of Corporate Sustainability Reporting 2011'. Online. Available HTTP: <http://www.kpmg.com/PT/pt/IssuesAndInsights/Documents/corporate-responsibility2011.pdf> (accessed 12 July 2013).

14 RIAA, 'Responsible Investment Annual 2011'. Online. Available HTTP: <http://www.responsibleinvestment.org/wp-content/uploads/2011/12/RI-Annual-2011-Report.pdf> (accessed 8 July 2013).

15 For example, N. Darnall, I. Seol and J. Sarkis, 'Perceived stakeholder influences and organizations' use of environmental audits', *Accounting Organizations and Society,* 2009, 34 (2), 170–87; R. E. Freeman, A. C. Wicks and B. Palmer 'Stakeholder Theory and "The corporate objective revisited"', *Organization Science*, 2008, 15 (3), 364–9; E. W. Orts and A. Strudler, 'Putting a stake in stakeholder theory', *Journal of Business Ethics*, 2009, 88 (4), 605–15.

16 K. Buysse, and A. Verbek, 'Proactive environmental strategies: a stakeholder management perspective', *Strategic Management Journal*, 2003, 24 (5), 453–70.

17 C. Liston-Heyes, and G. Ceton, 'An investigation of real versus perceived CSP in S&P-500 firms', *Journal of Business Ethics*, 2009, 89 (2), 283–96.

18 S. Hart and S. Sharma, 'Engaging fringe stakeholders for competitive imagination', *Academy of Management Executive*, 2004, 18 (1), 7–18.

19 Unilever, 'Sustainable Living Plan', 2013. Online. Available HTTP: <http://www.unilever.com/sustainable-living/uslp/> (accessed 12 July 2013).

20 E. Collins, K. Kearins and H. Tregidga, 'State of grace: can death be sustainable?', in S. Benn, D. Dunphy and B. Perrott, *Cases in Corporate Sustainability and Change*, Prahan, Australia: Tilde University Press, 2011, pp. 107–20.

21 For a comprehensive review of the concept of social capital and its implications for managers, see P. S. Alder and S. W. Kwon, 'Social capital: prospects for a new concept', *Academy of Management Review*, 2002, 27 (1), 17–40.

22 Extract from Vivendi Universal, 'Our Values'. Online. Available HTTP: <http://www.vivendiuniversal.com/vu2/en/who-we-are.cfm> (accessed 6 February 2002).

23 B. Burnes, 'Case Study 1: "Oticon – the disorganized organization"', in B. Burnes, *Managing Change: A Strategic Approach to Organizational Dynamics*, 3rd edn, London: Financial Times/Prentice Hall, 2000, pp. 319–28, p. 327.

24 A. Charles, 'Ten CEO Quotes to Live by', Fast Company, 2011. Online. Available HTTP: <http://www.fastcompany.com/1723702/spoken-true-leader-ten-ceo-quotes-live> (accessed 13 July 2013).

25 S. Sharma and M. Starik, 'Stakeholders, the environment and society: multiple perspectives, emerging consensus', Chapter 1, pp. 1–22 in S. Sharma and M. Starik, *Stakeholders, the Environment and Society*, Cheltenham: Edward Elgar, 2004, p. 7.

26 Vivendi Universal, 'Our Values'.

27 Ethical Corporation, 'Briefing Supply Chains; Patagonia Footprint', 2012. Online. Available HTTP: <http://www.patagonia.com/us/footprint/suppliers-map/> (accessed 12 July 2013).

28 See Patagonia, 'Used Clothing and Gear', 2013. Online. Available HTTP: <http://www.patagonia.com/us/ebay/used-gear> (accessed 14 July 2013).

29 D. Wright, *Patagonia: Leading Sustainability Case Study*, Brisbane: UQ Business School, 2005.

30 H. Buchner, 'Patagonia Restructures under "Patagonia Works" to Launch Internal Fund and Invest in Environmentally Sound Start-ups', Transworld Business, 2013. Online. Available HTTP: <http://business.transworld.net/129018/news/patagonia-restructures-under-new-business-model/> (accessed 15 July 2013).

31 Whole Foods Market, 'Whole Foods Market Caring for Communities', 2013. Online. Available HTTP: <http://www.wholefoodsmarket.com/mission-values/caring-communities> (accessed 15 July 2013).

32 K. Stock, 'Whole Foods Profits By Cutting "Whole Paycheck" Reputation', Bloomberg Business Week, 2013. Online. Available HTTP: <http://www.businessweek.com/articles/2013-05-08/whole-foods-profits-by-cutting-whole-paycheck-reputation> (accessed 15 July 2013).

33 H. Tibbs, 'The technology strategy of the sustainable corporation', in D. Dunphy, J. Benveniste, A. Griffiths and P. Sutton (eds) *Sustainability: The Corporate Challenge of the 21st Century*, Sydney: Allen and Unwin, 2000, pp. 191–216, p. 211.

34 R. Smithers, 'M&S Launches "Shwopping" Scheme', *Guardian*, 2012. Online. Available HTTP: <http://www.guardian.co.uk/money/2012/apr/26/marks-spencer-shwopping-scheme> (accessed 20 july).

35 Marks & Spencer, 'How We Do Business', 2013. Online. Available HTTP: <www.corporate.marksandspencer.com/howwedobusiness> (accessed 21 July 2013).

36 Marks & Spencer, 'Review of the Year', 2013. Online. Available HTTP: <http://planareport.marksandspencer.com/review-of-the-year/make-plan-a-how-we-do-business> (accessed 21 July 2013).

37 Hewlett-Packard, 'Commitment to the Environment', Hewlett-Packard Co., USA, 1998, p. 1.

38 Ibid.; see also HP 'About Environmental Sustainability'. Online. Available HTTP: http://www8.hp.com/us/en/hp-information/environment/sustainability.html#.UpQp26yz40E (accessed 24 November 2013).

39 C. Frankel, 'Into the fourth era', in *Earth's Company: Business, Environment and the Challenge of Sustainability*, Canada: New Society Publishers, 1998, pp. 81–94.

40 J. Elkington, *Cannibals with Forks: The Triple Bottom Line of 21st Century Business,* Oxford: Capstone, 1997.

41 J. Collett, 'Turning green into gold', *The Sun-Herald*, July 14 2013, p. 41.

42 A. Hoffman, *Competitive Environmental Strategy: A Guide to the Changing Business Landscape*, Washington, DC: Island Press, 2000, p. 163.

43 P. Evans and T. S. Wurster, *Blown to Bits: How the New Economies of Information Transforms Strategy*, Boston, MA: Harvard Business School Press, 2000.

44 Ibid., p. 229.

45 A. Spencer-Cooke, 'Hero of zero', Environmental Leadership Award 2000, *Tomorrow*, November–December 2000, 10 (6), 10–16, this quote p. 10.

Part IV
Pathways to sustainability: towards third wave corporations

7 The incremental path

- Setting the scene
- Incremental versus transformational change
- What is incremental change?
- Applying the phase model to incremental change
- Benefits of incremental change
- Potential pitfalls of incremental change
- Major issues in the movement between phases
- Steps involved in incremental change
- Conclusion

Setting the scene

For a significant part of the twentieth century, most managers used incremental change programmes to modify their organizations. Transformative change programmes were employed only in times of crisis, which were the exception rather than the rule. So the history of the development of systematic approaches to incremental change extends throughout the twentieth century and into the twenty-first. As a result, we now have a comprehensive set of tools available to make incremental change and we know some of the key ingredients for successful change programmes of this kind.[1]

Early in the twentieth century, scientific management theories led to an emphasis on technically- and operationally-focused change. Later, human relations theories dominated and the focus switched to an emphasis on changing the social systems of the organization through interventions such as supervisory training and motivational programmes. All of these approaches advocated making relatively slow-paced change. They also tended to ignore technological issues. However, in the 1970s incremental change theories began to address both social needs and technical efficiencies in a more balanced way. The dominant approaches became organization development (OD) and socio-technical systems (STS) theory. The STS approach developed in the UK and Scandinavia under the intellectual leadership of Trist and Emery while they were working from the Tavistock Institute of Human Relations in London. The approach was widely adopted after the Second World War, particularly in Scandinavia and Australia, where it became strongly linked to the industrial democracy movement.[2]

The STS approach derived from general systems theory in the natural sciences and used open organic systems as its metaphor for organizations. The diagnostic model was socio-technical systems analysis, which is a detailed approach to analysing both the technical and social systems. The ideal organization was a representative democratic community composed of work teams, learning through participative action research. STS theory strongly influenced the empowerment movement in the USA, particularly through the work of Davis, Cherns, James Taylor and others at the University of California, Los Angeles, and of Lawler and others at the University of Southern California. It also continues to influence action research in a range of countries, particularly in the Netherlands. STS theory consistently advocated incremental change as a necessary condition for workforce involvement.[3]

While STS and OD theories of change were developing in Europe, North America and Australia, in Japan quality management techniques were adopted with enthusiasm. The Japanese combined the TQM emphasis on statistical controls, stemming from the work of Deming and others, with the participatory shopfloor practices of the earlier human relations movement. The human relations movement advocated employee participation in decision making and strongly emphasized social factors. By including employees in the quality-improvement process, Japanese managers harnessed employee knowledge and competencies to overcome variances from ideal quality standards. The human relations/OD, STS and TQM approaches to change have all strongly supported incremental rather than transformative changes. Incremental change appeared ideally suited to the operating environments of many organizations in the late 1960s, 1970s and into the early 1980s, particularly when it achieved a balanced emphasis on both technical and human factors.

This emerging movement for incremental change was led by self-proclaimed management heretics (like Emery and Trist) who saw their mission as overturning the prevailing management orthodoxies of the time. The paradigm espoused by the Organizational Renewal Movement heretics contrasted significantly with the dominant managerial ethos of the 1960s and 1970s. Their criticisms were directed at inefficiencies in bureaucratic organizations, but even more at the dehumanizing and exploitative effects of bureaucratic managerialism on the morale and satisfaction of the workforce.[4] They advocated incremental change to shift organizations to be more effective in terms of the core business and more responsive to employee needs.

However, in the period from 1985 to 1999, under pressure from economic reforms, increasing globalization and international competition, many companies found that they were significantly out of alignment with their operating environment. For example, they found that their core technology was suddenly obsolete or that their major customer segment had shifted its preference to another type of product or service. In these circumstances, incremental changes were often insufficient to strategically reposition organizations. So in the late 1980s and the 1990s many organizations abandoned incremental change for radical, transformational change. Change of this kind is covered in detail in Chapter 8.

Many organizations have recently moved into a period of mid-range change: that is, many managers are recognizing that their organizations need the flexibility to move between the two approaches in order to stay in alignment with market conditions. Contemporary organizations need to be 'ambidextrous', that is, to have the ability to manage both incremental and revolutionary approaches to change. Hence we preface this chapter by acknowledging that the distinction between incremental and transformational change is somewhat artificial and that in most successful change programmes both approaches are used.

Incremental versus transformational change

In this chapter, we focus on those change approaches that are characterized by participative management and collaborative forms of work that require basic operational change and work redesign. However, our overall approach is not that we should go back to these past approaches but, rather, that they represent a part of our armoury of change that needs to be utilized under the appropriate conditions. For instance, when some of these change techniques are combined with value-oriented programmes such as The Natural Step and Total Quality Environmental Management, powerful forces for sustainability change are unleashed in organizations.[5] In other words, the approach to change that we advocate is not about pursuing the 'one best way' but, rather, of identifying the appropriate strategy for the appropriate situation. However, when it comes to the study of the environment and organizations, Orsato points out:

> The majority of literature on corporate environmental management assumes reformism as the guiding principle for organizational change. Incrementalism is the basic principle of the standards of environmental management systems such as the ISO 14000 series . . . These programs assume that through incremental improvements organizations would achieve eco-efficiency and, eventually, ecological sustainability.[6]

However, some advocates for sustainability question whether it can be achieved by changing corporations incrementally. In their view, incremental change is not enough: transformational changes are required to achieve sustainability.[7] For example, Hart and Milstein, in their prophetically titled article 'Global sustainability and the creative destruction of industries', argue that: 'the emerging challenge of global sustainability is a catalyst for a new round of creative destruction that offers unprecedented opportunities. Today's corporations can seize the opportunity for sustainable development, but they must look beyond continuous, incremental improvements.'[8] Building on the work of Joseph Schumpeter, these authors view incremental change as simply maintaining the status quo. Furthermore, they argue that at some point in the future, those organizations that have changed only incrementally will fail because they did not 'change the fundamental manner in which they provide products, processes and services'.[9] In their view, the operations of current businesses are so inimical to sustainability that only radical change will create a sustainable world.

Other recent studies examine the relationship between forms of organizational 'slack' and an organization's ability to respond to sustainability challenges. These studies too question the drive to efficiency characteristic of incremental change approaches and, in particular, the emphasis on removal of forms of organizational slack. These authors argue that research evidence points to the positive effects of organizational slack for the development of innovative capabilities and beneficial responsiveness. However, the more broadly held contrary view leans toward reducing slack on the grounds that efficiency and leanness are useful and functional for organizations. This may be the case for firms situated in economic systems that, as a whole, are relatively stable. In such circumstances, the relative system stability allows incremental change toward efficiencies derived from an increasingly lean resource base. However, under conditions of system instability, the benefits of efficiency may disappear and sustainability suffer, suggesting the need to qualify past findings in light of broader system conditions.[10]

In other words, lean and efficient organizations have received much attention and praise in recent years, but they may have a dark side that has so far been overlooked. They may lack the capabilities needed to respond to large-scale, disruptive and unpredictable events, particularly those connected with sustainability issues. Incremental change programmes may only compound this problem. So what really works best, incremental or transformational change?

We want to make it clear that making change of any kind is difficult. As Beer and Nohria state:

> Despite some individual success, change remains difficult to pull off, and few companies manage the process as well as they like. Most of their initiatives – installing new technology, downsizing, restructuring or trying to change corporate cultures – have had low success rates. The brutal fact is that about 70 per cent of all change initiatives fail.[11]

However, there are circumstances where incremental change can effectively create new values, structures and processes that support the building of sustainable corporations. Our collective experience of consulting and research in organizations indicates that incremental change is often a viable means to achieve sustainability outcomes – this is clear from organizations we have already discussed in this book, organizations as diverse as Scandic (hotels), Interface (carpets) and Rockcote (paints and coatings). In these organizations and in many others incremental change programmes have produced impressive results. The approach that we take in this and the next chapter is situational. We argue that managers should adopt the kind of change programme that suits the organization's specific situation. Significant gaps between corporate strategy and performance, or between a culture of Rejection and one of Strategic proactivity, for instance, do require larger, more robust transformational changes. Smaller gaps, new strategic opportunities, more minor culture shifts, capability development or changes in the workforce skills mix, however, may be achieved through incremental or continuous change initiatives. As Abrahamson states:

> To change successfully, companies should stop changing all the time. Instead they should intersperse major change initiatives among carefully paced periods of smaller, organic change using processes I call tinkering and kludging. By doing so companies can manage overall change with an approach called dynamic stability.[12]

So arguments for transformational change are compelling in some circumstances, but unconvincing in identifying it as the sole means to achieving sustainability outcomes. We agree with O'Reilly and Tushman, who argue that organizations need to become ambidextrous.[13] For instance, if increasing evidence on climate change and other ecological systems changes is consistently ignored by organizations and governments, and action towards sustainability not taken now, then the luxury of choice of type of change may disappear for many organizations[14] – full on transformational change may be the only option for organizational survival. Most organizations today, however, as they face up to sustainability issues, will need to be ambidextrous; that is, be able to manage incremental and transformational change simultaneously and/or sequentially.[15] Development of network relationships, for example, can lead an organization out of a firm-centric impasse and facilitate transformation and change – yet developing collaborative capabilities may be an aspect of an incremental change programme. So, in some ways, we acknowledge our separation of incremental and transformational as artificial in that we mean they may occur together and that both have key advantages. What is important is to recognize their need in the change programme, both individual and complementary.[16] Whether change is more incremental or more transformational, it is important to stress that change is ongoing and dynamic and that organizational change is shaped by the politics, the context and the substance of the change.[17] Taking the politics of a sustainability change programme, for example, into consideration, is clearly essential, given the range of stakeholder interests and spheres of influence. For example, government, lobby groups and NGOs are all involved in many decisions that need to be made by business leaders, particularly in relation to certain sectors.

The change strategy employed to make an organization sustainable must be situational and connected to, and driven by an organization's strategy. Without this, it becomes 'change for change sake'.[18] Incremental changes are best suited to organizations that require minimal strategic realignment. Where organizations are already meeting many of the demands of key stakeholders for sustainable practices, incremental strategies are effective in keeping the organization aligned to incremental changes in stakeholder expectations. So this chapter focuses on incremental change, showing the important role it can play in the development of the corporate capabilities, cultures and practices that lead to the creation of sustainable organizations.

What is incremental change?

Sometimes it helps to explain a concept by first defining what it is not. For our purposes, incremental change is not large-scale transformational or revolutionary change of the kind often associated with business process re-engineering, downsizing, corporate spin-offs, mergers/acquisitions or strategic unbundling. Incremental change does not include radical changes in strategy, structure, capability or organizational realignment. Rather, incremental change is planned and emergent, continuous and ongoing and for the most part impacts on the organization's day-to-day operational processes.[19] Incremental change includes changes to the way people work (job redesign; teamwork); changes to an organization's business-unit processes (quality management; STS redesign); and changes to reward systems, information systems and technologies. As Stace and Dunphy note: 'corporate wide total quality management, service quality and team building programs are often a feature of this type of organization change. Leadership is primarily consultative in style.'[20] Furthermore, incremental change can be used to generate new capabilities, for example, through multi-skilling or forming project teams or creating new values and modifying corporate culture (customer service, empowerment and leadership-development programmes).

Westpac Bank is a highly successful Australia-based bank that offers general, commercial and industrial banking services as well as insurance and financial services. It has consistently been rated as a leader in the banking sector on the Dow Jones Sustainability Index since 2003 and is listed in the Global 100 most sustainable corporations in the world.[21] Westpac has used incremental change strategies over the last decade to build its capabilities and reputation in corporate sustainability and responsibility. This approach was initially seen as an effective way to mitigate risk and repair consumer confidence in banks. Its approach has now grown into a comprehensive strategic programme for achieving corporate sustainability. As one executive stated: 'Achieving sustainability is a never-ending journey, the moment you think you are there, is probably when you are in most trouble.'[22] The Bank's success at pursuing its incremental sustainability change strategy can be attributed to a variety of factors:

- The development and incorporation of a values and goals statement that also elaborates on how the process of change should be managed and the integration of this into the mission and strategy of the organization.

- The creation of a culture of constant innovation including corporate sustainability and responsibility initiatives (for example, the development of green products; reduction of the organization's greenhouse gas emissions).
- The development of a workforce that takes initiatives both to shape the emerging business environment and to adapt rapidly and responsively to changing market, social and ecological conditions.[23]

We focus here on planned approaches to change.

The planned approach is very relevant to change for sustainability, as successful change results from the careful preparation and planning necessary for sustainability auditing and reporting.[24] This is particularly so, given the recent push towards integrated reporting which requires involvement from CFOs and the finance team, not previously involved in voluntary sustainability reporting.[25] In designing incremental change programmes, managers are faced by a variety of choices and options. They could attempt to pursue sustainability initiatives by developing corporate-wide programmes – based for instance on empowerment or The Natural Step[26] – or they could buy off-the-shelf programmes of the kind provided by consulting companies or tailor them in-house, or they could seek to encourage more organic, bottom-up initiatives where changes are initiated and trialled in pilot programmes in different parts of the organization.

These choices reflect the complexity of issues that managers face in implementing change programmes. One of these issues relates to the scope of the programme. The implementation of corporate-wide programmes can have a significant impact in raising awareness throughout the organization and lead to a variety of consistent initiatives. However, the broad scope of such programmes can also dilute valuable energies and disperse scarce resources. The result can be a loss of momentum. By contrast, pilot programmes can work spectacularly because resources are focused and the scope is limited. But they may not be subsequently diffused through the organization. Packaged change programmes offer organizations quick access to tools and methods for implementing change. After all, why reinvent the wheel? But they may not meet the needs of a particular organization and those in the organization can lose the opportunity to develop skills in change design.

There is no one recipe for successful change: the approach must be carefully chosen on the basis of an analysis of the situation and the availability of resources; so we suggest here some principles in designing incremental change programmes. First, where possible, organizations should look internally for change agents. The knowledge and capabilities need to be internalized so that organizational learning takes place and skills are retained in-house so that they can be used for future change programmes. If external experts are required, the organization should leverage their knowledge and capabilities and transfer these to internal change agents. Second, as much of the change programme as possible should be designed internally. If 'packaged programmes' are used, they need to be modified to suit the organization's unique culture and operating conditions. Change agents need a deep understanding and awareness of the culture of the organization before imposing a set of solutions on those who work there. Finally, significant outcomes can be achieved through small interventions. Donella Meadows states:

> Folks who do systems analysis have a great belief in 'leverage points'. These are places within a complex system (a corporation, an economy, a living body, a city, an eco system) where a small shift in one thing can produce big changes in everything.[27]

Applying the phase model to incremental change

Up to this point, we have discussed the need for incremental change and how it can be a powerful means to mobilize an organization's resources to achieve greater sustainability outcomes. In Chapter 1, we outlined a model of the phases of corporate sustainability. This model identified six phases in corporate progression towards full sustainability. These are:

1 Rejection
2 Non-responsiveness
3 Compliance and beyond
4 Efficiency
5 Strategic proactivity
6 The sustaining corporation.

These phases emphasize that there is an enormous difference in the readiness of organizations to move to sustainable practices. Some firms are highly advanced in terms of having sustainable human resource practices; others have scarcely given them a thought. The same is true in the area of ecological sustainability: some firms are actively working towards practices that sustain and renew the environment, while others continue to exploit the environment. Because traditionally the two kinds of sustainability have rarely been seen as connected, there can also be a lack of conjunction between an organization's current position on one dimension and on the other. The ideal of a fully sustaining corporation is outlined in Figure 7.1, the sustainability change matrix. The figure combines the scales of the two dimensions in the phases of corporate sustainability in a matrix. In the upper left-hand quadrant, we have those organizations with relatively few human and ecological sustainable practices, being actively rejecting, indifferent or simply minimally compliant to both human and ecological sustainability standards. The goal is to move corporations to the lower right-hand quadrant, which represents varying degrees of active involvement on the base of efficiency, strategic advantage or fully sustaining practices.

Figure 7.1 outlines the incremental changes that organizations could take in shifting from an unsustainable to a sustainable corporation position. These represent 'ideal type' incremental changes. We have not documented here all other possible incremental change scenarios; for instance, those organizations that have already made substantial progress on either ecological or human sustainability (quadrants 2 and 3) may also be able to take more evolutionary and incremental paths to sustainability. In the next section, we outline the benefits of engaging in incremental approaches to sustainability change.

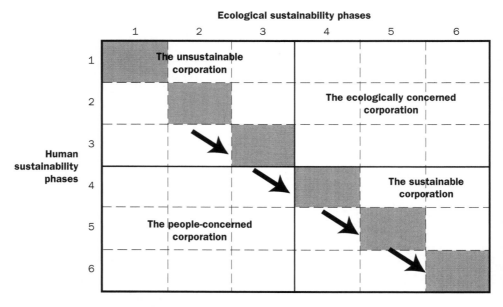

Figure 7.1 *The sustainability change matrix: incremental paths*

Benefits of incremental change

There are benefits for organizations that implement incremental changes. This section outlines a number of them.

The development of small wins

Whether planned or emergent, incremental change strategies allow organizations to achieve what Weick describes as small wins:

> A small win is a concrete, complete, implemented outcome of moderate importance. By itself, one small win may seem unimportant. A series of wins at small but significant tasks, however, reveals a pattern that may attract allies, deter opponents and lower resistance to subsequent proposals. Small wins are controllable opportunities that produce visible results.[28]

This strategy allows support to be built for the changes being implemented.

Take, for example, the case of the Australian operations of Panasonic Matsushita. Its incremental change approach was built on the 'small wins' model of establishing the change programme's credibility. Initially, its approach to sustainability started out as a series of informal meetings between a group of managers who believed that the organization could achieve savings by reducing waste and energy use. Within seven years this informal approach had developed into a planned and structured approach to pollution prevention through recycling, energy efficiency and supplier choice. In the process, it made significant cost savings as well as process and quality improvements. Having successfully achieved its first goal, the facility then implemented an environmental management system (EMS) to assess, manage and minimize the impact of its business operations on the environment.[29]

Many of the efficiency gains achieved by firms such as Scandic, IKEA and Fuji Xerox relied initially upon achieving straightforward cost efficiencies: 'picking the low-hanging fruit'. These easily gained benefits contributed to building momentum and became the basis upon which later successes were built.

The concept of small wins as a strategy can be applied to ecological efficiencies, process improvements and the development of broader

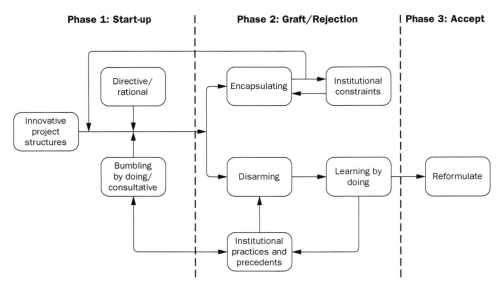

Figure 7.2 *Small wins*
Source: A. Griffiths and N. Haigh, 'Co-ordinating small wins as an effective mechanism for implementing eco-innovations', *Academy of Management Conference*, Best Paper, Organizations and Natural Environment, New Orleans, 2004.

cultural changes (see Figure 7.2). Research shows that, even when companies start out with a pro-innovation bias in attempting to introduce eco-innovations, differences emerge between companies based on the ability of the change agent to draw isolated and scattered innovations into a coherent, integrated programme.[30] Where organizations successfully make links between small wins, they create an atmosphere of learning by doing. This contributes to their ability to wind back entrenched institutional practices and creates a dynamic for deep, values-driven change. Integrated small wins become a means to generate systemic sustainability changes. Doppelt and Meadows, writing on the subject of change for sustainability, note that effective change requires a comprehensive understanding of organizational systems.[31] Furthermore, this research also shows that in those organizations where small wins weren't integrated, they became encapsulated by the existing norms, behaviours and cognitive values of the organizational members and were easily undermined by forces opposed to change. In these cases the eco-innovations simply withered away.[32]

Capability development

Another benefit of many incremental change strategies is their ability to extend and develop new technical, operational and human capabilities within an organization. Technical capabilities are developed primarily through the introduction of new technologies and multi-skilling. Operational capabilities are developed by giving employees the technical skills and authority to make product and process improvements. Human capabilities are developed through up-skilling, knowledge development and empowerment.

We take the case of Volvo to illustrate these points. Volvo's shift beyond compliance involved the development and integration of both ecological and human capabilities. This was achieved by the establishment of cross-functional project teams to work on corporate-wide key issues relating to sustainability; the implementation of broad communication and training programmes to educate employees and managers alike; and investment in R&D and technology. The performance of these programmes against sustainability goals was constantly reviewed, monitored and adjusted accordingly.[33]

Volvo executives were able to build on the existing corporate culture, which valued safety and social responsibility, by linking sustainability to their mission and values statements. Subsequently the programme focused on developing technical capabilities in product design, remanufacturing and recycling. These technical capabilities were embodied in the organization's standard operating and manufacturing procedures and policies. People capabilities were developed through team-working initiatives and the training of employees in sustainability-awareness workshops, and were built on existing projects which had encouraged widespread employee participation.

Positive culture changes

Incremental change programmes are often focused on culture-building activities. In its steel operations, One Steel implemented a pilot culture-change programme to assist with the spin-off of its steel-making operations into a new business. It centred on story-telling and developing positive future images of where the steel-making business was heading. This was designed as a powerful yet incremental means to build on the existing corporate culture. Shanahan and Maria state that 'we know that story-telling – particularly when used in industries heavily entrenched in rigid mental models – can succeed in removing obstacles to strategy development and process improvement when other methods fail'.[34] Story-telling and other culture-change programmes can open up lines of communication, create integration opportunities, commitment to new values and personal empowerment.[35] In *Dancing with the Tiger*, Nattrass and Altomare highlight the importance of stories for creating and generating values change. 'Stories help us make sense out of our experience.'[36] They are an important component of values and culture change in an incremental approach.

Particular organizational cultures influence the uptake of innovative practices in different ways. A study by Jones *et al.* found that corporate cultures with a 'human relations orientation' demonstrated higher readiness for change when it came to the implementation of a new information technology system. This was in direct contrast to those organizations that reported hierarchical, command-and-control-style cultures. Furthermore, those organizations that had developed reshaping capabilities – that is, change competencies – also showed greater readiness for change and higher usage of the IT systems once they had been implemented.[37] Incremental changes that build positive culture and values can enhance an organization's readiness for change and acceptance of new practices. This was also the case at Scandic corporation, highlighted previously. The successful redefinition of corporate values to 'profound caring' and the subsequent expression of this in greater stakeholder involvement and support depended on prior customer-orientated values.

Furthermore, there is a growing awareness of the importance of the understanding of subcultures within organizations and how these subcultures in turn understand issues associated with corporate sustainability. Recent research indicates that different groups across organizations and across levels within an organization may share similar values. Although this research is in an early phase, it shows that these values strongly overlap with understanding of corporate sustainability. Figure 7.3 highlights the direct relationship between the organization's overall culture/values score – which is primarily bureaucratic, and its understanding of corporate sustainability – which is dominated by an economic understanding. Furthermore, this leading research found that when this overall culture profile was broken down, it resulted in the emergence of five distinct organizational 'subcultures'. Each of these

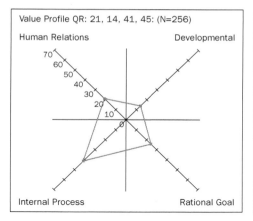

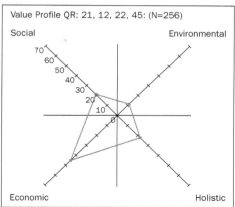

Figure 7.3 *Culture and corporate sustainability understandings profile for a transport company*
Source: M. Linnenlucke, 'Understanding Corporate Sustainability: A Quantitative Study about a Single Organization', Masters report, Queensland: University of Queensland Business School, Faculty of Business, Economics and Law, The University of Queensland, 2006.

subcultures corresponded with an almost identical plotting of understandings of corporate sustainability. One of the key implications of this path-breaking research is that when it comes to incremental, values-driven change, an understanding of a culture and the subcultures with an organization may be vital to tailoring effective incremental change processes to achieve greater sustainability outcomes and wider acceptance.[38]

In other research, the Network for Business Sustainability reviewed organizational practices that assist in building a culture of sustainability, defined as 'one in which organizational members hold shared assumptions and beliefs about the importance of balancing economic efficiency, social equity and environmental accountability'.[39] As shown in Figure 7.4, the researchers found that the practices could be grouped according to two dimensions: intent and approach. The intent dimension (vertical) encompassed a range of practices that encouraged both fulfilment and innovation, while the approach dimension (horizontal) included the formal and informal practices that were found to support a positive culture of sustainability.[40]

The alignment of this portfolio of practices along two dimensions highlights the inherent tensions between elements of organizational change that might support sustainability. So, for example, developing a

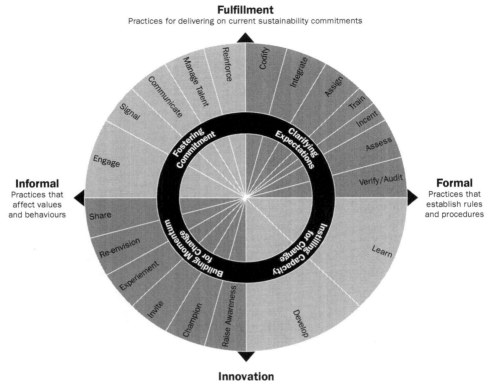

Fulfillment
Practices for delivering on current sustainability commitments

Informal
Practices that
affect values
and behaviours

Formal
Practices that
establish rules
and procedures

Innovation
Practices that move the organization further along the path to sustainability

Figure 7.4 *Practices that embed sustainability*
Note: Note that this framework is currently being refined and tools developed to support the assessment of these practices, available at www.nbs.net.
Source: Network for Business Sustainability, *Embedding Sustainability in Organizational Culture*, 2010, p. 14.

sustainability culture and then embedding it in the mainstream of the organization requires fulfilment in the form of delivery on established sustainability initiatives as well as innovating to develop new avenues such as products or processes that are more sustainable. Similarly, with the approach dimension there are tensions between the informal changes that are required, such as in values and norms, and the more formal systems of clarification and accreditation that we have described earlier. This portfolio of practices suggested from the Network for Business Sustainability research (see Figure 7.4) highlights the complexity of change for sustainability while emphasizing the multitude of practices that are available to the change agent to implement sustainability.

This research also acknowledges the critical aspects of change for sustainability that distinguish it from other change programmes. These include the fact that sustainability refers to a broader set of drivers that implicate cross-organizational involvement and a broader social agenda. As we have noted throughout this edition, the change agenda must apply across supply networks.

Other recent research confirms that a positive culture is important in fostering pro-environmental behaviour in employees alongside generating other benefits for the organization. For example, promoting of positive affect has been shown to increase not only more active environmentally responsible behaviour but creativity in a more general sense. This work also highlights the importance of promoting pro-environmental attitudes if employees' environmental behaviour is to change.[41]

Efficiency improvements

One of the key drivers for organizations to implement such practices is that incremental changes, when implemented successfully, can lead to improvements in operational performance. The drive towards eco-efficiency at Sony, for instance, brought about improvements such as a 50 per cent improvement in the ratio of recycled parts and materials, 50 per cent reduction in dismantling time and 50 per cent reduction in the use of styrene foam. These results came from implementing EMS in manufacturing operations and the design of products. But to recognize the relationship between improvements in environmental and other aspects of organizational performance, targeted measuring systems are required. Sony relies on utilizing greenhouse gas emissions and resource use as indicators, reporting, for example, that in fiscal year 2012 Sony's greenhouse gas emissions totalled approximately 17.41 million tons, down 30 per cent from fiscal year 2011. This decrease was attributable to the reduction of greenhouse gas emissions from sites, CO_2 emissions from product use and logistics. Sony's eco-efficiency index for greenhouse gas emissions in fiscal year 2011 was 0.64 times, compared with 0.96 times in fiscal year 2000, an improvement of approximately 50 per cent.[42]

Operational efficiencies are not limited to changes in technical production systems. The aspects of human sustainability clearly impact on organizational performance. In the twenty-first-century workplace, productivity is linked to aspects of human sustainability that go beyond work–life balance. Employees appear to perform better, including in terms of responding to change, if they are happy outside work, which may relate to spending time with friends and family or volunteering.[43]

Within the workplace, participation is clearly related to engagement in the change initiative. A recent 60-year review of quantitative studies on change recipients' reactions to change found evidence that change recipients who experienced high levels of participation report higher acceptance of new initiatives and exhibit overall support for the change.[44] Bartunek *et al.*'s work also demonstrates that there is a positive association between employee participation and understanding the meaning and benefits of a change.[45] Such studies add weight to the 30 years of case studies, anecdotal evidence and broad industry surveys which have shown the benefits of such practices in creating high-performance organizations.[46]

Rockcote: The Nerang Design Centre

Rockcote is a small, privately owned company that specializes in the generation of paints and architectural coatings for private and commercial use. Its newly established design centre at Nerang, on the 'Gold Coast' in Australia, highlights the links between eco-efficiency improvements and human factors in establishing and making a creative, green design-centre function. The Nerang Design Centre has quickly become an icon for green design in a commercial context. It has been created to exist in harmony with natural systems in order to optimize energy efficiency, water consumption, liveability and profitability. The entire site is environmentally sustainable; the first of its kind in Australia.[47] The view taken by CEO Bob Cameron during the design process was 'it doesn't cost any more to do something properly in the first place'. All rainwater is collected in rain tanks for human consumption. Waste from toilets and sinks is treated on site through a series of ponds, aquatic plants and fish, and then recycled using no fossil fuels. The building itself has been heavily insulated with clay and natural fibres, is situated on the site in such a way as to capture enough breeze and sunlight to render an air-conditioning system unnecessary and utilizes natural light and ventilation to increase staff productivity. New technology has been implemented to sense the levels of natural light and brighten or dim the internal lights accordingly. Organic waste from the staff lunchroom is composted on site. After hours, the showroom is made available free of charge for community functions, and the car park converts into a tennis court. The site is connected to mains water only to satisfy fire regulations and, more recently, a solar power system has been implemented, enabling Rockcote to sell power back to the grid.[48] The entire design and operation of the Nerang Design Centre is a series of eco-innovations, all brought together to create an entirely sustainable development, 'cutting

continued

edge, if not in the world, then certainly in Australia'.[49] The result is a commercial development operating 80 per cent cheaper than comparable traditional developments, with an environment conducive to greater staff productivity and creativity.[50] It is an example of what can be achieved through incremental change that encourages the full participation of staff in all aspects of planning and execution.

New organizational structures

Incremental change strategies can be used to generate new organizational structures, systems and reporting relationships while maintaining the online operational capacity of the organization. For instance, STS redesigns which result in what are now known as 'high-performance work organizations' have generated a sophisticated methodology for the implementation and evaluation of team-based organizations. These new organizations have flatter reporting structures; are reliant upon the devolution of responsibility and autonomy; have shifted from control to commitment-based systems and changed the way that production is organized. Creating high-performance work organizations can take years, but many organizations in Europe, the USA and Australia have benefited from the use of such team-based approaches to change. They represent powerful successful models which can be emulated. Citing the work of Ostroff and Schmitt, Stace and Dunphy note that the concepts of team-based organizations can be used to enhance new organizational structures such as networks. These organizations demonstrate the following characteristics:[51]

- they organize around processes by linking workflows and relying on teams[52]
- they keep hierarchies flat and remove the temptation to build control-orientated management systems
- they assign ownership of processes and performance to teams
- they link performance to customer satisfaction
- they combine managerial and non-managerial activities to encourage self-management
- they link customers and suppliers to teams
- they focus on developing trust and competencies.

Development of change competencies

Incremental change programmes are an excellent vehicle to develop change-agent skills and the change competencies of managers and employees. For example, incremental change provides environmental managers not only with the technical and process skills required for further change but also the opportunity to develop important skills needed for building and maintaining coalitions, designing educational programmes, extending leadership skills for culture change and negotiating with community representatives.[53] Daily and Huang argue that successful EMS implementation requires cultural changes.[54] Change agents can use opportunities around incremental change to create cultures which empower employees as well as implementing team-working initiatives which support sustainability.

For example, HP used the opportunity of its engagement with corporate social responsibility to develop, build and extend its HR competencies. As a direct result of harnessing diversity and unleashing the potential of its employees, HP has achieved significant and remarkable success in its corporate sustainability programmes.

Benefits of incremental change

- Development of small wins – small successes can be used to overcome areas of resistance and develop a powerful force for change.
- Capability development – incremental changes can be used to develop human and technical competencies.
- Positive culture change – incremental change can modify values and build commitment through employee involvement and participation.
- Efficiency improvements can be generated as a consequence of making process improvements, changes to product or work design.
- Creation of new organizational structures based on teams and virtual teams, and improvements in reporting systems and feedback loops.
- Development of change competencies.

Potential pitfalls of incremental change

The first major pitfall to threaten organizations that are changing incrementally is misfit: moving out of alignment with the firm's dynamic market environment. To avoid this, organizations need constantly to monitor and evaluate their current environments and develop competencies to anticipate future trends. Without such capabilities, they can become vulnerable to what Strebel refers to as 'breakpoints': significant events that face organizations with a major environmental discontinuity such as loss of a major market or a new technology that makes the existing technology obsolete.[55] Confronted with a crisis of this kind, the advocacy of incremental changes is usually a form of organizational complacency and dysfunctionality. When organizations experience turbulent and transformed conditions, incremental changes will fail to realign them with the new environments. Under these conditions, we advocate the use of transformational change strategies instead.

The gradualism of incremental changes means that they are susceptible to regression and abandonment, particularly if there is no clear link between the change programme and performance. Where success is not clearly evident, senior managers may withdraw their support from incremental changes and shift priorities for resources to other areas of organizational activity. Incremental changes do not usually occur in all parts of the organization at the same time or at the same pace. However, to attract continued managerial support, they must show significant performance improvements and clearly contribute to business results. Most of the cases that we have presented in this book demonstrate positive examples of successful change. However, not all cases have happy endings. In one energy company that we are familiar with, the change agent responsible for implementing sustainability programmes within the organization found that her time was spread too thinly across a range of projects in the organization. Innovations that she had started foundered as she switched her attention to other projects. The lack of resources meant that she was unable to establish clear performance improvements beyond some compliance activities. As a result, momentum was lost and the change programme petered out.

Employee cynicism over the 'latest management fad' can be fatal for incremental change programmes. Employees and managers alike 'batten the hatches' when senior executives launch the organization into the next alphabetically listed change programme. Abrahamson refers to 'permafrost' organizations[56] where change-fatigued middle managers block and actively resist initiatives from both below and above. Under these conditions, incremental change stands a significant chance of failure, disappearing like water into sand. A manufacturing organization that one of us researched, Bendix Mintex, had been through the 'alphabet soup' of change programmes. After many false starts it finally settled on a team-based approach to change. However, before this could succeed it needed to overcome employee cynicism about seeing this as just 'the latest fad'. It succeeded in overcoming the cynicism by including key opinion makers in the change process from redesign to implementation. Furthermore, it actively sought and encouraged employee suggestions on how the redesigned organization should work. By the time it began to implement the new redesign it had achieved a groundswell of support from the workforce, who wanted to see their own ideas put into practice. It became a successful team-based organization.[57] Table 7.1 outlines major threats to the success of incremental change programmes and how these can be overcome.

We have integrated some of Bob Doppelt's sustainability blunders and potential change solutions to dealing with these limitations of incremental change.[58]

Major issues in the movement between phases

Moving from non-responsiveness to compliance

The organizations in most need of change are those in the rejection and non-responsiveness phases. In our view, the movement from rejection

Table 7.1 *Overcoming limitations of incremental change*

Major issues	Action strategies
Lack of fit with external environment	Constant monitoring of the external environment of the firm and a preparedness to engage in transformational change if necessary.
Decreasing managerial support for change programme	Demonstrate and promote performance improvements. Develop small-wins approach, market success in order to win management support.
Change faddism	Maintain programme consistency and link the programme to overall corporate strategies and values statements.
Lack of a clear vision and programme objectives	Outline clear goals and priorities – provide clear support and encouragement for small wins that align with these goals.
Lack of learning mechanisms	Development of teams and processes whereby issues around incremental change success and failure can be drawn upon.

Source: B. Doppelt, 'The seven sustainability blunders', *System Thinker*, June–July 2003, p. 3.

(Phase 1) to compliance (Phase 3) is a transformational change of the kind we deal with in Chapter 8. So in this section we concentrate on the movement from non-responsiveness to compliance (Phase 2 to Phase 3). Non-responsive organizations tend to disregard the impact of their actions on the natural environment, the communities in which they are located and the value of their human capital. These corporations are economically, socially and ecologically blind or blinkered. In some cases, traditional values and a focus on operational and cost issues act as blinkers, resulting in a narrow view of what constitutes the firm's environment. Generally, business activities in these firms are concerned primarily with short-term profits, to the detriment of broader societal and environmental responsibilities. This may be across all the organization's activities or in particular areas. For example, some corporations don't apply the same 'home base' standards to their activities in other parts of the world, particularly third-world regions and countries. For example, Esmeralda Explorations Ltd was the owner of the Baia Mare Aurul gold mine. When a tailings dam burst, spilling 95 tonnes of cyanide into the environment, it denied responsibility, claiming that there was no connection between the spill and the poisoning of the Lapus and Somes rivers in Romania and the Tisza in Hungary.[59] One doubts whether it would have made the same arguments in its home country. More recently, Anvil Mining has been accused of assisting government forces in the Democratic Republic of Congo to massacre villagers who were disrupting activities in the area of the company's mining operations. The company issued a press release denying any involvement. An independent report by the United Nations had found that the company had lent vehicles, drivers and logistical support to local troops and had paid local troops.[60] The company maintained that it had done nothing wrong. Obviously, from these cases, significant challenges to the right to operate lie ahead for companies involved in such activities.

Non-responsive corporations are characterized by a blatant disregard for legislative and social standards. They may be willing to dump waste, clear-fell old-growth forests, engage in poor occupational health and safety (OH&S) standards and hide facts from the public about the damaging nature of their activities and/or products. However, there are many examples of organizations which once acted in this way abandoning these approaches and supporting significant sustainability initiatives. Given the willingness of the board, CEO, senior managers and major financial investors, these organizations can make the shift from non-responsiveness to compliance, using incremental change strategies. How is this to be achieved?

- Where there is organizational reluctance to initiate change, external pressure can be brought to bear on the organization through public protests, court action and third-party scrutiny or, increasingly, through pressure from investor funds. For instance, the Carbon Disclosure Project works with 722 institutional investors holding US$ 87 trillion in assets to help reveal the risk in their investment portfolios. It is the largest global holder of self-reported climate-change, water- and forest-risk data.[61] Increasingly, investors are avoiding non-sustainable companies.

- By ensuring that someone with authority in the organization takes charge of the change process. Non-compliance can have major effects on the profitability, risk liability and the reputation of the corporation. Consequently, the change agent responsible for the shift needs to be a senior manager who reports directly to the CEO and has the power and authority to implement the changes. This should be someone with credibility and integrity who is respected throughout the organization.

- By making a comprehensive evaluation of legislative and commercial obligations. The survey should cover legislative requirement areas such as pollution, waste and licensing, mining and logging, and OH&S and other workplace codes. Similarly, the organization needs to develop an understanding of its insurance risks, potential liabilities and obligations to bodies such as securities commissions. Some international agencies refuse to lend capital for development projects in third-world countries if the corporations involved cannot demonstrate that they are attempting to build local capacity and meet sustainability expectations.

- By undertaking a review of existing operations to see whether and where they fail to comply with the legislative requirements. Areas requiring immediate action are then targeted and resources allocated. It may be necessary to design and run training programmes and management awareness sessions, to institute searches for new technologies and to establish measurement and reporting systems. In some cases, decisions may be made to disengage the company from activities that involve future risks or are not cost-effective to operate.

- By using the human resources system to link management performance to these new goals in order to ensure that programmatic changes, such as OH&S initiatives, are accurately monitored and measured. Timelines and specified performance goals are set for the changes to be implemented. This phase requires standard project-management skills. Managerial remuneration may also be linked to sustainability performance as a means of bootstrapping the organization's performance.

- By putting feedback loops in place in critical compliance areas to ensure that compliance is monitored and managers are rewarded according to their performance against these standards.
- By using external auditing bodies to review and monitor corporate progress against plans. This may also involve the use of international agencies, such as the International Standards Organization and its ISO 14000 series as a basis for environmental management systems.

A summary of moving from non-responsiveness to compliance is provided in the box.[62]

Pathways from non-responsiveness to compliance

- Appoint a senior manager with authority and reputation to implement the change process.
- Undertake an evaluation of the key legislative requirements.
- Review existing operations and identify areas for immediate attention.
- Align programmatic changes to goals.
- Create feedback loops in critical compliance areas.
- Use auditing bodies to assess compliance.

This approach to incremental change is unusual because it is directive in character. Transformational strategies are more often associated with a directive approach to change initiated by senior executives. However, in ensuring compliance, significant responsibility for shifting the organization and its operations lies with senior management, who must institute and support clearly defined standards and rules. While there is a directive element in this change process, this does not exclude employee participation in making compliance-related procedures succeed. The recent accumulating research evidence demonstrates that when employees are engaged on sustainability issues they make significant and valuable contributions to the development of eco-innovations.[63] An example of this comes from Interface, the carpet company, which has used incremental change processes and employee involvement to move on a company whose products depended almost entirely on petroleum products. Its stylish Proscenium Collection uses a hybrid of polylactic acid (PLA) and nylon fibre. PLA is a bio-based renewable resource made from corn and other plant materials. The starch portion of these non-food-grade agricultural products is converted to sugar and fermented to produce lactic acid. This is then processed and polymerized to produce PLA, using 20–50 per cent less fossil fuel resources than traditional hydrocarbon resins. This means less greenhouse gases produced and also that the PLA can be naturally recycled.

Compliance to sustainable efficiency

For many corporations the incremental shift from compliance to efficiency is a natural extension of the capabilities, knowledge and practices developed in the earlier phase. For instance, compliance-monitoring systems – particularly attempts to reduce emissions – often result in organizations also implementing process improvements and installing new technologies that enable the organization to move beyond compliance. Similarly, we find that organizations investing in compliance activities also start to invest in resources, specialist knowledge and skills (developing environmental managers; shifting from a narrow personnel focus to a broader HR management focus) and new technologies (monitoring systems; human resource information systems). Such a transition involves a shift in focus away from issues such as pay scales and legislative compliance activities and towards the development of a more strategically orientated human resources function that contributes to gaining competitive advantage.

What are the incremental steps involved in shifting organizations from compliance to efficiency?

- Efficiency programmes often start on the periphery of an organization as innovative line managers use their business units to experiment with such practices as job redesign, teamwork or reorganization of the supply chain. This often occurs in problem plants – the poor performers – and is part of a push to improve performance. Sometimes, however, efficiency programmes may be initiated by a senior manager or CEO who develops a particular commitment to sustainability, inspired by programmes such as The Natural Step. For instance, Interface's Australian operations went from being the 'worst performer' to being its number one performing plant out of 27 plants scattered around the world, largely because of the CEO's personal enthusiasm for sustainability.
- Learning from the pilot experiments is normally brought together and evaluated. Successes and failures are talked about and initiatives extended. Managers who lead the changes in these business units walk the talk. Their actions and commitment are matched by their willingness to utilize the knowledge of employees, question current organizational orthodoxies and push responsibility down the line. Robert Eckert, CEO of Mattel, attributes its turnaround, in part, to a

'walk-the-talk' approach that encouraged employee empowerment and contributed to human capital development.[64]

- In both HR and ecological areas, incremental change results in an increased emphasis on capability development. Typical initiatives include education programmes, cross-sectional problem-solving teams, reviews of barriers and enablers and a willingness to try new ideas and suggestions. Meanwhile successes are monitored in both a tangible form (costs; waste; quality) and in an intangible form (stories; shifts in culture and values). These shifts often become part of the organization's folklore and help employees to develop a 'can do' attitude.

- We often notice that there is a point where the confidence-building activities, the devolution of authority, the education programmes and capability development all begin to crystallize. This becomes a critical leverage point. At this time there is the opportunity to shift the programme from a series of isolated small wins and to grow more independent support for organization-wide change. It is important to seize the opportunity and provide the resources needed to significantly expand the programme.

When this critical mass for change is harnessed, the programme develops its own momentum: for instance, efficiency gains are diffused to other parts of the organization. Problem areas outside the boundary of the business unit, such as product design and supply chains, now become open to influence and change. After the economic and other benefits of the efficiency changes have been demonstrated, the programme is championed by senior management and extended throughout the organization. As this happens, it is useful to dramatize and celebrate successes and reward key contributors to the change programme. These steps are summarized in the box.

Steps in moving from compliance to sustainable efficiency

- Look for efficiency opportunities at the periphery of the organization or in poorly performing plants.
- Collate pilot projects' experiences and evaluate.
- Increase capability development.
- Monitor success and incorporate success stories into organizational folklore.
- Identify leverage points and generate critical mass support.
- Look for opportunities to create programme momentum.
- Identify and work on problem areas.
- Extend the programme with management support.

Efficiency to strategic proactivity

With each additional incremental step, organizations can build increasing depth of technical and human capabilities. We also see changes in the organization's culture, such as increasing employee commitment, and more indicators of its movement towards high-performance activities. There is often also a direct attempt to increase diffusion of sustainability practices to suppliers and customers. For instance, in the HR area there is usually active recruitment and more retention of highly skilled people with strong sustainability values; challenging executive development programmes are developed and delivered and new opportunities are created for exciting and meaningful careers (as has been seen in the HP and Rockcote cases). In the ecological area, we see the emergence of strategic alliances with suppliers and customers and active engagement with community groups in the establishment of new products and services. This is exemplified by Scandic hotels, which promotes on its website the characteristics that suppliers to Scandic should aspire to in order to help Scandic deliver on its own value and sustainability commitments.

Our case study analysis indicates that the following characteristics assist in shifting a firm from efficiency to strategy by incremental processes:

- Senior level recognition that the efficiency gains achieved through value adding, and the capabilities developed along the way, are sufficiently valuable to be further integrated into the core strategic activities of the organization. The diffusion of strategic goals for sustainability to all key business units and managers within the organization. Along with that, responsibility for the attainment of sustainability goals is integrated into management reward and performance systems. For example, Queensland Rail, has agreed to integrate environmental sustainability throughout the organization, to the benefit of the environment, its people, customers and the community.[65]
- The allocation of significant corporate resources into key areas such as research and development, knowledge management, alliance formation, industry networking and social partnerships. Toyota and Honda have both invested significantly in research and development pertaining to fuel cells, hybrid technologies and lightweight materials. Both of these organizations are now recognized as having distinct advantages over their US competitors in the 'greening of the automobile'.[66]

- Systematic exploration of opportunities for strategic alliances. However, by this time, suppliers are accountable for the impact of their products and processes on sustainability outcomes. Training and resources are provided to those willing to change.
- Accreditation systems such as EMS, TQEM, design for environment, teamwork, communities of practice and networking become common features of organizational life. Operational and efficiency gains are constantly improved upon and linked to strategic objectives.
- Finally, corporate strategies are constantly revisited in light of the performance of products and services; new directions are initiated; there is openness to third-party auditing and systematic assessment of the impact of the organization on communities. Shell's 2005 Sustainability Report – with its self-criticisms – and Interface's commitment to third-party auditing of its eco-products testify to the increasing importance of scrutiny of an organization's sustainability claims and its link to management strategy.

These steps are summarized in the box.

Steps in moving from efficiency to strategic proactivity

- Senior-level support built on the gains made in the efficiency stage.
- Diffusion of strategic goals relating to sustainability to all parts of the organization.
- Allocation of corporate resources to key areas.
- Identification of strategic alliances and other emerging opportunities.
- Use of accreditation programmes.
- Strategies revised in light of performance.

Strategic proactivity to the sustaining corporation

Incremental change can also facilitate the shift from strategic sustainability to the sustaining corporation phase. We view these changes as cumulative. In becoming sustaining corporations, organizations do not abandon the strategic approach or the capabilities that they have acquired and built as they moved through prior phases. Rather, the shift from strategic sustainability to the sustaining corporation requires an expansion and modification of the value base of the organization. In particular, we identify three key changes:

- Change programmes that focus on shifting the behaviours and values of organizational members. These are designed to produce extensive culture change. For instance, employees may be rewarded for undertaking community projects or taking an organizational sabbatical working on ecological issues. For example, since 1984, Patagonia, a successful manufacturer of outdoor equipment, has committed 10 per cent of its annual profits to grass-roots environmental groups and has adopted the following mission statement: 'Patagonia exists as a business to improve and implement solutions to environmental issues.' As an expression of its values-based culture, Patagonia runs an internship programme for employees whereby they can work, fully paid, for up to two months in an environmental group of their choosing. Patagonia executives see these types of programmes as falling under the banner of their strategy – 'It's the right thing to do'.[67]

- The use of external parties to monitor, evaluate and encourage future performance: while not essential, this helps to create momentum for further change. Third parties can also be used to challenge prevailing assumptions and organizational complacency. Marks & Spencer, for example, has recently agreed to phase out all hazardous chemicals from its supply chain by 2020, working with Greenpeace as part of its Detox campaign to develop a commitment to implementing technologies such as cold batch dyeing, a process that, on average, uses 50 per cent less water and reduces carbon by 30 per cent.[68] More importantly, the sustaining organization will start to challenge others within its industry or supply chain to implement a broad sustainability agenda. For instance, Rockcote encourages and helps other organizations engage in eco-initiatives within its own geographic proximity. It has aligned itself with other eco-friendly companies to share resources and information and practical sustainability know-how. This is seen by all companies involved as a practical way of sharing information, learning by doing and removing the need for costly consultants.[69] As Bob Cameron, CEO of Rockcote states:

  > It would have taken us ages to figure out solutions to some of our waste water treatment issues . . . but when I saw what the others had done and saw the information that they complied, it all made sense on how we should do it.[70]

- A focus on design for environment, product and service innovation, and the education of consumers and supply-chain members on the role that they can play in creating viable alternative business models for sustainability and a sustainable society. Rockcote's Nerang Design

Centre, for example, exposes visiting customers experientially to high-quality eco-design and eco-products – the Centre itself is a visible demonstration of the economic, ecological and human value of moving to sustainability.

These steps are summarized in the box below.

Steps in moving from strategic proactivity to the sustaining corporation

- Build on previous capabilities from the efficiency and strategic stages.
- Focus on shifting behaviours and values to create large-scale cultural change.
- Use external parties to drive and challenge performance.
- Invest in innovation in product and process redesign, and consumer education.
- Diffuse sustaining practices to others in the supply chain and other organizations interested in benchmarking.

Steps involved in incremental change

In the previous sections of this chapter, we outlined some of the specific issues that organizations face when moving incrementally between the phases identified in Figure 7.1. In this section, we round off this chapter by identifying eight generic steps involved in creating sustainable organizations through the use of incremental change strategies:

Step 1: Begin with future workshops/search conferences. The incremental changes discussed in this chapter focus primarily on operational issues (such as product, process and people changes) and take place in strategic business units. However, starting change programmes at this level does not preclude having a vision or strategic direction. The cases of Scandic, IKEA and Patagonia all point to the importance of having a clear vision and strategic goals to move the organization or specific units forward. Future workshops and search conferences are tools that can be used to generate discussion, participation and commitment to the developing vision for sustainability, and to developing a plan for realizing the vision. They are also useful for identifying problem areas and potential strategic opportunities. Such events also act as leverage points to motivate and to harness employee energy to the change.

Step 2: Assess the organizations current position in relation to sustainability. This step addresses the questions: Where is the business unit currently in relation to sustainability practices? What are the barriers and enablers for making sustainability work? What influence will the existing corporate or unit culture have in facilitating or blocking sustainability initiatives? What are the activities that will need to be undertaken in order to shift the business unit from its present position to that outlined in the search conference? Information and employee engagement are key. For example, Marks & Spencer has arranged to survey 22,500 of its workers four times per year on workplace issues and financial literacy using mobile technology. To do this it has signed a one-year deal with social enterprise technology provider Good World Solutions to facilitate the communication. It will use Labor Link, technology that collates anonymous, quantitative survey results direct from the supply-chain workers.[71]

In some cases, assessing the current position also involves opening up the organization to external stakeholder evaluation and criticism. This stage also involves developing the business case for committing resources to sustainability.[72]

Step 3: Evaluate the type of change programme needed. This stage addresses the issue of the approach to be taken. Will the changes introduced be programmatic? That is, will the change programme seek coverage rather than depth – using change tools such as education programmes, The Natural Step workshops or competency training – or will the change approach encourage the emergence of organic innovations within identified business units? The choices made here will affect the types of change strategies used, resource needs and expectations for performance. On the whole, we advocate progressing through organic innovations that are piloted and then diffused through a more programmatic approach, although the type of change programme needed may differ for different countries and, potentially, for different organizational subcultures. The multinational bank the ING Group controls every aspect of its operations in the Netherlands through an EMS. This is more difficult in some countries; policies on investment concerning life sciences, coal energy and fur, for instance, are each considered separately.

Step 4: Identify change agents. We shall comment in more detail on change agents in Chapter 9. However, change agents should be enthusiastic, knowledgeable about business processes, and engender confidence and optimism. Furthermore, a team of change agents playing different facilitative, technical and coalition-building roles can have more impact than one change agent acting alone. For instance, at one manufacturing organization, the implementation of world-class manufacturing involved the formation of a change unit in which a variety of roles were played. The role of the senior executive leading the team was that of the strategist/political operator. It was his role to garner senior support and protect the change programme in its infancy. The operations manager played a task-focused role: he designed and implemented the change programme. His activities were directive and he was responsible for maintaining the momentum of change. His directive style of leadership was complemented by the change facilitator, who concentrated on the social relations side of the change. The change facilitator was assisted by a shopfloor employee, who was a key opinion maker. The change unit was coached by an external consultant, who also played an important role in gathering information and providing a template for action and training. These roles were coordinated and influential in creating a successful, multi-skilled unit that turned around a brownfield manufacturing site into one that was competitive and world class.

Step 5: Pilot new practices and innovations. In incremental change programmes there is usually time to pilot-test proposed changes. This allows competency deficiencies and operational problems to be identified and then addressed, rather like debugging a software programme before its widespread adoption. Once the effectiveness of pilot programmes has been established, they can be used to build broader support throughout the organization. Pilot programmes are also an ideal way to test the appropriateness of the tools, and redesign techniques and forms of participation that will be used in the subsequent full-scale incremental change programme. They are also useful in estimating the resourcing that will be needed when the programme expands.

Step 6: Harness further resources. When pilot programmes have been shown to be effective, diffusion of the changes requires access to further resources: time, money, people and management support. It is often best to start where people can readily be engaged and short-term wins can be achieved; later, areas of resistance within the organization need to be progressively incorporated into the programme. These areas may require a more intensive use of resources, particularly skilled change agents with high levels of interpersonal skills. If middle managers and supervisors are resistant to change, senior management support will be necessary to ensure that the programme is not sabotaged.

Step 7: Communicate and extend the programme. The success of the pilot needs to be communicated throughout the organization, and some of those involved in making the changes in the pilot situation should be used as change agents to initiate the changes elsewhere, working with line managers. At this stage, it is important that the change programme doesn't just become a proliferation of largely unrelated initiatives in different operations, but is integrated at the strategic level.

Step 8: Align organizational systems. For the successful initiatives to turn into truly programmatic changes, operating systems, reward systems, information systems and reporting structures will need to be modified. These modifications should be designed to enhance the robustness of the change and to prevent regression in the pilot site and diffusion areas. Without these broader changes, pilot sites can end up becoming 'islands of innovation in a sea of mediocrity'. As Shelton argues, they run the risk of 'hitting the green wall'.[73]

The steps of incremental change are summarized in the box.[74]

Eight steps of incremental change

1 Begin with future workshops/search conferences.
2 Assess the organization's current position in relation to sustainability.
3 Evaluate the type of change programme needed.
4 Identify change agents.
5 Pilot new practices and innovations.
6 Harness further resources.
7 Communicate and extend the programme.
8 Align organizational systems.

These eight generic steps by themselves do not guarantee the success of an incremental change programme. A great deal depends on the support given to the changes by senior management, readiness for change on the part of the workforce and the skill of change agents. However, omitting one of these steps can seriously affect the potential success of the change programme. A fully-fledged incremental change programme normally moves through all eight steps.

Conclusion

In this chapter, we have outlined some of the key characteristics of successful incremental change programmes. We have noted that incremental change strategies are useful for organizations seeking to move between one phase of sustainability and the next. However, as we discussed earlier in this chapter, not all organizations will be able to move forward fast enough on the path to sustainability by using incremental change strategies. The next chapter outlines transformational change strategies – that is, strategies that change the mind-sets, cultures, structures and products of organizations in radical ways to obtain sustainability outcomes.

Notes

1 Some of the key texts to emerge that deal with sustainability-driven change in organizations adopt an incremental systems-change perspective. See B. Doppelt, *Leading Change toward Sustainability*, Sheffield: Greenleaf Publishing, 2003; B. Nattrass and M. Altomare, *Dancing with the Tiger: Learning Sustainability Step by Natural Step*, Gabriola Island: New Society Publishers, 2002; D. Esty and A. Winston, *Green to Gold: How Smart Companies Use Environmental Strategy to Innovate, Create Value and Build Competitive Advantage*, Hoboken, NJ: Wiley, 2009; B. Willard, *The Sustainability Champion's Guidebook: How To Transform Your Company*, New Society Publishers, 2009; as well as many others such as *The Upcycle: Beyond Sustainability – Designing for Abundance*, by W. McDonough and M. Braungart, New York: North Point Press, 2013, which take a more radical approach.
2 D. Dunphy and A. Griffiths, *The Sustainable Corporation*, Sydney: Allen and Unwin, 1998.
3 D. Dunphy and A. Griffiths, 'Corporate strategic change', in M. Warner (ed.) *International Encyclopedia of Business and Management*, London: Thomson Learning, 2002, pp. 1169–75.
4 A. Griffiths and D. Dunphy, 'Heresies to orthodoxies: organizational renewal in Australia 1966–1996', *Management Decision*, 2002, 40 (1), 74–81.
5 Nattrass and Altomare, *Dancing with the Tiger*.
6 R. Orsato, 'The Ecological Modernisation of Industry: A Study of the European Automobile Field', Doctoral thesis, University of Technology, Sydney, 2001, p. 35.
7 See, for instance, the work of D. Korten, *When Corporations Rule the World*, San Francisco, CA: Berrett-Koehler, 1995; *The Post Corporate World*, San Francisco, CA: Berrett-Koehler, 1999.

8 S. Hart and M. Milstein, 'Global sustainability and the creative destruction of industries', *Sloan Management Review*, 1999, 41 (1), 23–33, esp. 24.

9 Ibid, p. 24.

10 A. Griffiths and M. Winn, 'Slack and Sustainability'. Paper presented to the *Academy of Management Conference*, Hawaii, 2005.

11 M. Beer and N. Nohria, 'Cracking the code of change', *Harvard Business Review*, 2000, May–June, 78 (3), 133–41, esp. 133.

12 E. Abrahamson, 'Change without pain', *Harvard Business Review*, 2000, July–August, 75–9, esp. 75.

13 C. O'Reilly and M. Tushman, 'The ambidextrous organization', *Harvard Business Review*, 2004, 82 (4), 74–81.

14 The Australian Business Roundtable on Climate Change warns that 'the longer we delay acting, the more expensive it becomes for business and for the wider Australian economy'. Australian Business Roundtable on Climate Change, *The Business Case for Early Action Report*, 2006, p. 2; while the Millennium Ecosystem Assessment, in its Statement from the Board, issues a stark warning: 'Human activity is putting such strain on the natural function of the Earth that the ability of the planet's ecosystems to sustain future generations can no longer be taken for granted . . . Nearly two thirds of the services provided by nature to human kind are found to be in decline worldwide.' Millennium Ecosystem Assessment, 'Living Beyond Our Means: Natural Assets and Human Well-Being', 2005, p. 2.

15 Readers who wish to understand in more detail the differences between incremental and transformational change can find excellent discussions and relevant research summaries in: B. Burnes, *Managing Change: A Strategic Approach to Organizational Dynamics*, Financial Times/Prentice Hall, London, 3rd edn, 2000, pp. 253–8; I. Palmer, R. Dunford and G. Akin, *Managing Organizational Change: A Multiple Perspectives Approach*, New York: McGraw Hill, 2006, pp. 74–86; D. Stace and D. Dunphy, *Beyond the Boundaries: Leading and Re-creating the Successful Enterprise*, Sydney: McGraw Hill, 2nd edn, 2001, pp. 103–26.

16 A. Ryan, I. K. Mitchell and S. Daskou, 'An interaction and networks approach to developing sustainable organizations', *Journal of Organizational Change Management*, 2012, 25 (4), pp. 578–594.

17 P. Dawson, 'The contribution of the processual approach to the theory and practice of organizational change', in D. Boje, B. Burnes and J. Hassard (eds) *The Routledge Companion to Organizational Change,* New York and London: Routledge, 2012, pp. 119–32.

18 Stace and Dunphy, *Beyond the Boundaries*, p. 64.

19 For further detail on the debates over planned versus emergent change, refer to K. Weick, 'Emergent change as a universal in organizations', in M. Beer and N. Nohria (eds) *Breaking the Code of Change*, Boston, MA: Harvard Business School Press, 2000; K. Weick and R. Quinn, 'Organizational change and development', *Annual Review of Psychology*, 1999, 50, 361–86.

20 Stace and Dunphy, *Beyond the Boundaries*, p. 110
21 Westpac, 'Sustainability and Community', 2013. Online. Available HTTP:
   <http://www.westpac.com.au/about-westpac/sustainability-and-community/
   reporting-our-performance/ratings-and-awards/> (accessed 9 September
   2013).
22 Quote from Noel Purcell, Westpac's Group General Manager for Stakeholder
   Communications. R. Kendall, 'Westpac now true CSR blue', *Ethical
   Investor*, 2005, December–January, 51, 6.
23 Stace and Dunphy, *Beyond the Boundaries*, p. 111.
24 C. A. Adams and P. McNicholas, 'Making a difference: sustainability
   reporting, accountability and organisational change', *Accounting, Auditing &
   Accountability Journal*, 2007, 20 (3), 382–402.
25 W. Stubbs and C. Higgins, 'Exploring the Inhibitors and Enablers of
   Integrated Reporting in Australia', paper presented at *Academy of
   Management Conference*, 9–13 August 2013, Ontonio, Florida.
26 See the work of R. Henrik, H. Daly, P. Hawken and J. Holmbery, 'A compass
   for sustainable development', *International Journal of Sustainable
   Development and World Ecology*, 1991, 4, 79–92.
27 D. Meadows, 'Places to intervene in a system in increasing order of
   effectiveness', *Whole Earth*, 1997, Winter, 78–84, esp. p. 78.
28 K. Weick, 'Small wins: redefining the scale of social problems', *American
   Psychology*, 1984, 39 (1), 40–9, esp. p. 43.
29 S. Benn, interview with D. Lett, Manager, Personnel and Administration, and
   A. Holmes, Supervisor – Local Purchasing, Panasonic Matsushita Pty Ltd,
   Penrith, Sydney, 29 August 2000.
30 A. Griffiths and N. Haigh, 'Co-ordinating small wins as an effective
   mechanism for implementing eco-innovations', *Academy of Management
   Conference*, Best Paper, Organizations and Natural Environment, New
   Orleans, 2004.
31 B. Doppelt, *Leading Change toward Sustainability*, Sheffield: Greenleaf
   Publishing, 2003; Meadows, 'Places to intervene in a system'.
32 Griffiths and Haigh, 'Co-ordinating small wins'.
33 J. Maxwell, S. Rothenberg, F. Briscoe and I. Marcus, 'Green schemes:
   corporate environmental strategies and their implementation', *California
   Management Review*, 1997, 39 (3), 118–34.
34 L. Rowledge, R. Barton and K. Brady, *Mapping the Journey*, Sheffield:
   Greenleaf Publishing, 1999; M. Shanahan and A. Maria, 'Creating change
   through strategic storytelling', *PRISM*, 1998, Q4, 99–108, esp. pp. 100–1.
35 Shanahan and Maria, 'Creating change through strategic storytelling'.
36 Nattrass and Altomare, *Dancing with the Tiger*, p. 43.
37 R. Jones, N. Jimmieson and A. Griffiths, 'The Role of Organizational Culture
   and Reshaping Capabilities in Creating Readiness for Change: Implications
   for Change Implementation Success', unpublished manuscript, Queensland:
   School of Management, Queensland University of Technology, 2001.

38 M. Linnenlucke, 'Understanding Corporate Sustainability: A Quantitative Study about a Single Organization', Masters report, Queensland: University of Queensland Business School, Faculty of Business, Economics and Law, The University of Queensland, 2006.

39 Network for Business Sustainability, *Embedding Sustainability in Organizational Culture*, 2010, p. 10. Online. Available HTTP: http://nbs.net/fr/files/2011/08/NBS_COrg_SystRev.pdf (accessed 20 September, 2013).

40 S. Bertels, L. Patania and D. Patania, 'Implementing Sustainability: How to Embed Sustainability in Organizational Culture', Report from Network for Business Sustainability, 2011.

41 M. Bissing-Olson, A. Iyer, K. Fielding and H. Zacher, 'Relationships between daily affect and pro-environmental behavior at work: the moderating role of pro-environmental attitude', *Journal of Organizational Behavior*, 2013, 34 (2), 156–75.

42 Sony, 'Environmental Indicators and Eco-efficiency'. Online. Available HTTP: <http://www.sony.net/SonyInfo/csr_report/environment/management/overview/index3.html> (accessed 9 September 2013).

43 See http://www.talentedheads.com/2013/06/11/gen-ys-version-of-work-life-balance-by-guest-blogger-conrad-liveris/ (accessed 2 October 2013).

44 S. Oreg, M. Vakola and A. Armenakis, 'Change recipients' reactions to organizational change: a 60-year review of quantitative studies', *The Journal of Applied Behavioral Science*, 2011, 47 (4), 461–524.

45 J. M. Bartunek, D. N. Greenberg and B. Davidson, 'Consistent and inconsistent impacts of a teacher-led empowerment initiative in a federation of schools', *Journal of Applied Behavioral Science*, 1999, 35 (4), 457–78; J. M. Bartunek, D. M. Rousseau, J. W. Rudolph and J. A. DePalma, 'On the receiving end: sensemaking, emotion, and assessments of an organizational change initiated by others', *Journal of Applied Behavioral Science*, 2006, 42 (2), 182–206.

46 For a review, see J. Pfeffer, *Competitive Advantage through People*, Boston, MA: Harvard Business School Press, 1995.

47 M. Hele, 'Rockcote paints it green – solutions for water and waste', *The Courier Mail*, 25 February 2005.

48 L. Moore, 'More than green', *The Courier Mail*, 11 October 2002.

49 Ibid.

50 L. Pregelji, 'The Creativity and Innovation Process at Rockcote', Master of Technology and Innovation Management Case Study, 2006; A. Griffiths, *Rockcote: A Case Study in Eco-entrepreneurialism*, Queensland: University of Queensland Business School, 2006.

51 Stace and Dunphy, *Beyond the Boundaries*, pp. 97–8.

52 See B. Doppelt, *Leading Change toward Sustainability*, pp. 114–15 for a commentary on the different roles that organisational members can play in sustainability teams.

53 N. Roome, 'Developing environmental management strategies', *Business Strategy and the Environment*, 1992, 1 (1), 11–23.

54 B. Daily and S. Huang, 'Achieving sustainability through attention to human resource factors in environmental management', *International Journal of Operations and Production Management*, 2001, 21 (12), 1539–52.

55 P. Strebel, *Breakpoints: How Managers Exploit Radical Change*, Boston, MA: Harvard Business School Press, 1992.

56 Abrahamson, 'Change without pain', p. 76.

57 J. Mathews, A. Griffiths and N. Watson, *Socio-technical Redesign: The Case of Cellular Manufacturing at Bendix Mintex*, New South Wales: Industrial Relations Research Centre, University of New South Wales Studies in Organizational Analysis and Innovation, University of New South Wales, 1993.

58 B. Doppelt, 'The seven sustainability blunders', *The System Thinker*, 2003, June–July, p. 3.

59 Greenpeace, 'Greenpeace Warns of Further Water Contamination in Romania and Hungary', press release, 14 March 2000; 'Cyanide Spill Mine Takes First Step towards Bankruptcy', Environment News Service, 16 March 2000.

60 United Nations Organisation Mission in the Democratic Republic Congo, 'Report on the Conclusions of Summary Executions and other Violations of Human Rights Committed by the FARDC in Kilwa on 15th October 2004', 2005.

61 Carbon Disclosure Project, 'About Us'. Online. Available HTTP: <https://www.cdproject.net/en-US/Pages/About-Us.aspx> (accessed 9 September 2013).

62 R. Staib, 'Environmental auditing', in R. Staib (ed.) *Environmental Management and Decision-making for Business*, New York: Palgrave Macmillan, 2005, pp. 263–70.

63 C. Ramus, 'Encouraging innovative environmental actions: what companies and managers must do', *Journal of World Business*, 2002, 37 (2), 151–67.

64 R. Eckert, 'Where leadership starts', *Harvard Business Review*, 2001, November, 79 (10), 53–62.

65 Queensland Rail, 'Environmental Sustainability'. Online. Available HTTP: http://www.queenslandrail.com.au/Safety/Pages/EnvironmentalSustainability.aspx (accessed 25 November 2013).

66 D. Elliott, 'Would You Buy a New Car From this Man?', *Time*, 30 January 2006.

67 Rowledge *et al.*, *Mapping the Journey*, p. 97; R. Walton, 'The diffusion of new work structures: explaining why success didn't take', in P. Mirvis and D. Berg (eds) *Failures in Organization Development and Change*, New York: John Wiley, 1977, pp. 243–61.

68 See http://www.edie.net/news/4/MS-promises-to-halt-toxic-chemical-release-from-supply-chain/23445/ (accessed 3 October, 2013).

69 Correspondence with Bob Cameron, CEO, Rockcote, 13 May 2006.

70 Ibid.

71 See http://www.edie.net/news/5/M-S-to-survey-supply-chain-staff-on-working-conditions/?goback=%2Egde_2901693_member_274751153#%21 (accessed 3 October 2013).

72 For a detailed outline of how this can be done, see D. Grayson and D. Hodges, *Corporate Social Opportunity: 7 Steps to Make Social Responsibility Work for Your Business*, Sheffield, UK: Greenleaf, 2004, pp. 101–39.

73 R. Shelton, 'Hitting the green wall: why corporate programs get stalled', *Corporate Environmental Strategy*, 1994, 2 (2), 5–12.

74 Interesting to note: Donella Meadows identified nine steps, while Bob Doppelt identified seven steps. Our approach differs because we specifically identified the criteria and methods adopted by organizations involved in the roll-out of incremental change strategies. In other words, we identify change strategies that are situationally appropriate for incremental change. The approach taken by both Meadows and Doppelt is generically applied to incremental and transformational change approaches.

8   The transformational path

- ○ **Why transformational change?**
- ○ **Steps towards transformational change**

Why transformational change?

For some organizations, the move to sustainability can be incremental. As outlined in the last chapter, there are many organizations which touch the earth lightly and already contribute substantially to the health and welfare of their workforce and the community. For these organizations, progress towards full sustainability can be a process of unspectacular but systematic and sustained development of awareness, policies and practices. These are the fortunate organizations.

There are many other organizations, however, that have been, or will soon be, subjected to unprecedented and unanticipated public pressures to make radical change. Why? Because some of their current policies or practices are revealed as plundering and polluting the planet, destroying the human capital assets of the organization or fracturing community relationships. We have given many examples throughout this book of organizations that have found themselves in such a situation and have had to respond by initiating radical, transformative change. In fact, some of today's leading corporate advocates of sustainability, whose managers have blazed a trail to sustainable practices, have been companies whose reputations suffered at some point because of unacceptable and unsustainable practices. Nike and Shell are obvious examples. Indeed, as we write, Shell is again under the spotlight with the Bodo community in the oil-rich Niger Delta, who have recently rejected a compensation offer from Shell for two oil spills in 2008.[1] In the example of Nike, the 'third party' not-for-profit groups have extended their campaign beyond their original targets to whole industry segments.[2]

We are moving into a period of history when organizations engaging in unsustainable operations will have their 'licence to operate' questioned by activist community groups or government watchdogs.[3] If organizations persist in these behaviours, they will be forced into crisis mode to extricate themselves, salvage their public image and retain market share. For instance, Monsanto's original drive to sustainability was undertaken both to strategically position itself out of low-margin industries and also to respond to the increasing public concern and community activism over its polluting habits. The community is increasingly suspicious of 'greenwash', so the change has to be more than simply a cosmetic makeover. In Chapter 5 we saw that Monsanto failed to address these concerns expressed by peripheral stakeholders, resulting in a perceptual gap between what the company was articulating and what the company was doing. This had extensive financial consequences for Monsanto. What is required sometimes is large-scale, transformative change: that is, a leap into a fundamental redefinition of the company or some significant aspect of it. This may involve developing a new definition of the business the company is in, a new strategic orientation or realignment, a new structure, a significant change in the workforce skill mix or profile and/or a substantive change in corporate culture. This may not mean change from those large companies which dominate the world stage in so many ways. As pointed out in a major report prepared by three of the world's leading associations for professional accountants, small companies have great power.

> New companies that are founded on sustainability as the fundamental guiding principle that drives every aspect of their business have the power to start a process that can transform entire industries.[4]

To date we have talked about companies having choices. However, in some cases, such as extreme weather events, the frequency and proximity of which seem related to climate change, some companies will have massive and transformative changes thrust upon them. These potentially could be disastrous for organizations. For instance, the New Orleans energy utility, Entergy, filed for bankruptcy protection following the near-complete shutdown of its operations and revenue following Hurricane Katrina. It was estimated that the company had lost its 337,000 electricity and natural gas customers and analysts predicted that even as things improved, it was reasonable to expect that its future customer base could be smaller.[5] In the face of dramatic environmental discontinuities, managers must think about the forms of adaptive capacity they need to build into their organizations.

Other companies may choose to change transformationally even though they are not subjected to external pressures to do so. Some of these will be companies whose managers see the significant business opportunities that are emerging in sustainable development and who wish to lead in taking up these opportunities. To do so they may have to reinvent the organization, for example, by moving from manufacturing petroleum-based products to manufacturing and recycling products based on natural fibres, while building a wholly new business operation that services and recycles. This is the story of DuPont, which has, since 1991, reclaimed millions of pounds of carpet. Some of the recycled content is used to manufacture products as diverse as carpet tiles and automobile parts.[6] However, central to DuPont's transformation has been the divestment of Conco and its shift towards life sciences investments.[7] In its current incarnation, DuPont has incorporated service provision of sustainable transformations into its business model and is working to promote the development of sustainable fibres. For example, its Sorona fibre, showcased in 2013 at New York Fashion Week, replaces a traditional petrochemical-based ingredient with one made with a renewably sourced material. According to DuPont, the production of Sorona fibre requires 30 per cent less energy and reduces greenhouse gas emissions by 63 per cent compared to the production of an equal amount of nylon.[8]

Other companies will be led by managers who are personally committed to contributing to a more sustainable world and who see their companies as instruments for accomplishing this. The move from a single-minded focus on creating short-term profits to embodying an ideological commitment to social justice and ecological diversity may also involve transformative change. The story of how Interface transformed its operations in Chapter 5 includes change of this kind as well.

We are addressing here what Robert Quinn refers to as 'deep change'. Quinn writes:

> Deep change differs from incremental change in that it requires new ways of thinking and behaving. It is change that is major in scope, discontinuous with the past and generally irreversible. The deep change effort distorts existing patterns of action and involves taking risks. Deep change means surrendering control.[9]

Corporate transformations are not to be initiated lightly, for they are difficult to accomplish, often risky for the careers of the change agents involved and can have significant impacts on the lives of others, not all of which may be positive in the short term. In fact some have questioned whether it is possible to manage such change at all.[10] In our view, it is often possible to bring about transformational change, and we have documented many successful cases.[11] However, the magnitude of the task is often underestimated by managers, who consequently under-resource the process and fail to assemble the skills required to accomplish large-scale, fundamental change. On the other hand, while transformative change involves risk, there are times when failure to initiate transformative change results in the business being out of business. Not doing anything can be a greater risk than initiating transformational change. In our first edition we quoted the words of Hart and Milstein: 'Managers that treat sustainable development as an opportunity will drive the creative destruction process and build the foundation to compete in the 21st Century.'[12]

Since then, we have been able to observe how these predictions concerning creative destruction are playing out. Take the role of SMEs, for instance. Burgeoning numbers of SMEs as an outcome of the creative destruction processes associated with rapid technology transition can be seen as a major sustainability problem, due to the resource challenges that SMEs face. However, in terms of transformational change, the SME supplier networks can be a major force as a source of sustainability innovation in specialist niches and through their actions as risk-averse buyers.[13] Take, for example, the Herdy Company in the UK. A Business in the Community Small Company of the Year, the Herdy Company's mission is to foster the local economy through selling its range of ethically sourced and produced giftware, promoting ethical sourcing while giving back to the local community.[14]

Given the magnitude and urgency of the changes needed to bring about sustainability in society, we are confident that over the next few years many organizations will have to undergo corporate transformation. The good news is that many already have done so over the last quarter century, due to the globalization of business, increasing competition and world economic recessions. Tough as these times have been, we have learned a great deal about how to reinvent organizations (and how not to). We can therefore draw on this experience and use what has been learned from it to manage the kind of transformational change needed to achieve full sustainability. In addition, we now know that 'long-living companies', that is, companies that survive for many years, undergo at least one significant period of transformational change and sometimes several. As mentioned earlier, de Geus has documented the histories of 27 companies that lasted from 100 to 700 years – companies such as DuPont, Kodak,

Mitsui, Sumitomo and Siemens.[15] Their ability to initiate and manage transformational change has been a major contributor to their longevity.

In addition, there are an increasing number of organizations whose basic corporate strategy is continually to transform or 'reinvent' themselves to maintain a competitive edge. Brown and Eisenhardt capture this well:

> For firms such as Intel, Wal-Mart, 3M, Hewlett-Packard and Gillette, the ability to change rapidly and continuously, especially in developing new products, is not only a core competence, it is also at the heart of their cultures. For these firms, change is not the rare, episodic phenomenon described by the punctuated equilibrium model but, rather, it is endemic to the way these organizations compete.[16]

Those organizations that see the development of new sustainable technologies, processes and products as central to their strategic success may choose to use continuous transformational change as a way of continuously dominating their emerging markets.

At a fundamental level organizational transformation may also involve paradigmatic change where the core values and assumptions underpinning decision making and practices are questioned and altered. Such innovation requires new models and frameworks to stimulate creative approaches to complex issues both to redress the ecological crisis and to create new products and practices to support organization and society.

One such model that takes a radically different approach to the three dimensions of the triple bottom line is Metabolic Organization (see Figure 8.1).[17] The design of Metabolic Organization is based on criticisms of the triple bottom line that argue that this is in practice a more sophisticated economic model where decisions and actions in the social and the environmental dimensions are still subordinated to economic rules and values. The framework of metabolic organization deliberately avoids direct linkage to and usage of economic terms, arguing that fiscal evaluation is a secondary function to strategic decision making and judgements.

Three integrated aspects comprise the model of Metabolic Organization: interdependence, metabolism and appreciation (see Figure 8.1). These aspects represent ongoing dynamic interdependent processes of organizing, rather than static structures of analysis at particular moments in time. It has been designed to be applicable at all scales of investigation, from individual through to global human organizing:

Figure 8.1 *Metabolic organization*
Source: © 2012 Robert Perey

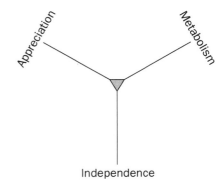

Independence

- *Metabolism* – metabolic processes concern nutrient consumption. They involve conversion of raw material to useful purpose for actors, with energy and waste as outcomes. Metabolism is further categorized into endometabolism and exometabolism, where endometabolism concerns the internal needs of an actor and exometabolism its external needs. Metabolism involves both biological/physical and social processes.
- *Appreciation* – involves the application of subjective preferences that actors have derived from their worldviews, drawing on their cultural contexts for determining their actions. Our moral frameworks define obligations to others, who and what is included or excluded from our moral order, and this includes nature. The appreciative process defines our preferences for actions and objects, including the processes of metabolism, and is strongly influenced by aesthetic sensibilities.
- *Interdependence* – describes the interrelatedness both socially and physically that an actor has with others. Where appreciation may be considered as the ideals or espoused activities and relationships, interdependence represents the actuals – what is both essential and already in place or needing to be in place. Interdependence maps the actor in their environment – maps them in their world.

This chapter outlines the practical process by which change agents can reinvent and reconstruct organizations into responsible instruments for creating products and services that contribute to a fulfilling life on a healthy planet. In the process, this makes a significant contribution to their own financial success and sustainability as viable organizations.

So, how is transformative change initiated and effectively implemented? We outline the steps involved in the process and give concrete examples of successes and failures.

Steps towards transformational change

Step 1: know where you are now

Transformative change involves reinventing the organization – creating a compelling image of a desirable future organization dramatically different from the current one. But before charging off into the future, it is important to know the starting point: the organization as it is now. This is not a minor task, particularly in a large, complex company. It is easy to assume that the organization's current strategic identity is known and understood – after all, many people in the organization may have been around for years. Yet everyone in an organization has a different experience of it – organizations are not primarily buildings, equipment, finance and organization charts. Rather, they are constructs in the minds of those who work in and with them, who buy from them and supply to them. They are primarily subjective realities, images that have been forged from individual and collective experience over time, and these subjective realities are usually partial and fragmentary and differ widely from one person to another. It is not enough to create a vision of the future and build an informed commitment to it. It is necessary first to build a shared understanding of the organization's current reality and of the need to radically shift that reality.

As Lynda Gratton notes:

> Working at the level of meaning in an organization requires a new way of thinking. To understand meaning it is not sufficient to simply consider what the organization is doing with regard to its tasks, the reporting structure or policy statements. We have to understand how the organization is perceived by its individual members. Working at the level of the 'unwritten rules of the game' provides us with such an opportunity. This level of analysis begins to answer questions about what is important around the organization, what people have to do to get on, what really motivates and excites individuals, and which factors send the most positive messages.[18]

So, up front of any transformative change programme we must assess the current reality.

How?

There are two basic sources for constructing a shared view of the organization's current situation. The first source is carefully chosen members of the organization, including, preferably, some who have left.

What can be gained from this source is a précis of the history of the organization, an outline of its defining formative moments. How did it come to be what it is? Who played key roles? To what extent were issues of sustainability taken into account along the way? The other source consists of representatives of key stakeholders – customers and suppliers, for example – who have dealt with the organization throughout its history. What is their experience of the organization? Have their expectations, particularly around sustainability (for example, pesticide-free food products), been met in the past? Are they being met now? To what extent are they currently expecting sustainable practices? Even if they are not, how would they respond to the development of such products and services?

There are various ways in which this information can be elicited; for example, through surveys, interviews, focus groups and analysis of organizational and community records. Sometimes valuable information about the expectations of external stakeholders can be gleaned from members of the organization who have roles that require regular contact with a key stakeholder group. Most organizations have a wealth of information about external stakeholder attitudes which is not accessed, integrated and assessed by the senior executive team, let alone made known throughout the organization as part of creating the consensual reality needed to launch a change programme.

An important part of assessing current reality is to identify the core cultural values of the organization and the entrenched behavioural mores that control much of day-to-day behaviour in the organization. Here a trained outsider can often make the most useful contribution by focusing a fresh, independent eye on the customary ways members of the organization undertake everyday business. The best observer is someone who is sensitive to the differences that often exist between espoused and enacted values – what people say they support versus what they actually do. Managers, for example, often express the view that 'people are our major asset' but their actual human resource practices may not reflect this stated belief. What are the prevailing views on sustainability issues held by the dominant coalition and other key groups such as trade union members, salespeople, maintenance workers, and research and development staff? What is the result, in practical terms, for the welfare of the workforce, for the community, for the environment?

'Telling it the way it is' can be confronting for many members of the organization. Some organizational members will have a strong personal stake in preserving fictional views of the organization's current reality, for their own identities are bound up in maintaining the fiction. For example, they may not welcome a realistic assessment of the organization's impact on the environment or of the human rights issues embedded in its supply networks. They may seek to 'shoot the messenger' who brings the disconfirming views. Remember the strenuous action of cigarette manufacturers who sought to disconfirm scientific evidence of the link between smoking and cancer. We emphasize strongly here that the basis for effective transformational change is widespread consensual agreement on the current organizational reality. It is necessary to be honest, sometimes brutally honest, to bring this about. This is easier to achieve when members of the dominant elite(s) are open to acknowledge different viewpoints and willing to absorb new information even when it challenges their traditional views. In fostering this openness, the credibility of the source of such information can also make a critical difference: respected external change agents with authority and expertise are more likely to be heard than insiders or outsiders without these attributes. A combination of confrontation by concerned community groups and, in parallel, a significant challenge from one or more sources whom executives respect and trust can provide the jolt needed to create the initial momentum for change.

In this regard, Byong-Wook Lee outlines some of the prevailing assumptions about waste in a Korean steel-producing operation. These assumptions had to be confronted before waste and the associated pollution could be significantly reduced. The commonly held views were that 'change of waste management is expected to have very limited effect upon the company's financial performance' and that 'there is little room to reduce wastes through changes in the steel making process'.[19] Neither view was accurate, but the beliefs were deeply entrenched in the traditional culture of the organization.

Halme points out that for any learning and change to occur around sustainability, the firm's managers need to understand how the core beliefs, basic assumptions and values of the organization relate to the impact of its activities on the natural environment. Where do they stand now and where do they want to be in the future? She argues that traditional management perspectives act only as cognitive defence mechanisms preventing the emergence of sustainability-related transformations.[20]

Step 2: develop the vision – the dream organization

Transformative change is an opportunity to rethink the *raison d'être* of the organization. Organizations are organic entities, social systems, which take on a life of their own, often independent of those who brought them into being. They are shaped initially by the purposes of their founders but modified by external social pressures, by momentous and sometimes unanticipated events. Organizations sometimes actively shape the economic, physical and social environments in which they operate; they both shape and are shaped by these forces. They sometimes lead changes in their environments; more often they lag behind.

Organizations are, however, human creations, held in place by the values and actions of those in and around them. What has been created by human thought and action can also be recreated. However, to use an analogy, remanufacturing is a different process from manufacturing. In remanufacturing, the physical basis of metals, for example, may have been changed by heat, vibration and wear. In remanufacturing, therefore, different processes have to be invented to produce the same or similar outcomes that result from manufacturing from raw materials. The same is true of transformative change: changing an organization that has already developed a history and a culture requires a different approach from creating a new organization. We are intervening in a system that has already developed powerful properties and processes of its own and these processes are usually deeply embedded in the minds, emotions and lives of the members of the organization and its external stakeholders. Changing the organization involves changing those in it, often including ourselves; it often also involves changing the expectations of those outside.

The first step in transforming an organization is to creatively imagine one or more future realities (scenarios) that the organization will face. The future is usually three to ten years out – the time chosen depends fundamentally on an estimate of how long it will take investments made now, in capital, human and technical capabilities, to be realized. This scenario planning begins with an identification of: (a) the major current trends that are likely to affect the future viability, success and sustainable contribution of the organization; and (b) who the critical stakeholders are likely to be in the future, for they may be different from those the organization relates to now. Scenario planning of this type first emerged in the Royal Dutch Shell Group in the 1970s and has since been elaborated and widely used under the general heading of 'strategic scenarios analysis'.[21] It is widely used: for example, the US power industry has created scenarios that apply to the development of industry technology in a world experiencing climate change and resource uncertainty.[22] At the VERGE 2013 conference, Shell International's chief economist described the scenario-mapping discipline at Shell, which models scenarios to enable emerging economies to grow while creating a more resilient society. Bery focuses on the food–energy–water stress nexus and the constraints brought about by climate change. Shell believes that dealing with this stress nexus will govern a firm's licence to operate in the world over the next 30 to 50 years and argues that companies need to recognize that they will be operating in a world that will not be dominated by the rich countries.[23]

In constructing future scenarios, it is neither necessary nor wise to eliminate alternative scenarios for one 'most likely' scenario. Rather, a vision may be elaborated for the most likely scenario, but parallel visions roughed out for 'best case' and 'worst case' scenarios. The purpose of the exercise is not simply to create a strategy for the future but also to create a purposeful process of engaging people inside and outside the organization in scoping out possible new paths ahead – to engage them in a critical debate about possible alternative futures. The aim is to build the commitment of all critical stakeholders to a challenging new future role for the organization.[24] At the same time, it is important to avoid locking the organization into an irrevocable path to a future that may never eventuate. The organization needs to be proactive, to create direction and momentum, but also to retain the flexibility to adapt to unanticipated developments.

A critical part of this process of strategic realignment is to move from an identification of key future stakeholders to an imaginative construction of how their expectations may affect the organization in the future. This is an opportunity to engage these stakeholders in a dialogue about how they view their future – to give them voice. It is important also that as many members of the organization as possible are in a position to hear for themselves these voices from the stakeholders or their representatives.

This exercise leads into a definition of the most critical issues facing the organization. The natural next step is to ask: What will these anticipated changes mean for our organization? What problems will we face? What opportunities will be available to us? What values will we stand for?

These questions centre on defining a new identity for the organization and developing an innovative strategic intent to guide the organization in its future decision making. An important facet of this process is defining a set of core values in which human and ecological sustainability have a central place.

However, this does not mean that organizational learning around sustainability can take place only once a value change towards a more ecocentric understanding has taken place. Halme's work investigating how learning occurs in relation to environmental management issues in two different organizations that are culturally homogenous challenges earlier findings that change for sustainability can progress only once the underlying values have been changed. Her research indicates that in fact learning around environmental values and beliefs progresses through action. As she says:

> The present findings indicate that in order to learn new environmental core values and beliefs, the organization must engage in action because learning from experience as well as testing and refining new ideas in practice are essential for the emergence of new knowledge.[25]

As noted elsewhere in this book, numerous organizations are now adopting triple-bottom-line performance criteria or comparable approaches that reflect a significant broadening of values and acceptance of a multiple-stakeholder approach. Involving forward-thinking stakeholders in the process of renewing the corporate vision and strategic intent is an important part of building 'relationship capital'. Creating an engaging dialogue with key stakeholders ensures that their interests are taken into account and that they recognize this. It also enlists their active support for the emerging changes in the organization's operations.

As Halme's research on organizational learning for sustainability shows: 'If the company allows different perspectives to be expressed and actions on the basis of those perspectives to be taken, then weak signals have a greater likelihood to trigger environmental learning'.[26] The central challenge of transformative change is to unleash the imagination of organizational members and stakeholders so that they collaborate in creating a vision that breaks out of existing cultural assumptions to create a prototype for a truly sustainable and sustaining organization. Whereas incremental change can often be successfully generated and led entirely by people internal to the organization, transformative change almost always needs input from outsiders. The outsiders need to be informed, radical, lateral thinkers who can and will challenge existing assumptions about the current organizational pattern and accepted best practice. It is only to be expected that change for sustainability will have a stronger affective component than other change programmes, with emotions such as frustration coming to the fore with more frequency.[27]

The vision must be spelled out as clearly as possible and personally endorsed by senior management. However, at this stage it represents a new identity, a change of direction, an idea in process to be explored, tested and progressively given shape through future action. It must also be formulated in a way that speaks to the hearts and minds of the key players in the organization and to stakeholders whose support will be needed for it to be realized. It has to have a clear relationship to the core business strategies of the organization. For example, the GE EcoImagination portfolio presents GE as a rational, scientifically informed and forward-looking company that can both help save the planet and make money for its investors.[28]

Step 3: identify the gap

Having reached this point, now is the time to pull back from the dream and to create a realistic assessment of the gap between the organization's current situation and where the new vision seeks to position it in the future. The Corporate Sustainability Matrix around which this book is constructed provides a way of estimating and describing the gap as well as indicating how to move forward. To do this, you need to work independently through the human sustainability column and the ecological sustainability column – an organization may be at a different stage in each of these areas (refer to Appendix). It is possible for the same organization to have a highly strategic approach to human sustainability (Phase 5) but to be lagging in terms of compliance in the ecological sustainability area (Phase 2) – for example, a mining company which has first-rate human resource policies but which has environmentally destructive operations.

The outputs of Steps 2 and 3 above supply the information needed to position, in the matrix, where the organization is now and where it aspires to be, and over what time span. The differences between current and envisioned future positions in the matrix define the gap to be bridged. Let's take the case of a bank, for example, which has systematically built its HR strategies over a ten-year period, using them to attract and retain some of the best talent in the industry. The bank has also been concerned about its contribution to the community and also used its community relations to support its progressive, 'concerned and caring' image. This places it in Phase 5, strategic proactivity (HS5), in the area of human sustainability. However, it has given little thought to its environmental impact. It uses huge amounts of paper, most of which is not separated for recycling. It constantly updates its computers, printers and so on, but commits them by truckloads to landfill. It is discussing developments in the ethical investment fund area but has not yet launched such a fund or developed an alliance with another financial institution that has. This places it, for ecological sustainability, in Phase 2, non-responsiveness (ES2). So its overall position on the Sustainability Change Matrix (see Figure 8.2) is at point A. Now it aspires to be a leader in the introduction of both human and ecological sustainability practices by moving towards HS6 and ES6. Clearly it needs, at the most, incremental change in the human sustainability area. But its transformational change programme needs to centre on ecological sustainability, where it has a lot of ground to make up before it reaches its ideal position at or near point B. The gap between the current phase and the desired future phase defines the bridge the organization must cross in order to emerge transformed.

If the organization is complex, having divisions and units with differentiated operations, market environments and cultures, the process of

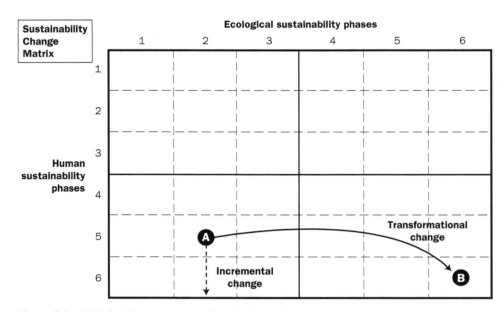

Figure 8.2   *Bridging the gap: what kind of change?*
Source: Adapted from D. Dunphy, J. Benveniste, A. Griffiths and P. Sutton, *Sustainability: The Corporate Challenge for the 21st Century*, Sydney: Allen & Unwin, 2000, p. 256.

positioning on the matrix may need to be analysed for each differentiated unit. This implies that the organization may have to pursue a complex change strategy that is a mix of both incremental and transformative change, depending on the current character of the subunits. The more differentiated the change strategy in this regard, the higher will be the cost of coordinating across ongoing strands of the change programme. Resources, human and financial, need to be allocated to ensure that the various change initiatives move the organization as a whole on its chosen trajectory, rather than spinning off on their own orbits.

The most obvious output of this stage of the design process is a realistic assessment of the nature of the gap to be bridged – the gap between the organization's current commitment to and performance on key sustainability indicators and the new vision for the future. This gap may be substantially different for human and ecological sustainability and may also differ from one part of the organization's operations to another.

If the process has been well managed to this point, an important secondary output is that commitment to change is already building among key opinion leaders within the organization and significant external stakeholders. Transformative change is always a political process and a central task of change agents is to build active support among constituent groups, or at least to receive tacit acceptance of the desired changes. This is not always possible: there are usually individuals and groups who have a significant stake in the existing order, the status quo, and whose interests are threatened by change. It would be naive not to expect active and passive resistance from them. What is often harder for change agents to accept, however, is the resistance that often comes from some of those who are disaffected from the status quo and who stand to *benefit* from the proposed changes. Some people cannot project themselves into a future world, cannot assess realistically how their interests will be served by change, or actually prefer to remain locked in, complaining, to the security of a known if debilitating role rather than break the chain and be free. We cannot make people change; we can only provide opportunities for them to change themselves.

Step 4: assess the readiness for change

For those who have been intensely involved in the diagnostic process described in Steps 2 and 3, it is easy to assume that the organization as a whole is poised and ready for change, or that, if there are points of resistance, these will simply fade away as the change proceeds. This is usually far from the truth. Planning change is the easy part; intervening in an ongoing system that is alive, has its own compelling logic of which we are only a small part, is a huge challenge. Even formal authority has limited validity in a transformative change process. Ordering people to change is seldom effective; change by memorandum and edict usually fails. Leadership, not management, is the critical element in transformative change. Leadership at all levels is vital in creating the bursts of energy that must spark responses in opinion leaders and build momentum for change. This is an issue we will deal with in more detail in our final chapter.

Transformative change may involve authoritative action, even coercion, but its success depends ultimately on emotional contagion across the living networks of human relationships that make up an organization. There must be a compelling intellectual agenda for change, but that is not enough to transform deeply entrenched behavioural patterns built up over years of repetitive action. People are more than minds; they have hearts and spirits as well and the agenda for change must also appeal to people at emotional and spiritual levels. The sustainability agenda has the potential to do this. For example, most parents care about the world that their children and grandchildren will inherit. Most people want to work for organizations that are seen to be making a contribution to community life. We seek meaning and purpose in our lives: the great opportunity that faces managers and change agents in the move to sustainability is to actualize the opportunity this represents to enhance the sense of meaning people derive from coming to work each day. A transformative change programme can catalyse meaning and provide opportunities for the development of wholeness through purposive and fulfilling work.

As Debashis Chatterjee points out: 'Organizations are not merely structures of units and departments but living fields of creative intelligence of the people who constitute the organization.'[29]

However, we caution change agents about the 'one size fits all' approach to selling and motivating for sustainability-driven transformation. In our research and consulting experience, we have identified at least four different sustainability change drivers. These include:

1   The emotional pitch (mentioned above): This appeals to people's need and desire to leave the world a better place for their children and future generations. However, this message may not appeal to all stakeholders and may not generate the conditions for change readiness.

2 The financial-risk pitch: This often appeals to senior executives and argues a case for change readiness based on the risk of losing capital and reputation.
3 The classic business case for sustainability: This is built on the premise of delivering measurable benefits such as operational efficiencies (see Chapter 4).
4 The opportunity case: This case outlines the prospective opportunities that become available for organizations when they adopt a different mind-set on sustainability issues (see Chapter 5).

Step 4 involves identifying the important internal and external organizational stakeholders whose attitudes and actions could affect the success of the proposed change programme, and working out how their interests may be affected by the changes. It may be appropriate to consult with them beforehand if this has not already happened. Again, where possible, the change programme should be modified to ensure that the interests of as many key players as possible are served by the unfolding programme of change. However, in transformative change, there are usually some groups whose entrenched interests will be threatened. If this is the case, positive alternatives can sometimes be developed to reduce the win–lose nature of the situation. If not, then conflict can be expected and strategies developed to minimize the threat their opposition will represent for the repositioning of the organization. We stress that transformative change is a political process characterized by conflict and power plays. Those initiating the change need to develop a clear understanding of the sources of their authority and power to initiate and carry through the desired changes, build political alliances to support their initiatives and anticipate potential sources of opposition and indifference. Sustainability is a relatively new ideology and support for it cannot be assumed but needs to be won progressively.

Step 5: set the scene for action

There are three additional issues that need to be addressed in creating a base for effective action: awareness of the need for change; identifying change leaders; and assembling the resources needed for the change programme.

Before change can happen, those in the organization must be aware of the need to change. In creating an awareness of the need to change, it makes sense to start where there is the most potential energy for change, that is, with those who are already aware of and committed to the changes. In today's organizations, there are usually articulate advocates of sustainability who understand at least some of the key issues and who are impatient for change. There are also others who are aware but tend to be 'covert' believers, less articulate but waiting for encouragement and clear opportunities before becoming involved. The awareness-building process can start by bringing these people together and identifying the potential contributions they can make to the change process both individually and collectively. One of their most important resources will be the informal networks of others in the organization whom they can influence, so creating a process by which the 'ripples' of awareness can spread out through the natural links between people in the organization. In the early 1990s, for example, Scandic Hotels, the hotel chain in Scandinavia which we discussed earlier, embarked on a change programme to improve the environmental and economic performance of all its hotels. In the first year alone, employees identified more than 1,500 potential innovations which resulted in significant savings and reduced the hotels' environmental impact. In 1997 Scandic was rated in the top 100 most desirable companies to work for in Sweden and successfully attracted large numbers of environmentally conscious guests.[30] By 2003, Scandic had trained over 9,000 employees in sustainability-awareness programmes as a way of institutionalizing sustainability in the culture of the organization. This example adds to the evidence that social learning is crucial to the wholesale implementation of sustainability, as it draws on a collective and collaborative approach to learning around social issues.[31]

Another important step in building awareness is to open windows on the world and on the future for those in the organization. The more that those in the organization can be given access to leading thinkers and organizational practices in corporate sustainability, the more compelling the case for sustainability becomes and the more engaged they will be. Lectures, seminars, site visits, articles, videos and books can all help to build a compelling case for change. They are an important part of creating an intellectual agenda for the change programme.

But effective change programmes require leadership and resources as well as ideas. The next task therefore is to identify change leaders at all levels of the organization, to bring them together around creating a practical agenda for change and to win their commitment to make the change happen. This team (or partnership of several teams) will become the guiding coalition driving the change programme. To be effective, this group needs to have representatives of all key power groups, formal or informal, in the organization that have the capability to make the programme succeed or fail. It needs to include at least one member of the top team so that its work is linked to the core business strategies of the organization. The change leaders include those who have the requisite technical knowledge in areas such as human resource management, corporate social responsibility and the natural environment. They also need to have the EQ (emotional intelligence) skills required to work effectively with people and the SQ (spiritual intelligence) skills needed to provide the wisdom to make sound choices in the face of complex problems.[32] We shall discuss the role and relevance of these factors in more detail in Chapter 9. However, an excerpt from an article by a leading researcher and educator, Paul Shrivastava, reinforces our argument for this holistic approach to change for sustainability.

> Sustainable organizing and managing require an astute combination of cognitive, physical, and emotional or spiritual skills. Managers work long hours, and they travel extensively (Bunting, 2004). Despite the norm of 40-hour work week, managers routinely put in 60 to 70 hours each week. Managerial work may be 'office' work, but it often includes physical engagement (meetings, presentations, site visits, inspections, audits) and can be physically strenuous (Feldman, 2002). Dealing with people (staff, clients, the public, environmentalists, government agencies) involves emotional work. Sustainable managing requires high physical and emotional stamina. Managing sustainably is more than a set of disembodied analytical techniques. It is primarily physical. It is infused with emotional engagement and passion. Managing sustainably with passion involves using analytical skills, physical stamina, and emotions to accomplish and exceed goals.[33]

However, even the best managers and leaders cannot accomplish effective large-scale change without the necessary resources of time, personnel support and finance. Some of the best-planned change programmes fail because senior executives believe that key personnel can simply act as change agents in their 'spare time' and that change programmes do not need the kinds of resources that would be considered essential to a well-run operational task of similar magnitude. Managing a large-scale organizational change programme is equivalent to an engineering project such as creating a new mine, building a skyscraper or installing an organization-wide IT system. Because there may be no visible end-product, justifying the time involved and the provision of the necessary resources often demands building a convincing case for equivalent support.

If enthusiasm has been engendered for change, those who assume leadership can readily underestimate the time needed for deep change. Lynda Gratton, through UK-based The Leading Edge Research Consortium, has had the opportunity to monitor several transformational change processes in leading companies. One of the companies studied was Glaxo Wellcome, the world's largest drug company by sales. Its position was challenged because of cost cutting in drug purchases and the introduction of 'managed care'. In 1988 Glaxo chairman Richard Sykes and his senior team reviewed their business strategy, deciding to move away from a single-product focus to the concept of disease management, closer partnerships with their customers and speedier delivery of drugs. Gratton details how it took two years of intensive targeted activity to transform the company's functional, hierarchical structure to a process-driven, customer-focused culture with effective multidisciplinary teams. Only then, two years later, did the company begin to pick up the performance benefits it had aspired to; over this period it also created a stable of new drugs to fuel its continuing success in the future. But it was really the late 1990s before the new culture it had envisaged ten years earlier was hard- and soft-wired into the organization and the benefits fully realized. Deep change takes real time.

While incremental change can often be effectively undertaken with resources internal to the organization, transformative change usually requires the use of competent, qualified and experienced external consultants. Cultural shifts require a rethinking of cherished assumptions, the challenging of existing patterns of behaviour and the generation of novel alternatives. In this process, it is valuable to have the assistance of parties who have not been socialized into the current corporate culture and who have moved across a variety of organizations in different industries. Organizations undergoing cultural change have characteristics of both chaos and order and this is becoming a normal pattern of corporate change in a much more dynamic and unpredictable world.[34]

Step 6: secure basic compliance first

We want to stress here that securing compliance with legal requirements and the legitimate expectations of stakeholders is the necessary base from which transformational change to more advanced stages must be made. No matter how urgent the need to move the organization forward to other stages of sustainability, it is dangerous to skip this stage – dangerous because failure to comply with legal requirements for health and safety, for example, could lead to costly lawsuits and a damaged corporate reputation. For multinationals, this involves ensuring that their operations do not impact negatively on local peoples and their environment, particularly in conditions where governance is problematic. For example, as we write this, Shell is beginning compensation talks with villagers in Southern Nigeria concerning oil spills in 2008. The villagers are claiming millions of dollars for compensation and clean-up costs.[35] Shell has been in operations in Nigeria for 50 years and has been dogged by accusations of corruption and careless environmental management for much of that time.

It is not only dangerous to skip this stage but also irresponsible because the health and safety of employees, of the community and the environment is the first responsibility of any organization in the twenty-first century. In addition, transformational change inevitably creates disorder that can increase the risk of non-compliance. Consequently, it is important to create clear guidelines for compliance first and to build a tight control system that is actively maintained at a grass-roots level. This needs to be backed up by clear managerial accountability to hold compliance in place when everything else is changing. It is vital to ensure that compliance norms are internalized and to create a working set of operational procedures to reduce corporate risk to a minimum. Contingency plans for damage control also need to be in place in case the compliance procedures fail (for example, in a mining operation, a tailings dam collapses in an unprecedented downpour, despite well thought-out measures to prevent this).

It is not only compliance with legislation that is important: as we have previously pointed out, companies must also meet the strong expectations of stakeholders even if these do not have legal standing. For example, Monsanto set out to model sustainable development via selling GMOs but experienced global outrage when it was recognized that many farmers in developing countries would not be able to buy seeds of this type and would have to rely on conventional seeds, which would not make them competitive.[36]

Compliance is the base platform on which sustainability can be built. We outline here the necessary tasks to be performed in achieving compliance:

- Identify potential risks through undertaking a risk analysis.
- Establish the priorities for risk reduction.
- Decide who will take charge of the compliance-generating process, keeping in mind that this is an opportunity to begin to identify and

develop change leaders for later stages in the path to sustainability. Create a task force to plan and guide the process.

- Estimate the resources needed to achieve compliance and assemble these resources.
- Develop a coordination and communication plan that links line and staff responsibilities.
- Set criteria for success and construct an ambitious schedule for completion.
- Establish a monitoring and review process that is understood, transparent and widely reported.

In a transformational change process, the priority is to achieve compliance effectively and rapidly. This can be accomplished by creating a number of task forces in important areas of sustainability such as OH&S, Equal Employment Opportunity, water and energy conservation, and then having these task forces operate in parallel. (In an incremental change programme, these key compliance areas might be tackled sequentially.) The cost of organizing in parallel lies in the need for greater coordination across the teams to ensure that the end result is a well-integrated and mutually consistent set of policies and procedures. Therefore there is a need for an effective liaison role in linking the teams together as they work on their focal issues.

Step 7: move beyond compliance

With an effective compliance base in place, it is now time to put the organization into fast-forward mode. At this point it is useful to return to the sustainability matrix and to confirm the decision, made in Step 1 above, to move towards either the phase of 'strategic sustainability' or to 'the sustaining corporation' (see Figure 7.2). In addition, the gap between where the organization is now and where it aspires to be needs to be reviewed. Now is the time also to outline the major steps through which the change programme should move and the time-frame for this. The resulting change programme must be challenging but achievable. For example, if significant cultural change is needed, then the schedule would normally cover three to five years.

There are two possible transformational change paths to take at this point: to attempt to take the organization in a leap forward either to Phase 5: strategic proactivity, or to Phase 6: the sustaining corporation. Obviously the latter is the goal involving the biggest stretch, but both involve moving rapidly through Phase 4: efficiency. This has significant implications; for instance, it may be possible to pick up some of the key achievements of the efficiency phase along the way but there is a real risk that transformational change of this order will actually work against making efficiency gains, at least in the short term. The speed and extent of large-scale transformational change often brings significant inefficiencies because of the level of disorganization involved. Similarly, the larger leap from the compliance phase to the sustaining corporation runs the additional risk of losing some of the advantages to be gained in the strategic proactivity phase. It is possible to lose strategic focus and direction and so place the sustainability of the organization itself at risk. It seems that this is what happened at Monsanto.

We wish to stress that transformational change, unlike most incremental change, involves significant risks. These risks should not be taken lightly, as they can endanger the viability of the firm itself and can damage the careers of many involved. There are situations, however, when these risks are warranted: for example, when the core business of the organization is clearly no longer ethical (cigarette companies); when the firm's production processes need to be completely replaced because they are dangerous to the workforce and society (organochlorines); or when there is a significant strategic opportunity that demands major reorganization (alternative energy generation).

The critical questions to be answered in this step are: Where are we going in terms of sustainability? How fast must we make the changes? Can we assemble the resources needed to make this schedule realistic? Where are the critical gaps in our expertise that we must fill? Where is the most resistance likely to occur? How will we know we are succeeding? The answers to these questions form the outline of the emergent change programme. Other useful questions are: Can we identify positive models for the changes we need to make – either within our own organization or in other organizations? What other organizations have attempted to travel this path? Can we access them and assess their level of success? Were their attempts successful or unsuccessful? Where they were successful, what can we learn from their achievements? Where they were unsuccessful, what can we learn from their mistakes? Site visits are often useful in making these assessments and maximizing learning from the experience of others.

In drawing up the programme for change, it is vital to ensure that the sustainability goals adopted are integral to the overall business plan for the organization. Sustainability must be a business imperative, not simply an add-on or option. In transformational change, sustainability initiatives can contribute significantly to business performance, particularly to future corporate repositioning. von Weizacker *et al.* give a multitude of examples of companies that have dramatically reduced their use of resources and at the same time significantly increased their profitability.[37] In addition, sustainability initiatives can be important in securing the support of key stakeholder groups for the organization's strategy of repositioning itself in new markets. However, other stakeholders may perceive some sustainability initiatives as a threat to their interests. For example, suppliers who find their materials or products bypassed for others with more sustainable characteristics may be alarmed to see their business being diminished. As stated before, transformational change is always a political process. It is important therefore to understand which stakeholders will be important for success and to attempt to secure their support or, if necessary, neutralize their opposition.

The questions to answer at this stage are: Where will this change programme or its outcomes add value for this particular group of stakeholders? How could it diminish value, as the stakeholder perceives it? How can the positive value proposition be most effectively communicated to each stakeholder group? How can any negative perceptions be managed to ensure that the programme of change is not undermined by any resulting opposition?

Step 8: establish the performance criteria for 'compliance plus'

If the change programme is to be seen to contribute significantly to the core business of the organization and to the well-being of the community and the environment, then we need to define the criteria for performance. How shall we judge whether the programme is successful? What performance criteria shall we use for this?

There are two kinds of performance criteria to use; the first is 'output criteria'. What are the outputs we are seeking in terms of such factors as decreased waste or community contribution? The second kind of performance criteria is 'process criteria'. What characteristics of the process of change are we seeking to create (for example, the progressive engagement of key interest groups in the change programme or a more collaborative set of relationships between different organizational units)?

Many change programmes fail to define performance criteria at all and, as a result, they falter or fail. If we don't know what we are trying to achieve or fail to reach agreement on the goals of change, confusion and chaos will reign. Most successful change programmes define output criteria and this helps to keep them on track. But in our experience few change programmes define process criteria. However, the quality of the developing change process can be critical in achieving sustainable performance. There is a tendency in transformative change programmes to sacrifice the quality of the change process in the interests of achieving the desired performance outputs quickly. The result can be resentment, cynicism and a failure of key groups to engage and commit to longer-term performance.

Output criteria relate to the following kinds of performance for existing products and services:

- reduced costs, increased profitability
- added quality
- innovation, flexibility, and speed of initiation and response to market shifts
- increased market share.

In addition, other criteria may relate to the process of strategically repositioning the organization:

- entry to new markets
- development of new products and services
- industry leadership
- enhanced public profile and reputation
- creation of a new industry.

Beyond these traditional measures of effective business performance, other criteria might be:

- elimination of waste and sources of pollution
- building workforce capability to contribute to the development of sustainable operations
- building workforce commitment to continue to build the company's future sustainability performance
- development of new environmentally beneficial production processes
- contributing to strengthening community relationships
- increasing stakeholder support, including licence to operate and increased trust
- significantly reducing the organization's ecological footprint.

An example of an initiative which will be measured according to these criteria is the agreement made by Unilever to buy oil derived from algae in a new commercial partnership with Solazyme, a start-up that bio-engineers algae to make oils, proteins and complex sugars. It will be used in products such as Dove, much criticized for its dependence upon palm oil, and will contribute to Unilever reaching its goal to have fully sustainable sourcing by 2020.[38]

These outputs may significantly increase the real wealth of the organization. An important issue to be decided early in the change programme is, therefore, how these benefits are to be distributed among the organization's stakeholders. The traditional answer for a listed company is that the increased wealth would be divided between the shareholders and reinvestment in the company's future growth, usually in the form of capital assets. In the new world of business that we have been describing, capital assets are becoming less important than intellectual capital and stakeholder relationships assume greater significance. Therefore, the increased wealth represents an opportunity to invest in the further development of the capabilities of employees and in strengthening key stakeholder relationships, rather than increased investment in buildings and hardware. This is the route followed by organizations such as HP, Scandic and Westpac and is central to how they generate added value through sustainability initiatives.

Process criteria are ways of assessing whether the change process itself is generating the quality of relationships and capabilities needed to sustain future change. Criteria that may be used here include:

- progressive engagement of key individuals and groups, both internally and externally
- development of concrete, actionable plans for delivery of the outputs above
- progressive development of skilled and committed change leaders at all levels
- a climate of trust and more collaborative relationships between organizational subunits
- a culture of non-defensive learning.

An important issue to be addressed in regard to process quality is the style of change leadership that will be adopted to bring about the desired transformation. Research on change programmes shows that as the scale and speed of change increase, there is a shift to more directive styles of leadership.[39] In addition, the research also shows that the majority of organizational members understand the necessity for this and support it. So, in large-scale transformational change, it is not necessary or appropriate that all decisions be made participatively. The executive team needs to decide early in the change programme what issues will be dealt with by executive decision and are therefore non-negotiable. Safety, for example, is generally regarded as a non-negotiable value. Similarly, the team should decide what kinds of decisions will be made participatively, that is, where individuals, groups, stakeholders or their representatives will be encouraged to participate, influence or determine outcomes. The rationale for this decision-making approach needs to be clearly understood throughout the organization. However, if management is to take a decisive lead, its actions must consistently model its rhetoric.

Step 9: launch and manage the transformational change programme

The reader may be wondering whether we would ever get to this point, that is, of doing what we set out to do. Is all this taxing groundwork necessary? Why not simply get on with it and launch the change programme in the first place? We can only reiterate that launching transformative change programmes is a risky endeavour and that a great deal of the success comes from careful preparation in advance. While this preparation consumes time, it can be carried out efficiently and significantly raises the chances of a successful outcome. Managing a change programme has some similarity to painting a house: a large part of the business of doing a first-rate job lies in the careful preparation of surfaces and selection of the appropriate paints. The painting is the easier part.

Below we outline some of the key steps in a programme designed to move the organization rapidly along the path to sustainability:

- Create and communicate the main focus of the programme so that all in the organization understand the direction and rationale for change (for example, SC Johnson – A Family Company; Honda – The Power of Dreams).
- Map the main subprojects in sufficient detail to clarify for change agents how the change is expected to happen, ensuring that the link to business strategies is clear.
- Build a network of change agents (line and staff personnel, internal and external consultants); break the overall change programme down

into projects that can be handled by multidisciplinary task forces led by these change agents.

- Establish a change coordination team consisting of executives and other strategically located change agents; clarify authority for decision making and accountabilities against goals and timelines; pay particular attention to the roles of front-line supervisors and ensure that they have a clear role to play.
- Monitor the emerging trajectory of change and remediate where necessary; the monitoring should be of both output and process performance criteria; seek and respond to grass-roots feedback.
- Create and celebrate early wins and publicly reward those responsible for them.
- Progressively enlarge the sphere of engagement – go with the energy; remember that opposition is a natural part of the engagement process (apathy and cynicism are more serious threats).
- Create momentum, feeding in resources where necessary.
- Communicate and dramatize success; foster transparency and truth.
- Ensure that, as the capabilities for organizational reshaping develop, they are reinforced and progressively translated into intellectual capital.
- As change goals are reached, consolidate them in new operational systems under the control of committed and competent operational managers (not change agents) and operational teams.
- Ensure that the operational managers achieve efficiencies as the new systems are debugged and routinized.
- Check that key stakeholders perceive that the promised value propositions are being delivered; consolidate their support.
- Build reward systems that reinforce and renew the core values of the new culture and reinforce the behaviours that support the emerging system. These behaviours then become the cultural norms supporting the next stage of sustainability development. It is vital that achievement of sustainability outcomes is a major criterion in staff assessment for career advancement.

Step 10: maintain the rage

In a dynamic world, change is an ongoing process. When the goals have been achieved, the change process may become incremental rather than transformative, but change continues. Organizations ossify unless they continue to change with their environments. Therefore it is essential to continue the processes of environmental monitoring and identification of emerging stakeholder interests around issues of sustainability. The organizational members need to ensure that the organization maintains its leading-edge position; it is easy to fall behind the leading edge through becoming complacent.

Those organizations that move to the stage of becoming sustaining corporations can improve their performance even further by contributing to a growing industrial ecology. An industrial ecology is an active network of organizations for exchanging ideas, products and services in sustainable ways. The best-known example of this is an eco-industrial park in the town of Kalundborg in Denmark. Several companies in the town created a system of exchange whereby the by-products ('wastes') from one company's operation became a resource or raw material for another's.[40] Networks and alliances of organizations like this, working actively to promote and model sustainable practices, are epicentres for the development of the new sustainable economy. As their success becomes apparent, they contribute to a developing climate of political and community support for the enhancement of human capability and environmental regeneration. Any optimistic scenario for the future depends on widespread transformational change designed to bring about a different form of economy to that existing today. Networks of transformed organizations are a major dynamic for transforming the economy as a whole.

In the box below, we have outlined ten steps to creating a successful transformational change programme. These steps are distilled from the experience of many change agents working on a range of transformational change programmes and adapted to the task of moving organizations rapidly towards sustainability. They are a useful guide, but in reality, as we have noted, the change process will be more chaotic than this indicates. Nevertheless, the steps can help us assess our progress in managing change and they set a direction to work towards. Leadership is the decisive factor that determines whether we succeed, and we turn to that next in Chapter 9.

Ten steps to creating a successful transformational change programme

1 Know where you are now.
2 Develop the vision – the dream organization.
3 Identify the gap.
4 Assess the readiness for change.
5 Set the scene for action.
6 Secure basic compliance first.
7 Move beyond compliance.
8 Establish the performance criteria for 'compliance plus'.
9 Launch and manage the transformational change programme.
10 Maintain the rage.

Notes

1 ABC News, 'Nigerian Community Rejects Shell Compensation Offer', 2013. Online. Available HTTP: <http://abcnews.go.com/International/wireStory/ nigeria-community-rejects-shell-compensation-offer-20250479> (accessed 24 September 2013).
2 Consider the correspondence between Oxfam and Nike, available at https://www.oxfam.org.au/explore/workers-rights/nike/talking-with-nike/ (accessed 25 September 2013).
3 J. Elkington, *Cannibals with Forks: The Triple Bottom Line of the 21st Century Business*, Oxford: Capstone, 1999; United Nations Organisation Mission in the Democratic Republic of Congo, 'Report on the Conclusions of the Special Investigation into Allegations of Summary Executions and other Violations of Human Rights Committed by the FARDC in Kilwa on 15th October 2004', 2005.
4 CICA, AICPA and CIMA, 'SMEs Set Their Sights on Sustainability: Case Studies of Small and Medium-sized Enterprises (SMEs) from UK, US and Canada', 2011. Online. Available HTTP: <http://www.aicpa.org/interest areas/businessindustryandgovernment/resources/sustainability/downloadable documents/sustainability_case_studies_final%20pdf.pdf> (accessed 10 September 2013).
5 M. O'Driscoll, 'Entergy reeling after Katrina, Rita', *Greenwire*, 26 September 2005.
6 BSD Global, 'DuPont'. Online. Available HTTP: <http://go.webassistant. com/ep/cont_pub_view_item.lhtml?-Token.cID=100159&-Token.ID=13947 &-Nothing> (accessed 6 March 2013).
7 S. Hart and M. Milstein, 'Global sustainability and the creative destruction of industries', *Sloan Management Review*, 1999, 41 (1), 23–33.

8 Environmental Leader, 'DuPont Sustainable Fiber Hits Fashion Week Runway', 2013. Online. Available HTTP: <http://www.environmentalleader.com/2013/09/10/dupont-sustainable-fiber-hits-fashion-week-runway/> (accessed 10 September 2013).

9 R. Quinn, *Deep Change: Discovering the Leader Within*, San Francisco, CA: Jossey-Bass, 1996, p. 3.

10 I. Palmer and R. Dunford, 'Who Says Change Can Be Managed? Positions, Perspectives and Problematics', unpublished paper presented at the *International Research Workshop 'New Ways of Thinking about Organizational Change: Discourses, Strategies, Processes, Forms'*, University of Sydney, 26–27 November 2001.

11 D. Dunphy and D. Stace, *Under New Management: Australian Organizations in Transition*, Sydney: McGraw-Hill, 1990; D. Stace and D. Dunphy, *Beyond the Boundaries: Leading and Re-creating the Successful Enterprise*, 2nd edn, Sydney: McGraw-Hill, 2001.

12 Hart and Milstein, 'Global sustainability and the creative destruction of industries'.

13 S. Moore and S. Manring, 'Strategy development in small and medium sized enterprises for sustainability and increased value creation', *Journal of Cleaner Production*, 2009, 17 (2), 276–82

14 About Herdy, see http://www.herdy.co.uk/about/about-us (accessed 24 September 2013).

15 A. de Geus, 'The living company', *Harvard Business Review*, 1997, March–April, 51–9.

16 S. L. Brown and K. M. Eisenhardt, 'The art of continuous change: linking complexity theory and time-paced evolution in relentlessly shifting organizations', *Administrative Science Quarterly*, 1997, 42 (1), March, 1–34, esp. p. 1.

17 R. Perey, 'Metabolic Organisation: Reframing Ecological Sustainability', paper presented to the annual conference of the Academy of Management, Orlando, Florida, 9–13 August 2013.

18 L. Gratton, *Living Strategy: Putting People at the Heart of Corporate Purpose*, London: Financial Times/Prentice-Hall, 2000, p. 18.

19 B.-W. Lee, 'Waste costing for a Korean steel producer', in K. Green, P. Groenewegen and P. S. Hoffman (eds) *Ahead of the Curve: Cases of Innovation in Environmental Management*, Dordrecht, Netherlands: Kluwer Academic Publishers, 2001, esp. pp. 63–7, 71.

20 M. Halme, 'Corporate environmental paradigms in shift: learning during the course of action at upm-kymmene', *Journal of Management Studies*, 2002, 39 (8), 1087–109.

21 Stace and Dunphy, *Beyond the Boundaries*, pp. 71–3.

22 Electric Power Research Institute, 'Program on Technology Innovation: Electric Power Industry Technology Scenarios', report prepared for Global Business Networks, 2005.

23 J. Makover and S. Bery, 'The stress nexus of food, energy, and water', *Greenbiz*, 2013. Online. Available HTTP: <http://www.greenbiz.com/video/2013/05/22/food-energy-water-stress-nexus> (accessed 10 September 2013).

24 Gratton, *Living Strategy: Putting People at the Heart of Corporate Purpose*.

25 Halme, 'Corporate environmental paradigms in shift', p. 1103.

26 Ibid, p. 1101.

27 Ibid.

28 GE Imagination at Work, Online. Available HTTP: <http://www.ge.com/about-us/ecomagination> (accessed 7 March 2014).

29 D. Chatterjee, *Leading Consciously: A Pilgrimage towards Self Mastery*, Oxford: Viva Books and Butterworth-Heinemann, 1999, p. 39.

30 B. Smith and J. Yanowitz, 'Sustainable innovation and change: the learning-based path to growth', *Prism*, 1998, 4th Quarter, 35–45.

31 J. Dlouhá, A. Barton, S. Janoušková and J. Dlouhý, 'Social learning indicators in sustainability-oriented regional learning networks', *Journal of Cleaner Production*, 2013, 49 (0), 64–73.

32 D. Goleman, *Emotional Intelligence*, New York: Bantam Books, 1996; D. Zohar and I. Marshall, *Spiritual Intelligence: The Ultimate Intelligence*, London: Bloomsbury, 2000.

33 P. Shrivastava, 'Pedagogy of passion for sustainability', *Academy of Management Learning & Education*, 2010, 9 (3), 443–55, 446; D.C. Feldman, 'Managers propensity to work longer hours', *Human Resource Management Review*, 2002, 12 (3); 339–357; M. Bunting, *Willing Slaves: How the Overwork Culture is Ruling our Lives*, New York: HarperCollins, 2004.

34 See D. Hock, *Birth of the Chaordic Age*, San Francisco, CA: Barrett-Koehler, 1999.

35 The West Australian (2013) 'Shell in Compensation Talks over Nigeria Oil Spills', *The West Australian*, 7 September 2013. Online. Available HTTP: <http://au.news.yahoo.com/thewest/business/a/-/world/18815947/shell-in-compensation-talks-over-nigeria-oil-spills/> (accessed 9 September 2013).

36 The Nuffield Council on Bioethics, 'Genetically Modified Crops: The Ethical and Social Issues', 1999. Available at http://www.nuffieldbioethics.org/sites/default/files/GM%20crops%20-%20full%20report.pdf (accessed 24 September 2013).

37 E. von Weizacker, A. B. Lovins and L. H. Lovins, *Factor 4: Doubling Wealth – Halving Resource Use*, Sydney: Allen and Unwin, 1997.

38 V. Delgrano, Unilever on target to meeting 2020 sustainable sourcing goal. See http://www.2degreesnetwork.com/groups/supply-chain/resources/unilever-target-meet-2020-sustainable-sourcing-goal/ (accessed 3 October, 2013).

39 Stace and Dunphy, *Beyond the Boundaries*, pp. 106–18.

40 H. Tibbs, 'Industrial ecology: an environmental agenda for industry', *Whole Earth Review*, 1995, September–October, 120–34.

9 **Leading towards sustainability**

- Facing up to the future
- Dealing with complexity
- Theories of leadership
- A model of phase leadership
- Key factors in change agent competency
- Owning your power and changing corporate culture
- Putting the jigsaw puzzle together

Facing up to the future

Leadership is the creation of new realities. In this final chapter we discuss the leadership of change and the roles that different kinds of change agents can play in constructing the new reality of the sustainable corporation. Transforming the way we do business is no minor task and will require the inspiration, energies and skills of more people than are currently engaged in the task. If we are to create a sustainable world, we need many more effective leaders.

In raising the issue of change leadership, we cannot ignore how much easier it is to accept the status quo, to respond to our fear of change and our desire for certainty, to opt out rather than to engage actively in attempting to change the organizational world. Most of us, if we are honest, would rather let someone else lead in this kind of endeavour. Change of the order we are advocating here threatens us with uncertainty and chaos. It is much easier to hold on to traditional ways of doing things and to accept the leadership of others who don't question the status quo. The past, because of its familiarity, seems to offer us security – more security, at least, than a divergent and uncharted future. However, as we have argued throughout this book, many past practices are unsustainable. If we want the world we know and love to survive we must change it. If we are to survive and thrive ourselves we too must change. To change, however, requires the rawest kind of courage.

Choosing to lead change similarly involves courage, risk taking and the development of high levels of skill. These are the focus of our discussion in this chapter. The chapter is also designed to help you answer some basic questions about your own potential role as a leader of sustainable change:

- How do I equip myself to be an effective leader?
- Where shall I start?
- Who can I work with to have the most impact?

Dealing with complexity

Sustainability leadership means dealing with complexity.[1] The complexity includes varying interpretations of what sustainability might mean, trade-offs between the social, environmental and economic elements of sustainability, the wide range of stakeholders involved and varying government regulations dealing with such matters add up to a complicated portfolio of issues for change leadership. One way of dealing with this complexity is to consider sustainability as not one particular state but rather a process which change agents frequently refer to metaphorically as a journey. Throughout this book we have outlined what we see as the major phases that mark key stages on the journey that moves from opposition to commitment. As we have described it, the intentional movement toward achieving sustainability starts with Phase 3 compliance and moves through Phases 4 and 5 to Phase 6, the sustaining corporation.

What we have found in our research and summarized in this book is that the sustainability goals, organizational actions and interventions and types of effective leadership vary from phase to phase. The successful sustainability leadership qualities at Phase 3 compliance are dramatically different from, say, those that are effective at Phase 5 strategic proactivity. Not only do the leadership requirements vary but the prevailing discourse around the change process changes from phase to phase also; each phase has its own language, particularly around the dialogue of change toward sustainability, which is shaped by and shapes the core issues emerging in that phase.

So what are the major leadership differences that emerge in the evolution of the sustainable corporation? To answer this question we first briefly review the major theoretical orientations to leadership in the social science literature in order to show how these theories describe important and distinctive features of leaders at each phase.

Theories of leadership

Transactional leadership. In transactional leadership, the leader influences others, using an exchange relationship which appeals to the self-interests of others in the relationship.[2] Transactional leaders set up reward systems for behaviours that meet their expectations and, if well designed, these reward systems help to create a consistent and reliable set of rewards linked to the organization's goals. The transactional leader's interpersonal behaviour then acts as another set of rewards, reinforcing at a day-to-day level the impact of the reward systems.

Distributed leadership. Recent contributions to leadership theory debunk the 'great person' or heroic theories of leadership, arguing that leadership as the capacity to influence others is a concept that extends well beyond character and authority. Distributed leadership occurs within group situations and involves more than one leader. The basic idea is that different individuals can exercise leadership functions within a group or organization at different times; no one individual dominates.[3]

Enabling leadership. Some scholars argue that modern organizations are so complex that notions of traditional leadership do not do justice to the role of those in organizations who do not specifically lead themselves but who enable or guide others to do so.[4] Enabling leaders create the structures, rules, interactions and cultural characteristics that support the leadership actions of others who use these to further their change objectives.[5]

Transformational leadership. Transformational leadership is evident in leadership behaviours that demonstrably transform and have the ability to motivate others to perform their best. Such leaders go beyond their own interests for the sake of the organization as a whole.[6] Transformational leaders are visionary, enthusiastic and confident. Transformational leadership has been strongly identified with change agents who are responsible for organizational innovation, including sustainability innovations.[7]

Complexity leadership. Complexity leadership is a relatively new contribution to leadership theory that derives from recent developments in complexity theory. Leadership in complex systems is viewed as an outcome of many interactions between people in the system and emerges as people try to create order from what may be an uncontrolled and somewhat chaotic process. Complexity theory challenges linear, mechanistic views of organizational behaviour and traditional top-down models where leaders direct the behaviour of those below them in the hierarchy.[8]

Each of these theories of leadership has relevance in explaining what effective leadership for sustainability might mean. We now relate these theories of leadership to the differing manifestations of leadership across the phases of the sustainability journey.

A model of phase leadership

Leadership of the compliance phase: transactional/distributed

In the compliance phase, sustainability is defined as meeting governmental legislative and statutory requirements and the legitimate demands of stakeholders representing communities and the ecology. Once these demands are taken seriously by senior executives, transactional leadership is important because it rewards organizational members for 'keeping to the rules' and acting according to the norms rather than finding ways around them. Compliance is largely about putting in place new rules around ethical behaviour in areas such as occupational health and safety, emissions monitoring and community relations. Transactional leadership establishes basic trust in the organization and its leaders, as employees feel that they are 'getting a fair go', being appropriately rewarded for observing ethical norms and that there is consistency between the values the organization espouses and what it rewards.

However to effectively achieve the institution of both explicit rules and accepted norms, i.e. to create a culture of compliance, the compliance phase also must begin the process of building in leadership capability at all levels of the organization. People at all levels must start to take initiatives in ensuring that the organization is compliant. Compliance is not just about ensuring that the rules are kept, it is also about interpreting how the rules can be applied in specific, sometimes novel situations to ensure that the purposes for which the rules were instituted are achieved.

Leadership of the efficiency phase: distributed/enabling

In the efficiency phase, sustainability is interpreted as minimizing waste and maximizing use of productive resources, without necessarily redefining the strategic direction of the organization. Leaders must be planners, fostering the efficient deployment of finance and other resources internally, analysing the efficiency of day-to-day operations and identifying and minimizing waste of plant, equipment, materials and human resources. Externally, emphasis is placed on negotiating changes with those in the supply chain and delivery systems which also reduce or eliminate waste and pollution and increase efficiency.

At the efficiency phase, leadership continues to be distributed, as increasing efficiency in the use of resources requires action at all levels of the organization. No one leader can oversee the multitude of changes that need to be introduced, but reward systems which rely on transactional leadership can continue to reinforce new norms and behaviours, as long as they are modified to align with the new, more efficient operational approaches.

But in addition, enabling leadership becomes increasingly important. At the compliance phase, a traditional command-and-control, authority-based leadership approach can be relatively effective but, as organizations move beyond compliance, internal commitment becomes increasingly important and novel solutions that depart from the status quo are needed. Enabling leaders encourage this.[9] They also create active networks across boundaries for information sharing and the emergence of new ideas[10] as well as managing the conflicts that arise around the dialogue about adopting new approaches to old ways of operating.[11] They move resources to the point in the organization where they are needed to make change happen. Through their authority, networked connections and access to organizational resources, enabling leaders can raise the power of others to achieve far more than they would otherwise be able to do by their own efforts alone.

Taylor, for instance, notes that:

> proponents of this theory have suggested that enabling leadership suits senior leaders who are patient, comfortable with uncertainty, open to new ideas, proficient in systems thinking and have a propensity to control change.[12]

The combination of senior enabling leaders who back up the actions of the work of other distributed leaders at various levels throughout the organization brings the efficiency phase to a successful conclusion.

Leadership of the strategic proactivity phase: enabling/ transformational

In the strategic proactivity phase, enabling leadership continues to be important. Senior executives in particular work to maintain and expand the culture of voluntarism built at the previous phase. At the efficiency phase, the emphasis was in finding new and improved ways of doing what the organization already does. The strategic proactivity phase requires a significant shift in mind-set, requiring radical rethinking of the organization's strategies so as to make sustainability central. There is an emphasis on consistently pursuing the opportunities presented by emerging new industries such as alternative energy production or new products such as biodegradable plastics. This kind of radical thinking is needed throughout the organization.

But it is at the strategic proactivity phase that transformational leadership comes into its own. Making sustainability central to the corporation's business strategies usually requires a major strategic reorientation, including a radical rethinking of the nature of the business the enterprise is engaged in and of its product and/or service mix.

Transformational leaders work actively with organizational members and stakeholders to develop shared visions; they initiate new organizational directions, modify organizational culture and work through inspiring and motivating others. They move organizations from one system state to another and can have a marked positive impact on organizational performance.[13]

Leadership of the sustaining corporation phase: transformational/ complexity

In the sustaining corporation phase, the organization is not content to pursue sustainability only for its business advantages but also adopts an ethical viewpoint that sustainability is worthwhile in its own right. It goes beyond traditional views of the nature of the corporation as existing primarily to make returns for shareholders, to a view which sees the corporation as an integral cell in the ecology and society as well as the economy. As such, it regards the function of the 'cell' to contribute to the health of the planet and society on which its own health depends. It therefore actively supports a wider range of activities than is customarily the case and engages with a wider range of stakeholders.

In the sustaining corporation, the development of a shared vision is still vital and the activities of the organization are in a process of continuous transformation so that the corporation can remain on the leading edge of change toward a sustainable world. Therefore there is still a powerful need for transformational leadership. However, the organization itself and the external relationships and networks that it contributes to and relies on are increasingly complex. This requires a new kind of leadership to come to the fore – complexity leadership.

Sustainability and sustainable development are systems-based concepts and the full development of sustainability depends on recognizing the systemic context of production and consumption.[14] The natural and social environments are complex open systems of which we are part and therefore, if organizations are to be truly sustainable, corporate leaders must learn to operate within that complexity and with respect for it.[15] Modern organizations are themselves complex adaptive systems; the move to sustainability increases their level of complexity and also complexifies the leadership task.

The preceding discussion leads us to suggest that leaders of sustainable organizations emphasize heterarchy rather than hierarchy, and heterogeneity rather than homogeneity; ensure that knowledge is distributed across the organization rather than focused in expert and specialized areas; and recognize the need for dynamism and creativity rather than stability and predictability.[16] Such thinking reflects the growing influence of chaos and complexity theory on organization studies and leadership theory, which themselves are responses to the changing world characterized by these qualities.

Key factors in change agent competency

What do we need to be effective change leaders, given the range of leadership styles we may need to adopt in order to promote change? Are there practical skills or personal qualities that will help us to mould our own favoured approach to suit the particular organizational need? We need clarity of vision, knowledge of what we wish to change and the skills to implement the changes. But none of these can be fully effective without maturity and wisdom. In the end it is who we are, not what we know or can do that makes the crucial difference in effecting organizational change. Ideally, change agents need the following characteristics and practical ways of dealing with the complexity challenges that currently face us in the implementation of sustainability.

Goal clarity

'I know what outcomes I want to produce.' Yes, we do need to know what we want to achieve, but our understanding of the goal doesn't have to be precise when we begin. What we need is a 'strategic intent', a direction, a deep, intuitive response to the organizational situation in which we find ourselves, an aspiration to nudge our organizational world a little closer to the ideal of sustainability. This aspiration does not necessarily require transformative leadership, but it does entail a clear understanding of core values and core purpose on the part of the leadership team.[17]

Role clarity

'I know what to do to produce change.' Of course, when we start, we often do not know what to do. We may not have a clue about what to do to make change happen. This is a paradox we face as change agents – we need to find a viable and effective role to play in midwifing the future, but everything seems to conspire to block us. Nike for instance, initially floundered in finding its response to the boycotts and activism associated with poor working conditions in subcontractor factories in developing countries such as Vietnam. However, in 1998 Nike established a global corporate responsibility function and created the specific role of Vice-President of Corporate Responsibility, covering areas such as labour compliance, global community affairs, stakeholder engagement and corporate responsibility, strategic planning and business integration. In 2013 the role has become one of Vice-President Sustainable Business and Innovation who reports directly to the CEO. Responsibilities include 'enabling the company to thrive in a future state sustainable economy through closed loop business models'.[18] Nike has also developed an internal and external contract factory monitoring programme as well as a number of other measures designed to integrate corporate responsibility more tightly into the business.[19]

Similarly, at Hewlett-Packard, every design team has an Environmental Product Steward who is responsible for advising on reducing the environmental impact across the product life-cycle. These Stewards are charged with the specific role of taking the Hewlett-Packard Design for Environment guidelines to the practical level.[20]

Relevant knowledge

'I have or can access the knowledge required to produce the outcomes I want.' Corporate change processes demand depth of knowledge, and in the area of sustainability that knowledge is often not gained easily. Sustainability cuts right across traditional disciplinary boundaries. In a particular project, for example, we may need knowledge of the political processes of the organization; information on the human rights issues along the supply chain; technical knowledge about energy conservation, water purification, chemical pollutants; and knowledge about the attitudes of key external stakeholders. It would be an unusual person who had this knowledge at the beginning of a change programme. But we don't need all the knowledge before we start; we can acquire it as we go along, in partnership with others more knowledgeable than ourselves in some of these areas.

Nike is a firm which illustrates this principle of learning as we go (or 'learning through action', as Halme puts it).[21] Take Nike Inc. President and CEO Mark Parker's comments on the 2010–11 sustainability report, in which he acknowledges the role of continuously setting targets in pursuing innovation:

> We have continuously invested in reducing our environmental and social impacts within our own business and supply chain and have made substantial gains over the last decade. We know we cannot achieve our bold sustainability goals simply by delivering incremental improvements. We need to deliver innovations that rapidly evolve the way things are done at Nike, in our industry and throughout business.[22]

Relevant competencies and resources

'I have or can assemble the skills and resources to make it happen.' Again, we may not have the skills we need when we first take up a role as an organizational change agent. Acquiring skills is a lifetime endeavour. So, we need to be realistic about the skills we have and start the change process in a way that builds on our current skill level. However, the only effective way to learn skills is through experimentation and practice. To acquire them, we take faltering steps at first but, with practice, our steps become firm and purposeful. Mentors and models help, so, if we are relatively unskilled, another criterion of where to start the change process is to find others who do have the necessary skills and work with them. To begin, we need only a subset of the skills demanded by the full change programme and, if we work with others, we do not need the full repertoire of skills ourselves.

Self-esteem

'I believe I can do it.' Sometimes this one is the toughest call of all, but a passionate belief in the profound importance of the change we are initiating is a great help. Being a change agent is not for the faint-hearted. Emotional resilience is a fundamental requirement. We are often called on to persist in the face of adversity, derision, contempt and anger. Changing entrenched power structures can be a career-threatening experience. But then, abandoning the cause of sustainability is a planet-threatening experience. If we choose to undergo some adversity, at least in the end we have the satisfaction of knowing that we stand for life, for hope, for a viable future for us all.

If we believed we need the five characteristics so starkly listed above without the added provisos, we would never start to try to change corporations. These are ideals to be worked towards; they set a direction for our learning – they are not the starting line we must cross in order to begin. They define mastery in this field, and we discuss below the path to mastery: it is a long path and we learn primarily by doing. If we choose well, we also learn by apprenticeship to others more experienced and skilled than ourselves and by finding models and mentors. But definitely by doing.

We need to learn to live with ambiguity and a degree of chaos. Managing corporate change is rather like white-water rafting or surfing. The first lesson is not to try to control the environment but to move with it. Like rafting or surfing, success in change leadership comes from being willing to change our internal psychological world.

Achieving mastery

But that's only Change Leadership 101. As in any field of serious endeavour, learning of this kind is a lifetime commitment. We start as novices and may achieve mastery, but that takes effort, time and commitment. Table 9.1 outlines the stages in achieving mastery as a change agent. Moving through these stages opens us to a series of opportunities rather than problems.

Starting with self-leadership

Being a leader of change means living in and between two worlds. One is the world of inner experience, of personal meaning, of selfhood. The other is the outer world of action. The inner world is the real challenge for change agents. Paradoxically, the secret to changing the world about us is discovered only within ourselves.

Recent research on leadership effectiveness reinforces the notion that change leadership requires particular kinds of psychological strengths.

Table 9.1 *Stages in achieving mastery as a change agent*

1 Novice: learning 'the rules'
We seek clear guidelines for how to act in different situations; for example, many novices are drawn to The Natural Step programmes, which offer simple rules for instituting sustainable practices. We seek the codified knowledge of others who have done it.

2 Advanced beginner: beyond rules to strategies
We realize that in many situations, the rules don't work. Making change is more complex than we thought. Rules become more blurred and evolve into thoughtful strategies.

3 Competence: disciplined effectiveness
We develop a 'feel' for the complexity of change, select cues and respond to them on the basis of our accumulating experience. Our knowledge now is more tacit; our strategies are now evolving to include deeper levels of awareness.

4 Proficiency: fluid, effortless performance
We have internalized the strategies and they are backed up with high levels of skill. Intuition now dominates and reason is secondary.

5 Mastery: acting from our deepest intuition with confidence and flow
We become one with the changes we are making and are changing ourselves and our organizational world at the same time. Our inner and outer worlds are one. What we do often seems effortless and spontaneous.

For example, Luthans draws on developments in positive psychology – a field which emphasizes building on people's personal strengths rather than focusing on their weaknesses. He reviews research into the contribution of personal strengths to performance improvement in the workplace. He finds that these characteristics include realistic hope, optimism, subjective wellbeing/happiness and emotional intelligence.[23] These are the characteristics of mature, emotionally healthy human beings as well as of effective change agents and leaders.

Building or assembling the skills needed for diagnosis and action

Self-leadership is necessary, but it is not enough. As well as self-knowledge and an empathetic understanding of others, effective change leaders need skills.

First on the list are skills associated with effective diagnosis. If we are to attempt to change an organization we must first understand where the organization is on the path to sustainability and where it needs to go. Making the right diagnosis is as important in achieving organizational well-being as it is in achieving individual physical health. One of the major challenges for organizational change agents is that they usually have to make the analysis themselves and they have to do it on the run and *in situ*. It would be nice if our organizational change efforts began with a neatly packaged Harvard Business School case analysis, but unfortunately they don't.

If we work in the organization, then we are part of what we are analysing. Our viewpoint will be biased by the position we occupy – the view from below is always different, for example, from the view from above; the industrial engineer's view is different from that of the salesperson in the field. On the other hand, if we are external to the organization – for example, a consultant – we may have a more open mind; but we don't have the advantage of inside information. Whatever our role, as we start actively to find out more about the organization, looking at records, interviewing personnel and so on, we are already intervening in the ongoing system.

So we are studying a dynamic system of which we are part or become a part as we study it. We can't put it in a laboratory, take it apart and analyse it under a microscope. All we can do is immerse ourselves in it, understand that our own view will be biased and try to offset that by an empathetic identification with others who occupy very different positions. We can also gather data that can expand or contradict our biases. Moving around the organization helps, as does cultivating an open mind, observing and listening. The skills of action research are the most useful. In some cases we may wish to add more formal means of analysis such as surveys and financial analysis. These can help, but are no substitute for being there with full awareness.

More specifically, the action research and diagnostic skills we need are:

- *A well-developed, systematic theoretical position*, a framework or multiple frameworks; that is, a model of how organizations operate which helps us select the kind of data that are useful for understanding and for future action. This model is always partial and limited and so we must be open to revising it on the basis of experience.
- *A model of the ideal sustainable organization* combined with openness to others' ideal models. The future is mostly a collective creation, emerging from the active dialogue and interaction of interested parties. We need to be as clear as we can on what we want so that we can engage fully with others in that dialogue; but we need to be open to any emerging shared vision. Of course, there may be competing visions and resistance to visions in general: conflict is simply an element of the unfolding drama through which the future is defined; conflict is a signal that something important is at stake; it is a measure of progress on the path, not the end of the path.
- *The ability to question and listen to others* for factual, value-based and emotive information; all three kinds of information are useful. Moving to sustainability necessarily involves values and emotions as well as facts.
- *The ability to use varied data sources and methods of analysis*, to apply critical insight and make balanced judgements. If we want to make a map, it is useful to view the landscape from different viewpoints – triangulation increases accuracy.
- *The ability to convey a concise diagnosis* to others in their terms. The emerging field of sustainability studies is already developing its own language – professional and technical jargon; some of this is useful as shorthand and for technical precision. But if we are to influence others, we need to be able to translate what is important into the everyday language of the workplace.
- *The ability to monitor and evaluate the change process*: the process of diagnosis does not stop when the action begins. Diagnosis

becomes even more crucial in checking whether we are achieving what we set out to achieve and whether we need to change the path we travel along as we reach a fuller understanding of where we need to go.

Diagnostic skills help to define the path to sustainability. Moving down that path requires change agents to develop other skill sets too, particularly the skills of effective communication, of managing stakeholder relationships and project management:

- *Skills of effective communication*: the willingness to listen and ask skilful questions; the ability to adopt multiple viewpoints; the commitment to keep people informed and 'in the picture'; the ability to communicate clearly and simply with others in speech and writing; the ability to use images and emotions as well as facts in communicating with others.
- *Skills of managing stakeholder relationships*: direction setting (visioning) and defining the scope of responsibilities for parts of the vision; influencing and networking; delegating; developing, mentoring and coaching others; performance management and monitoring; team building.
- *Skills of project management*: making and taking opportunities; updating technical and organizational knowledge; problem solving; resourcing.

Relevant to each of these skill sets are communication skills that can convey the value proposition of sustainability to different stakeholders.

Figure 9.1 summarizes our analysis of the skills needed to become an effective change agent. These skills will be in great demand as more organizations embrace what Hirsh and Sheldrake refer to as 'inclusive leadership'.[24] Inclusive leadership, as they define it, derives from adopting the stakeholder perspective on organizations. It involves managers developing and maintaining an interactive exchange with all those who have a stake in the organization: investors, employees, suppliers, customers, the community and representatives of the environment and future generations. Organizations need to perform instrumental tasks and to reach financial objectives. But this is most effectively achieved by creating a wider set of outcomes that meet the needs of key stakeholders.[25] The skills of relationship building will be particularly critical as organizations move forward on the path to sustainability.

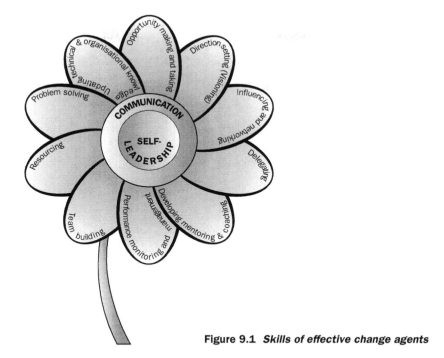

Figure 9.1 *Skills of effective change agents*

Creating dialogue and shared scenarios

One of the central tasks of change agents is the creation of visioning capabilities in the organization. Gratton writes that 'the capacity to create and develop a vision of the future that is compelling and engaging [is] at the very centre of creating a human approach to organizations'.[26] But where does the vision come from?

Vision emerges from dialogue – both inner dialogue within ourselves and dialogue within the organization and with its external stakeholders. The task of the change agent is to work with others to create new meaning, for new meaning creates new realities. This is the process that Weick calls 'sensemaking'.[27] Dialogue is not chatter but, rather, engagement at the deepest level with ourselves and with others. Dialogue begins with cultivating awareness and with listening; it continues with responsiveness and an exchange that is a catalyst for creative change.[28]

Dialogue can change people's perceptions of themselves and of their organization. From these new perceptions a sense of collective identity and purpose emerges that can renew or transform the existing culture of the organization. If this happens, the leadership of change passes from the handful of change agents who began the change process to a much larger network within the organization. Leaders create leaders. So was the case in an exemplar organization of change for sustainability which we have studied: Yarra Valley Water.

Sustainability leadership at Yarra Valley Water

Yarra Valley Water (YVW) is widely recognized in Australia as a leader in corporate sustainability. It is a water utility, owned by the government of the State of Victoria, which delivers water and sewerage services to over 1.6 million people in the northern and eastern suburbs of Melbourne.

YVW's ability to deliver innovative projects and to demonstrate industry leadership is the outcome of over a decade of commitment to learning and change in the organization's operations. Central to this change have been ongoing initiatives to create a more open and collaborative organizational culture that fosters innovation and creativity.

YVW has created ongoing processes of corporate reinvention and renewal that have improved customer service and led to innovations resulting in significant efficiencies. Central to this success has been a systematic programme designed to develop leaders who have a constructive leadership style which supports openness and initiatives from all levels of the organization. As a result, from 2007 to the present YVW has been winner or runner-up for many high-performance business awards (such as service excellence), but also for many environmental awards.

Until 2001, YVW was a conventional hierarchical and bureaucratic government organization dominated by a traditional engineering mentality. In that year a new CEO, Tony Kelly, asked an international consulting company to carry out an organizational culture audit.

As a result of discussion of the survey results, the organization established a new set of goals around building a high-performance culture. According to the HR Manager, Anne Farquhar, this culture would be underpinned by constructive behaviours that have been shown to facilitate high-quality problem solving and decision making, teamwork, productivity and long-term organizational effectiveness.[29] A major change programme was instituted to achieve this goal – a programme which has been continuously developed since that time. In 2003 YVW established 'environment' as one of four key elements in the organization's strategic intent and since then has continued to integrate environmental considerations into core business decisions. The organization has also developed and integrated a number of sustainability tools and approaches from around the world, including The Natural Step, Life Cycle Assessment and stakeholder consultation.

continued

The 12-year journey to date can be documented through regular culture audits which show consistent movement away from the aggressive and defensive behaviours which characterized the old culture, toward a set of highly constructive behaviours prevailing now. Data from Human Synergistics, the international company conducting the surveys, shows that of 2,065 organizations surveyed, YVW 'now sits in the top 2% of organizations that have a mindset to change and a focus on long term effectiveness'.[30]

Leadership of the culture-change programme began with the incoming CEO, Tony Kelly, and an outstanding Human Resources Manager, Anne Farquhar. After the first Human Synergistics survey, Kelly worked with his senior team to develop the strategic intent for the organization and to gain the team's commitment to model in its own behaviour the change from aggressive/defensive behaviour to open, constructive behaviour. The senior team demonstrated personal commitment to cultural change and modelled the behavioural changes needed to support others in similarly modifying their behaviour and so shifting the culture of the organization. Internal and external change agents were used to coach and develop personnel at all levels and the repeated surveys monitored the impact of these interventions.

This new cultural environment encouraged questioning of traditional approaches to water collection and distribution, as well as other organizational practices, and eventually resulted in major improvements in efficiency and in effectiveness (such as improved customer feedback). A wide range of sustainability achievements include providing recycled water to more than 100,000 homes and the development of partnerships that aim to reduce nutrient contamination of local waterways by 80 per cent.[31]

In terms of the leadership theories outlined earlier in this chapter, the behaviour of the executive team can be characterized as 'enabling' and 'transformational'. Creating enabling structures rewarded upward feedback of innovative ideas and enhanced increased autonomy for decision making throughout the organization. On this base there was a radical rethinking of the way in which the enterprise conducted its business and impacted on the ecological environment and on the communities in which it operated. Transformational leadership became the norm throughout the organization and was reinforced through a strong emphasis on targeted training and development.

The Yarra Valley Water example demonstrates how leadership that focuses on building in a capacity for continuous organizational renewal and the creation of a constructive culture expedites an ideal environment for both business success and for innovation in ecological and human sustainability.

Source: P. Crittenden, S. Benn and D. Dunphy, 2011,
'Yarra Valley Water: Learning and chnage for sustainability',
Prahhan, Victoria, Tilde University Press, pp. 147–161.

Our own experience in working with effective change leaders at all levels of organizations is that they have a profound belief in the capability of others. This belief manifests itself through challenging others to contribute even beyond what they thought was their best and supporting them in doing this. Typically, others say of such leaders: 'You know, he (she) believed in me more than I believed in myself. Through him (her) I learned that I could accomplish much greater things than I ever thought possible.' This is true empowerment and it is part of the process of creating organizations where everyone has the opportunity to lead in developing a sustainable workplace that offers exciting and meaningful work.

However, some conflicts of interests in organizations are intractable. When this is the case, leadership becomes the art of achieving what you believe is the best possible outcome in the circumstances, even if that does not match your ideal. Negotiations and compromise may be necessary to produce small wins that can be built on later. A general rule for change agents is that if you can't go around it, over it or under it, then negotiate with it.

Identifying and dealing with resistance to change

All change agents encounter resistance to the changes they attempt to introduce. There is an extensive literature on resistance to change and how to deal with it. Much of it is written for senior executives and embodies the assumption that positive change is mainly initiated by senior executives, who encounter resistance to change from middle management or the workforce. Our own experience is that senior executives are as resistant to change as anyone else and the initiative for change often comes from elsewhere in the organization. The reality is that most people resist change when others are attempting to change them; few do when they feel that they are in charge of change.

People are particularly likely to resist change when they see it as threatening their interests and when they believe that their knowledge and skills may be made irrelevant as changes take place. As we move towards sustainability, there will be those whose interests are threatened and whose current knowledge and skills become obsolete. Not all resistance to change is irrational. As change agents we need to understand that change is a political process in which people's power and status are implicated. There will always be those whose identification with the old order is so strong that they will actively oppose or passively resist change towards the new. There can also be legitimate disagreements – value conflicts – about the best way to proceed in progressing sustainability: disagreements about priorities, about facts such as the potential danger of certain substances, about strategies and tactics for moving forward. As change agents, we need to work to create an evolving consensus among interested parties. Active engagement of those who will be affected by the changes is often the most effective way forward. However, it does not always work. There can be delays, obfuscations, side-tracks, subversions. As in all fields of endeavour, persistence is a large part of success and persistence comes from a deep commitment to a meaningful view of the future.

Contributing to living networks

An important part of making change happen is networking with like-minded people. Change agents spend real time in building networks to provide information about the systems they are working in, to act as channels of influence and for support in what is an emotionally demanding endeavour. But where do we find like-minded people?

Values researcher Ray has identified three major groups in the USA, whom he refers to as modernists, heartlanders and cultural creatives. The modernists embrace mainstream materialist values, try to acquire property and money, are value winners and are cynical about idealism and caring for others; the heartlanders hold conservative values, reject modernism, favour traditional gender roles and fundamentalist religion, and are volunteers who care for others; the cultural creatives reject modernism and support the values of an integral culture that seeks to integrate life on the basis of diversity. They have a well-developed social consciousness, are optimistic and committed to family, community, internationalism, feminism and the environment. They are concerned about health, personal growth and spirituality. Cultural creatives share with modernists openness to change and, like heartlanders, care about community and personal relationships.[32] Ray's surveys estimate that 47 per cent of the US population are modernists, 29 per cent are heartlanders and 24 per cent are cultural creatives.

We expect that a disproportionate number of leaders in sustainable change programmes will be drawn from the ranks of the cultural creatives. Clearly, what Ray calls integral culture is a value set that supports the views we have espoused in this book. Ray argues that there are about 50 million cultural creatives in the USA and that they are the leading edge of cultural change in the country. We are not alone.

Who are the leaders/change agents?

We have outlined the personal characteristics and skills of effective change agents. But what roles do change agents occupy and how do these roles affect the contributions they can make to the sustainability movement? Our list follows, and then we discuss how their distinctive contributions can make corporate sustainability a living reality.

Change agent roles

- Internal:
    - line roles: the board of management, the CEO, the senior executive team, other managers and supervisors, general employees;
    - staff support roles: HR, OD (organization development), industrial engineering and environmental specialists, life scientists and IT specialists.
- External: politicians, bureaucrats and regulators; investors; professional business consultants; customers; community activists, concerned citizens and intellectuals; environmentalist activists; those who speak for future generations.

What are their distinctive roles?

We now take up the issue of how the various roles listed above can contribute to sustainability initiatives. As outlined, we divide them into roles internal to the organization and external to it. All these roles can make a distinctive contribution to moving organizations towards sustainability; in collaboration, they can have an irresistible impact. We begin our discussion with roles internal to the organization.

The internal roles consist of 'the line' and 'staff support'. The line consists of the board of management, CEO, senior executive team, other managers and supervisors and general employees.[33] The staff support roles consist of specialist professionals who provide support to those in the line. We will deal with the line roles first.

Boards of management

Boards of management can play a crucial role in setting the operating rules for an organization. Directors have heavy legal responsibilities and may be liable to major penalties if the organization is not compliant. They also have ultimate responsibility for appointing the CEO and signing off on the firm's business strategies. The relationship between the board and the CEO appears to be critical if an organization is to act more responsibly towards its stakeholders.

Boards of management often lack sufficient diversity to deal effectively with the shift from sole focus on shareholder value to meeting the expectations of a wider set of stakeholders. The changes we are advocating mean that the membership of boards needs to change so that they sample the diversity of stakeholders whose interests the board must now represent. Corporate sustainability has implications for corporate governance.

Line managers

Line managers include the CEO, senior executives, managers and supervisors or team leaders. Gratton views the line manager's role in the change process as being courageous enough to create broad involvement, to support the process of change and to ensure that HR is centrally important to the business.[34] The CEO and senior executive team's central task is to ensure that sustainability strategies are an integral part of business strategy and that they contribute to profitability, to customer satisfaction as well as to the welfare of other stakeholders. Their role involves communicating that corporate objectives include sustainability and outlining what this means for the integrity of organizational structures, processes, products and services. Their actions must also match policy statements rather than contradict them: it is important that they model what they are espousing, allocate resources to support the change process and ensure that measures of business-unit performance include progress on sustainability goals. As strategies are implemented successfully, line managers also have the responsibility for seeing that the resulting learning is communicated across the organization so that successful sustainability innovations are adopted and adapted.

Siemens provides us with the example of an organization which has successfully implemented a strategy around sustainability with line management playing a key role in its ongoing development.

Sustainability leadership at Siemens

As noted in Chapter 5, Siemens is a company which has taken sustainability as a guiding principle of its corporate strategy. But strategy must be constantly renewed and implemented to be effective; leaders develop strategies and translate them into ongoing practice to achieve the intended results.

To design, coordinate and manage the sustainability initiatives, Siemens established in 2009 the Siemens Sustainability Advisory Board, a Sustainability Board and a Sustainability Office. The Siemens Sustainability Advisory Board is a panel of outside consultants consisting of nine independent individuals from science and industry. They are drawn from a variety of disciplinary backgrounds and from different continents. The Advisory Board meets at least twice a year and these external thought leaders provide independent external guidance and advice for Siemens sustainability policy development and initiatives.

The Siemens Sustainability Board is the central steering and decision-making body in charge of sustainability. It is chaired by the member of the company's Managing Board who is also Chief Sustainability Officer. The Board is staffed by representatives of the four sections of Siemens and of all relevant specialist functions.

The Sustainability Office is responsible for implementing sustainability strategy and for coordinating company-wide programmes and initiatives.

The members of these bodies and other leaders throughout the organization form an ongoing sustainability network which interacts closely with executives in charge of company units to develop programmes and initiatives, to establish targets and to define performance indicators. Key performance indicators for these sustainability objectives are an important part of management performance measures. Contribution to the development of the Siemens' Environmental Portfolio is a factor in the bonuses paid to members of the Managing Board. Similarly, executive compensation depends in part on achieving specific targets defined in the compliance programme.

Thus the actual implementation of sustainability programmes is ultimately the responsibility of the heads of operational units (sectors, divisions, business units, clusters and regions), who are supported in this by leaders of specialized functions such as Environmental Protection and Corporate Citizenship. In this sense, therefore, sustainability leadership at Siemens takes place through regular managerial processes, as for other areas of the business.[35]

In terms of the leadership theories outlined earlier in this chapter, the leadership approach at Siemens can be characterized as 'transactional' and 'enabling'. The behaviour of leaders is transactional in that it reinforces the new norms and behaviours relating to sustainability, particularly through changing the reward structures. It is enabling through supporting the creation of active networks across boundaries: networks that increase information sharing and the emergence of new ideas and innovations in the area of sustainability practice.

The CEO

The role of the CEO is vital in terms of both symbolic and practical leadership. It is no easy role.

The CEO of a public company faces the dilemma that many market analysts and investment funds seek short-term returns and, as yet, place far too little emphasis on the importance of the issues we have discussed in this book. The CEO who is attempting to build a sustainable and sustaining corporate culture faces a daily performance evaluation by a share market which traditionally places little value on this. As we have discussed, ethical investment funds have demonstrated consistently superior returns and the size of these funds is growing. Nevertheless, the CEO must deliver in the short term and find resources to invest in the future. This is no easy task, particularly in a recession; sometimes it feels to CEOs that they are running up an escalator that is moving in the opposite direction. Nevertheless, many CEOs manage to generate short-term gains by 'picking low-hanging fruit' while quietly investing in building the capabilities of the corporation to generate medium- to long-term performance, including performance due to sustainability initiatives.

Hart and Quinn saw CEOs as playing four kinds of leadership roles in the change process: motivator, vision setter, analyser and taskmaster.[36] These roles are directed respectively to people, the future, the operating system and the market. They investigated the typical roles played by CEOs and linked these roles to three measures of firm performance: short-term financial performance, growth and future positioning of the organization, and organizational effectiveness (non-financial measures of performance such as employee satisfaction, product quality and social responsibility).

Hart and Quinn found that CEOs used the taskmaster role the most but the role did not influence any of the three performance measures. The analyser role, directed at creating improved efficiency, and the vision-setter role were significant predictors of business performance and organizational effectiveness, but not of short-term business performance. The motivator role was, however, a particularly strong predictor of organizational performance on all three dimensions. The research results also demonstrate that those CEOs who used all four roles achieved higher levels of performance than CEOs who did not.[37] Being an effective CEO demands a varied role repertoire and the flexibility to move in and out of different roles as the needs of the situation change. These qualities of the CEO are the qualities of any organizational leader, writ large: all leaders need to be able to understand the issues (analyser), inspire others (vision setter) and help others to focus their energy (motivator).

We have recognized that both incremental and transformative changes can facilitate organizational sustainability. If it is the profound transformational change associated with redesigning the organization around sustainability principles that is chosen as appropriate, then, above all, the CEO and other corporate figures must be able to face the realities of what the organization is and what it needs to change. One example is the drive to micro-franchising taken up by corporate leaders of organizations such as Unilever. Based on the famous example of Grameen Bank, whose micro-finance operations have successfully assisted many thousands of poor, mostly female clients to borrow money interest-free to establish their own business, micro-franchising targets the Bottom of the Pyramid (BOP) section of the market. Tex Gunning, the global head of BOP Strategy for Unilever, argues that his vision of Unilever micro-franchising not only leaves a smaller environmental footprint but has the capacity to end child malnutrition.[38]

Other managers, supervisors and team leaders contribute to the strategic process and actively translate the strategies into practical action plans. If they are to be effective, these plans will include achievable but challenging sustainability goals and involve the introduction of processes and systems that embody ecological and human sustainability principles. Supervisors and team leaders, in particular, are the critical front line of both incremental and transformational change. Their support and feedback is vital to a successful change programme.

At any level of the organization, leaders who recognize the importance of sustaining the diversity and interconnectedness of life forms and who value their employees and the wider community, by definition must address organizational issues of gender, diversity and power.

General employees

These often see themselves as having more limited power than executives and managers. They certainly have more limited authority; but general employees make or break organizational strategies. A strategy that is not translated into the moment-to-moment, day-to-day operational work of the organization is like a bird without wings – it never gets off the ground.

Green Mountain Coffee Roasters, the largest purchaser of Fair Trade Certified™ Coffee in the world for the second year running and winner of McDonald's Best of Sustainable Supply Award 2012, provides a good example of the power of employee commitment to make a difference in the sustainability strategy of the firm. As we discussed in a previous edition, this firm places a strong emphasis on employee engagement and commitment in maintaining its business success, claiming that, taking a number of its 600 employees on an annual trip to coffee-growing cooperatives in Vera Cruz and Oaxaca, Mexico has given them an appreciation for how hard the coffee growers work and has dramatically raised staff awareness of the value of the firm's long-held commitment to social and environmental issues.[39] According to its new CEO, Brian Kelley:

> Sustainability does mean different things to different companies. But at the end of the day, having a sustainable supply chain, having a community and employee base that is fundamentally on board and committed to it, and having products that deliver it – those are three common strategies. It's very hard to get all three working in harmony. The alchemy of it is not a simple thing. You've got to put this mix together and make it work.[40]

Staff support roles

Staff support roles are usually occupied by specialists who do not have the authority held by line managers. Their impact is achieved through expertise and influence rather than authority. HR and OD specialists, industrial engineers, environmental specialists and IT specialists are particularly important in making change happen.

HR specialists are an integral part of the change-planning process, including working with and to the senior executive team. They must also be active in creating and maintaining the guiding coalition that leads the change process and they need to provide technical expertise on HR issues such as performance reward systems, and the training and skills development needed to build the competencies required to progress through the sustainability phases.

OD specialists are particularly important in the organizational reshaping process. Not all organizations have OD specialists or, if they have, refer to them in this way. By OD specialists we mean change agents with highly specialized skills around the process of corporate change. They are professionals with training and experience in techniques such as team building, conflict resolution, counselling and intergroup relations. They are accustomed to working with the hot human process of change as it occurs; they take emotional reactions as a normal part of any significant change process and are not fazed by them. They are accustomed to working in ambiguous situations where they have little authority and to collaborating with others to design the ongoing process of change. Working on the edge of chaos and keeping organizational change processes on track and productive is their speciality.

Industrial designers and engineers

In manufacturing and other industry sectors, specialists with an engineering or industrial design background play key roles in process design, planning and operations. Where they have a grounding in business process re-engineering this can prove invaluable in redesigning product flows to make them more efficient and sustainable. Their grasp of the technical knowledge needed in moving to sustainability can combine with the skills of HR and OD specialists to be a winning combination. Where such specialists have a working knowledge of the principles developed by the 'cradle to cradle' design experts Bill McDonough and Michael Braungart, they can be instrumental in redesigning the firm's business model around the 'eco-effective' concept of zero waste.[41] In this model, the firm owns the molecules or the building blocks of the products, which are then continually recycled according to market demand. Cars, for instance, would be returned to the manufacturer. Materials would either be composted or recycled into new models. The concept is dependent upon design for ready disassembly and the minimal use of toxic materials.[42] Designers working according to the 'biomimicry' principles developed by such experts as Janine Benyus can also radically reconceptualize the firm's business model in order to integrate sustainability.[43]

IT specialists

IT is an enabler of corporate success. No large, complex modern organization can afford to lag behind the leading edge of change in IT, particularly with the rapid development of e-commerce and virtual organizations. IT specialists are vital to the construction of the computer-based systems needed for coordination and control of a wide variety of processes, including complex supply chains. They need to understand the imperative for building sustainable systems and the requirement for them to be both efficient and user friendly. IT specialists can easily become lost in their world of rapidly changing technology and lose touch with the firm's business imperatives. Sustainability-oriented organizations work to overcome this.

As an organization progresses through the six phases of sustainability, there is an increasing requirement for a more holistic and integrated approach to both human resources and environmental management. This means that the HR and environmental management functions, in particular, must change and eventually merge or collaborate closely with a mutual understanding of how their efforts contribute seamlessly to the emerging philosophy and practice of sustainability.

External change-agent roles

In the sustainability movement, external change agents have played major roles in bringing pressure to bear on organizations to adopt more sustainable strategies. This external pressure has been at times adversarial in both the human and ecological areas of activity. While there will be a place for adversarial activists in the foreseeable future, a shift in emphasis has taken place as more organizations move beyond compliance to launch sustainability initiatives on a voluntary basis. New collaborative alliances are taking place across the boundaries of organizations and external change agents have important roles to play in these alliances. Major and minor consulting companies have also moved to set up specialized practices to provide advice on a variety of sustainability issues.

Politicians, bureaucrats and regulators

The role of politicians, bureaucrats and regulators is to create 'third wave' economies that support 'third wave' organizations. This means having the courage to challenge the narrow assumptions of 'second wave' economists who dominate departments of finance in most Western economies. It means being open to the new fields of ecological economics, industrial ecology and intellectual capital. The countries making most progress in this regard are the Netherlands, Germany, Finland and Denmark. Japan, too, has highly developed national strategies in place concerning product stewardship. These countries are already creating national policies that shift first- and second-wave corporations forward into the growth industries of the third wave and are developing new export industries in, for example, alternative energy generation.

Investors

Investors control the flow of capital to corporations directly and through brokers and funds. There is no more powerful pressure for change than the withdrawal of investment from public companies or the flow of capital to them. It is vital therefore that investors support companies that are working to implement sustainability policies and withdraw investment from those that are not. Companies with sustainable policies give better returns overall than those without such policies, so, on financial grounds alone, this is a viable investment policy. Customers can exert similar pressures through shifting their buying to favour sustainable products and services. As these products and services are healthier, this is also a sensible pattern of consumer spending. Consumers are increasingly demanding transparency in terms of ingredients and components in products (for example, information on genetic modification of foods). Supporting increasing transparency makes an important contribution to advancing the sustainability movement because transparency makes informed consumer choice possible.

Community activists

Community activists, concerned citizens, intellectuals and scientists also have important roles in demanding transparency in company operations, assembling the best available knowledge about the impact of particular kinds of products and services (for example, chemicals) and bringing external pressure to bear on companies that avoid their responsibilities to their workforces, communities or the environment. In addition, as more companies move to an 'inclusive leadership' approach that welcomes the participation of a range of stakeholders in achieving corporate sustainability, there are emerging opportunities to collaborate on new initiatives. Community activists also have a vital role in speaking for the natural environment – they are often closest to it and best able to provide a voice to protect it.

Green Mountain Coffee Roasters, for example, began to improve its environmental performance in 1989 when it formed an environmental committee and created a rainforest nut coffee to support the Rainforest Alliance, a non-profit dedicated to protecting ecosystems. The company has grown increasingly active in the countries where coffee is grown and, as noted, has been a pioneer and leading participant in the Fair Trade movement, which pays coffee growers stable, fair prices.[44]

Future generations

Finally, we have included future generations as change agents. The unborn generations are not, of course, yet present and so are unable to act for change that will serve their interests. They need spokespersons to stand for intergenerational equity. In our view, those best equipped to play this role are parents, educators, youth leaders and others who strongly identify with the children of the future and can speak for them.

Building alliances of change agents

Many change agents feel isolated and unsupported in working towards the creation of a sustainable future. Their activities often have little impact and are lost in the ongoing operations of large-scale, complex organizations. As the sustainability movement advances, there are increasing opportunities to lead by forming alliances between change agents working within an organization and others outside it. Such alliances can create a pincer movement of pressure for change in the first three phases of sustainability and so build momentum for compliance and for the movement towards compliance plus. In the latter three phases they can create increasing momentum by linking initiatives in different parts of the organization and in the community – initiatives that otherwise might be struggling on their own. It is vital to keep in mind that this is a social movement that extends beyond the corporation and, like all social movements, its success demands a disciplined cooperation, despite inevitable differences of values and skill bases.

Constructing the sustainability agenda

In Figure 9.2 we have summarized some of the challenges the change leader, whether of the SME or the large enterprise, will need to address.[45]

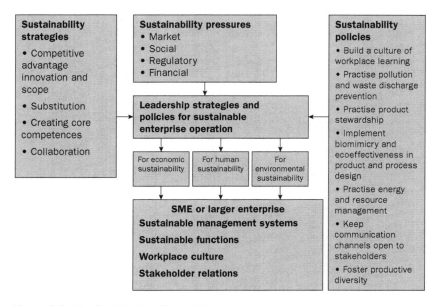

Figure 9.2 *Idealised leadership model*
Source: Modified from R. Kerr, 'Leadership strategies for sustainable SME operation', *Business Strategy and the Environment*, 2006, 15, 30–9.

So what is the agenda for collaborative action between change agents if they are to address these challenges? Below we summarise the main points of the sustainability agenda we have discussed through the book. The first outlines the internal agenda; that is, the changes in the workforce itself that are needed to build a relevant base of human capabilities. The next one outlines the external agenda, that is, the move towards stakeholder involvement and participation. The third box outlines the agenda for the ecological environment, that is, the changes that need to take place in the corporation so that it does not damage but restores and renews the natural world.

Human sustainability: the internal agenda

- Adopt a strategic perspective to workplace development.
- Build the corporate knowledge and skill base (intellectual and social capital) of employees – develop human potential.
- Foster productive diversity in the workplace (OH&S, gender equity, participative decision making, work–life balance).
- Develop the capability for continuing corporate reshaping and renewal, including visionary change leadership.
- Create communities of practice to diffuse knowledge and skills.
- Provide relevant expertise in the best way to organize work for high performance and satisfaction.
- Represent employees' concerns to management, while simultaneously giving employees an increased role in organizational decision making.

Human sustainability: the external agenda

- Reinterpret strategy around a wider range of stakeholders and develop cooperative strategies with them (responsiveness).
- Add, rather than subtract, value for all relevant stakeholders.
- Build a culture of workplace learning and commitment to a 'generative society' through a declared and enacted value base.
- Initiate and sustain an ongoing dialogue with stakeholders to define key elements of social responsibility – set priorities (accountability).
- Define social goals, develop action plans to reach these goals, monitor and disclose performance against key performance indicators (transparency).

continued

- Seek genuine feedback on performance from stakeholders – welcome and learn from criticism.
- Win, by responsible informed action, the support of all stakeholders for the organization's continued existence and growth.

Achieving ecological sustainability

- Design a production system that is an integral part of the ecology (like an earthworm).
- Conduct life-cycle assessment and develop a policy of resource stewardship.
- Eliminate waste and pollution, particularly by product redesign and developing an industrial ecology.
- Form active partnerships with 'green', human rights and other community groups.
- Appoint independent experts to monitor the corporation's environmental 'footprint' (environmental auditing).
- Link action on human sustainability with action on ecological sustainability to create an integrated, seamless approach to corporate sustainability.

Owning your power and changing corporate culture

Corporate culture is strategy in action.[46] Culture arises out of the collective experience of the members of an organization; it provides a framework of meaning to interpret the stream of events which people encounter in the workplace so that they can make sense of their work and their role in the organization and society. Culture is a guide to action – at best a living expression of the strategic intent of the organization. The role of change leaders is to actively engage in the process of meaning making so that they are an integral and powerful part of the process of cultural redefinition that must take place in order to create sustaining organizations in a sustainable society.

In this change process, actions are often more powerful than words, though words have an important place. Symbolic events are frequently the focus for significant shifts in cultural awareness. Part of the role of the change leader is to become an actor in the unfolding drama of change towards sustainability.

The art of cultural co-evolution is the art of managing dynamic complexity over time. Connecting things is relatively easy – the skill is in finding ways for them to connect in an organized, indirect, limited, yet coherently meaningful way.

As change agents and change leaders, we are only one source of influence in a complex, changing reality. Nevertheless, let us not underestimate the potential transformative power that we represent. As Korten has stated:

> The transformative power of the organism – both human and nonhuman – is the ultimate source of all that has value in the fulfillment of our own being. It includes not only the whole of the natural living capital, by which the planet's life support system is continuously regenerated, but also the human, social and institutional capital by which we utilize the wealth of the living planet to serve our needs and by which we may ideally come to lend our own distinctive capacities to further life's continuing journey.[47]

Change leadership involves owning our own power and using it responsively and responsibly.

Putting the jigsaw puzzle together

We began this book with an analogy. We wrote that constructing the sustainable organization of the future is like assembling pieces of a jigsaw puzzle. We have identified a range of organizations which represent parts of the puzzle because they have already begun inventing the future. No individual or group has yet grasped the whole picture; not all the parts of the puzzle are in existence; but when we make an inventory of what this organization is doing here and what another is doing there, the bigger picture emerges. We have used the sustainability phase model as an overlay to the puzzle – we think it clusters the pieces in a way that delineates an integral part of one section of the final picture. We all have a role to play in helping to put the puzzle together, in unfolding the 'implicate order'. We can lead where we are now, by fulfilling the potential of the roles we hold in the organizations of which we are a part. If we act with integrity, standing with courage for the planet, for a healthy society and for future generations, our leadership will contribute to creating a new organizational reality – the sustaining corporation that contributes to creating a fully sustainable world.

Notes

1 In this section of the chapter we draw from our work in D. Dunphy and S. Benn, 'Leadership for sustainable futures', in R. By and B. Burnes (eds), *Organizational Change, Leadership and Ethics*, London and New York: Routledge, 2012.

2 B. M. Bass and P. Steidlmeier, 'Ethics, character, and authentic transformational leadership behaviour', *Leadership Quarterly*, 1999, 10 (2), 181–217.

3 C. Pearce and J. Conger, 'All those years ago: the historical underpinnings of shared leadership', in C. Pearce and J. Conger (eds), *Shared Leadership*, Thousand Oaks, CA: Sage Publications, 2003, pp. 1–17.

4 R. Marion and M. Uhl-Bien, 'Leadership in complex organizations', *Leadership Quarterly*, 2001, 12 (4), 389–418; D. A. Plowman, S. Solansky, T. E. Beck, L. Baker, M. Kulkarni and D. V. Travis, 'The role of leadership in emergent, self-organization', *The Leadership Quarterly*, 2007, 18 (4), 341–56.

5 R. Marion, 'Complexity theory for organizations and organizational leadership', in M. Uhl-Bien and R. Marion (eds), *Complexity Leadership: Conceptual Foundations*, Charlotte, NC: Information Age Publishing, 2008, pp. 1–17.

6 B. Avolio and B. Bass, *Multifactor Leadership Manual*, Menlo Park, CA: Mind Garden Inc, 2004.

7 For a comprehensive review see A. Taylor, 'Sustainable Urban Water Management: The Champion Phenomenon', PhD thesis, Monash University, Melbourne, Victoria, 2010. Online. Available HTTP: <http://arrow.monash.edu.au/vital/access/manager/Repository/monash:34939?queryType=vitalDismax&query=taylor+sustainable+water+management> (accessed 12 September 2013).

8 L. Metcalf and S. Benn (2013) 'Leadership for sustainability: an evolution of leadership ability', *Journal of Business Ethics*, 2013, 112 (3), 369–84. Available at: http://link.springer.com/article/10.1007/s10551-012-1278-6.

9 Plowman *et al.*, 'The role of leadership in emergent, self-organization'.

10 H. Ibarra and M. Hunter, 'How leaders build and use networks', *Harvard Business Review*, 2007, 85 (1), 40–7.

11 Taylor, 'Sustainable Urban Water Management'.

12 Ibid, p. 2.

13 Q. Jones, D. Dunphy, R. Fishman, M. Larne and C. Canter, *In Great Company: Unlocking the Secrets of Cultural Transformation*, Sydney, Australia: Human Synergistics, 2006.

14 A. Tukker, S. Emmert, M. Charter, C. Vezzoli, S. Stø, M. Andersen, T. Geerken, U. Tischner and S. Lahlou, 'Introduction', in A. Tukker (ed.), *System Innovation for Sustainability 1: Perspectives on Radical Changes to Sustainable Consumption and Production*, Sheffield: Greenleaf Publishing, 2008, pp. 1–13.

15 A. Montuori and R. Purser, 'Ecological futures: systems theory, post-modernism, and participative learning in an age of uncertainty', in D. Boje, D. Gephart and T. Joseph (eds) *Postmodernism and Organization Theory*, Newbury Park, CA: Sage, 1996, pp. 181–201.

16 Ibid.

17 I. Palmer, R. Dunford and G. Akin, *Managing Organizational Change: A Multi-Perspective Approach*, 2nd edn, New York: McGraw-Hill, 2009.

18 Nike, 'Our Sustainability Strategy', 2012. Online. Available HTTP: <http://www.nikeresponsibility.com/report/content/chapter/our-sustainability-strategy#topic-sustainable-innovation> (accessed 12 September 2013).

19 Nike, 'Nike Names New VP of Corporate Responsibility, Maria Eitel Becomes President of the Nike Foundation', press release, 21 October 2004. Online. Available HTTP: <http://www.csrwire.com/press_releases/24945-Nike-Names-New-VP-of-corporate-responsibility-Maria-Eite-Becomes-President-of-the-Nike-Foundation> (accessed 12 May 2006).

20 HP, 'Design for Environment', 2013. Online. Available HTTP: <http://www8.hp.com/us/en/hp-information/environment/design-for-environment.html#.UjCJ9JH85Mo> (accessed 11 September 2013).

21 M. Halme, 'Corporate environmental paradigms in shift: learning during the course of action at upm-kymmene', *Journal of Management Studies*, 2002, 39 (8), 1087–109.

22 Nike, 'FY 10–11 Sustainable Business Performance Summary', 2012. Online. Available HTTP: <http://nikeinc.com/news/nike-inc-introduces-new-targets-elevating-sustainable-innovation-within-business-strategy> (accessed 12 September 2013).

23 F. Luthans, K. Luthans, R. M. Hodgetts and B. C. Luthans, 'Positive approach to leadership (PAL): implications for today's organizations', *Journal of Leadership Studies*, 2002, 8 (2), 3–20; F. Luthans, 'Positive organizational behaviour: developing and managing psychological strengths for performance improvement', *Academy of Management Executive*, 2002, 16 (1), 57–72.

24 B. Hirsh and P. Sheldrake, *Inclusive Leadership: Rethinking the World of Business to Generate the Dynamics of Lasting Success*, Melbourne: Information Australia, 2001.

25 Ibid., pp. 211–12.

26 L. Gratton, *Living Strategy: Putting People at the Heart of Corporate Purpose*, London: Financial Times/Prentice-Hall, 2000, p. 17.

27 K. E. Weick, *Sensemaking in Organizations*, Beverley Hills, CA: Sage Publications, 1995.

28 For a more extended discussion of the nature of dialogue, see E. H. Schein, *Process Consultation Revisited: Building the Helping Relationship*, Reading, MA: Addison-Wesley, 1999, pp. 201–18.

29 P. Crittenden, S. Benn and D. Dunphy, 'Case 13: Yarra Valley Water: learning and change for sustainability', in S. Benn, D. Dunphy and B. Perrott,

Cases in Corporate Sustainability and Change: A Multidisciplinary Approach, Prahran, Victoria: Tilde University Press, 2011, pp. 147–62; Q. Jones, D. Dunphy, R. Fishman, M. Larne and C. Canter, *In Great Company: Unlocking the Secrets of Cultural Transformation*, 2nd edn, Sydney, NSW: Human Synergistics Aust P/L, 2011, Chapter 5, pp. 219–78.

30 Human Synergisitics, personal communication, 2012.

31 Yarra Valley Water, 'Next Generation Water Services', available at http://www.yvw.com.au/Home/Aboutus/Nextgenerationwaterservices/index.h tm (accessed 3 October 2013).

32 Quoted in D. C. Korten, *The Post-corporate World: Life after Capitalism*, San Francisco, CA: Kumarian Press and Berrett-Koehler Publishers, 1999, p. 215; P. H. Ray and S. R. Anderson, *The Cultural Creatives: How 50 Million People Are Changing the World* (illustrated edn), New York: Harmony Books, 2000.

33 Of course, many organizations today do not have 'a line' in any simple sense – the term comes from traditional bureaucratic organizations. We use the line/staff distinction as a simple descriptive classification system.

34 Gratton, *Living Strategy*.

35 R. Sayers, 'Sustainability at Siemens', CS and Strategy Australia, April 2012. Also see Siemens, 'Sustainability'. Online. Available HTTP: <http://www. siemens.com.au/sustainability> (accessed 25 November 2013).

36 S. Hart and R. E. Quinn, 'Roles executives play: CEOs, behavioral complexity, and firm performance', *Human Relations*, 1993, 46, 543–75; also reviewed in R. E. Quinn, *Deep Change: Discovering the Leader Within*, San Francisco, CA: Jossey-Bass, 1996, 5, pp. 148–51.

37 This result holds true regardless of firm size or the level of competitiveness of the firm's environment.

38 S. Hart, *Capitalism at the Crossroads*, Upper Saddle River, NJ: Pearson Prentice Hall, 2005.

39 Green Mountain Coffee Roasters, 'Case Study Employee Origin Trip: Going to Source', Online. Available HTTP: <http://www.gmcr.com/sustainability/ peopleandcommunities/people/employeeorigintrip.aspx> (accessed 24 November 2013).

40 Green Mountain Coffee Roasters, 'CEO's Dialogue', 2012. Online. Available HTTP: <http://www.gmcr.com/Sustainability/Overview/CEO.aspx> (accessed 12 September 2013).

41 W. McDonough and M. Braungart, *Cradle to Cradle: Remaking the Way We Make Things,* New York: North Point, 2002; W. McDonough and M. Braungart, *The Upcycle: Beyond Sustainability – Designing for Abundance*, New York: North Point, 2013.

42 B. Doppelt, *Leading Change towards Sustainability*, Sheffield: Greenleaf Publishing, 2003.

43 J. Benyus, *Biomimicry: Innovation Inspired by Nature*, New York: Harper Perennial, 2002.

44 D. Roth, '100 best corporate citizens for 2006', *Business Ethics Magazine*, 2006, 20 (1), Online. Available HTTP: <http://www.thecro.com/?q=node/63 (accessed 6 March 2014).

45 I. Rankin Kerr, 'Leadership strategies for sustainable SME operation', *Business Strategy and the Environment*, 2006, 15 (1), 30–9.

46 P. Bate, *Strategies for Cultural Change*, Oxford: Butterworth/Heinemann, 1994.

47 D. Korten, *The Post-corporate World*, p. 117.

Appendix

The corporate sustainability checklist

Characteristic	Activities
	Compliance
Vision/goals	Develop an integrated, organization-wide plan for sustainability
	Implement systematic and ongoing improvement in industrial relations, OH&S, EEO, EMS and community services
Change agents	Ensure top-level commitment
Key activities	Select and develop change agents and nominate responsibilities
	Identify and regularly update the organization on the risks of non-compliance with current legislation, possible future legislation and public opinion
	Organize workshops to define compliance roles
	Clarify roles of top management, compliance officers and other stakeholders
	Assign staff responsibilities to improve existing IR, EEO, OH&S and Environmental Management Systems
	Develop staff training systems
Corporate policies/ strategies	Foster an understanding of business ethics across the organization
	Work toward a comprehensive sustainability strategy
	Foster an individual sense of responsibility for the environment and the need to be alert to potential sources of pollution and resource waste
	Minimize adverse environmental effects of all activities and take steps to minimize waste and conserve energy

Corporate policies/ strategies (cont)	Take necessary measures to prevent avoidable accidental releases of pollutants
	Provide advice on the safe handling, use and disposal of the company's products
	Examine product liability requirements
	Take employee suggestions and feed back into account
	Minimize risk using a precautionary approach
	Build and sustain reputation
	Build a learning platform for the organization
Stakeholder relations	Establish positive relationships with community and government
	Avoid greenwash by reporting conscientiously
	Enlist NGOs as environmental and social monitors
	Establish volunteer relationships
	Assist public authorities in establishing well-founded environmental regulations
Human capabilities	Create OH&S, EEO, IR and community relations policies and involve employees in ongoing improvement
	Implement employee training programmes for OH&S
	Implement employee awareness programmes for human rights and EEO obligations
	Develop human sustainability auditing and reporting capabilities
	Identify human rights, OH&S and IR obligations of members of the supply chain
	Establish relations with a third-party professional to conduct external audits
	Ensure ongoing compliance through implementing ISO 9000
Ecological capabilities	Implement environmental awareness programmes
	Develop ecological auditing and reporting capabilities
	Identify the environmental obligations of members of the supply chain
	Ensure ongoing capacity to address compliance through the implementation of voluntary standards or continuous improvement systems such as ISO 900I
Tools/techniques	Develop a Sustainability Plan which covers the management and operation of facilities and the design, manufacture and delivery of products and services

Tools/techniques (cont) Involve employees in planning for the development of the Sustainability Plan

Establish auditing and reporting systems

Develop relationships with relevant regulators

Communicate Sustainability Plan aims, objectives and benefits to employees and suppliers

Press suppliers to be compliant through face-to-face meetings

Ensure that contractors working on the organization's behalf apply acceptable human environmental sustainability standards

Ensure that any transfer of technology is accompanied by the information needed to protect the environment

Assess in advance the environmental and human sustainability implications of new processes, products and other activities

Production/service systems

Identify legislation and standards associated with all production and service systems

Ensure assessment, monitoring and reporting systems are in place to address compliance requirements relevant to all products and services

Efficiency

Vision/goals

Generate cost savings via the pursuit of efficiencies in ecological and human sustainability areas

Generate efficiencies by reducing costs; adding value and innovation

Develop an organization-wide approach that seeks to shift from cost to innovation in order to capture sustainable competitive advantages

Change agents

Allocate change-agent roles to operational and line managers with relevant technical expertise

Ensure top level commitment

Develop change programmes that generate efficiencies in specific areas – through the use of programmes – TQM, The Natural Step; EMS

Pilot programmes and look for opportunities to widen their sphere of influence

Corporate policies/strategies	Develop a systematic approach to the management and pursuit of efficiency. Look for 'small wins' and use them to spread the project, create a more programmatic approach Create corporate incentive schemes that reward employee performance and start to build social capital De-layer through the use of teams with the aim of increasing workplace commitment/outsource non-core activities
Structures/systems	Establish assessment systems to address OHS and community issues, i.e. start to develop internal structures for external stakeholder information management Implement HRIS systems in order to track human resource performance Assess and report on social/environmental impacts beyond compliance requirements Establish environmental management systems and link into corporate-wide systems Assess product risk and other liability issues and look at building into value-adding and innovation approaches (eco-design)
Stakeholder relations	Identify key external stakeholders and engage in dialogue, symbolic activities Form alliances with suppliers and subcontractors in order to deliver on environmental criteria for product/service efficiency Focus on the customer and look to add value to products by moving features to services Build new capabilities though shared learning experiences with other organizations Seek to build human capability through collaborative arrangements with other organizations
Human capabilities	Develop increased returns from human resources; develop a systematic approach to human resource management Identify required competences in middle managers and commence competence development Focus on appropriate employee skills development (communication, systems analysis, conflict management, problem solving) Reorganize in multi-skilled teams where appropriate

Human capabilities (cont)	Establish systems for employee empowerment Calculate cost/benefit ratios for human resources
Ecological capabilities	Develop the skills required to identify and pick off low-hanging fruit Start to develop competences in eco-design, supply chain management and procurement practices Develop and use systematic tools and measurement systems
Tools/techniques	Develop and use proven programmes – TQM; The Natural Step Implement TQEM and EMS Develop corporate-wide reporting systems for knowledge sharing
Production/service systems	Minimize environmental load and life-cycle impacts Ensure packaging/design impacts along the supply chain Commit to take back products at the end of their life Review all material and energy flows in physical and monetary units in order to identify efficiencies

Strategic proactivity

Vision/goals	Scan the environment (present and future) to identify (1) potential threats to the sustainability of existing products and services, (2) potential opportunities for creating innovative sustainability products/services Ensure business activities generate competitive advantages through the pursuit of sustainability Develop a vision that defines core sustainability competences and values
Change agents	Benchmark against industry best practice Encourage feedback on new ideas in order to generate strategic insights Implement interpersonal skills training with a focus on developing the change competences of the organization Develop systems of knowledge sharing among employees Work to develop close relationships with stakeholders – internal and external Work towards establishing enabling organizational structures – teams, virtual teams and networks Aim to develop long-term sustainability competences

Corporate policies/strategies	Integrate human and ecological sustainability systems to create dynamic core competences
	Align the corporate vision on sustainability with practical policies and strategies for action
	Formalize the commitment to sustainability at board level
	Develop management plans and set targets for the integration of environmental, financial, human competences, and knowledge management
	Create cross-functional sustainability integration teams
	Use TBL/Balanced Scorecard to demonstrate corporate performance
	Promote research and development into next-generation environmentally sound products and services
	Constantly undertake stakeholder analysis
Structures/systems	Develop systems for capturing and utilizing employee knowledge
	Develop systems for training, development and transfer of knowledge that focus on core competences
	Develop structures – teams, project teams, virtual teams and communities of practice – that enable the pursuit of sustainability
	Align supply chains, stakeholders and logistics systems; examine e-commerce potential
	Develop performance management systems that monitor and reward sustainability performance of business units
Stakeholder relations	Define and communicate strategic interests and potential benefits with stakeholders
	Develop codified rules for the management and coordination of relationships
	Develop strategic relationships with NGOs, community organizations and other corporations
	Collaborate with non-profits and other commercial organizations and build reputational capital
	Leverage partnerships for sustainability, such as communities of practice
	Develop key components of innovation competition
	Work with communities of practice to develop knowledge base – become an agent for change

Human capabilities	Support work–life balance for employees
	Provide diversity training
	Empower people by giving them the tools and motivation to innovate and express values through work
	Implement career and benefits planning
	Develop flexible workplace practices such as telecommuting or work sharing and video-conferencing; utilize new information technology to create project and virtual teams
	Ensure that good architecture provides a pleasant working and living environment
Ecological capabilities	Develop capabilities for monitoring and acting on a broad range of ecological and social information
	Develop key relations with stakeholders
	Incorporate core competences on design/technology into strategies
Tools/techniques	Use Triple Bottom Line reporting or Balanced Scorecard
	Conduct culture-building activities
	Initiate strategic competitor analysis
Production/service systems	Establish and incorporate systems of industrial ecology
	Develop industrial ecology synergies through supply chain management
	Increase focus on research and development

The sustaining corporation

Vision/goals	Review basic corporate values; create a codified set of company values
	Ensure top-level support for a strong sustainability position
	Re-examine organization values against changing external expectations by active workshopping with stakeholders
	Codify corporate values
	Broaden stakeholder analysis to include society as a whole, future generations and the natural world
Change agents	Ensure that the senior executive team deeply internalizes and acts on sustainability principles
	Build strong collaborative networks between internal and external change agents to create momentum on progressing sustainability

Corporate policies/strategies	Build on the sustainability achievements of previous stages
	Use external bodies to conduct social and environmental audits; cultivate transparency and accountability
	Communicate achievements to employees, the community and other organizations and share learning with alliance partners – build reputational capital
	Develop new market opportunities; provide customized services
	Contribute to maintaining the biosphere
Structures/systems	Develop a networked, flexible corporate structure
	Form alliances and emphasize collaboration
	Create a strong corporate culture around core sustainability values
Stakeholder relations	Develop a shared vision with non-profit organizations
	Share employee work hours with non-profit partners
	Encourage active engagement in community activities
	Be proactive in pursuing sustainability agenda with governments and other community bodies
Human capabilities	Build the personal and professional capability of the workforce; build intellectual capital within the organization and in collaboration with alliance members
	Include ethical concerns in staff performance measures
	Ensure staff relations are based on potential for contributions, not status; support participative decision making
	Ensure staff recruitment policies are proactive towards minority groups; foster workforce diversity and equal opportunity
	Ensure highest standards in workplace health and safety
	Adopt family-friendly policies
	Develop higher-order employee capabilities (process skills, self-confidence, sharing)
Ecological capabilities	Contribute to ecological renewal
	Be proactive in negotiating with other corporations for the design and production of more sustainable products
	Assist smaller corporations to be more responsible by sharing knowledge and expertise
	Use life-cycle assessment to reduce packaging, eliminate waste, increase dematerialization

Tools/techniques	Consolidate and integrate the systems adapted in earlier phases
Production/service systems	Redesign products to ensure environmental safety
	Redesign supply chains to become material processing loops to eliminate waste and pollution
	Dematerialize physical products where possible to emphasize service activities

Source: B. Nattrass and M. Altomare, *The Natural Step for Business*, Gabriola Island, BC: New Society Publishers, 1999; Social Venture Network, *Standards of Corporate Social Responsibility* at www.svn.org/organization.html accessed 18 April 2002.

Further reading

Benn, S. and Bolton, D., *Key Concepts of Corporate Social Responsibility*, London, Thousand Oaks, New Delhi, Singapore: Sage.

Benn, S., Dunphy, D. and Perrott, B. (eds), *Cases in Corporate Sustainability and Change*, Prahran, Victoria: Tilde University Press, 2011.

Chandler, D. and Werther, W., *Strategic Corporate Social Responsibility* (3rd edn), Los Angeles, London, New Delhi, Washington: Sage, 2014.

Diamond, J., *Collapse: How Societies Choose to Fail or Survive* (2nd edn), New York: Allen Lane Penguin, 2011.

Grace, D. and Cohen, S., *Business Ethics* (5th edn), Oxford: Oxford University Press, 2013.

Kurucz, E., Colbert, B. and D. Wheeler, *Reconstructing Value: Leadership Skills for a Sustainable World*, Toronto, Buffalo, London: Toronto University Press, 2013.

Marshall, J., Coleman, G. and Reason, P. (eds), *Leadership for Sustainability*, Sheffield: Greenleaf Publishing, 2011.

Index

References to figures are shown in *italics*. References to tables are shown in **bold**. References to notes consist of the page number followed by the letter 'n' followed by the number of the note, e.g. 254n74 refers to note no. 74 on page 254.